A COMPLETE GUIDE

PHILADELPHIA, BRANDYWINE VALLEY & BUCKS COUNTY

FIRST EDITION

PHILADELPHIA, BRANDYWINE VALLEY & BUCKS COUNTY

David
Langlieb

The Countryman Press
Woodstock, Vermont

To Sol Langlieb and Egon Sensky

ISBN 978-1-58157-087-8

Cover photo by David Langlieb
Interior photographs by the author unless otherwise specified
Maps by Mapping Specialists Ltd., Madison WI, © The Countryman Press
Book design by Bodenweber Design
Composition by Christine Cantera Design

Published by The Countryman Press, P.O. Box 748, Woodstock, VT 05091

Distributed by W. W. Norton & Company, Inc., 500 Fifth Avenue, New York, NY 10110

Printed in the United States of America

10 9 8 7 6 5 4 3 2 1

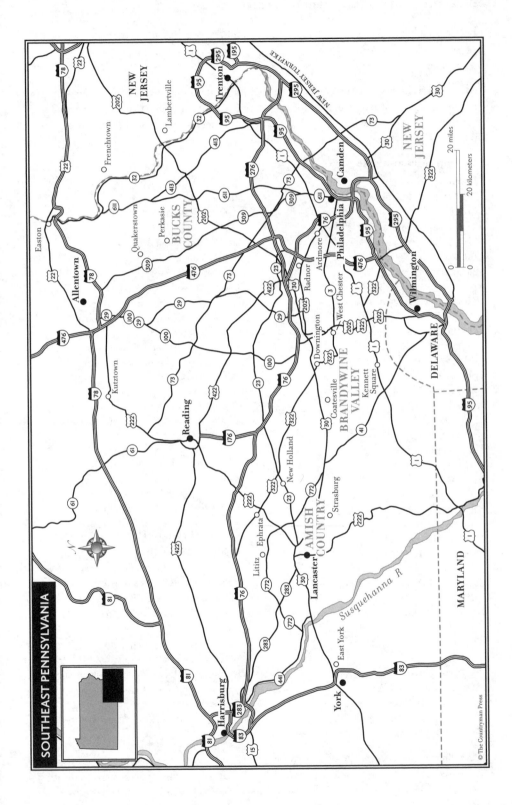

SOUTHEAST PENNSYLVANIA

NEW JERSEY

NEW JERSEY

DELAWARE

MARYLAND

BUCKS COUNTY

BRANDYWINE VALLEY

AMISH COUNTRY

Lancaster

NEW JERSEY TURNPIKE

Susquehanna R

Easton
Allentown
Kutztown
Reading
Harrisburg
York
East York
Lititz
Ephrata
New Holland
Strasburg
Coatesville
Kennett Square
Downington
West Chester
Ardmore
Radnor
Philadelphia
Camden
Wilmington
Trenton
Lambertville
Frenchtown
Quakerstown
Perkasie

20 miles

20 kilometers

© The Countryman Press

CONTENTS

ACKNOWLEDGMENTS

I received so much help at every turn that I cringe thinking where I'd be without it. The initial encouragement from Gabrielle Ohayon, Slater Gray, Mark Robinson, and Sebastian Mankowski was crucial. Huge thanks are owed to Jeanette Duffy, who drafted a sidebar and gave several chapters her rigorous consideration while putting up with a lot. My classmates at the Fels Institute provided indispensable support and made eating and drinking my way around Philadelphia a pleasure. I enjoyed every one of those meals, and getting to know all of you truly was the highlight of my year. The same goes for my old college friends who helped me through this process.

Professor Gary McDonogh somehow found time to offer feedback while working on a thousand projects of his own. Kim Grant is a saint and wonderful editor. Maria McCollester reviewed much of the text and helped me revisit key establishments until I got them right. Kim R. Ford provided a seasoned palate and sparkling conversation that only got better when it bordered on outright hostility. Meredith Brett (and parents!) gave me new perspective on Bucks County, and Katie Thomas filled in the blanks of Amish Country. Abbie Lamb Siskin and Eric Siskin offered content guidance and made me believe in love. Liz Garrison was a calming influence when the going got tough. La Vida Johnson ate the vegetables I couldn't stand and taught me good manners. Ed DeSeve broadened my perspective on the region's history. The ever-reliable Sarah Lorr and Milan Mitra remain the salt of the earth. And whatever I now know about women's clothing stores is owed entirely to Liz Roller. There are many others: Esther Agbaje, Mike Bruckner, Lauren Dawson, Kate Dempsey, Justin Evilsizor, Brittany Gibbs, Rachel Gormley, Andrew Gooch, Meredith Guillot, Lauren Hoberg, Suzanne Hughes, Chris Kingsley, Kate Meeley, and Maura O'Brien to name just a few.

Special thanks are also owed to Deke Castleman, who for reasons I still don't fully understand went out of his way to support me in this field when I was a dopey kid bouncing around Las Vegas. There's no way this book could have existed without him. The same goes for Anthony Curtis. More than anything, I'm grateful to Mom, Dad, Grandma, and Madeline for their unconditional love and support.

And a final thank you to the dozens upon dozens of innkeepers, shop owners, antique dealers, barflies, and local residents throughout the Delaware Valley and Pennsylvania Dutch Country who enthusiastically filled the gaps in my knowledge and helped me produce the best text that I could. Any inaccuracies are my own, but the pithy observations and useful recommendations are mostly theirs.

INTRODUCTION

The case for visiting the Delaware Valley begins with its history. No other region presents the American story with such gravitas. What transpired in Philadelphia at the 1787 Constitutional Convention was a milestone event in the course of human progress, authoritatively documented in historic attractions around the Old City and Society Hill neighborhoods. Still, the region's history is about more than lawyers and businessmen writing a constitution. Its age and cultural identity made it a part of every triumph, every argument, every wrong turn and eleventh hour save in American history. To visit greater Philadelphia today is to taste the fruits of the experiment devised within the city itself nearly 225 years ago. Philadelphia is a rich city, a poor city, a city of first-generation immigrants and descendents of William Penn. The stone houses, small towns, and rolling hills of the countryside go back just as far, rendering a different, but no less authentic glimpse at the evolution of American life.

My favorite Delaware Valley attractions tell this history in an unconventional way. The Hagley Museum hoists up early American industry for inspection and understanding. The Fairmount Park mansions speak to the surprisingly tumultuous lives of the original Pennsylvania elite. Johnson House adds dimension to the story of the Underground Railroad. The Mercer Museum in Bucks County and the Christian Sanderson Museum in the Brandywine Valley breathe new life into generations of Americana. Best of all is Eastern State Penitentiary, which brings together Gothic architecture, Al Capone, ghost stories, and just a dash of well-intentioned Quaker naiveté. Beat that, Empire State Building.

The cultural sphere is equally remarkable. The Philadelphia Museum of Art is a destination in and of itself. The Barnes Foundation in the Main Line suburb of Merion (for now) displays an impressionist and early modern collection that any museum in the world would die to have. And there are unconventional curiosities everywhere from sculpture at Rodin to the macabre Mütter Museum. The list goes on and on. In the pages that follow, I have attempted to capture all that I love about the region—from the shoebox-sized hoagie shops in South Philadelphia to the 47,000-square-foot duPont mansion in the Brandywine—with details and observations that do justice to their unique appeal.

Compiling this guidebook has given me the chance to dabble in everything, and I recommend you do the same to the extent that your time frame allows. Weekend in the New Hope hills and catch a Phillies game on the way home. Camp outside Quakertown one night, and book a suite at the Philadelphia Sofitel the next. This is the birthplace of American freedom, after all. Exercise some yourself.

A few additional thoughts:

- Traveling out from Center City, the Delaware Valley gets rural quickly. There are even countrified pockets within the city itself. Deer trot freely around Fairmount Park, for example, which is rather extraordinary considering the dense urban neighborhoods that surround it.

- Philadelphia is chronically underrated in so many ways. Its restaurants, museums, and public spaces are finally getting some of the recognition they've long deserved. One stereotype that has yet to be shattered is that of the cranky, hostile Philadelphian. This is a shame. Generally speaking, folks who live here are among the kindest, most generous, and least pretentious people you could hope to meet. Honestly.

- While Philadelphia has improved considerably over the past couple decades, it is still a 1.5-million-person city with a big-city crime rate. Stay alert and consider your surroundings. Center City and Chestnut Hill are fine day or night. Northern Liberties, Manayunk, Fairmount, Queen Village, and Bella Vista are generally safe as well. Germantown is the only neighborhood referenced repeatedly in this book that should be avoided at night, though it is safer during the daytime. University City is safe and well policed, but the rest of West Philadelphia can be dangerous (stay east of 50th Street at night). No matter where you are, keep your belongings secure, travel in groups when possible, and know your route ahead of time to avoid getting lost.

- As a corollary to the above, Bucks County is an excellent place to get lost. I'm half serious about this; some of the most interesting things I've seen in the course of researching this book (weird signs, hidden trails, animal life, etc.) occurred after a wrong turn in Upper Bucks. I hesitate to over-romanticize country roads, but it's true.

- To be perfectly honest, I have never understood the appeal of the wet-bottom shoofly pie sold in Amish Country. The other Pennsylvania Dutch foods are fantastic.

Sumptuously ornamented City Hall

THE WAY THIS BOOK WORKS

This book has six chapters. The first discusses the region's history, with the spotlight on Philadelphia. Subsequent chapters delve further into the individual histories of their subjects, including the final chapter, which touches on Amish history prior to the settlements in Lancaster County.

Advance planning is encouraged, but the book's contents are designed to be useful even on a whim. All contact information, operating hours, etc., was checked close to publication time. Still, it never hurts to call restaurants or museums to verify information, particularly if you're going out of your way. A special note must be made about Chapter 3, which covers Philadelphia's peripheral neighborhoods and Main Line suburbs. Since so many areas in this chapter are non-contiguous, pay close attention to the neighborhood designations. A restaurant in Queen Village is a considerable drive from Morris Arboretum in Chestnut Hill even though both are within the city limits.

If you are planning ahead, browse through the text a little and see what looks appealing. You may find a restaurant, hotel, or cultural attraction that you had not considered. If, on the other hand, it's almost dinnertime and you need to find a restaurant five minutes from your hotel, consult the index, which is organized by location, cuisine, and price.

Price ranges approximate how much a hotel or restaurant will cost. Lodging prices vary from day to day and season to season. Big conventions in Philadelphia drive up room rates significantly. Bed & breakfast rates in the countryside are generally more stable, but weekend bookings at many places require at least a two-night stay. Midweek, you can always book a single night. In the dining sections, price ranges reflect the cost of a three-course meal, including appetizer, entrée, and dessert for one person. They are not inclusive of alcoholic beverages, tax, and gratuity.

Prices

	Lodging	*Dining*
Inexpensive	Up to $80	Up to $15
Moderate	$80 to $150	$15 to $30
Expensive	$150 to $230	$30 to $50
Very Expensive	$230 and up	$50 or more

1

History

Annals of a Region

THE EARLY DELAWARE VALLEY

Before there was William Penn, before there was Benjamin Franklin, and before there was the Eagles' offensive line, there was Johan Björnsson Printz. The Printz name is nowhere to be found in most American history textbooks, but his was the original political link between Europe and the Delaware Valley. Massive in size and voluble in temperament, Printz left his native Sweden in 1643 to become royal governor of New Sweden, charged with administering the small group of Dutch and Swedish settlers who had arrived a few years before.

This is not to credit Printz with founding greater Philadelphia, or even with the Swedish settlement in the New World. The idea actually originated from the Dutch West India Company, the second of two Holland-based trading companies that sought dominion over the flow of goods between Europe and the Americas throughout the 17th century. The Dutch traders saw in the Swedes a way to expand their influence in North America southward from the New Amsterdam (Manhattan) settlement. The Swedish monarchy, soaking in the afterglow of its triumphant performance during the Thirty Years' War and anxious to join the lucrative world of international trade, was happy to go along. The arrangement was brokered in 1637 by Dutch trader Peter Minuit, who also served as New Sweden's colonial administrator before Printz arrived six years later.

A first wave of settlers founded Fort Christina (named for the Swedish queen) in present-day Wilmington, Delaware, and commenced trading. Their earliest partners were the Leni-Lenape, an associated group of Native Americans from three regional tribes. The relationship between the Swedes and the Leni-Lenape was peaceful. The Indians lived in decentralized villages of minimal governance and agrarian, hunter-gatherer economies. The Swedes, who were vastly outnumbered by the Lenape, were content to live quietly and trade clothes, beads, and tools for food and furs. The settlements grew slowly along the Delaware River and colonists harvested crops like corn and tobacco. Governor Printz moved north towards present-day Philadelphia, building himself a large home.

But barely a decade after its founding, New Sweden began to fall apart. Minuit died on an early voyage back to Europe and with him went the colony's most enthusiastic and skilled administrator. Even more devastating was the fundamental problem of New Sweden's purpose. If it was merely an outpost for the Dutch West India Company, then why was the Swedish crown investing so much domestic treasure? Alternatively, if New Sweden was a full-fledged colony designed to boost Sweden's international prestige, then why was the early settlement so small and unambitious? Either way, enthusiasm for the venture was low. Swedes back home felt little connection, either socially or economically, to their countrymen on the other side of the Atlantic.

New Sweden was soon folded into the Dutch territories, which was a logical end to the experiment in Swedish colonialism. The Dutch governed the loose federation of Delaware Valley settlements for roughly 12 years, at which point the English handily wrested power away through a combination of migration and combat. In 1674 a treaty was signed ending the Dutch-English war, and all settlements in and around the Delaware Valley were ceded to the English.

There remain vestiges of New Sweden in greater Philadelphia to this day, most notably Old Swedes' Church and an American Swedish museum in the southeast part of the city. There are also numerous allusions to the area's Native American inhabitants, including several neighborhoods (Manayunk, Shackamaxon, Passyunk, etc.), which draw their names from Lenape vocabulary.

Much of today's historical literature on greater Philadelphia glosses over the early Swedes and Lenape as irrelevant to the region's critical narrative. It is true that Philadelphia would eventually occupy a unique and central place in the American story, largely independent of whether or not the Swedes had ever set foot in North America. Even so, one cannot help but wonder how long these different but seemingly amiable peoples might have lived in peace had history allowed.

Penn with the Leni-Lenape

Penn and Colonial Philadelphia: Any Responsible Migrant

Penn loudly advertised his willingness to accept any responsible migrant—proving only that he believed in some kind of God (not necessarily very fervently), engaged in no very conspicuous criminal activity, and was willing to work hard enough to stay off the charity rolls. In short order, Pennsylvania had gain[ed] a widespread and well-deserved reputation as a haven for eccentricity which would never have been tolerated in cavalier Virginia, much less Puritan New England.

—Peirce Lewis and Ben Marsh,
"Slices Through Time: The Physical and Cultural Landscapes of Central and Eastern Pennsylvania,"
The Philadelphia Region

Shortly after the English assumed control of the Delaware Valley, what would become the territory of Pennsylvania was granted to William Penn by King Charles II. The land was a debt payment owed to Penn's father. His son, an English Quaker and social progressive, immediately went to work designing Philadelphia to anchor his colony in the southeast. It was an ambitious project in several respects.

First, Philadelphia sought to merge the tranquility of the countryside with a small but active commercial core. Penn was a realist and understood that his city would need a merchant class to power its economic engine. But he was also a lover of large estates and green space, and planned for an agrarian base within Philadelphia as well. He was concurrently dissatisfied with the chaos he found in most European cities, where streets seemed to wind and wander incoherently and where many towns lacked a vital center. Penn drew the roads between the Delaware and Schuylkill Rivers as a perfect grid, with a public square in each city corner and a fifth in the middle. He also had surveyors divide Philadelphia's land into large plots. It would be, he famously declared, "a green country town."

The second, more ambitious aspiration of Philadelphia was a shared morality. It could be said that tolerance above all else was Pennsylvania's organizing principle, and Philadelphia was no exception. Penn had been jailed in England for his Quakerism and envisioned for his New World colony a citizenry that shared his aversion to bigotry. He ignored a segment of his church that argued for Philadelphia to become exclusively Quaker. Penn also paid the Lenape a reputedly fair price for their land, and made an effort to speak the native tongue, of which he grew fond.

Penn's twin goals of low-density living and a tolerant ethic met with mixed success. In many ways, the first goal proved to be the more elusive. His original group of First Purchasers—mostly middle and upper class Englishmen who sought adventure and profit in the New World—were interested in clustering around the east part of town, close to the commercially useful Delaware River port. Penn had tremendous problems selling land on the less desirable west side, which lacked easy access to the Delaware. Even worse, the demand for real estate on the east side convinced early Philadelphians to rapidly subdivide the long, sprawling plots that Penn had so deliberately drawn. He was able to distribute the population as he wished during Philadelphia's infancy, but the city charter enacted in 1701 severely curbed Penn's influence and market forces took over. When he died in 1718 (broke and distraught), his city stood under-inhabited in the west and densely packed in the east. Penn's expansive vision would pay dividends for Philadelphia in later years, but the early settlers wasted little time deviating from the grand plan.

Philadelphia's early social dynamics were nuanced. By the standards of the era, the city was indisputably broadminded. Whites in Philadelphia (including Catholics and minority-sect Protestants) rarely faced religious bigotry, something that could not be said about other colonial cities like Boston and New York. On the other hand, slavery was not abolished until 1780, despite pockets of Quaker opposition.

The city saw brisk expansion and transformation during the first half of the 18th century. The concomitant growth of industry, trade, and the arts moved Philadelphia into the realm of world-class cities. Specifically, furniture manufacturing, printing, and the trade of wholesale goods fortified the era's prosperity. Farming thrived as well, both within the city limits and beyond. All sectors found strength in the city's diversity of European immigrants, who were mostly German, Scots-Irish, English, and Welsh during this period. The bridges between the New and Old World further augmented the market for international trade, and the city enjoyed an expansion in the production of bigger and better ships.

It was around this time that Philadelphia was introduced to Benjamin Franklin, a rare breed of public intellectual and American Renaissance man who epitomized the promise of Philadelphia's second act, just as Penn had embodied its first. Born in Boston, Franklin settled in Philadelphia in 1723 after he grew tired of apprenticing at his brother's newspaper. He soon became the heart and soul of Philadelphia's burgeoning civil society. Within 10 years of his arrival, Franklin founded a community organization and a library company, published the *Pennsylvania Gazette*, and completed the first edition of his *Poor Richard's Almanac*. He would go on to establish the American Philosophical Society, organize a fire company, serve on Philadelphia's first hospital board, found a university, map America's postal routes, and invent bifocals (among other things). His energy and prolificacy in colonial America were virtually unequalled.

Revolution and the Aftermath

Franklin spent considerable time in Europe during the 1750s and 1760s, and was in England when Parliament approved the Stamp Act in 1765. The act hit cities like Philadelphia especially hard, since it taxed paper goods such as books and newspapers that were most popular in cosmopolitan centers. Quick protest led to its repeal, but the Townshend Revenue Acts of 1767 levied new import taxes on goods like glass, paint, and tea. After early ambivalence, Philadelphians rose to fight Townshend duties.

Philadelphia possessed two key ingredients that made it a hotbed of Revolutionary sentiment: first, a citizenry that felt sufficiently removed from England (both generationally and spatially) for Parliament and the king to command minimal loyalty. Its non-English immigrant population had cooperated with the sons and daughters of the original colonists to build a city that, while not unlike European towns in certain respects, also enjoyed its own culture and local allegiance. Second, Philadelphia had a cadre of influential lawyers and merchants versed in ideas of the Renaissance and the Enlightenment, who could provide the intellectual groundwork for the cause. Of course, there were also many loyalists to the English crown, as well as pacifist Quakers who might have agreed with rebel principles but opposed fighting militarily. Both groups would cause difficulties once the war effort began in earnest.

In September 1774, the First Continental Congress gathered at Carpenters' Hall in Philadelphia and forged the Articles of Association to boycott British imports. The delegates also arranged for a Second Continental Congress to meet in May 1775, by which time the colonies were essentially at war with England. Over the next six years, Philadelphia was both a seat of government and a city at war. Franklin had returned to Philadelphia by 1775. His patience with the British was exhausted and his belief in the sovereignty of the United States solidified. After his election to the Second Continental Congress he served on the drafting committee for the Declaration of Independence. The final document was signed on July 4, 1776, making Philadelphia America's birth- place. Fleets of British troops soon arrived at the American shore.

Philadelphia should not have been a terribly difficult city to defend. While Penn's noble design predicted a peaceful future and eschewed city walls, Philadelphia's location 50 miles inland from the Atlantic Coast (a perpetual trad- ing disadvantage in competing with Boston and New York) kept it safe from a surprise attack. Nevertheless, a threat soon came from the north. Washington's Continental Army suffered early and bru- tal defeats in New York, which forced the general to retreat southward as the

The Continental Army is long gone, but the whitetail deer remain in Valley Forge.

English pursued. By the later months of 1776, a British attack on Philadelphia seemed all but inevitable and the Second Continental Congress fled to Baltimore. Most Philadelphians left the city as well.

The exodus was premature. Washington held the line in the Battle of Trenton, the Congress returned, and life resumed. It was a different life than Philadelphians had grown accustomed to, however, as suspicion of traitorous activity consumed the city. The insta- bility affected the city's defense, and Philadelphia found itself unable to raise the large local militias that helped protect Boston and other New England cities. The British Army sought to take advantage, and General William Howe refocused his efforts on southeastern Pennsylvania in the summer of 1777. The colonists' troubles came to a head on September 11 of that year at the Battle of Brandywine near Chadds Ford. Washington was beaten out- right, losing twice as many soldiers as the Brits, and failing to stop Howe's northeastern march. After another lopsided victory in the town of Paoli, the British captured Philadelphia. Washington attempted to recover at the Battle of Germantown a week later, but his sneak attack five miles outside the city was easily quashed. As the Continental Army retreated to Valley Forge to nurse its wounds and the Continental Congress moved west to York, exiled Loyalists flooded back to the city. Howe was able to blunt the flow of food and supplies out of Philadelphia to Valley Forge, where Washington's army camped through the winter.

But the British left Philadelphia voluntarily in the spring of 1778 when its troops were needed elsewhere. The Americans emerged from Valley Forge stronger and better trained than they had been before. A new alliance with France increased troop levels, and Washington moved on New York. The Continental Congress returned to Philadelphia for the third (and final) time. The region played a diminished role in the war's last three years, though Loyalist sentiment caused significant headaches for both the city and continental government until the siege of Yorktown in 1781. At war's end, celebration came to Philadelphia. It was America's largest city, ravaged by war, but ultimately triumphant.

The Articles of Confederation, ratified on March 1, 1781, called for a Confederation Congress to legislate the new government. After six difficult years under the Articles, a constitutional convention was convened in Philadelphia in May 1787 to sort through the problems. Entire volumes have been written about the extraordinary events that transpired at the Philadelphia Convention, relating not only to the constitutional debates and compromises that occurred inside the State House, but also to the delegates' interplay with the city. Throughout the spring and summer, delegates debated in the daytime, spent the evenings in the taverns, and drew energy from the city's hopeful masses (though a rule of secrecy prohibited specific discussion about the process). It was also, quite appropriately, Franklin's finest hour; his statesmanlike hold over the convention convinced reluctant delegates to work past their differences. And his vigorous opposition to slavery, while unable to move the convention's consensus, revealed his common decency. Franklin died less than three years after the convention, with the city and the Constitution forever in his debt.

Bucks and the Brandywine: The Early Years

A quick step back to the late 17th century, the time of William Penn's initial visit to the Delaware Valley. In the course of designing Philadelphia, Penn also established two other counties: Bucks (derived from Buckingham) County to the north and Chester County to the west. These sleepy provinces developed in a more leisurely, less deliberate manner than

Philadelphia's Delaware River waterfront today

the city. Philadelphia was Penn's calculated experiment, carefully planned and monitored. Bucks and Chester were his organic creations; consciously drawn, but allowed to develop with minimal interference from their draftsman.

Bucks is where Penn ultimately decided to build his estate, known as Pennsbury Manor and situated in the southeast corner of the county on the Delaware River. (When Penn wished to visit Philadelphia, he tended to sail down the Delaware by boat.) Early Bucks County maps reveal that many of his First Purchasers settled to the north, west, and south of Pennsbury Manor on relatively small plots of land, at least as compared with the larger plots given to settlers farther west in Bucks or on the northeastern fringe of Philadelphia County. Land adjacent to the Delaware was the choicest, though enough people lived in the south-central part of the county to support a small town, known as "New Town" in 1684 and "Newtown" today. Other small villages sprang up around the same time, and in 1692 the county began designating legal townships such as Bristol, Buckingham, and Solebury (today home to New Hope).

The original purchasers in Bucks County were demographically similar to the Philadelphians: mostly English, with German, Scots-Irish, and Welsh families mixed in. Life for the early Bucks settlers was difficult. Smallpox broke out in 1702 and then again in 1703. Penn had returned to England shortly after the founding, and land disputes caused friction among the settlers. These early conflicts underscored the region's tremendous potential. Bucks County offered its early settlers fertile soil, a wealth of stone and lumber, and an advantageous location near Philadelphia and New York. Eighteenth-century residents were primarily farmers, but many artisans settled in Bucks as well. Their early successes predicted the county's vital contributions to the American Arts and Crafts movement, particularly in Doylestown and New Hope.

By 1800, approximately 27,500 people lived in Bucks County. It had survived the early growing pains and was well on its way to becoming the pleasant medley of towns and villages that it is today. Roads linked the population centers, which included Solebury in the east, Bristol and Bensalem in the south, and Doylestown in the middle. These were small hamlets, with merchants selling mostly farming equipment, seed, tools, furniture, and crafts. Northern settlements remained universally rural.

As Bucks County developed along the Delaware, other contiguous villages sprang up wherever arable land and easy access to Philadelphia could be found. Thirty miles west of the city flowed the narrow Brandywine River, from Pennsylvania into Wilmington, Delaware, where Governor Printz's original Swedish colony had begun. Wilmington had emerged as a remarkably diverse immigrant city; it maintained a Swedish and Finnish character that had been diluted in Philadelphia shortly after English colonization. Wilmington's diversity extended to other European cultures, and in 1799 a Frenchman named Pierre Samuel du Pont arrived on its shores, an escapee of post-revolution France. Pierre's son Irénée would go on to become America's preeminent gunpowder producer, and the du Pont name would become forever linked with Wilmington.

The Brandywine villages were anchored by Wilmington in the south, but the river flowed down through Chester County, Pennsylvania, the third county founded by Penn upon his land grant from the king. What would eventually become known as the Brandywine Valley was a diffuse set of rural towns that took advantage of the river's ample fish supply. The northwest end was also the stage of a bitter argument between the colonists and the Indians, who did not believe they had sold Penn the site of a town past the northwest fork. Land disputes around the Brandywine continued through the French and Indian Wars in the 1750s, at which point the last vestiges of the Lenape and other regional tribes left the Delaware Valley.

The most egregious act, which expanded the colonial territory north of Bucks County, was the 1737 "Walking Purchase," in which Penn's sons produced for the Indians a dubious treaty stating that they were entitled to whatever land could be walked west from a point on the Pennsylvania side of the Delaware River in a day and a half. With the help of colonial administrator James Logan (whose house, Stenton, you can still tour today—see Chapter 3), they cleared paths through the Pennsylvania woods and employed the fastest runners they could find. Leaving aside the issue of the treaty's authenticity, the "walk" extended nearly twice the distance that a real walk could have covered in that length of time.

Troublesome Times Take Hold

Philadelphia was America's capital city through the country's first two presidencies, and you can visit the spot where presidents Washington and Adams lived and worked near the Liberty Bell Center. It is now a relatively peaceful corner of Market Street, but Philadelphia at the turn of the 19th century was beset by conflict from all sides. There were the political disputes—addressed but not settled in the nascent Constitution—questions of slavery, federalism, and later a bitter fight between Philadelphia's Nicholas Biddle and President Andrew Jackson over the United States Bank. But such debates seemed largely academic in the summer and fall of 1793, when the populace fell collectively ill with yellow fever. The disease spread with such intensity and rapidity that just weeks after the initial diagnoses, those who could afford to decided to flee. The city's preeminent physician and Founding Father, Benjamin Rush, advocated bloodletting, a practice that greatly diminished the body's capacity for fighting disease. Roughly 10 percent of Philadelphians died during the epidemic.

The fever returned periodically during these early years. For Washington and Adams, however, a more durable nuisance was Philadelphia's increasing affinity for the Republican Party and its anti-federalism. The nation's first and second presidents advocated a strong national government, while a growing majority of Philadelphians preferred a decentralized model favored by anti-Federalists. Somewhat paradoxically, most local offices were held by Federalists. It was a complex dynamic: as a northern port city, Philadelphia held a natural sympathy for mercantile interests that were represented by the Federalists; but its considerable agrarian base and libertarian instincts endeared many to the Republicans. In the great presidential election of 1800, anti-Federalist Thomas Jefferson defeated incumbent Adams in part by winning the city and securing more Pennsylvania electors.

In spite of the political turmoil and a budding rivalry with New York, it was also an age for building. By James Monroe's presidency, Philadelphia had completed its Water Works along the Schuylkill River, which was the most beautiful and technologically advanced piece of infrastructure of its day. (The Water Works today is a must-see attraction for those touring Fairmount Park.) Philadelphia also began constructing a transportation network. Early roads and bridges paved the way for the railroads, which would, in the latter half of the century, fundamentally redefine the region.

The seeds had been planted. Modern roads, a growth in the housing stock, and new technology predicted the Industrial Revolution and the subsequent labor movement (both of which would thrive in Philadelphia). The seeds were also planted for coming social change, as increasing numbers of blacks migrated north to find jobs in eastern industrial

The Fairmount Water Works

cities and new immigration from overseas further variegated Philadelphia's fabric. One of the strongest trends was the trend outward; new neighborhoods cropped up west of the Schuylkill, and along the northeast banks of the Delaware. These industrial villages were outside the city lines, but quickly filled with Eastern European and Irish immigrants. These neighborhoods, with names like Manayunk, Frankford, and Port Richmond, would be the areas most impacted by the Industrial Revolution. Factories operated close to residents' homes and communities solidified.

Of course, wars often revise (or at the very least interrupt) whatever economic and social trends dominate a period. There was a brief pause in Philadelphia's progress during the War of 1812, but a truly pivotal point arrived in 1860 when the big question—the question that had been left off the table in Philadelphia some 73 years before—was answered through warfare.

From Civil War to Civil Society

Much as it is today, Pennsylvania was a swing state in the election of 1860. Abraham Lincoln found himself running a close four-way race in a country bitterly divided by region and ideology. Slavery had caused such deep splits that in all but a few states the victor was predetermined. Without winning Pennsylvania and at least one other large state, there would be no way for Lincoln to capture a majority of the electoral college (he worried intermittently about New York and Ohio as well). Candidates did not campaign themselves in Lincoln's era, but he dispatched allies to speak on his behalf in greater Philadelphia. Lincoln's promoters rarely emphasized his opposition to the expansion of slavery, which had only tepid support in the region, but rather touted his advocacy for a steep tariff to protect Philadelphia's industrial workforce. On the strength of this promise Lincoln carried Philadelphia, won Pennsylvania, and secured the presidency. Mere months into his term, shots were fired at Fort Sumter in Charleston, South Carolina, and the Civil War began.

As during the Revolutionary War, public opinion in Philadelphia was split. It also turned on a dime; many Philadelphians flirted with sympathy towards the southern cause but were likewise susceptible to Lincoln's appeals to patriotism. Philadelphia's cultural

Ulysses S. Grant, immortalized in Fairmount Park

identity remained complex. It bordered Delaware, a slave state (though loyal to the Union), and abolitionist sentiment never quite permeated the general public the way it did in many New England towns. That said, close to 100,000 Philadelphians served in the Union army throughout the war, and the city supported numerous military hospitals for Union soldiers. Philadelphia also produced two Union generals: the mediocre George McClellan and the more virtuous, albeit staid, George Meade. General Meade's triumphal return to Philadelphia after a major victory at the Battle of Gettysburg sealed the city's support for the Union. As the war slogged on, a gradual but unmistakable move towards Lincoln's Republican Party occurred.

The war ended, Reconstruction of the American South commenced, and the Delaware Valley entered a magnificent era. It was in post–Civil War Philadelphia that William Penn's grand designs realized their true potential. Population increases resulting from the Industrial Revolution caused New York and Boston tremendous overcrowding problems. But Philadelphia had room, and rather than stuffing its populace in hastily constructed apartment buildings, it built throngs of single family row-homes. While the city was by no measure immune to low wages, child labor, and other problems of the era, the quality of life for the average Philadelphian was relatively high. It helped that local industries tended to employ skilled and semi-skilled workers who commanded better pay than their counterparts in the New York City sweatshops.

Rural Pennsylvania joined in the economic expansion. Mill towns along the Delaware River in Bucks County grew swiftly, capitalizing on their natural resources and location between New York and Philadelphia. The mid-19th century construction of the Delaware Canal linked the steel-producing city of Easton in the Lehigh Valley with Bristol in Lower Bucks, where the materials were used locally and sent downriver.

In 1876 Philadelphia celebrated the Centennial in Fairmount Park, which had expanded north and west of downtown. It was America's first world's fair, and incorporated over two hundred structures into its design. More than 10 million people from across the country and around the world came to Philadelphia that year to take in the city's cultural attractions and see exhibitions like Westinghouse's air brake and Bell's telephone. The exposition embodied Philadelphia's renewed confidence and status as a premier American city. It was, in some sense, an egalitarian sequel to the Constitutional Convention.

Next came the railroads, which soon transformed the Delaware Valley into a true metropolitan area. With an expanding upper class, a demand for suburbs was born. And while many distant neighborhoods already existed, the Main Line railroad (today the R5 line) made them accessible. This late-19th-century period brought the first significant wave of wealthy Philadelphia families to Main Line neighborhoods like Wynnewood, Bryn Mawr, and Gladwyne. Some purchased second homes and others moved entirely. Lower Bucks County evolved as an alternative, though it remained more rural than Montgomery and Delaware Counties. The Brandywine Valley retained its unique identity as a harbor from both the city and the inner suburbs. Kennett Square had incorporated in 1845, and West Chester's leisurely growth gave the Brandywine area a manageable, small-town appeal.

Main Liners and their inner-city contemporaries enjoyed a diverse regional economy that insulated greater Philadelphia from a national slump. Textiles, cigars, ice cream, beer, cleaning products, telephones, metals, and hats—Philadelphia made them all. High rates of home ownership persisted and neighborhoods flowered. An art museum and a grand city hall were constructed. Civic institutions formed throughout tightly knit ethnic communities of north and south Philadelphia as second-generation immigrants inched their way towards the middle class. At the turn of the 20th century, Philadelphia and her environs were enjoying a sustained boom. How long could the good times last?

The Bosses and the Bust

Philadelphia remained a Republican town since the closing days of the Civil War, but its party machine was as ruthlessly corrupt as the Tammany Hall Democrats in New York. Philadelphians found it difficult to get energized about politics, and this collective apathy alongside brisk economic growth made the city highly vulnerable to municipal fraud and graft. In the early 1900s, muckraking journalist Lincoln Steffens called Philadelphia "corrupt and contented."

There were many party bosses and competing factions, but none eclipsed the power amassed by William Vare's machine in South Philadelphia. Perched from his seat in the U.S. Congress, Vare lorded over the city, securing millions of dollars worth of city contracts for family and friends. A reform movement enjoyed occasional success, but could never hold the reins of power for more than a couple years before the party machine redoubled its efforts and fought its way back into office. Finally, in 1929, Vare suffered a fatal political defeat and Philadelphia's political machines began to dissolve (though current residents will attest that cronyism has yet to disappear entirely).

New problems bubbled to the surface. Philadelphia's proclivity for corrupt municipal governance had rendered the city's infrastructure woefully inadequate to support its continued growth. The temperance movement threw a new wrench into law enforcement, as bootlegging and organized crime flourished despite occasional police raids on the city's speakeasies. The municipal problems had been mitigated by a bustling economy and large tax base. But when the Great Depression hit, years of corruption caught up with Philadelphia. A bloated city payroll was pared down, public works projects got axed, and the city's social service providers found themselves unprepared to meet the tremendous need. Starvation and poverty ravaged the peripheral neighborhoods.

Some of the region's wealthiest residents fell the farthest. The Main Line was a particularly bizarre sight; its bankers and stock brokers, at one time among the wealthiest people in the entire country, woke up the morning after Black Tuesday to find they were virtually penniless. One such Main Line child named Thacher Longstreth (who would go on to run two unsuccessful races for Philadelphia mayor) wrote in his biography *Main Line WASP* about leaving the 30-room Haverford mansion where he was raised: "The upkeep was simply beyond our suddenly depleted means, and so we were forced to close the mansion and move in to the carriage house in the rear.... If you haven't been through it yourself, it's hard to understand what it's like to be wiped clean-clean. Our family went from an income of $50,000 or $60,000 a year to exactly $997 in 1935." Such stories were not uncommon in Philadelphia's upper-crust suburbs.

The Great Depression also marked the end of Philadelphia's Republican domination. The city helped re-elect Franklin Delano Roosevelt on his New Deal platform, and reform Democrats found support in local races. The economy picked up and municipal services improved. In 1940 the city hosted the Republican National Convention, probably the second most famous political assembly in Philadelphia's history, where GOP delegates nominated the moderate Wendell Wilkie over isolationist Robert Taft, helping sow the seeds for American involvement in World War II.

As with many industrial cities, the wartime economy propelled Philadelphia out of the Depression once and for all. Its factories hummed day and night; by war's end Philadelphia

A Girard Avenue trolley, returned to service in 2005 with rebuilt World War II–era streetcars

manufacturers would perform a staggering $1 billion worth of work for the Department of War. In South Philadelphia, the United States Navy Yard worked at capacity, building new ships and repairing old ones. Nearly 200,000 Philadelphians served in World War II, and countless others contributed their labor to the effort at home, including many women. The war also stimulated the research potential of academic institutions like the University of Pennsylvania, where engineers developed the world's first electronic computer.

The Post-War Shift

When Philadelphia's World War II veterans returned from overseas, they found a city teeming with potential. Generally speaking, the war brought out the best in Philadelphia. Downtown had rebounded marvelously from the Depression and new office buildings anchored the Center City core. The outskirts were flush with factories, stores, parks, and housing. A new city charter wiped away the most antiquated organizational barriers to governing Philadelphia, and a reform faction brought competence and credibility to City Hall.

Philadelphia seemed primed for a full-blown resurgence, but the city's recovery met with social and economic trends destined to change its course. Returning veterans found an improving city, but they also found opportunities where none had existed before. The G.I. Bill allowed thousands of Philadelphia veterans to educate themselves into white collar jobs. Others obtained small business loans and grew their own companies. Industrial work remained gettable, but was no longer an ambitious breadwinner's only option. The post-war order generated a new class of Philadelphia professionals: accountants, dentists, lawyers, engineers, and businessmen whose emergence soon personified 1950s America.

On the heels of the G.I. Bill came mass production of the automobile and highways. It would only be a matter of time before legions of Philadelphia's middle class families left the city and settled in the suburbs. The Main Line, Philadelphia's oldest string of suburban neighborhoods, evolved quickly from a retreat for the fabulously wealthy into a middle and upper middle class bastion (to be sure, certain communities remained wealthier than others). Bucks County developed along similar lines, while suburban developments sprouted in Chester County's Brandywine towns and all along northern Delaware. The city's population peaked in 1950 at 2.07 million people. It was down to 1.69 million by 1980.

There was also a racial dimension to the population shift. The vast majority of suburban flight involved white families, who left behind neighborhoods that were increasingly black and increasingly poor. By the 1970s, flight had become something of a self-fulfilling prophecy; the middle class households and small businesses that left the city took the tax base with them, further straining the city's social service budget and stimulating more flight. Racial tensions in newly integrated neighborhoods complicated an already fragile balance. The situation exploded in 1964 when North Philadelphia's Columbia Avenue business district was razed and looted after charges of the largely white police force abusing black residents.

Such discord was hardly unique to Philadelphia, and the suburbanization story is so well ingrained and so often told that the natural tendency is to exaggerate the impact of flight. Many neighborhoods were unquestionably decimated, but others held firm. Those communities that weathered a difficult era with strength and grace today constitute some of the most vibrant places in the city.

It is also true that Philadelphia did not suffer as badly as other Northeastern and Midwestern cities that had been completely blindsided by changes in the 1950s and '60s. A functional public transit network helped, as did thoughtful planning that stoked an emerging modern economy centered on financial services, legal services, education, and health care. Tourism played a key role too, as the Park Service restored Independence National Historic Park and its colonial-era buildings in advance of the 1976 Bicentennial. Philadelphia's manufacturing base surely dwindled, and its population declined. But on Philadelphia's worst hour of its worst day it remained the economic engine of Pennsylvania. And that worst hour is long gone.

An Urban Renaissance

Spend just a single day in the city, and you'll feel it: Philadelphia is hitting its stride. There is a palpable energy on the city's streets, inside its museums, theaters, galleries, and bars. New restaurants are opening, public squares buzz with activity, and once-abandoned blocks are completely occupied and lovingly maintained.

Why are these wonderful things happening? Philadelphia is more livable. A new generation of young people enamored with urban living has leant some pep to a world-class city all too often inclined to hide under its insecurities. Philadelphia has always been a fine place to visit, but its attractions require exploration, rediscovery, and growth. After a few difficult decades, Philadelphia is in the midst of being rediscovered, and the results are tangible: There is more to do, more to see, and more fun to be had.

The 21st-century Philadelphia skyline

The city has also made its peace with the suburbs, which have come to view themselves as a part of a metropolitan area rather than an out-and-out escape. Main Line residents cherish their local institutions, but often spend evenings in Philadelphia. Likewise, city residents can be found weekending at New Hope bed & breakfasts or appearing at the fall mushroom festival in Kennett Square. Dutch Country farmers make weekly trips to West Philadelphia to sell produce at city-sponsored fruit and vegetable markets, and Doylestown lawyers take weekend bicycle trips to the ends of Upper Bucks County. It has become clear to all concerned that southeast Pennsylvania has much to offer everyone. The Delaware Valley has been through a great deal over the last three hundred years, but continues to relearn the lesson Benjamin Franklin memorably instilled in a young association of English colonies as they considered revolution: ultimately, we're all in this together.

2

Downtown Philadelphia

Birthplace of the Revolution

While it served as the model for many American cities, no city center is quite like downtown Philadelphia. A hundred miles north is Manhattan, an organic creation by origin that did not acquire its grid until 1811. To the south is Washington, D.C., carefully drawn by Pierre L'Enfant and Andrew Ellicott at the city's birth. Philadelphia went a third way. It was diligently planned and almost instantly renovated. William Penn's grand design for a broad grid to anticipate large green estates was chopped to bits mere decades after its creation. Early settlers kept the grid, but subdivided the land into smaller parcels and built narrow new side streets to adapt.

Walk around downtown Philadelphia for five minutes and the upshot of this history will be clear. What is between 3rd Street and 5th Street? Fourth Street, yes. But also St. Peters Way, Lawrence Court, Leithgow Street, Orianna Street, and a handful of other byways that start and stop at different points throughout the grid, built by private landowners and tailored to serve their individual parcels. A bird's-eye view of downtown Philadelphia more closely resembles a jigsaw puzzle than a checkerboard.

It can get confusing, but there are good reasons to celebrate this. Abstractly, it humanizes Philadelphia's early years when her grand ambitions were forced into extemporaneous adjustment. But more tangibly, this history birthed a fascinating place. It is a city of nooks and crannies, a city with stories around every corner and along every street. An old city by American standards, it is also a textured city. It was a witness to and a participant in every stage of the country's growth, from colonization to present day. And its downtown developed in concert with the arc of American history.

To be sure, important elements of Penn's original design remain. The city's five public squares stand in all four corners and the center of downtown as originally intended and give Philadelphia ample public space and geographic coherence. Large estates are rare, but downtown is decidedly green. Smaller municipal parks complement the public squares and a national park occupies its most historic seven blocks. Fairmount Park, the city's master work, begins in the northwest portion of downtown Philadelphia before it spreads into the periphery.

Downtown is beautiful in other ways. It is an architectural grab bag, with distinct styles that reflect varied tastes and different eras of the city's development. Federal or Colonial architecture characterizes old residential blocks, picturesque Greek Revival and Victorian buildings dot the historic district, and modern glass towers fill the skyline. Public art is everywhere, the fruition of deliberate government efforts to mandate and incentivize its growth.

Downtown Philadelphia is often referred to as Center City, which, depending on whose definition you use, encompasses the same basic area: the Schuylkill River to the west, the

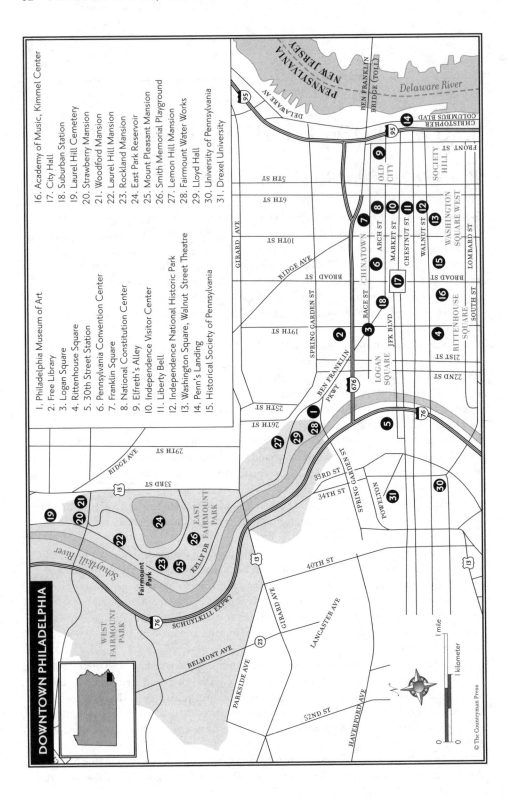

DOWNTOWN PHILADELPHIA

1. Philadelphia Museum of Art
2. Free Library
3. Logan Square
4. Rittenhouse Square
5. 30th Street Station
6. Pennsylvania Convention Center
7. Franklin Square
8. National Constitution Center
9. Elfreth's Alley
10. Independence Visitor Center
11. Liberty Bell
12. Independence National Historic Park
13. Washington Square, Walnut Street Theatre
14. Penn's Landing
15. Historical Society of Pennsylvania

16. Academy of Music, Kimmel Center
17. City Hall
18. Suburban Station
19. Laurel Hill Cemetery
20. Strawberry Mansion
21. Woodford Mansion
22. Laurel Hill Mansion
23. Rockland Mansion
24. East Park Reservoir
25. Mount Pleasant Mansion
26. Smith Memorial Playground
27. Lemon Hill Mansion
28. Fairmount Water Works
29. Lloyd Hall
30. University of Pennsylvania
31. Drexel University

© The Countryman Press

Delaware River to the east, South Street to the south, and Spring Garden Street to the north.

Within downtown Philadelphia lie several distinct neighborhoods. On the east side by the Delaware River are **Old City** and **Society Hill**, where every street corner seems to have played some role in the American Revolution. Old City is anchored by Independence National Historical Park and includes Philadelphia's most famous attractions like the Liberty Bell and Independence Hall. It has also evolved into a hub for dining and nightlife, which is highly convenient for visitors looking to fuse educational tourism with a plain old good time. Society Hill is comparatively quiet and residential. Landmarked townhomes, where the early American elite lived and dined, blend seamlessly into the contemporary streetscapes. During spring, summer, and fall, the clop and clatter of horse-drawn carriages around Old City and Society Hill provide a fitting din. The southern limits of Society Hill give way to the contrastive South Street district, an offbeat strip of bars, restaurants, tattoo parlors, clothing stores, and specialty shops that attracts a younger demographic.

Just east and a bit north of Old City is Philadelphia's **Chinatown.** While physically smaller than Chinatowns in New York and San Francisco, the neighborhood's streets hum with activity, and its restaurants stay open late. Chinatown's centerpiece is the beautiful Friendship Arch at 10th Street. The western edge of Chinatown gives way to the Philadelphia Convention Center, an informal eastern boundary of **Penn Center,** Philadelphia's high-rise business district. Here are Center City's skyscrapers, a glistening cluster of office buildings, hotels, and condominium towers.

Chinatown bustles day and night.

Below Chinatown is attractive, mostly residential **Washington Square West**, a sleeper area for gourmet restaurants and shopping. The western half is known as the "Gayborhood," the heart of Philadelphia's gay and lesbian culture.

South of Market Street and west of Broad is **Rittenhouse Square.** The square itself constitutes Philadelphia's second most famous park, and perhaps the city's most beloved. Summertime in Rittenhouse Square is magical, as its lush vegetation and fountains form a perfect urban oasis, synchronically accessible and secluded. The proximate neighborhood is appropriately grand, boasting top restaurants and some remarkable hotels.

North of Rittenhouse Square is the **Logan Square** neighborhood, alternately referred to by its main arterial road: the Benjamin Franklin Parkway, which runs from City Hall to the Philadelphia Museum of Art. The Parkway is itself a sight to see, its broad, tree-lined avenues intended to evoke the Champs-Élysées. High rises and townhomes are scattered throughout the area, but it is best known for its museums. The Franklin Institute, the Academy of Natural Sciences and the Rodin Museum are all on the Parkway.

TRANSPORTATION

Getting There

Commercial air traffic comes through **Philadelphia International Airport** (www.phl.org), which is served by all major airlines and is a hub for US Airways. The airport is located on the southern edge of the city, roughly 8 miles from downtown. A leader among American airports in environmentally responsible growth, PHL is rapidly becoming a modern facility, with renovation and expansion a constant over the last 10 years. Rental cars are available from all national companies and taxi service to downtown Philadelphia is a flat $28.50 per ride. Limousine service runs $50–$75 for a single trip. Some hotels clustered around the airport offer free shuttle service, but downtown hotels do not. The thrifty choice is to take regional rail on the Southeast Pennsylvania Transit Authority (SEPTA) for $5.50 per person (the R1 line has two stops downtown). Keep in mind that SEPTA trains stop running just after midnight and don't start again until 5 A.M., so red-eye fliers will need alternate transportation. SEPTA bus service is also available.

Rail travel to Philadelphia is convenient from most East Coast cities via **AMTRAK** (215-369-1069 or 1-800-872-7245; www.amtrak.com), but AMTRAK trains stop at 30th Street Station in West Philadelphia, so connection to downtown requires a short cab ride or train connection. **Greyhound** (215-931-4075 or 1-800-231-2222; www.greyhound.com) has a 24-hour bus terminal at 10th and Filbert Streets in downtown Philadelphia, which it shares with regional bus line **Peter Pan** (1-800-333-9999; www.peterpanbus.com). The supremely budget-sensitive can visit **Gotobus.com** to reserve tickets for "Chinatown buses," which run frequently from Chinatowns in New York, Washington, D.C., and Boston at bargain basement rates. The $20 round-trip from New York to Philadelphia is a college student staple. New bargain-priced lines **Megabus** (www.megabus.com) and **Bolt Bus** (www.boltbus.com) also offer incredibly inexpensive fares up and down the Northeast corridor. You generally need to reserve these tickets in advance, so check the Web sites for availability.

By car, Philadelphia is accessible via I-95. The Vine Street exit on the southbound side will deposit you in the heart of town. The Schuylkill Expressway (I-76) runs east-west and is the most direct route into the city from many suburbs. The Benjamin Franklin Bridge runs directly into the east part of Center City from southern New Jersey, via I-676 over the Delaware River. While lacking a traditional beltway, Philadelphia is encircled by a series of interstates that serve essentially the same purpose. I-276 links the suburbs north of the city, and touches both I-476 in the west and I-95 in the east. The latter hooks around the south part of town to complete the circle. All these roads hit I-76, which empties into the city. For those willing to endure traffic lights, US 30 and US 1 offer direct access to Philadelphia from the west and south, respectively.

Philadelphia is 100 miles from New York City, 100 miles from Baltimore, and about 130 miles from Washington, D.C.

Getting Around

Philadelphia's downtown is a grid, with the exception of the Benjamin Franklin Parkway, which runs diagonally from City Hall to the Museum of Art. Numbered streets run north-south, with low numbers on the east side. Major crosstown streets have an arboreal theme (Chestnut, Walnut, Spruce, Pine, etc.). Broad Street is the major north-south artery, and carries traffic in both directions. Market Street serves a similar function running crosstown, though it only allows west-east traffic on the west side of the city. Market and Broad meet at City Hall, a beautiful and historic building that nonetheless creates a rather large impediment to vehicular travel. The resulting intersection is a muddled, synthetic traffic circle that is best avoided if possible. Congestion in Philadelphia is a problem during rush hour but manageable the rest of the day. Be especially leery of I-76 and I-95 from 5 P.M. to 7 P.M.

Taxis are easy to find on Friday and Saturday nights circling the city's hotspots, and you have a decent chance of snagging one midday around most of downtown. Base fare is $2.70, and each mile is $2.30, plus a flat $0.50 gas surcharge tagged onto every ride. Taxi companies include Olde City Taxi (215-338-0838), Quaker City Cab (215-728-8000), and Yellow Cab (215-922-8400).

During the spring and summer you can ride purple, natural gas–powered **Philly Phlash** trolleys (www.phillyphlash.com) across town from the Penn's Landing waterfront as far west as the Museum of Art. Rides are $2 each, or $4 for an all-day pass. Trolleys run from 10 A.M. to 6 P.M. when operational. Look for the Phlash's colorful logo on poles all along Market Street and the Ben Franklin Parkway to designate the route's 21 stops.

Another option for getting around is public transit on **SEPTA** (215-580-7800; www.septa.org), which operates subway, bus, rail, and trolley lines. There are two subway lines—the Broad Street line running north-south and the Market-Frankford line running east-west. The subways can be useful, but Philadelphia is more of a bus town when it comes to mass transit. There are 110 bus routes, most of which run from 5 A.M. to 1 A.M. The system's strongest suit is arguably regional rail (see Chapter 3), which is unhelpful for getting around downtown. At one time trolley service was a key component of Philadelphia's transit infrastructure, but most trolleys have been replaced with buses. A few holdouts remain to serve West Philadelphia. Subways, buses, and trolleys cost $2 per ride, with exact change or token required. You can save $0.55 a ride by purchasing tokens ahead of time; unfortunately, functional token machines cannot be found at every station. Those who plan on taking the subway often should buy several tokens upon arrival. A 24-hour day pass is $5.50 and can be used for all buses, subways, and trolleys, plus one ride on any regional rail line.

Even with all these options, the best way to get around downtown Philadelphia is on foot. Streets are small, navigable, and above all interesting. You can walk the length of downtown, from the Delaware River to the Schuylkill in under an hour.

Independence Visitor Center in the heart of historic Philadelphia

Touring

No matter how you intend to tour downtown Philadelphia, your first stop should be **Independence Visitor Center** (1-800-537-7676; www.independencevisitor center.com; 6th and Market Sts.). The center is stocked with detailed, up-to-date information about the region's major attractions and screens short films on America's founding to whet your historical appetite. The friendly staff can help you book a tour, reserve tickets for shows or attractions, or direct you to a particular part of town. Computer portals allow you to research restaurants, museums, and even book a last-minute hotel room or rental car. On Saturday mornings, the center's ballroom holds Breakfast with Ben (215-965-7676; www.breakfastwithben.com) for kids and parents to talk with Dr. Franklin over eggs, muffins, fried potatoes, and juice. Make your reservation at least one day in advance.

The center is located on Independence Mall, between the Liberty Bell and the National Constitution Center in **Independence National Historical Park** (www.nps.gov/inde). The park's seven-block footprint is loaded with historical attractions. It has been managed by the National Park Service since its 1956 founding, so nearly all are free of charge. A perfunctory tour of the park attractions can be completed with a visitor's center map and a little curiosity.

By Boat

Spirit of Philadelphia (1-866-455-3866; www.spiritofphiladelphia.com). Lunch, dinner, moonlight, and themed cruises along the Delaware River. The ship leaves from Penn's Landing.

By Bus or Trolley

The venerable **Philadelphia Trolley Works** (215-389-8687; www.phillytour.com) runs double-decker buses and trolleys throughout downtown all day, shuttling tourists between attractions with company guides narrating along the way. You can ride these burgundy

A "Ride the Ducks" amphibious vehicle turns onto South Street.

buses and Victorian-style trolleys for 24 hours upon purchase for a single fee ($27 for adults, $10 for children under 13). Twenty stops are scattered around Center City, as far east as the Delaware River and as far west as Fairmount Park. The entire loop takes an hour and a half. Using the bus or trolley makes sense if you plan to stay on board for the whole tour. Attractions on the east side are so close to one another that during high-traffic seasons it can be faster to walk. Service operates from the morning to late afternoon. Passes can be purchased on board, at the Visitor's Center or online.

Philadelphia also offers amphibious touring via **Philadelphia Ride the Ducks** (1-877-887-8225; www.phillyducks.com). The funny looking vehicles start at 6th and Chestnut Streets, tour the historic district, and dip into the Delaware River for a spell. Kids love the duck tours, which are both humorous and informative.

And if time allows, consider taking a tour of Philadelphia's beautiful and storied public murals with **Mural Arts Tours** (215-389-8687; www.muralarts.org). Center City tours occur only during the first week of the month on Wednesdays and weekends (other tours explore different city neighborhoods). Be sure to call ahead to confirm a tour date.

By Bicycle or on Foot

Biking downtown Philadelphia is tricky business. Attractive crosstown byways like Pine Street are very narrow, and drivers tend to be aggressive. A bit more luck can be had on wider arterial roads like Market and Broad Streets, but traffic also moves quickly and can be hazardous. One surprisingly good downtown bike route is Christopher Columbus Boulevard, which runs north and south on the east side by the river and Penn's Landing; it serves fast-moving vehicular traffic but also has designated bike lanes. During warmer months you'll catch a refreshing breeze off the Delaware.

Philadelphia is actually a very good city for biking; it's just that the best routes are found outside downtown. (See Chapter 3 for suggestions, including the picturesque Schuylkill River Trail.) Because of this, renting a bicycle in Center City is difficult. There are two reliable rental options just outside the downtown boundaries:

Breakaway Bikes (215-568-6002; www.breakawaybikes.com; 1 Boathouse Row). Breakaway Bikes is a good bike shop in Center City at 1923 Chestnut Street, but the company also operates a rental booth in Fairmount Park on Boathouse Row. It is very close to downtown, just past the Art Museum on Kelly Drive. Call for directions on how to rent.

Trophy Bikes (215-222-2020; www.trophybikes.com; 3131 Walnut St.). Just barely over the Schuylkill River in West Philadelphia at the base of the Left Bank apartment complex. Tandem bikes are also available for rental with a reservation.

Of course, the best way to explore downtown Philadelphia is on foot. Enterprising types can just pick up a complimentary street map from the Visitor Center, which notes major attractions. Between Memorial Day and Labor Day you'll find performers scattered throughout the historic attractions at storytelling benches, spinning the occasional yarn. Additionally, the privately managed **Center City District** (www.centercityphila.org) has done a very effective job installing color-coded signage throughout the area. Easily recognizable "Walk!Philadelphia" postings on city sidewalks direct pedestrians to nearby attractions with easy-to-read maps and arrows. These signs are ubiquitous in downtown Philadelphia, and very useful in a pinch. Look for one if you get lost.

Downtown also offers guided walking tours to suit all tastes:

Centipede Tours (215-735-3123; www.centipedeinc.com). Comprehensive themed tours of historic Philadelphia, with guides in colonial-era costumes. Other tours are available as well, including Center City beyond the historic area.

Constitutional Walking Tour (215-525-1776; www.theconstitutional.com). Guided tours of historic Philadelphia that leave from the Visitor Center. The route hits all the big Old City attractions, and you can take it any day of the week between Memorial Day and Labor Day, plus weekends during the fall and early spring. The Constitutional Foundation, which runs the tour, lays out a good walking route for a self-guided tour of the historic district on its Web site.

Ghost Tour of Philadelphia (215-413-1997; www.ghosttour.com/philadelphia.html). Candlelit tours of creepy sites around Society Hill and vicinity. Washington Square's grisly history is especially disturbing.

Lights of Liberty Show (1-877-462-1776; www.lightsofliberty.org). A unique and impressive spectacle, Lights of Liberty is a combination show and walking tour around Independence National Historic Park. It employs high-tech light and sound effects to tell the story of the American Revolution. Show dates vary. There are between two and five show days a week from May–October.

Philadelphia Society for the Preservation of Landmarks (215-925-2251; www.philalandmarks.org). The Society offers a wide variety of themed tours in Center City and beyond, including numerous architectural walking tours.

By Carriage

'76 Carriage Company (215-925-8687; www.phillytour.com). Three different horse-drawn coach rides around historic Philadelphia, with varying length and scope. The shortest tour does just the Park, the longest includes Old City and Society Hill.

LODGING

Downtown Philadelphia has many quality hotels to suit all budgets and tastes, including a few bed & breakfasts. Visitors need not worry about astronomical rack rates for downtown hotels (as in Manhattan) or deceptively remote "downtown" inns clustered outside the urban core (as in Washington, D.C.). To be sure, there are a number of fine hotels on the edge of the city, but if you wish to stay downtown you should find it neither difficult nor prohibitively expensive. Center City's stock of hotel rooms rocketed up in the late 1990s, in part because of the city's broad resurgence and partly in anticipation of the 2000 Republican National Convention. Center City hotels retain decent occupancy rates—around 73 percent—but there are usually more than enough rooms to go around. One significant new hotel had not yet opened at press time: a **Four Points by Sheraton** at 1201 Race St. in Chinatown.

Lodging is organized by neighborhood. If your primary interest is in Philadelphia's historical attractions, choose a hotel on the east side of downtown, in the Old City or Society Hill neighborhoods. Alternatively, stay on or around the Benjamin Franklin Parkway for proximity to museum row and Fairmount Park. If you prefer to dabble in both, consider staying near Rittenhouse Square or the Convention Center. Hotels here are often the best values in the city, and Philadelphia's downtown is easily walkable. One obvious caveat: when big name conventions and special events come to town like the Philadelphia Flower Show, room rates at hotels adjacent to the Convention Center inevitably spike up.

In 2003, the **Greater Philadelphia Tourism Marketing Corporation** (www.gophila.com) debuted its "Philly's More Fun When You Sleep Over" campaign, aimed at filling the city's hotel rooms with travelers from nearby areas who typically visit Philadelphia for the day. The slogan gets it right. Philadelphia is a fine day trip, but there is far more to do than can be crammed into a single day by even the most workmanlike visitor. Check out the Web site for packages at Center City hotels that include discount coupon books and free parking. It is also a good site to visit prior to your trip, just to see what's going on.

Rates

Inexpensive	Up to $80
Moderate	$80 to $150
Expensive	$150 to $230
Very Expensive	$230 and up

These rates do not include room taxes or special service charges that might apply during your stay. All hotels are handicapped accessible unless otherwise noted. Total hotel taxes come to 14 percent.

City Hall/Penn Center

Courtyard Philadelphia Downtown
215-496-3200 or 1-888-887-8130
www.marriott.com
21 N. Juniper St., Philadelphia, PA 19107
Price: Expensive
Credit Cards: Yes

Among Philadelphia's most triumphant conversions, the Courtyard completed a protracted metamorphosis from Beaux-Arts municipal building to Beaux-Arts hotel in 1998, after standing vacant for 10 years. It was once the City Hall Annex, a distinction preserved with an entrance plaque and the moniker of the downstairs Annex Grille and Lounge. The Philip A. Johnson Library—named for the famous American architect who designed the building—is a comfortable place to read or decompress and has a nice stock of coffee table books. Rooms are elegant and comfortable, with plush chairs and ergonomically designed work space.

Crowne Plaza Philadelphia City Center

215-561-7500 or 1-800-972-2796
www.crowneplaza.com
1800 Market St., Philadelphia, PA 19103
Price: Expensive to very expensive
Credit Cards: Yes

Its renovations completed in the spring of 2008, this stylish, centrally located luxury hotel is popular with both tourists and business travelers. Amenities are first rate and include wireless Internet throughout the property, a 24-hour fitness center, and outdoor pool deck. The Crowne Plaza's specialty is a good night's sleep—all guest rooms are fitted with extra-cushy beds and calming accoutrements like eye masks and sleep CDs.

Doubletree Philadelphia

215-893-1600 or 1-800-222-8733
www.doubletree.com
237 S. Broad St., Philadelphia, PA 19107
Price: Very expensive
Credit Cards: Yes

The Doubletree towers over Broad Street, offering some superlative views on the north side and easy access to the Avenue of the Arts theater district. The lobby underwent a recent facelift and boasts a comfortable modernity that matches the guest rooms. The downstairs Standing O Bistro and Bar is unusually lively for a hotel bar, often peopled late into the evening by the after-theater crowd lingering over nightcaps. The Doubletree also draws lots of business travelers.

Marriott Residence Inn

215-557-0005 or 1-800-331-3131
www.residenceinn.com
1 E. Penn Square, at Market & Juniper Sts., Philadelphia, PA 19107
Price: Expensive to very expensive
Credit Cards: Yes

Not to be confused with the Courtyard Marriott next door, the Residence Inn is an all-suite property housed in the former Market Street National Bank. The hotel was a centerpiece of Philadelphia's downtown redevelopment in 2000–2001, when the slender 25-story art deco building (mostly shuttered at the time) was converted. The free breakfast and indoor pool are handy amenities, and many of the 269 suites peer out over the city skyline. Suites also have kitchens. As with all Residence Inns, hotel employees will do your food shopping if you ask.

Park Hyatt Philadelphia at the Bellevue

215-893-1234 or 1-800-233-1234
www.parkphiladelphia.hyatt.com
Broad St. and Walnut St., Philadelphia, PA 19102
Price: Very expensive
Credit Cards: Yes

In its way, the Bellevue is as iconic as the Liberty Bell or Art Museum. Now over a century old, the magnificent French Renaissance building is the crown jewel of Broad Street and one of the most sumptuous hotels in Philadelphia. It has been the choice of presidents, entertainers, ambassadors, kings, and queens for much of its history. Like Philadelphia, the Bellevue has had its ups and downs—it closed for part of the 1980s due to an economic downturn—but has shown resilience time and again. Under the steady management of the Hyatt brand since 1996, the Bellevue has a top-story bar and restaurant Nineteen (XIX) overlooking the city, an excellent sporting club/fitness center, and 24-hour room service.

Ritz-Carlton Philadelphia

215-523-8000 or 1-800-542-8680
www.ritzcarlton.com
10 S. Broad St., Philadelphia, PA 19102
Price: Very expensive
Credit Cards: Yes

Awe-inspiring is the only way to describe the Ritz, Philadelphia's most impressively converted Neoclassical Revivalist wonder. The Ionic columns, portico, and marble lobby (recently renovated and dramatically modernized) once belonged to the Girard Trust Company. If you try hard you can imagine the space in its former life as a bank. The Ritz coddles its guests with amenities and service, particularly those who upgrade to Club level rooms and get their own personal concierge. The 1,900-square-foot penthouse suite, with private elevator, is among the most renowned hotel rooms in the city. If you can't bear to leave at the end of your stay, consider purchasing a condominium in the nearly completed Ritz-Carlton Residences tower next door.

Convention Center

Hilton Garden Inn

215-923-0100 or 1-800-774-1500
www.hiltongardenphilly.com
1100 Arch St., Philadelphia, PA 19107
Price: Expensive
Credit Cards: Yes

The Hilton occupies a middle market niche for Convention Center hotels between the budget Travelodge and the posh downtown Marriott. Bright, business-friendly guest rooms are practically appointed and well-priced. Nearly half the guest rooms are junior suites that come with an extra television set and extended living space. All rooms have refrigerators, microwaves, and coffeemakers, and are on the seventh story or higher since a parking garage occupies all the space below. The Tenth Floor Grill serves basic American fare.

Loews Philadelphia Hotel

215-231-7333 or 1-866-563-9792
www.loewshotels.com
1200 Market St., Philadelphia, PA 19107
Price: Expensive to very expensive
Credit Cards: Yes

Loews Philadelphia Hotel, still bearing the initials of the Philadelphia Savings Fund Society

The letters "PSFS" still hang atop this famous Philadelphia landmark, suggesting its previous association with the Philadelphia Savings Fund Society, America's oldest bank. The building, completed in 1932, will look instantly familiar to students of International-style architecture as an original and eminent example of modern design in the United States. The tower was rescued by the Loews hotel corporation in the late 1990s after the bank went belly up. Today's Loews is a study in contrasts: the unornamented, machine age exterior now encloses a conspicuously extravagant hotel with a deluxe spa and flat-screen televisions in the rooms. But it is fitting. The original structure was considered exceptionally cutting edge for its time, so today's ultramodern hotel is its logical heir. It is also a fun place to stay, with distinct, colorful rooms and one of the city's finest in-house fitness centers. A daily breakfast buffet at the SoleFood restaurant downstairs serves an impressive spread for around $20.

Philadelphia Marriott

215-625-2900 or 1-800-320-5744
www.philadelphiamarriott.com

1201 Market St., Philadelphia, PA 19107
Price: Expensive to very expensive
Credit Cards: Yes

A practical choice for conventioneers, the labyrinthine Marriott feeds right into the Pennsylvania Convention Center. It also possesses a wide variety of meeting rooms, lounges, and halls, including the 33,000-square-foot Grand Ballroom. Renovations are ongoing, which engenders an air of confusion, but outstanding service and a central location keep the place humming. Upgrade to "Concierge-level" guest status and avail yourself of breakfast, hors d'oeuvres, and drinks at an exclusive top-floor lounge. A Starbucks on the ground level and the Hard Rock Café across the street are the more egalitarian hangouts.

Logan Square
Embassy Suites
215-561-1776 or 1-800-362-2779
www.embassysuites.com
1776 Benjamin Franklin Pkwy.,
Philadelphia, PA 19103
Price: Expensive to very expensive
Credit Cards: Yes

During its years as an apartment complex, basketball player Wilt Chamberlain lived in this cylindrical 28-story building. Embassy Suites acquired the property in the early 1990s, and gave it a bright lobby, while outfitting its multi-room suites with sofa beds and efficiency kitchens. Each one has a balcony, some with Parkway/Art Museum views, and others overlooking the Center City skyline. Suites are a spacious 750 square feet, making this hotel a smart choice for families. Check for offers, which include tickets to kid-popular attractions like the Philadelphia Zoo.

Four Seasons
215-963-1500 or 1-800-332-3442
www.fourseasons.com/philadelphia
1 Logan Square, Philadelphia, PA 19103

Price: Very expensive
Credit Cards: Yes

A brighter, airier interpretation of high luxury lodging than you'll find at other Philadelphia hotels, the low-rise Four Seasons uses soft woods, light granite, and cream-colored walls where her competitors invoke dark mahogany and black marble. The free-flowing ground floor hooks around a courtyard with fountains and foliage, viewable through large windows. The hotel is a peaceful retreat at the busy end of the Ben Franklin Parkway, though it buzzes a bit on Sundays when locals and visitors descend for brunch at the Fountain restaurant or Swann Lounge. The Four Seasons provides every service and amenity imaginable, and its on-site spa is among the city's most revered.

Sheraton Philadelphia City Center
215-448-2000 or 1-866-716-8103
www.starwoodhotels.com/sheraton
17th and Race Sts., Philadelphia, PA 19103
Price: Expensive to very expensive
Credit Cards: Yes

The vast and open foyer with an oblique glass roof welcomes guests to one of few Philadelphia hotels that provides for business and leisure travelers with equal exertion. The location just off the Ben Franklin Parkway puts you within manageable walking distance from the Museum of Art, but don't be surprised to see convention activity spill over into the hallways and the lobby bar. This is among Philadelphia's largest hotels with close to eight hundred rooms, and the facilities have been modernized by Sheraton since the company acquired the hotel from Wyndham in 2006. It recently added a Philips Seafood restaurant, a Maryland import known for its crab cakes.

Windsor Suites Philadelphia
215-981-5678 or 1-877-784-8379

www.windsorhotel.com
1700 Benjamin Franklin Pkwy.,
Philadelphia, PA 19103
Price: Expensive to very expensive
Credit Cards: Yes

Perched near the base of the Ben Franklin Parkway, the Windsor is a combination hotel and apartment complex. Studio suites are a good size for small groups and come with kitchens. Larger one-bedroom suites run $30–$50 extra per night. The best rooms include functioning balconies with views of the Parkway, and the seasonal rooftop pool is a nice amenity. Ask for a suite with a recently renovated bathroom since improvements are ongoing.

Old City

Best Western Independence Park
215-922-4443 or 1-800-624-2988
www.independenceparkinn.com
235 Chestnut St., Philadelphia, PA 19106
Price: Expensive to very expensive
Credit Cards: Yes

A historic slice of Chestnut Street construction, this 36-room hotel is on the National Register of Historic Places and could not feel less like a multinational chain. The building has been in use since 1856 and once housed a brewery. The subsequent conversion from industrial space to inn created nicely sized, high-ceilinged guest rooms (up to 17 feet), a rarity in this dense part of Old City. Most rooms are outfitted with Federal-style furniture.
Complimentary breakfast is served under a sunken glass enclosure, allowing just the right amount of morning sunlight.

Hyatt Regency at Penn's Landing
215-928-1234 or 1-800-233-1234
www.pennslanding.hyatt.com
201 S. Columbus Blvd., Philadelphia, PA 19106
Price: Expensive to very expensive
Credit Cards: Yes

Interstate 95 separates this luxury hotel from the historical attractions of Old City, so many guests are business travelers. A sea of dark suits floods the second-floor event rooms during the daytime and the Keating's River Grill during happy hour. But the Hyatt also offers packages including breakfast and a late checkout, which work for leisure travelers with a car or who are willing to stroll. Views from the tower overlook either Center City or the Delaware River waterfront.

Omni Hotel at Independence Park
215-925-0000 or 1-800-843-6664
www.omnihotels.com
4th St. and Chestnut St., Philadelphia, PA 19106
Price: Very expensive
Credit Cards: Yes

The lobby lounge at the Omni is one of Philadelphia's more elegant places to enjoy a strong drink and a light meal. A ground-level view of Chestnut Street activity makes for good people-watching as you relax by the fireplace, piano, and plenteous flora. Plant life is a theme at the Omni, extending to the restrained but classy guest rooms, which have either two queen beds or a king and a plush sleeper-sofa. Taken as a whole, the Omni is among Center City's most appealing luxury hotels. And it is doubly appealing if you can secure a high-floor view of the park. When offered, packages including a dining credit at the neighboring Buddakan restaurant are a great value.

Penn's View Inn
215-922-7600 or 1-800-331-7634
www.pennsviewhotel.com
14 N. Front St., Philadelphia, PA 19106
Price: Expensive
Credit Cards: Yes

Something completely different from the high-rise luxury hotels downtown, the Penn's View is a family-owned, 52-room

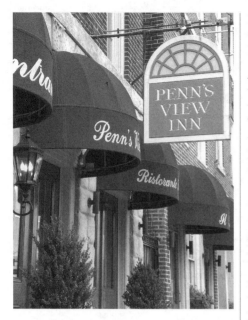

The wonderful Penn's View Inn

boutique hotel, just off the Delaware River in the heart of historic Philadelphia. It is also one of downtown's most romantic lodging options. Standard rooms are on the small side, but offer either little terraces—a rarity in Philadelphia—or handsome exposed brick décor. Premium rooms are larger and have the choicest views; they also come with working fireplaces and whirlpools. The Penn's View neatly merges a cloistered intimacy with a first-class service standard. Frequent guests are welcomed by name and the small staff always goes the extra mile. Your stay includes a continental breakfast with fresh waffles and fruit. The wine bar off the lobby, decorated with murals of Renaissance Italians playing mandolins, is a lovely place for a glass before dinner.

Thomas Bond House
215-923-8523 or 1-800-845-2663
www.winston-salem-inn.com/philadelphia
info@thomasbondhousebandb.com
129 S. 2nd St., Philadelphia, PA 19106

Price: Moderate to expensive
Credit Cards: Yes
Handicapped Access: No

A 12-room Georgian structure renovated in the Federal style, the house once belonged to Pennsylvania Hospital co-founder Dr. Thomas Bond, whose portrait hangs above the lounge's fireplace. The lounge and breakfast rooms are outfitted with Chippendale furniture common in Philadelphia's elite residences during the colonial era. Rooms have mostly pencil post or high poster beds, and the Thomas Bond Jr. and Sr. suites boast fireplaces and full baths with whirlpool jets. The clever Benjamin Franklin Room on the fourth floor has a borrowed window in between the bath and bedroom, allowing light to pass through (though its pitched ceiling makes it a poor choice for tall guests). Weekday mornings guests get a continental breakfast with pastries and fruit. Weekend breakfasts are prepared hot and might include egg and breakfast meat on Saturdays, and something heavier like stuffed French toast on Sundays. Wine and cheese is served every day from 5:30 to 6:30 P.M.

Rittenhouse Square
Hotel Sofitel Philadelphia
215-569-8300 or 1-800-763-4835
www.sofitel.com

Comfortable furnishings at Thomas Bond House

120 S. 17th St., Philadelphia, PA 19103
Price: Very expensive
Credit Cards: Yes

The French influence is everywhere from the brasserie to the bathroom soap, but the Sofitel also has a fun, unstuffy energy. Rooms are 400 square feet—big for Center City—and bathrooms have separate marble shower/bath combos. Soft lighting characterizes the public areas along with stone trimmings like the registration desk topped with blue Brazilian granite. Leisure travelers appreciate the hotel's proximate location to the pleasures of Rittenhouse Square and the Walnut Street shopping district. The design incorporates the old Philadelphia Stock Exchange Building.

The Latham Hotel

215-563-7474 or 1-877-528-4261
www.lathamhotel.com
135 S. 17th St., Philadelphia, PA 19103
Price: Expensive to very expensive
Credit Cards: Yes

The lobby of this one-hundred-year-old boutique hotel is bathed in marble, and the Beaux-Arts structure was once a residential building for the city's moneyed elite. The Latham maintains a European character, even after adapting old spaces to new uses like the fitness room and business center. Some rooms are larger than others, and most have a Victorian feel—sixth-floor rooms are just a bit more modern in style. The Latham boasts one of the most comprehensive amenity packages within its price bracket, right down to the uniformed doormen.

Radisson Plaza Warwick Hotel

215-735-6000 or 1-888-201-1718
www.radisson.com/philadelphiapa
1701 Locust St., Philadelphia, PA 19103
Price: Moderate to expensive
Credit Cards: Yes

Travelers give up some of the convenience to Philadelphia's historical attractions by staying in Rittenhouse Square, but get more space for their touring buck. Besides, the Radisson's recently completed renovation has it looking every bit as refined as luxury hotels that go for double the price on the east side of town. Rooms are now lustrous and modern, complete with firmness-adjustable beds. The Prime Rib, one of the city's best steakhouses, is right downstairs.

The Rittenhouse

215-546-9000 or 1-800-635-1042
www.rittenhousehotel.com
210 W. Rittenhouse Square., Philadelphia, PA 19103
Price: Very expensive
Credit Cards: Yes

Lavish, generously sized accommodations and the highest service standard distinguish this luxury hotel from even its upmarket competitors. It is magnificently appointed, from the mahogany and marble lobby dotted with fine art to the guest room armoires. A stay at the Rittenhouse affords you not only a bed with down pillows and a park view from every room, but Philadelphia's most exhaustive list of complimentary services. It is partly the hotel's small size—just 98 rooms and suites—that allows the famously attentive staff to meet guests' every need. Its prime location on the square makes the Rittenhouse among Philadelphia's most romantic hotels, as well as a popular spot for weddings. Restaurants on-site include the world-renowned Lacroix, and a Smith and Wollensky steakhouse.

Rittenhouse 1715

215-546-6500 or 1-877-791-6500
www.rittenhouse1715.com
reservations@rittenhouse1715.com
1715 Rittenhouse Square St., Philadelphia, PA 19103

Neighborhood: Rittenhouse Square
Price: Very expensive
Credit Cards: Yes

Avail yourself of the city's highest luxury standard at this 23-room boutique hotel on a thin side street just off Rittenhouse Square. A mere sampling of the amenity list: European towels and bathrobes, marble baths, pillow-top mattresses, Molton Brown toiletries, plasma televisions with 100-channel cable, and round-the-clock concierge and food delivery service. Rittenhouse 1715 flawlessly unites two Georgian townhouses with a hundred-year-old carriage house, creating a property that feels sumptuous and organic. Rooms and suites are slightly different from one another in layout and design, though all achieve an inviting elegance that is equal parts contemporary and classic. Guests enjoy daily white wine receptions in the early evening set in the handsomely furnished drawing room, which abuts an innovative nook garden. Deluxe continental breakfast is included every morning.

The Presidential Suite Living Room at Rittenhouse 1715. Courtesy Rittenhouse 1715

Westin Philadelphia
215-563-1600 or 1-800-937-8461
www.westin.com
99 S. 17th St., Philadelphia, PA 19103

Price: Expensive to very expensive
Credit Cards: Yes

Sleek luxury lodging in the shadows of One Liberty Place, Philadelphia's original skyscraper. The hotel is perfectly situated for both business and leisure travelers, halfway between Rittenhouse Square and City Hall. The Westin's famously comfortable beds, a cozy second-floor lounge, and a good fitness center are just a few highlights. Rooms are outfitted with flat-screen televisions and a solid lineup of business amenities. The glass hotel tower once housed the Philadelphia Ritz-Carlton before its move to Broad Street.

Society Hill
Sheraton Society Hill
215-238-6000 or 1-800-325-3535
www.sheraton.com/societyhill
1 Dock St., Philadelphia, PA 19106
Price: Expensive to very expensive
Credit Cards: Yes
A low-rise property that blends seamlessly into the rowhouses and cobblestone streets of Society Hill, the Sheraton doubles as a small museum. During the hotel's construction, archeologists uncovered mugs, vases, and other antiquities dating back to Philadelphia's colonial period. These are on display in the lobby. Despite its low height, the hotel is deceptively large, so request a room near the elevators. The top-floor pool is a unique perk. Ceiling skylights let you gaze at I. M. Pei's Society Hill Towers while doing the backstroke.

Washington Square West
Alexander Inn
215-923-3535 or 1-877-253-9466
www.alexanderinn.com
12th St. and Spruce St., Philadelphia, PA 19107
Price: Moderate to expensive
Credit Cards: Yes

The art deco Alexander is smaller than

most Center City hotels and is revered for its outstanding customer service. Located in the heart of the city's gay and lesbian cultural attractions, it is popular with gay travelers while appealing to a diverse clientele (families, conventioneers, etc.) that appreciates the quality and value.

Completed at the turn of the 20th century after an eight-year construction period, the hotel's stained glass, marble, and millwork are all original. Its 48 European-style rooms spread over seven floors are all non-smoking, and 36 include bay windows. An "Expanded Continental" breakfast features fresh fruit, yogurt, cereal, granola, and breakfast pastries.

Alexander Inn, a friendly choice in Center City

Morris House Hotel

215-922-2446
www.morrishousehotel.com
info@morrishousehotel.com
225 S. 8th St., Philadelphia, PA 19106
Price: Expensive to very expensive
Credit Cards: Yes

A rare and beloved treat, the 15-room Morris House Hotel achieves a tranquility that belies its Center City location. It is also a seamless union of new and old, perfectly exemplified in the hotel's Colonial-style exterior complemented by an entrance pediment with a clear glass tympanum. Perhaps the hotel's greatest feature is its courtyard garden, insulated from street noise and marked by a dogwood tree, among other flora. The garden is an understandably popular place for weddings, and guests can also take daily breakfast—which includes pastry from gourmet bakery LeBus—outside when the weather allows. Some rooms feature four-poster beds and period furniture. One that does not is the gorgeous bi-level presidential loft suite, which has a more modern flavor. The house is also a big slice of Philadelphia history, and Morris family heirlooms can be found throughout.

Value Choices

Aside from **Apple Hostels of Philadelphia** (1-877-275-1971; www.applehostels.com; 32 S. Bank St., Old City), where a bed in a shared dormitory-style room is around $30 a night, rack rates downtown start at $115–$125. The following hotels, all reliable national chains, typically offer rooms for under $200 per night:

Comfort Inn at Penn's Landing (215-627-7900 or 1-877-424-6423; www.comfortinn.com; 100 N. Columbus Blvd., Philadelphia, PA 19106). A touch isolated from centermost Old City, the Comfort Inn's courtesy shuttle makes the short trip for hotel guests on demand. Room rates are significantly lower than at similarly appointed hotels just a few blocks away, and bargain rates can be found with a little digging on discount travel Web sites. Hotel rooms are functional and guest services include an exercise room and continental breakfast.

Hampton Inn (215-665-9100 or 1-800-426-7866; www.hamptoninn.com; 1301 Race St., Philadelphia, PA 19107). Newer and better maintained than similarly priced Center City hotels. Primarily a business hotel within easy walking distance of the Convention Center, the Hampton makes sense for budget-minded tourists who don't mind staying in an unattractive—though perfectly safe—part of town.

Holiday Inn Express Midtown (215-735-9300 or 1-800-972-2796; www.himidtown.com; 1305 Walnut St., Philadelphia, PA 19107). Standard guest rooms are spacious for the price at this Washington Square West hotel, and an overnight stay includes hot breakfast. The hotel is virtually equidistant from Independence National Historical Park, Rittenhouse Square, and the Convention Center.

Holiday Inn Historic District (215-923-8660 or 1-800-972-2796; www.holiday-inn.com/phlhistoric; 4th St. and Arch St., Philadelphia, PA 19106). Location is the selling point at this affordable hotel, no more than a half mile from every major attraction in Old City and Society Hill. The rooftop pool is eight stories up, making it Old City's highest. The Holiday Inn is entirely nonsmoking.

Philadelphia Travelodge (215-564-2888 or 1-800-578-7878; www.travelodge.com; 1227 Race St., Philadelphia, PA 19107). Just north of the Convention Center and within skipping distance of Chinatown. The four-story hotel has 50 rooms that have coffee makers, cable television, and complimentary Internet access. Rates are low for the area, but only a bargain if easy access to the Convention Center is your top priority.

CULTURE

Architecture

Trying to assign Center City Philadelphia a "universal" architecture is a fool's errand. The city's old age, combined with its diversity and penchant for change have created a downtown that is simultaneously rich in architectural history and impossible to pin down stylistically. But the variety inherent in Philadelphia's architecture is part of what makes the city such a delightful place to tour.

The earliest post-Penn residences could be described as modified Georgian. Colonial-era homes throughout early America drew from Georgian architecture, incorporating strict symmetry, redbrick shells, and arched Palladian windows. Georgian architecture itself overlaps almost entirely with Palladian design, the style popularized during the Italian Renaissance and subsequently borrowed by Great Britain. The emergence of this style in an English colony should come as no surprise, though there are differences between English Palladian buildings and the average colonial-era Philadelphia row-home. Most notably, the Quaker ethos of humble practicality tended to tone down the ornamentation. There are certainly examples of elaborate Palladian features in downtown Philadelphia, but they are mostly reserved for special buildings such as **Christ Church** and **Independence Hall.**

Many Society Hill residences are preserved or rehabilitated Federal-style structures, and some of the housing stock dates back centuries. The low-rise Federal rowhouse is as distinctly Philadelphian as the city's architecture gets. A more grandiose example of the style is the old **Pennsylvania Hospital** at 8th and Pine Streets, where the brick facade is augmented by white marble.

Philadelphia also took part in the Greek Revival wave that swept the country through the first half of the 19th century. This was a proud time for the city, a peak of its financial and cultural prowess relative to the rest of the country, and the august Greek columns and imposing geometry of the style fit the era like a glove. The **Second Bank of the United States** and the **Merchant's Exchange** in Old City are famed examples of Greek Revival architecture in America. Neither structure serves its original purpose today, but both have been maintained.

The emergence of Greek Revival architecture in Philadelphia overlapped with the construction of Gothic Revival churches and residences, especially in the rapidly developing western side of Center City. It is here that you can find **St. Mark's Church**, its tall, narrow lancet windows and Gothic ornamentation nestled into a similarly striking block. While many architecture buffs readily tour the earlier-developing eastern side of town (not without cause) the Rittenhouse Square vicinity produced some eye-catching Gothic Revival buildings in the latter half of the 19th century when the eastern neighborhoods were mostly full.

Many of Philadelphia's great industrial-age buildings were done in Second Empire style, which filtered across the Atlantic Ocean in the mid to late 19th century. The American trend towards elaborate Victorian design corresponded with a growing demand for extravagant buildings in central Philadelphia such as **City Hall**, the **Masonic Temple**, and the **Union League**. Equally extravagant is the **Pennsylvania Academy of the Fine Arts** from acclaimed Philadelphia architect Frank Furness. The Academy is both a superb art museum and a multicolored, intensely creative Gothic-style structure.

The turn of the century brought a bevy of new architectural influences to Philadelphia. Beaux-Arts ushered in new buildings with ornate exterior sculptures. The Queen Anne style, with its distinctive medieval chimneys and bay windows became a staple of the era's new residential properties. The flagship **Wanamaker** department store was completed in 1911, with a boxy exterior design that gave way to a palatial five-story interior. Today the building is occupied by **Macy's**, and is as awe-inspiring as ever.

A tour of downtown Philadelphia cannot ignore the area's notable modern and post-modern architecture, a stew of buildings assembled after the Second World War. Changes in commercial and residential markets catalyzed a desire for more high-rise buildings, and 21st-century Center City has an easily identifiable skyline. At downtown's heart, Penn Center's collection of distinctive commercial skyscrapers is encircled by a growing number of residential towers. The first two buildings to surpass the 500-foot height of City Hall were the **Liberty Place** towers, completed in 1987 and 1990, which might be described as modernist interpretations of New York's Chrysler Building. Liberty Place One was Philadelphia's tallest structure until last year, when the **Comcast Center** edged it out at 975 feet. As the city's newest sky-

I. M. Pei's Society Hill Towers

scraper, the Comcast Center is an environmentally friendly "green" building with 56 floors of commercial tenants and lots of ground-level public space.

There has been high-rise development in Center City neighborhoods as well. The most familiar example since its controversial debut in 1964 is **Society Hill Towers:** I. M. Pei's triumvirate of rectilinear apartment buildings, which rise above the community's genteel townhouses. Center City has also produced interesting low-rise buildings since the war's end. For a look at influential postmodern architecture, visit Philadelphia native Robert Venturi's **Guild House** on 7th and Spring Garden Streets at the northernmost edge of Center City. Guild House demonstrates Venturi's fondness for the "Decorated Shed"—an ordinary, even unattractive looking building that features symbolic ornamentation.

Venturi still has an architectural firm in the city in the northwest Manayunk neighborhood, but he is just one of the many famous architects born in or based out of Philadelphia. Frank Furness, referenced earlier, designed some of Philadelphia's most spectacular Victorian Gothic buildings during the late 19th century. Louis I. Kahn lived in Philadelphia for much of his life, studied at the University of Pennsylvania, and developed a unique interpretation of the International style that utilized natural elements. Kahn's most famous Philadelphia building is outside Center City: the **Richards Medical Research Laboratories** at UPenn (see Chapter 3). The charming **Louis Kahn Park** was built in his memory in Center City's Washington Square West neighborhood. It stands at 11th and Pine Streets and hosts free concerts during the summertime.

Philadelphia's modern history also features a talented urban planner: Edward Bacon—father of actor Kevin—who headed the Philadelphia City Planning Commission through the 1950s and '60s. These were sanguine days for city planning in America, when urban renewal seemed within the reach of a capable bureaucrat. Bacon, like Robert Moses in New York, was a controversial figure who managed to drive numerous high-impact projects. He is responsible for downtown's Penn Center, among other Philadelphia developments.

There is a lot more to the region's architecture, of course, from the beautiful Victorian homes in West Philadelphia to the old industrial buildings in the north, to the mansions of wealthy Main Line suburbs like Gladwyne. Architecture aficionados should visit the Athenaeum in Society Hill (see "Libraries") for an all-encompassing look.

Art

Philadelphia has a proud art tradition. In 1959, the city enacted one of America's first Percent for Art ordinances, which sets aside a percentage of the budget for any public construction project to fund public art on the project site. The program has spawned hundreds of pieces since its inception, and many are scattered around downtown. The city has a **Public Art Program** office (www.publicartphiladelphia.org) to coordinate Percent for Art. Its Web site has a useful rundown of each piece of public art in Philadelphia, and you can use the site's information to map your own walking tour.

Percent for Art was joined in 1984 by the **Mural Arts Program** (www.muralarts.org), which sought to wipe out graffiti by using blank or blighted urban canvasses for large public murals. The program has achieved tremendous success at beautifying and revitalizing communities through creative, colorful art that speaks to neighborhoods' individual histories. Today, no city on the planet has more public murals than Philadelphia. The majority of murals are outside downtown, but the program Web site links to a cartographic tool developed by the University of Pennsylvania to help search for murals within a given area, including Center City.

"Moonlit Landscape," at 8th and Christian Streets south of Center City; one of many murals in Philadelphia from the Mural Arts Program. Everyone has a favorite.

Another wonderful installation is the **Magic Gardens** mosaic in the vicinity of South and 10th Streets (www.philadelphiasmagicgardens.org). The color and creativity makes it well worth the short walk from the South Street bar and restaurant district.

And finally, check out the cutting edge of public art on the **Comcast Center Video Wall** (1701 Arch St.). Walk into Philadelphia's newest skyscraper and you can't miss it, right behind the security desk. The wall panels transform into a 2,100-square-foot, high-definition video screen that shows short video clips in phenomenal color and clarity. While you're at the Comcast Center, visit the gourmet food court on the lower level.

See "Galleries" and "Museums" for more on Center City art.

Film

Philadelphia is blessed with the **Ritz** theater chain (www.ritztheaters.com), which operates three cinemas in Old City. Ritz shows mostly independent first-run films, and sells discount tickets for students and seniors. Center City's other movie theater is the **Roxy** in Rittenhouse Square, which shows both classic films and wide-release blockbusters. The Roxy is very old school—your ticket comes off the kind of numbered roll used at church raffles or carnivals. Also, the **Tuttleman IMAX Theater** at the Franklin Institute shows feature films on a four-and-a-half- story-high IMAX Dome screen. Big-budget popcorn flicks make the most of the effect.

Ritz at the Bourse (215-440-1181; 400 Ranstead St.)

Ritz East (215-925-2501; 125 S. 2nd St.)

Ritz Five (215-440-1184; 214 Walnut St.)

The Roxy (215- 923-6699; 2023 Sansom St.)

Tuttleman IMAX Theater (215-448-1111; 222 N. 20th St.)

Celluloid Synopsis

Visitors have been scampering up the "Rocky Steps" at the Philadelphia Museum of Art since the film's 1976 premiere. Since that time, Philadelphia's reputation as a cinematically friendly locale has soared, with dozens of productions following in the weathered fighter's boxing boots. See if already planned visits acquire extra meaning, or take a cinephile's trek of your own to some of these Philadelphia and surrounding areas made famous in film.

With its ominous history and ambiance, **Eastern State Penitentiary** is a film set waiting to happen. The creative team behind 1995's *12 Monkeys* capitalized on this, and used Eastern State as the mental institution that housed Jeffrey Goines, played by Brad Pitt in a breakthrough role.

The city served as backdrop and namesake for the 1993 film *Philadelphia*. Pop your iPod ear buds in and listen to Bruce Springsteen's "Streets of Philadelphia" while stopping off at the **Pickwick Pharmacy** (1700 Market St.). Denzel Washington as Joe Miller made a diaper run here, clashing with a customer and raising self-doubt about his decision to represent AIDS patient Andrew Beckett, played by Tom Hanks.

Pennsylvania native M. Night Shyamalan is known to feature the Philadelphia area in his films, particularly in 1999's *The Sixth Sense*. Walk by the intersection of **23rd Street and St. Albans Place,** where Haley Joel Osment as Cole Sear lived and first bonded with Dr. Malcolm Crowe, his furtive therapist played by Bruce Willis. In 2002, *Signs* took over the streets of Bucks County's **Newtown.** Mel Gibson as Reverend Graham Hess visited local veterinarian Ray Reddy, played by Shyamalan himself, on **State St.** And Paul Giamatti brought Cleveland Heep's rescue mission of a wayward water nymph, Bryce Dallas Howard, to life just across the street from the Bloomsdale section of **Bristol** in 2006's *Lady in the Water*.

If you're interested in a thorough look at Philadelphia's cinematic claims to fame, take the **Philadelphia in the Movies** tour (www.film.org). Check close to your visit, as tours are constantly changing. Local production has been on the rise since 2007, when the Film Production Tax Credit Program was signed into Pennsylvania law. Tours last around two hours and include a seat on a coach bus, allowing your legs to rest for that victory climb up the museum steps.

Galleries

There are galleries all around Center City, but the most concentrated cluster is found in Old City, along 2nd and 3rd Streets between Chestnut and Race. To see the Old City arts scene come alive, stop by between 5 P.M. and 9 P.M. on the first Friday of every month for Old City's First Friday celebration, organized by the **Old City Arts Association** (www.oldcityarts.org). Many galleries offer complimentary wine and finger food, and on clear evenings the energy spills into the streets. First Fridays draw an eclectic crowd, from

Main Line art lovers to college kids looking for a quick buzz before the evening's partying begins.

Along similar lines, keep your eye out for Center City Gallery Night, sponsored by the **Center City District** (www.centercityphila.org). Gallery Nights are less frequent occurrences than First Fridays, but an enjoyable way to see downtown galleries outside Old City. Here are just a handful of downtown's many galleries:

Art Alliance (215-545-4302; www.philartalliance.org; 251 S. 18th St.). The old Rittenhouse Square home of Christine Wetherill Stevenson, heiress to a paint fortune and a devoted supporter of the arts in Philadelphia. The Italian Renaissance–style mansion actually plays host to multifarious artistic pursuits, including play readings and music events. The galleries feature ambitious and unique exhibits of all kinds, from photography to porcelain sculpture to jewelry design. There is typically a $5 admission charge, but Fridays are pay what you wish. Stay for lunch at Gardenia, a nice little on-site restaurant.

The Clay Studio (215-925-3453; www.theclaystudio.org; 139 N. 2nd St.). Devoted exclusively to ceramics, the Clay Studio also offers classes and workshops for all experience levels and ages.

F.U.E.L. Collection (215-592-8400; www.fuelcollection.com; 249 Arch St.). Fans of MTV's *The Real World* television program may recognize the F.U.E.L. building as home base during the 2004–2005 season in Philadelphia. The large Neoclassical structure was eventually converted into a bright, two-tiered gallery that presents the work of fresh, up-and-coming artists.

The Galleries at Moore (215-965-4027; www.thegalleriesatmoore.org; 20th St. and the Ben Franklin Pkwy.). Moore College of Art and Design, an all-women undergraduate institution, uses these on-site galleries to display contemporary art, with an emphasis on pieces done by female artists. Undergraduate and alumni work is often featured as well. Open every day except Sunday.

Philadelphia Sketch Club (215-545-9298; www.sketchclub.org; 235 S. Camac St.). The club itself dates back to 1860, when Philadelphia was in the early stages of its emergence in the fine arts. The small oil painting exhibition has been a club tradition for nearly a century and a half and takes place in the early spring. While you're here, take a walk up Camac Street, which is partly made of wooden blocks.

Sande Webster Gallery (215-636-9003; www.sandewebstergallery.com; 2006 Walnut St.). An always interesting collection of mostly non-figurative art in a slightly offbeat, free-flowing space. The gallery also specializes in archival framing.

Vivant Art Collection (215-922-6584; www.vivantartcollection.com; 60 N. 2nd St.). A busy, high-ceilinged space featuring West African masks and pottery.

Wexler Gallery (215-923-7030; www.wexlergallery.com; 201 N. 3rd St.). A roomy, modern gallery emphasizing glass art and studio furniture. Always has something intriguing and unexpected.

Carpenters' Hall

Historic Homes and Sites

Bishop White House

215-965-2305

www.nps.gov/inde/bishop-white-house.htm

309 Walnut St., Philadelphia, PA 19106

Open: Hours vary, call ahead

Admission: $2

Bishop White was an early rector of Christ Church (see "Churches") and a crucial figure in Philadelphia's religiopolitical history. During the 1793 yellow fever epidemic, White remained in the city to aid the sick. His Federal-style house was a model of luxury in the 18th-century city, the parlor often playing host to gatherings for early Philadelphia's social elite.

Carpenters' Hall

215-925-0167

www.carpentershall.org

320 Chestnut St., Philadelphia, PA 19106

Open: Jan. and Feb., Wed.–Sun. 10–4; Mar.–Dec., Tues.–Sun. 10–4

Admission: Free

It's hard to imagine the First Continental Congress meeting in such a small space, especially if you've seen today's Capitol Building, but it's true. In September 1774, 56 representatives from 12 colonies convened here and addressed a list of grievances to King George III. It is also where the Pennsylvania Provincial Conference voted on the resolutions of the Second

Continental Congress and made
Pennsylvania a state. The site now houses a
small collection of historical exhibits and
colonial-era tools.

City Hall
215-686-1776
15th and Market Sts., Philadelphia, PA
19107
Open: Mon.–Fri. 9:30–4:15; tours every
weekday at 12:30; elevator rides to the top
of the tower all day
Admission: Tours are $10 (including the
tower); rides up the tower are $5

City Hall, located in the heart of
Philadelphia and in the exact geographic
center of William Penn's plan for the city,
rises over 510 feet in the air. Until the mid-
1980s there was an unspoken agreement
among Philadelphia's developers not to
build anything higher than City Hall, but
the current cluster of skyscrapers testifies
to the many recent breaches of that rule.
The building, widely panned by critics and
journalists when it first opened in 1891, has
come to be known as one of the nation's
most iconic examples of Second Empire
architecture. It is also known for Alexander
Milne Calder's 37-foot-tall statue of
William Penn that caps off the peak of the
colossal structure. Penn faces east towards
Penn Treaty Park, where he agreed to the
original peace treaty with the Lenape
Indians. The daily weekday tour is a comprehensive trip around the building's interior and takes roughly two hours. If you are
short on time, take the elevator ride up the
tower. On the way, you'll see the internal
workings of City Hall's great clocks. If it's a
clear day, you can see up to 40 miles of vista
from the observation deck. Even without
the tour or elevator ride, the premises can
be a fun diversion—on weekdays there's
occasionally some kind of press conference
or protest going on.

Congress Hall
215-965-2305
www.nps.gov/inde/congress-hall.htm
6th and Chestnut Sts., Philadelphia, PA
19106
Open: Daily 9–5
Admission: Free

Sixteen years after the American
Revolution was catalyzed at Carpenters'
Hall, the freshly elected U.S. Congress met
at Congress Hall to administer the federal
government. Philadelphia housed the leg-
islature for 10 years (1790–1800) while
L'Enfant and Ellicott worked on
Washington, D.C. Today you can tour the
restored House of Representatives on the
ground level and the Senate on the second
floor.

Declaration House
215-597-8974
www.nps.gov/inde/declaration-house.htm
7th and Market Sts., Philadelphia, PA 19106
Open: Daily 10–4
Admission: Free

Yes, it was on this site that Thomas
Jefferson drafted the famous Declaration of
Independence. And yes, the current
Jefferson exhibit presents a thorough history of the document and of Jefferson himself. But this isn't the real house where it
happened! The real Declaration House, part
of which Jefferson rented from a local
bricklayer to write the Declaration of
Independence, is long gone. The site was
vacant until the house was reconstructed in
1976 to celebrate the Bicentennial.

Elfreth's Alley
215-574-0560
www.elfrethsalley.org
information@elfrethsalley.org
Front and 2nd Sts. between Arch and Race
Sts., Philadelphia, PA 19106
Open: Mar.–Oct., Mon.–Sat. 10–5, Sun.
12–5; Nov.–Feb., Thurs.–Sat. 10–5, Sun. 12–5

Admission: Free to visit; museum is $5 adults, $1 children

Advertised as the oldest residential block in America, Elfreth's Alley housed colonial Americans as early as 1702 in an original Philadelphia neighborhood. Today, its Federal-style brick homes are so exquisitely restored and cared for that the street almost resembles a movie set. Walk down the alley any time you choose, but be courteous and quiet since people still live here. The museum is in House 126, midway down the block. Tours are free every July 4th.

Franklin Court

215-965-2305
www.nps.gov/inde/franklin-court.htm
314–322 Market St., Philadelphia, PA 19106
Open: Daily 9–5
Admission: Free

This is a great attraction, and the site of Ben Franklin's first Philadelphia home. The home is now gone, but Philadelphia architect Robert Venturi cleverly designed a pseudo-skeleton of the building, which makes for an interesting tour. Franklin Court's underground museum offers great insight into Franklin's scientific curiosity. An adjacent building considers his early attempts to build fire-resistant homes. There is also the courtyard, a pleasant public space at the nexus of the Independence Hall area. On the whole, the imaginative design of the spot is a fitting tribute to an intensely creative man.

Independence Hall

215-965-2305
www.nps.gov/inde/independence-hall-1.htm
Chestnut St. between 5th and 6th Sts., Philadelphia, PA 19103
Open: Daily 9–5
Admission: Free; tours leave every 15–20 minutes

An obvious must-see for most visitors,

Elfreth's Alley, among the oldest residential streets in America

Independence Hall was the hub of the American Revolution, and played a key role in the subsequent birth of the nation. It was here that the Declaration of Independence was signed, where the Second Continental Congress convened to firm up the revolution, and where the nation's founders eventually junked the Articles of Confederation and drafted the Constitution. Delegates to the Constitutional Convention met in the Assembly Room, which has been mostly recreated but still contains George Washington's "Rising Sun" chair, the perch from which he governed the convention. Independence Hall is also a good place to start a tour of Philadelphia, in part because of its central location and in part because the events that occurred here serve as an appropriate historical starting point for the neighboring attractions. The free tours, led by engaging park rangers, run a brisk 30–40 minutes. You need tickets, which can be picked up at the Independence Visitor Center. To be safe, call the center prior to your trip to reserve tickets if you intend to visit during a peak tourist season.

Liberty Bell Center

215-965-2305
www.nps.gov/inde/liberty-bell-center.htm
6th and Chestnut Sts., Philadelphia, PA
19106
Open: Daily 9–5
Admission: Free

As with most instantly recognizable symbols and monuments, actually seeing the Liberty Bell is a bit anticlimactic. The bell was made in England in 1751, and rang over the Pennsylvania State House in the run-up to the Revolutionary War. It might have escaped the history textbooks but for a group of abolitionists who used it to symbolize the struggle for freedom during the 1830s. The bell stands at the end of an exhibition on civil rights movements and the struggle for liberty throughout American history. The attraction's popularity and recently heightened security measures make seeing the bell a potentially time-consuming activity. Beat the lines by coming very early or very late in the afternoon.

Masonic Temple

215-988-1900
www.pagrandlodge.org
1 N. Broad St., Philadelphia, PA 19107
Open: Tours leave Tues.–Fri. at 11, 2, and 3, and Sat. at 10 and 11; schedule can vary, call ahead
Admission: Adults $8, children and seniors $5

The Pennsylvania branch of the Freemasons, America's oldest fraternal order, completed this exceptionally ornate edifice in 1873. Still, the history of the Masons in American and Pennsylvania goes back much farther. Benjamin Franklin was an active Pennsylvania Mason who served as Grand Master in the mid-18th century. And George Washington was a Pennsylvania Mason throughout his entire presidency. The tour is an architectural feast, since the Freemasons modeled each hall in a differ-

ent design style. Egyptian Hall is a favorite, its magnificent ornamentation complemented by proper hieroglyphics, and some of the first electrical lighting in Philadelphia, installed in the late 19th century. Area lodges still use the facility today for meetings. Corinthian Hall is where representatives from all Pennsylvania lodges meet quarterly to discuss organization business and vote. Portraits of past and recent Grand Masters are on display throughout the building—each serves a two-year term, so there are several. The Masonic Temple is both a sight to behold and an absorbing look at American civil society.

Pennsylvania Hospital

215-829-3370
www.uphs.upenn.edu/paharc/collections
800 Spruce St., Philadelphia, PA 19107
Open: Mon.–Fri. 8:30–4:30; guided tours on Thurs. and Fri. at 10 and 1, but call ahead
Admission: Free to see; guided tour has a $4 suggested donation

America's first hospital, this perennially under-visited attraction is a window into colonial-era medicine, when anyone with an impressive-sounding superstition could pass as a doctor. The highlight of the tour is the surgical amphitheater, where bystanders watched primitive surgery being performed under a circular skylight. Without gas or electric lights, operations were only attempted between 11 A.M. and 2 P.M. on sunny days. The historical portion of the hospital is no longer used, but is attached to a functioning hospital managed by the University of Pennsylvania. To arrange a tour, call a day ahead.

Physick House

215-925-7866
www.philalandmarks.org
info@philalandmarks.org

321 S. 4th St., Philadelphia, PA 19106
Open: Thurs.–Sat. 12–4, Sun. 1–4
Admission: Adults $5, students and
seniors $4

Physick House is remarkable architecturally as a rare free-standing 18th-century
dwelling in Society Hill, but its most famed
occupant was even more extraordinary.
Philip Syng Physick, known as the father of
American surgery, fashioned countless
advanced medical techniques and treated
the likes of John Marshall and Dolley
Madison. A surgical tool collection is on
display inside. Note the fanlight over the
double-door entrance and other traditional
Federal ornament. Physick acquired the
house from wealthy importer Henry Hill,
who built himself 32 rooms spread over
three floors. Like Bishop White House, this
is a fine example of the lifestyle that the
upper class enjoyed during the late-colo-
nial and post-colonial era. It is owned by
the Philadelphia Society for the
Preservation of Landmarks and is sometimes reserved for private events, so call
ahead to plan a visit.

Powel House
215-627-0364
www.philalandmarks.org
powelhouse@philalandmarks.org
244 S. 3rd St., Philadelphia, PA 19106
Open: Thurs.–Sat. 12–4, Sun. 1–4
Admission: Adults $5, students and
seniors $4

This classic Georgian home was owned for a
period by Samuel Powel, Philadelphia's first
mayor. His wife's popularity as a party
organizer, along with the spacious parlor
and dining rooms, brought colonial-era
luminaries to the house to eat, drink, and
unwind. The interior of the mansion looks
much as it did in the late 18th century, with
plaster ceilings and a mahogany staircase.
It was a threat to demolish the Powel House
in 1930 that catalyzed the organization of

the city's landmark preservation society. As
with the Physick House, it is best to call
well in advance to reserve a tour.

Todd House
215-965-2305
www.nps.gov/inde/todd-house.htm
401 Walnut St., Philadelphia, PA 19106
Open: Tues.–Sun. 10–4
Admission: $2

A counterpart to Bishop White's striking
abode, Todd House portrays the less extravagant quarters kept by Philadelphia's early
professional class. The Todds were a typical
Quaker couple who lived unpretentiously,
but Mr. Todd passed away and his wife
Dolley married eventual president James
Madison. The home survived as an ordinary
Philadelphia townhouse with modest furnishings and decoration.

Thaddeus Kosciuszko National Memorial
215-597-9618
www.nps.gov/thko
301 Pine St., Philadelphia, PA 19106
Open: Wed.–Sun. 12–4
Admission: Free

Hero of the Revolutionary War, Thaddeus
Kosciuszko left his native Poland in 1776 to
offer his services to the American
Revolutionary Army. The general performed brilliantly, fortifying key American
strongholds at Saratoga and West Point. He
returned to fight for Polish independence
after the war, but was exiled by the Russian
regime and sailed into Philadelphia in
November 1797. His memorial stands
where Kosciuszko lived during his five-
month stay in Society Hill, where he met
frequently with vice president and loyal
admirer Thomas Jefferson. The restored
house displays General Kosciuszko's second-story bedroom as it appeared during
his time in Philadelphia, with sketching
tools, utensils, and military medals.

Libraries
Athenaeum of Philadelphia
215-925-2688
www.athenaonline.org
219 S. 6th St., Philadelphia, PA 19106
Open: Weekdays, 9–5
Admission: Free

A research library and gallery of changing exhibits, the Athenaeum is a one-stop shop for architectural history buffs and is especially useful for those interested in Philadelphia architecture. The building's design is appropriately significant as America's initial foray into the Renaissance Revival style. Scottish American architect John Notman, whose Philadelphia portfolio includes Laurel Hill Cemetery and St. Clement's Church, outfitted the Athenaeum with attention-grabbing floor-to-ceiling windows in the building's midsection.

Free Library of Philadelphia
215-686-5322
www.library.phila.gov
19th St. and Benjamin Franklin Parkway, Philadelphia, PA 19103
Open: Mon.–Wed. 9–9, Thurs.–Sat. 9–5, Sun. 1–5; Closed on Sun., Jun.–Sept.
Admission: Free

The Free Library's founding in 1891 was a watershed moment in Philadelphia's history—a long overdue effort to bring literacy and learning to the masses. The original branch at City Hall and subsequent locations on Chestnut and Locust Streets gave way to today's Neoclassical Revival edifice on the Ben Franklin Parkway. More than a million books can be found on this central branch's shelves, including some rare first editions. Locals and tourists alike can be seen crossing its pink marble hallways and poking around the remarkable music collection. A grand renovation and expansion awaits the necessary funding. You can see the proposed models in the foyer.

Historical Society of Pennsylvania
215-732-6200
www.hsp.org
1300 Locust St., Philadelphia, PA 19107
Open: Tues. and Thurs. 12:30–5:30, Wed. 12:30–8:30, Fri. 10–5:30
Admission: Adults $6, students $3

Not a facility to browse casually, but if you have a specific research interest related to Pennsylvania history and wish to find obscure source material, then the Historical Society was made for you. This is the kind of place that can dig up 150-year-old community newsletters. It makes for fascinating research for those who have roots in Pennsylvania, and especially in and around Philadelphia.

Library Company of Philadelphia
215-546-3181
www.librarycompany.org
1314 Locust St., Philadelphia, PA 19107
Open: Mon.–Fri. 9–4:45
Admission: Free

Another Franklin hobbyhorse, and the first subscription library in the country, the Company holds a wealth of material on American life prior to 1900. A free gallery hosts changing exhibits, which are reliably thorough. Its nondescript building on Locust Street attracts minimal attention from locals, but the resources within make it a treasure trove for scholars.

Library Hall
215-440-3400
www.amphilsoc.org/about/libhall.htm
104 S. 5th St., Philadelphia, PA 19106
Open: Mon.–Fri. 9–5
Admission: Free

Home to an original copy of the Declaration of Independence and Lewis & Clark's travel journals, the Georgian-styled Library Hall is a research facility and a collection for the highly exclusive American Philosophical

Society. Gallery exhibitions on-site give you a taste of the scholarship contained inside. Philosophical Hall on the opposite side of 5th Street is the society's headquarters.

Museums

The Academy of Natural Sciences

215-299-1000
www.acnatsci.org
webmaster@ansp.org
1900 Benjamin Franklin Parkway, Philadelphia, PA 19103
Open: Mon.–Fri. 10–4:30, Sat.–Sun. and holidays 10–5
Admission: Adults $10, children and seniors $8

The Academy is a popular natural history museum, primarily drawing families with children. Premier attractions include a live butterfly exhibit, a mummified body, Dinosaur Hall, and the Fossil Prep Lab, where retrieved fossils are cleaned and readied for study. Dino-material occupies part of two floors, including a section devoted to the Philadelphia region's important role in the development of paleontology. The wild yak, puma, bison, and other life-sized animal dioramas are organized by continent. This isn't as grand a spectacle as the Museum of Art or as interactive a collection as the Franklin Institute, but it is a fun and educational way for a family to spend an hour or two.

African American Museum in Philadelphia

215-574-0380
www.aampmuseum.org
info@aampmuseum.org
701 Arch St., Philadelphia, PA 19106
Open: Tues.–Sat. 10–5, Sun. 12–5
Admission: Adults $8, children and seniors $6

Centered around a four-gallery collection of changing exhibits on African American history and life, the museum's content is invariably fresh. Recently, the museum has hosted photography, archeological history, and new media exhibitions. The permanent exhibit on the ground level recounts early African history in and around present-day Egypt and Ethiopia, where the ancient Egyptians, Nubians, and Askum lived. The auditorium hosts performances, workshops, and other special events. A massive research collection of artifacts and rare documents relating to the African American experience can be seen with an appointment. The museum is an affiliate of the Smithsonian and was completed in 1976 as a part of the Bicentennial.

Atwater Kent Museum

215-685-4830
www.philadelphiahistory.org
15 S. 7th St., Philadelphia, PA 19106
Open: Wed.–Sun. 1–5
Admission: Adults $5, children and seniors $3

Philadelphia itself is a veritable history museum, but it is a history about the American founding. Visitors more interested in the city's history should check out Atwater Kent. The museum opens with an oversized floor map. An expansive second-floor exhibit walks you through Philadelphia's social history and includes the city's 1701 charter. Norman Rockwell's *Saturday Evening Post* covers and other Americana are strewn throughout. Kent himself was in the radio business, which explains the downstairs radio exhibition. The museum is housed in a Greek Revival building that was once the Franklin Institute.

Betsy Ross House

215-686-1252
www.betsyrosshouse.org
239 Arch St., Philadelphia, PA
Open: Daily Apr.–Oct. 10–5; closed Mon. Oct.–Mar.
Admission: Adults $3, children $2

Perfectly pointed brick, tight winding staircases, and an authentic simplicity characterize the Betsy Ross House, marked from the street by the 13-starred flag flying above. Ross was a thrice-widowed Quaker who eventually joined the Free Quakers in support of the Revolutionary War effort. She was a resilient woman who went on to produce the original American flag at the behest of George Washington. What is remarkable about the house is its humble functionality: a reminder that middle class Philadelphians lived a modest existence during the Revolutionary era, even those friendly with the commander of the Continental Army. Be warned that there is some debate over whether or not Ross actually lived there. Informative displays and family heirlooms dot the walls. Don't look for the original flag, though. It's at the Smithsonian in Washington, D.C.

Federal Reserve Bank of Philadelphia
1-866-574-3727
www.philadelphiafed.org
100 N. 6th St., Philadelphia, PA 19106
Open: Mon.–Fri., Hours vary by season
Admission: Free

Macroeconomists have struggled mightily to make central banking an engaging and digestible topic, which makes the Philadelphia Fed's "Money in Motion" exhibition all the more impressive. A small exhibit, it is high tech and interactive, incorporating games and animation into its tutorial on the United States economy. It's also practical: plug your credit card debt and interest rate into the Debt Calculator and see how long you'll be paying it off.

Fireman's Hall Museum
215-923-1438
www.firemanshall.org
firemus@aol.org
147 N. 2nd St., Philadelphia PA 19106
Open: Tues.–Sat., 9–4:30, with extended hours on the first Fri. of each month

Admission: Donation suggested

One reason William Penn designed Philadelphia with broad avenues and large estates was his experience in densely packed London during the Great Fire of 1666. His efforts were mostly for naught, and Philadelphia filled up quickly, which is why one of Ben Franklin's many brainchildren was the city's original volunteer firefighting company. Fireman's Hall Museum follows the evolution of firefighting in Philadelphia and elsewhere, with a terrific collection of old tin helmets, water pumps, and firefighting tools. The highlights are original horse- and steam-powered fire trucks, some over two hundred years old. The museum is housed in a real 19th-century firehouse.

Franklin Institute Science Museum
215-448-1200
www.fi.edu
20th St. and Benjamin Franklin Parkway, Philadelphia, PA 19103
Open: Daily 9:30–5
Admission: Adults $14.25, seniors and students $13.25, children $11.50; IMAX extra

This one is very nifty. Few museums manage to combine an interactive experience with an educational component as well as the Franklin Institute, and it has been doing so long before interactive learning became hip—the Institute is over 175 years old. The legendary walk-through heart is every bit as cool as it sounds, but the museum has a great deal more to offer. Exhibits on Ben Franklin's countless inventions, the Fels planetarium, the oversized pendulum, the world's largest pinball machine, and the weather station are all top-flight presentations in their own right.

Independence Seaport Museum
215-925-5439
www.phillyseaport.org
seaport@phillyseaport.org

The boat shop at Independence Seaport Museum

211 S. Columbus Blvd., at Walnut St.,
Philadelphia, PA 19106
Open: Daily 10–5
Admission: Adults $10, children and
seniors $7

A celebration of local nautical history and
shipbuilding, the Independence Seaport
Museum is a good attraction for families
with children. Start with a tour of the 17th-
century Delaware River and the ships that
brought over the original Swedish colonists
to the Delaware Valley. The flagship exhibit
in the museum's rear explains the chal-
lenges of boat construction and includes a
functioning boat shop where you can watch
the restoration of old boats in action. On
the upper level, see the actual logbooks
from the HMS *Talbot* and HMS *Jupiter*.
Other notable displays examine trade with
China, and the U.S. Navy at the turn of the
20th century. The USS *Olympia*, which
helped fight the Spanish-American War, is

parked on the docks out back, and you can
tour the inside of the Olympia and also the
USS *Becuna* submarine for no additional
charge. The Seaport Museum is a little isolated from the rest of historic Philadelphia,
but can be combined with a visit to the
Penn's Landing waterfront.

Mütter Museum

215-563-3737
www.collphyphil.org
museum@collphyphil.org
19 S. 22nd St., Philadelphia, PA 19103
Open: Daily 10–5, extended hours on Fri.
Admission: Adults $12, children and
seniors $8

A fascinating and unsettling collection of
human skulls, organs, tumors, and other
excised matter, the Mütter Museum offers
all the anatomy of medical school with none
of the student loans. The exhibition area,
located within the College of Physicians of

Philadelphia, is not especially large, but the contents are astounding and magnificently presented. The Mütter is especially interested in the rare, so typical displays concern things like conjoined twins and teratology. For the social scientists there is a look at the history of presidential health care, which incorporates the actual cancerous lesion removed from Grover Cleveland's jaw. While it takes its purpose and history seriously, the Mütter also has a sense of humor about itself (the gift shop sells plastic syringe pens and eyeball lollipops). No photography allowed in the museum, but the image of an 8-foot colon will remain etched in your mind forever.

National Constitution Center
1-866-917-1787
www.constitutioncenter.org
visitorcomments@constitutioncenter.org
525 Arch St., Philadelphia, PA 19106
Open: Mon.–Fri. 9:30–5, Sat. 9:30–6, Sun. 12–5
Admission: Adults $12, seniors $11, children $8

Philadelphia's newest major museum, the National Constitution Center is an educational and imaginative tour of America focused around the constitutional questions that shaped the country's history. The museum's hub is a theater-in-the-round, where a combination live-action and video presentation paints the broad strokes of America's founding. Encircling the theater is the museum's permanent exhibition, an admirably comprehensive and nuanced presentation of American history. These displays are creative and interactive, like the sculpture examining national highways and the inherent tensions of federalism. The experience concludes at Signers' Hall, where life-sized bronze statues of the Constitution's signers pose stroking their chins and chatting among themselves. Note the anti-Federalist Virginians huddled in

the corner, and Alexander Hamilton on his lonesome. The Constitution Center also has a large gallery for temporary exhibits.

National Liberty Museum
215-925-2800
www.libertymuseum.org
liberty@libertymuseum.org
321 Chestnut St., Philadelphia, PA 19106
Open: Daily 10–5, closed Mon. in the winter, spring, and fall
Admission: Adults $7, seniors $6, children $2

One of the historic district's most intriguing and ideological museums, it boasts four floors on the past, present, and future of peace and diversity. Exhibits include the wall of Nobel Peace Prize winners, and a "Tyrant vs. Hero" display revealing history's worst despots and most courageous freedom fighters. There is also a room of White House china, and some terrific glass art.

New Hall Military Museum
215-965-2305
www.nps.gov/inde/new-hall.htm
Chestnut St., east of 4th St., Philadelphia, PA 19106
Open: Hours vary, call ahead
Admission: Free

Housed in what was once the headquarters of the American War Department is this collection of Revolution-era rifles, model ships, and related materials, which tell the story of the early American Marines, Army, and Navy. A video presentation on Revolutionary War battles and the political conflict adds context, as does a display on the political difficulties the Founders confronted in convincing the new republic to support a standing peacetime army.

Pennsylvania Academy of the Fine Arts
215-972-7600
www.pafa.org
118–128 N. Broad St., Philadelphia, PA 19102

Open: Tues.–Sat. 10–5, Sun. 11–5
Admission: Adults $10, children $6

The country's first art school and art museum, the Pennsylvania Academy of the Fine Arts is a too-often overlooked treasure. While not as imposing as the Philadelphia Museum of Art, the Academy's landmarked building is an unhurried, peaceful place to take in colonial and modern American realism. The star attraction is the American Painting of Modern Life gallery that builds to Thomas Eakins's "The Gross Clinic," his renowned and shocking portrayal of late-19th-century surgery. Eakins was a native Philadelphian who studied and taught at the Academy and his portrait of Walt Whitman (also on display) was the poet's favorite. Benjamin West's work is also featured prominently. Especially memorable is his chaotic "Death on the Pale Horse," which occupies the better part of an entire wall and was the first work of his purchased by the Academy. In 2003, the museum opened the Samuel M. V. Hamilton Building next door to the original museum. The Hamilton Building, an automobile factory in its former life, offers space to temporary exhibits, sculpture, and assists with the Academy's educational function.

Philadelphia Museum of Art
215-763-8100
www.philamuseum.org
visitorservices@philamuseum.org
26th St. and Benjamin Franklin Parkway, Philadelphia, PA 19130
Open: Tues.–Sun. 10–5, extended hours on Fri.
Admission: Adults $14, seniors $12, children $10; Sun. is pay what you wish

The caramel-colored marvel of the Ben Franklin Parkway, the Philadelphia Museum of Art is internationally acclaimed for its two hundred galleries worth of art, touching on most eras in recorded human history and nearly all corners of the globe. The presentation mingles decorative arts with paintings and sculptures to create a fluid, visually energizing space. Masterpieces found inside include works by Van Gogh, Barberini, Picasso, Rubens, and Brancusi. Tour the fine art, but leave time for the themed period rooms like the Japanese teahouse, and classics like the Kienbusch Collection of Arms and Armor. The building itself is part of the attraction and a magnificent example of Greek Revival architecture. Its founders, unable to raise enough money to construct the entire museum at once, had the wings constructed first, cleverly anticipating that the city would not allow such an obviously incomplete structure to crown the city's most attractive parkway. Outside are the famous steps used for Rocky Balboa's triumphant run in the movie *Rocky*; Sylvester Stallone's Rocky statue stands at its base, off to the side. The museum's Azalea Garden in the rear features 12 beds of trees, shrubs, and flowers. In 2007, the museum opened the Perelman Building, a renovated art deco annex of mostly changing exhibits that allows the museum to display more of its collections. Perelman is typically less crowded than the main building.

Rodin Museum
215-763-8100
www.rodinmuseum.org
22nd St. and Benjamin Franklin Parkway, Philadelphia, PA 19101
Open: Tues.–Sun., 10–5
Admission: $3 suggested donation

Come and soak in this exceptional collection of work from Auguste Rodin, the expressive French sculptor most famous for *The Thinker,* a cast of which can be found at the museum's entrance. His controversial attempts at sculpting French writer Honoré de Balzac occupy an entire room, perhaps the most intriguing part of the exhibition. This museum is the largest collection of Rodin's outside France, and includes an original cast of his intense *Gates of Hell* bronze. Make sure not to miss the on-site garden.

Rosenbach Museum and Library
215-732-1600
www.rosenbach.org
info@rosenbach.org
2010 Delancy Place, Philadelphia, PA 19103
Open: Tues.–Sun. 10–5, extended hours on Wed.
Admission: Adults $10, seniors $8, children $5

Brothers Abraham and Philip Rosenbach helped pioneer the business of rare book dealing in America and Abraham's old Rittenhouse Square townhome is now a museum and library devoted to original prints and art. The recently expanded Rosenbach includes rarities like James Joyce's *Ulysses* manuscript, Ben Franklin's *Poor Richard's Almanac,* and Maurice Sendak's original illustrations from the popular children's book series *Where the Wild Things Are.* Near the third-floor libraries is a re-creation of poet Marianne Moore's living room, complete with her animal miniatures and autographed baseballs. Tour guides are deeply knowledgeable about the history of American book dealing and the house's sundry art collection. If you care to use the museum's books or historical papers for research, call ahead to schedule an appointment.

Second Bank of the United States
215-965-2305
www.nps.gov/inde/second-bank.htm
420 Chestnut St., Philadelphia, PA 19106
Open: Daily 9–5, but call to confirm
Admission: Free

Andrew Jackson vetoed a rechartering of the Second Bank in 1836, leaving the country's credit system to neglect, and closing the handsome Philadelphia building (modeled after the Parthenon, with grand Doric columns). The National Park Service took over the bank building in 1939, eventually converting it into a small museum for portraits of the Founding Fathers, the young republic's financiers, and other colonial- and Revolutionary-era figures. Famous American artist Charles Willson Peale is credited with producing many.

United States Mint
215-408-0114
www.usmint.gov
5th and Arch Sts., Philadelphia, PA 19106
Open: Mon.–Fri. 9–3 except federal holidays
Admission: Free

The Mint is open to the public for limited hours on weekdays, but call ahead to be sure. A self-guided tour explains Philadelphia's crucial role in establishing America's first national currency, and offers a look at the production floor itself. This is the fourth building to serve as the Philadelphia mint, pumping out billions of coins for circulation every year, nearly half of them pennies. Its output exceeds that of any other mint in the country. Leave the camera in the hotel room, though. Photography is strictly prohibited and you will be turned away.

Music and Dance
It has been said that Philadelphia's early stoicism stunted its artistic growth. If true, the city has since regained all the lost ground and then some. A commonly cited turning point is 1912, when the creative and energetic Leopold Stokowski became conductor of the Philadelphia Orchestra, transforming it into an ensemble now recognized as one of America's best. Broad Street south of City Hall was designated Philadelphia's "Avenue of the Arts" in 1993

to mark the city's renewed commitment to a dynamic arts district. You'll find Philadelphia's foremost performance venues along this strip.

Academy of Music (215-893-1999; www.academyofmusic.org; Broad and Locust Sts.). A timeless Philadelphia institution from architect Napoleon LeBrun, the Academy of Music opened in 1857 during the industrial boom to bring the city's cultural reputation added prestige. It lives today as it did then, as a palatial Italian-style opera house and a magnificent place to experience music. The Victorian chandelier incorporates almost eight thousand crystals into its design. A recent renovation sought to restore the Academy's original feel by reimagining the interior lighting. The Academy is no longer home to the Philadelphia Orchestra, but hosts top-tier ensembles from around the world, plus performances by the Opera Company of Philadelphia, the Pennsylvania Ballet, and occasional musical theater. Operations have merged with those of the Kimmel Center, so visit the Kimmel box office to pick up tickets for either venue.

Curtis Institute of Music (215-893-5261 or 215-893-5252; www.curtis.edu; 1726 Locust St.). This esteemed conservatory hosts solo and chamber music recitals in its Field Concert Hall. Its students also perform regularly at the Kimmel Center and Prince Music Theater.

Electric Factory (215-627-1332; www.electricfactory.info; 421 N. 7th St.). Rock music venue that reproduces Philadelphia's celebrated (if short-lived) Electric Factory of the late 1960s and early '70s. Like the original, the space is a converted space, with high ceilings that make it seem bigger than it really is. The crowd tends to be young.

Theater of the Living Arts (215-922-1011; www.livenation.com; 334 South St.) underwent a transformation from movie house to concert hall in 1987, and is now a fair place to see indie rock bands or a rare comedy headliner. Modestly sized and standing room only unless you can snag a seat by the bar. It is right on South Street, so there is plenty to do in the immediate vicinity.

Kimmel Center (215-790-5800; www.kimmelcenter.org; 260 South Broad St.). The coiled glass shell anchoring south Broad Street marks the Kimmel Center, heralded as Philadelphia's finest performance venue to open since the Academy of Music. The Philadelphia Orchestra and the imaginative Philly Pops play at Verizon Hall, the Center's triple-tiered, cello-shaped auditorium and the largest venue on-site. Other resident dance, music, and theater companies perform in the adaptable Perelman Theater. Even if you are not interested in attending a performance, the center is worth a quick tour. You can ride the elevator up to the Dorrance H. Hamilton Roof Garden for a pleasant panoramic view of the city's east side. The Center's design creates an indoor plaza between the two auditoriums that provides auxiliary services like as ticketing, a café, and public space.

Trocadero Theatre (215-922-5483; www.thetroc.com; 1003 Arch St.). An absolutely beautiful Victorian-era throwback in the heart of Chinatown, this onetime vaudeville house now plays host to inexpensive rock concerts. The multi-tiered balcony and high ceiling make for excellent sightlines and sound, but try not to get stuck behind one of the support columns. On Movie Mondays, the Trocadero shows recently released films for just $3, which includes a bar credit.

You can find performances by venue, or contact the music and dance companies them-

The Kimmel Center on the Avenue of the Arts

selves. Opera and ballet are typically performed at the Academy of Music. The Philadelphia Orchestra moved from the Academy to the Kimmel Center in 2001.

Chamber Orchestra of Philadelphia (215-545-5451; www.chamberorchestra.org)

Opera Company of Philadelphia (215-893-3600 or 215-732-8400; www.operaphilly.com)

Pennsylvania Ballet (215-551-7000; www.paballet.org)

Philadelphia Chamber Music Society (215-569-8080; www.philadelphiachambermusic.org)

Philadelphia Dance Company (215-387-8200; www.philadanco.org)

Philadelphia Orchestra (215-893-1999; www.philorch.org)

Nightlife

Not since before the colonial era has Philadelphia wanted for drink. It progressed from the early taverns and later speakeasies into a perfect bar city with something for absolutely everyone. Philadelphia has enough room for hazy dives like **Oscar's Tavern** (215-972-9938; 1524 Sansom St.), the Ritz-Carlton's plush wine and Scotch lounge **The Vault** (215-

523-8000; 10 S. Broad St.), and everything in between. All Philadelphia bars that serve food are nonsmoking.

Old City is a good place to begin a drinker's tour. The four-block radius around the 2nd and Chestnut Street intersection has emerged as Center City's weekend frat party. It's a younger crowd, with throngs of 20- and 30-somethings who barhop and club-hop until they're sent home. Cramped but fun **Rotten Ralph's** (215-925-2440; 201 Chestnut St.) has a good beer and cider selection downstairs. For a bite with your brew, try **Triumph Brewing Company** (215-625-0855; 117 Chestnut St.), where tasty late night "small plates" are served alongside eight beers made on-site. A personal favorite for cheap well drinks (by Old City standards, that is—figure $4.50 for a strong vodka tonic) is **Nick's Roast Beef** (215-928-9411; 16 S. 2nd St). Nick's is known for good sandwiches, a casual atmosphere, and the 8-foot fish tank behind the bar.

Old City stretches southward and becomes Society Hill, where you'll find **Dark Horse** (215-928-9307; 421 S. 2nd St.), a handsome wood and brick English/Irish tavern. Dark Horse is a casual place perfect for a burger and a Smithwicks draft. Go a little farther south and hit the bouncy South Street district. There are several great watering holes to choose from on South, like the sports bar **Manny Brown's** (215-627-7427; 512 South St.), and the **Blarney Bar & Grill** (215-413-8294; 328 South St.), a lively Irish pub with over two hundred beers from around the world.

Night falls and Continental Mid-town heats up

Leaving the easternmost end, Center City bars draw more diverse crowds. The nautically themed **Misconduct Tavern** (215-732-5797; 1511 Locust St.) attracts a smattering of middle-aged professionals and younger graduate students who come for the inexpensive microbrews. The exposed-brick walls and plasma televisions complete the hybrid experience. Just around the corner, with similarly outstanding food and beer variety is **Good Dog Bar and Restaurant** (215-985-9600; 224 S. 15th St.), its beloved signature burger injected with bleu cheese. For something completely different, try **Vintage Wine Bar** (215-922-3095; 129 S. 13th St.), where five-dozen reasonably priced wines are served by the glass. And never discount **Dirty Frank's** (215-732-5010; 347 S. 13th St.), the finest dive bar in Center City, marked only by the exterior mural of famous Franks—Sinatra, Frankenstein, Congressman Barney Frank, etc.—and a guaranteed boozy good time among fun-loving Philadelphians.

Downtown's space limitations generally mean limited amenities, but you can usually get a dart game going at **Black Sheep** (215-545-9473; 247 S. 17th St.), a multi-tiered Irish pub that serves filling Sunday brunch and makes a great basket of fries. Nearby, **Cavanaugh's Rittenhouse** (215-665-9500; 1823 Sansom St.) is a fun place to watch football. Two more notables, a little bit off the beaten track: **Ten Stone** (215-735-9939; 2063 South St.), a distinctly British bar and restaurant with a reddish-orange glow on the southwest corner of downtown, and tiny **Mace's Crossing** (215-564-5203; 1714 Cherry St.) for cheap beer and a good jukebox near the virtually pub-less Ben Franklin Parkway.

The bar scene is inexpensive fun, but Center City also has a stable of comedy clubs, lounges, and hotspots for after-hours revelry. Some possibilities:

Chris' Jazz Café (215-568-3131; www.chrisjazzcafe.com; 1421 Sansom St.). Philly's premiere jazz club, with a dark, relaxed ambiance, snug booths, and music that goes all night every day but Sunday. Food is available and cover charges are low.

Continental Mid-town (215-567-1800; www.continentalmidtown; 1801 Chestnut St.). Look for the gigantic martini olive hanging off a retro diner; if it's a clear weekend night, you'll likely find a long line snaking under it. This is Stephen Starr's second Continental, and like the more reserved Old City version (215-9236069; 138 Market St.) it's a combination restaurant-lounge. The colorful, splashy Mid-town has become a real hotspot, and late nights the second floor gets packed.

Helium Comedy Club (215-496-9001; www.heliumcomedy.com; 2031 Sansom St.). Shows are Wednesday through Saturday (two shows on Friday and Saturday nights) plus Open Mic nights on Tuesday.

J. L. Sullivan's Speakeasy (215-546-2290; www.jlsullivans.com; 200 S. Broad St.). A sleek sports lounge with white marble tabletops and flat-screen TVs everywhere. Booths have individual televisions, but the secluded luxury suites are even more fun. The lounge is located downstairs in the Bellevue building where noted Philadelphia jazz club Zanzibar Blue once stood.

Laff House (215-440-4242; www.laffhouse.com; 221 South St.). Open Mic on Wednesday, two shows on Thursday and Friday, and three on Saturday nights, including a midnight show.

Mahogany on Walnut (215-732-3982; 1524 Walnut St.). A dark cigar bar that delivers the goods: Scotch, wine, posh leather chairs, and a thick mist of cigar smoke. A good cigar shop—Holt's—is right below.

The Piano Bar (215-563-4704; www.cascamorto.com; 1939 Arch St.). Has a friendly neighborhood feel, with black walls and wood trimming that makes it look much older than it is. Linger over a beer and request your favorite song from the talented roster of pianists. Smoking is allowed.

Vango Lounge and Skybar (215-568-1020; www.vangoloungeandskybar.com; 116 S. 18th St.). A young, aggressively hip restaurant-lounge with Japanese fusion cuisine, a wall of translucent vodka bottles, private booths, bottle service, and a rooftop deck.

Religious Sites
Arch Street Meeting House
215-627-2667
www.archstreetfriends.org
4th and Arch Sts., Philadelphia, PA 19106
Open: Mon.–Sat. 10–4
Admission: Suggested donation $2

This one is a real treasure. The nation's largest active meeting house, it serves not only the local Quaker community but attracts members of the Society of Friends from all over the country for a yearly meeting. The art and history exhibit is a great resource for those wishing to learn about the traditions of Quakerism. Check out the reproduction of an original map of Pennsylvania, and note the names of the major landowners, some of which now grace the entrances to Philadelphia's civic institutions.

Cathedral Basilica of Saints Peter and Paul
215-561-1313
www.sspeterpaulcathedral.catholicweb.com
1723 Race St., Philadelphia, PA 19103
Open: Daily
Admission: Free

Majestic both inside and out, this Italian Renaissance cathedral draws on different materials to achieve one of Philadelphia's premiere architectural feats. Look for the chocolate brownstone exterior, its entrance marked by four stone columns capped with Corinthian pilasters. The crown of the cathedral is a 60-foot-high copper dome, turned green patina over the years, since the cathedral dates to the mid-19th century. Pope John Paul II visited in 1979.

Christ Church
215-922-1695
www.oldchristchurch.org
2nd St. just north of Market St.
Open: Mon.–Sat. 9–5 and Sun 12:30–5; services Sun. at 9 and 11 and Wed. at noon
Admission: Suggested donation $3. Tours of adjacent burial ground are $2 and offered daily on the hour, 10–3

Christ Church has not missed a single service since its opening in 1695, and that includes the 2007–2008 renovation when scaffolding crammed the aisles. The Georgian-style building is as beautiful as any in the city, and steeped in history. This was the house of worship for George Washington, John Adams, Benjamin Franklin, and Betsy Ross, who could only afford a pew situated directly behind a column with an obstructed view. The church's most distinctive choice is its clear glass windows (rather than stained glass). This is owed to Franklin's Enlightenment influence, which favored a connection to nature over isolation. Franklin rests in the burial ground next to his wife and son.

Free Quaker Meeting House
215-965-2305
www.nps.gov/inde/free-quaker.htm
500 Arch St., Philadelphia, PA 19106
Open: Call for hours

While ostensibly similar to Philadelphia's many other utilitarian meeting houses, this church was frequented by an idiosyncratic band of Quakers who split from the pacifism of mainstream Quakerism and endorsed the Revolutionary War. Visiting hours vary by season, so call ahead.

Mikveh Israel
215-922-5446
www.mikvehisrael.org
44 N. 4th St., Philadelphia, PA 19106
Open: Mon.–Thurs. 10–5, Fri. 10–3, Sun. 12–5
Admission: Free

Mikveh Israel is the second oldest Jewish congregation in the country, and an active Sephardic synagogue. Its cemetery includes gravesites for prominent Philadelphia Jews and Jewish veterans of early American wars. Visitors can see the sanctuary and changing exhibitions in the gallery. The synagogue is affiliated with the National Museum of American Jewish History at 5th Street (www.nmajh.org). A new $150 million museum from architect James S. Polshek is scheduled to open in 2010.

Mother Bethel African Methodist Episcopal Church
215-925-0616
www.motherbethel.org
motherbethel@aol.com
419 Richard Allen Ave., S. 6th St. between Pine and Lombard Sts., Philadelphia, PA 19147
Open: Museum open and guided tours offered Tues.–Sat. 10–3
Admission: Free, but donation requested

The first African Methodist Episcopal Church in America, Mother Bethel holds an important place in both the spiritual lives of its congregants and in the course of American history. It sits on the oldest piece of land continuously owned by American blacks, and served as a Philadelphia focal point for anti-slavery and civil rights activism. Church founder and bishop Richard Allen was a former slave and a hero of the early struggle for emancipation. Careful observers will find symbolism spread throughout the church. Every seventh flower on the sanctuary carpet is a lighter shade of green to signify God's resting on the seventh day. The on-site museum includes the church's original pews, wooden ballot boxes used to elect bishops, and a mural depicting Allen's journey and the church's founding.

Old Pine Street Presbyterian Church

215-925-8051
www.oldpine.org
mary@oldpine.org
412 Pine St., Philadelphia, PA 19106
Open: Mon.–Fri. 10–noon and 2–3
Admission: Free

The most interesting feature here is the cemetery, where the bodies of Revolutionary War soldiers are buried under weathered headstones. It is a fitting spot for such a cemetery, as the church itself was heavily damaged by British troops during the war but has since been beautifully restored. The structure, originally Georgian, was transformed into a Greek Revival masterwork with Corinthian columns, a yellow facade, and large blue doors.

Old St. Joseph's Church

215-923-1733
www.oldstjoseph.org
germane@oldstjoseph.org
321 Willings Alley, Philadelphia, PA 19106
Open: Mon.–Fri. 9–4; mass on Mon.–Sat. at noon, Sat. at 5:30, several times Sun.
Admission: Free

The third church built on this site, Old St. Joseph's was Philadelphia's original Catholic establishment. Following the dictates of Penn's doctrine of religious freedom, Old St. Joseph's served as an important historical test of the government's progressiveness. It survived anti-Catholic rioting in 1844. The style integrates Gothic and Greek Revival flourishes.

Old St. Mary's Church

215-923-7930
www.ushistory.org/tour/tour_stmary.htm
oldstmary@verizon.net
252 S. 4th St., Philadelphia, PA 19106
Open: Mon.–Sat. 9–4:45; mass on Sat. at 5 and Sun. at 9 and 10:30
Admission: Free

Society Hill's other Catholic church, established 30 years after St. Joseph's, Old St. Mary's is a brick Gothic building with stained-glass windows. Various Founding Fathers visited the church during the Revolutionary War; the music and spirit of the congregation earned plaudits from John Adams. The church and attached cemetery also blend beautifully into the rest of the block.

St. Clement's Church

215-563-1876
www.s-clements.org
2013 Appletree St., Philadelphia, PA 19103
Open: Tours are given Mon.–Fri. 10–3; call ahead to arrange
Admission: Free

An Anglo-Catholic stone church constructed with a Romanesque design, featuring a Gothic-style High Altar, and many beautiful paintings and statues. Incredibly, a 1929 street widening required the church to be moved 40 feet to the west—a task accomplished over three days.

St. Mark's Church

215-735-1416
www.saintmarksphiladelphia.org
1625 Locust St., Philadelphia, PA 19103
Open: Call ahead
Admission: Free

No Philadelphia structure quite screams "Gothic Revival" like St. Mark's Episcopal Church in Rittenhouse Square. The construction plans were approved by the Cambridge Camden Society in England as a way to guarantee fidelity to the essence of 14th-century Gothic design. In addition to the ornamentation, note the lush garden on-site and bright red doors out front.

St. Peter's Episcopal Church

215-925-5968
www.stpetersphila.org
313 Pine St., Philadelphia, PA 19106
Open: Mon.–Fri. 8:30–4, Sat. 8–5, Sun. noon–5
Admission: Free tours offered on weekends, but must be arranged ahead of time

The church was founded in 1761 by Philadelphians frustrated with overcrowded Christ Church in Old City, and a lottery was sanctioned to raise the construction budget. The building is an unpresumptuous Palladian venue, built mostly from brick. Atypically, the pulpit and altar are on different sides of the aisle. Noted Philadelphians like bank president Nicholas Biddle and painter Charles Willson Peale are buried on the grounds.

Seasonal Events

Something is always going on in Philadelphia. The **gophila.com** Web site has it all listed and easily searchable, from the smallest neighborhood crafts fair to the spring's internationally renowned flower show. Listed below are some of the biggies. A few are citywide events, a few are limited to one neighborhood, and a couple take place at the **Pennsylvania Convention Center** (215-418-4700; www.paconvention.com; 1101 Arch St.), which is in the process of expansion.

Elfreth's Alley Fete Day and Deck the Alley

215-574-0560
www.elfrethsalley.org
Front and 2nd Sts. between Arch and Race Sts.
Time: June and early December

There are two seasonal events on this old cobblestone street in Old City: the first is Fete Day, held on the second weekend in June, when Elfreth residents open their doors to the public. Guides sport colonial-era dress and usher visitors through the Alley's houses.

Then, on the second Friday in December, the residences are opened again for Christmas-themed "Deck the Alley" tours. Admission is charged for both.

Equality Forum

215-732-3378
www.equalityforum.com
Citywide event
Time: Late April to early May

A weeklong event held every spring, Equality Forum combines gay, lesbian, bisexual, and transgender rights symposiums with art exhibits, social events, films, and street fairs around the city. Now 16 years old (formerly known as PrideFest Philadelphia), it has grown quickly and is now an internationally seasoned event, with featured speakers and entertainers from around the world.

Jam on the River

215-636-1666
www.jamontheriver.com
Penn's Landing, Philadelphia, PA
Time: Memorial Day weekend

Memorial Day weekend in Philadelphia means high energy concerts on the edge of the Delaware. The event attracts top-flight bands, and you couldn't ask for a more perfect backdrop than the Penn's Landing waterfront.

Mummers Parade

215-336-3050
www.mummers.com
Broad St., from South Philadelphia to City Hall
Time: New Year's Day

Every New Year's morning Philadelphians wipe what little sleep they got the previous evening out of their eyes and head straight for Broad Street to either watch or participate in the Mummers Parade. Members of the region's social clubs don the most lurid costumes they can imagine and strut up from South Philadelphia to City Hall. Later in the day, prizes are given for the best string bands and performances by the colorfully dressed Fancy Brigades. The tradition has its roots in medieval England and the early Scandinavians in

A taste of the 2008 Mummers Parade

the Delaware Valley who often caroused through the area on Christmas Day. The word "Mummer" is German for "disguise," which is a reference to the Mummers' atypical attire. The parade and performances last all day and constitute a truly one-of-a-kind event. The party extends into the wee hours along 2nd Street in Pennsport southward from the Mummers Museum.

Philadelphia Flower Show

215-988-8800

www.theflowershow.com

Time: Early March

The country's best-known indoor flower show, the event is held annually in early March to mark the beginning of spring. Regional horticultural societies expend great time and effort putting creative twists on the annual theme. It takes place in the Pennsylvania Convention Center. See the wide variety of flowers judged and buy some from one of the many vendors.

Philadelphia Live Arts Festival and Philly Fringe

215-413-1318

www.pafringe.org

Time: Early September

Barely a decade old, the Live Arts and Fringe Festival is 16 fun days of modern dance, theater, street busking, and sundry performance art throughout the city (some events are downtown). It has been growing steadily in size and popularity since its 1997 debut, and attracts participants and even spectators from around the globe. Live Arts dance and theater acts are invited to perform and ticket prices are generally higher for these events (though still very reasonable). Fringe artists, on the other hand, can be anyone, so performance genre and quality varies a bit. No matter who acts, sings, dances, or puppeteers, the season is always rich with creativity and energy.

Rittenhouse Square Fine Art Show

1-877-689-4112

www.rittenhousesquarefineartshow.org

Time: June and September

A juried art show featuring paintings, sketches, sculpture, and mixed media from top artists (both local and non-local) who gather around the Square to display their best work for two weekends a year. The June event is the oldest outdoor art show in the country.

Sunoco Welcome America Festival

215-636-1666

www.americasbirthday.com

Time: Late June to early July

Fireworks, food, concerts, dance performances, outdoor movies, and tons of other events make Philadelphia's 4th of July celebration one of the country's best. Almost everything is free and attractions are scattered around the city during the week leading up to Independence Day. The Ben Franklin Parkway is a festive place to be on the holiday, and the whole shebang closes with fireworks on the Delaware River. Venues change from year to year, of course, so check up ahead of time.

Theater

There is a significant theater presence on the Avenue of the Arts, but also a pocket of mostly smaller venues west of Broad near Rittenhouse Square.

Arden Theater Company (215-922-1122; www.ardentheatre.org; 40 N. 2nd St.). Reliably high-quality theater at this 360-seat Old City playhouse. Each season mixes productions of classic plays and musicals with new works. The Arden also puts on children's theater.

Forrest Theatre (215-923-1515; www.forrest-theatre.com; 1114 Walnut St.). Philadelphia was once a testing ground for new Broadway shows, and productions came to auditoriums like the Forrest to work out the kinks before premiering in New York. Now it mostly works the other way, as successful Broadway productions are performed at the Forrest Theatre once they attain threshold popularity. Recent productions include Avenue Q and A Chorus Line.

Merriam Theater (215-732-5446; www.merriamtheater.org; 250 S. Broad St.). The University of the Arts owns this 1,800-seat theater, which showcases everything from splashy musicals to celebrity headliners. The building dates back to 1918, when it was known as the Sam S. Shubert Theater, named for the New York producer.

Prince Music Theater (215-569-9700; www.princemusictheater.org; 1412 Chestnut St.). The Prince hosts mostly musicals and cabaret shows, and the typical season will include a healthy mix of throwbacks and new or experimental productions. Formerly a movie theater, the Prince screens movies during Philadelphia film festivals.

Society Hill Playhouse (215-923-0210; www.societyhillplayhouse.com; 507 S. 8th St.). The emphasis is on breezy musical comedies at this cozy 223-seat main stage. The more intimate Red Room is a venue for mostly local works and single performer acts.

St. Stephen's Theater (215-829-0395; www.lanterntheater.org; 10th and Ludlow Sts.). Attached to a Gothic Revival church and playhouse for the Lantern Theater Company—a gifted group that puts on four shows a year and hosts a periodic lecture series to further explore the plays' subject matter. All sorts of productions, from Shakespeare's classics to new works.

Suzanne Roberts Theatre (215-985-0420; www.phillytheatreco.com; 480 S. Broad St.). Suzanne Roberts is the newest theater on Broad Street, and home to the Philadelphia Theatre Company. The main stage auditorium is a modern space that works very well for plays, with 365 seats including a cozy five-row mezzanine. The Theatre Company puts on top-quality productions of recently written American theater, including musicals. A small concessions stand sells wine and snack-sized panini.

Walnut Street Theatre (215-574-3550; www.walnutstreettheatre.org; 9th and Walnut Sts.). The oldest theater in the United States, this Classical Revival venue is one of the more exceptional places in Philadelphia to see a show. Nicely sized at around 1,000 seats with excellent acoustics, it is as suitable for a talky Neil Simon play as a flashy Andrew Lloyd Webber musical. It was the site of Jimmy Carter and Gerald Ford's first presidential debate in 1976 and currently hosts four to five productions a season. "Day of" tickets are steeply discounted, and available most weekdays and some weekends, depending on the popularity of the show. It is nearly always worth taking a chance; there are bars and movie theaters within walking distance, so the ticketless are never stranded with nothing to do.

Wilma Theater (215-546-7824; www.wilmatheater.org; Broad and Spruce Sts.). Among the Avenue of the Arts' newest theaters (the current space opened in 1996), Wilma productions are first rate, ambitious, and a little more offbeat than what you'll find at her neighboring playhouses. The 300-seat showroom is an attractive, comfortable space. While there isn't a bad seat in the house, a few rows back is best.

Restaurants and Food Purveyors

Many things have happened to Center City Philadelphia since the late 1980s—safer streets, lower wage taxes, cleaner subways, and nicer hotels—but few changes have been as dramatic as the evolution of its dining scene. Twenty-five years ago, quality downtown dining was a difficult thing to find. The handful of noteworthy restaurants (internationally renowned Le Bec-Fin, for example, which still exists today in a new location) had an exception-that-proves-the-rule quality about them. They were also invariably expensive.

But urban revitalization and the rising cachet of a Center City address brought empty nesters and young families downtown who love to eat out. The restaurateurs naturally followed, and at some point during the last decade Philadelphia became a great dining city. The trendy restaurant movement established a particularly strong toehold courtesy of Stephen Starr, a New Jersey native and former club owner who has opened more than 10 restaurants since his 1995 debut. Starr serves fusion menus in jaunty, ultramodern dining rooms that a new generation of locals have come to know as an identifiable component of Philadelphia dining.

Another component is the BYOB bistro. The late 1990s and early 2000s ushered in dozens of imaginative new restaurants that served affordable Italian, Mediterranean, and New American food without corkage fees for patrons armed with their own wine. New bistros open all the time in Center City, and competition has generated more ambitious menus and different cuisines. The Philadelphia BYOB is a revelation to many expatriated New Yorkers and Washingtonians accustomed to good restaurants with underwhelming and overpriced wine lists. It also leaves extra money for recognizing good service. Just recently, *Zagat* named Philadelphians the most generous tippers in the country.

The only rub is the Pennsylvania Liquor Control Board. Due to an antiquated Depression-era law, the state of Pennsylvania holds monopoly power over retail sales of wine and hard liquor (beer can be sold by private businesses). The state-run **Wine & Spirits** (www.pawineandspirits.com) shops that you will see scattered around Philadelphia are the only legal retail level wine dealers in the state. Their selection and prices are mediocre, though variety has improved a little bit recently. In a pinch, here are some locations:

Wine & Spirits Shop (215-560-4215; 1913 Chestnut St.)

Wine & Spirits Shop (215-627-9463; 227 Market St.)

Wine & Spirits Shop (215-560-4380; 1218 Chestnut St.)

It is technically illegal to purchase a bottle of wine outside of Pennsylvania and consume it within. But if your trip to the Delaware Valley includes stops in the Brandywine or Bucks County, consider purchasing a few bottles of wine from one of the excellent wineries out there if you plan on subsequent BYOB dining in Philadelphia. Wineries operate outside the state monopoly (see Chapters 4 and 5 for some options).

Cheesesteak Ruminations

No food is so closely identified with Philadelphia as the cheesesteak, a 6- to 12-inch soft Italian roll loaded with thin sliced steak and topped with onions and melted cheese to taste. The cheesesteak was a Depression-era invention of Pat and Harry Oliveri, the original proprietors of **Pat's King of Steaks** in South Philadelphia (215-468-1546; 1237 E. Passyunk Ave.). Pat's still occupies one side of a decades-old war with neighboring steak shop Geno's Steaks (215-389-0659; 1219 S. 9th St.) over who serves the best cheesesteak in Philadelphia. Geno's is certainly flashier, and its neon signs are an iconic presence in South Philly. Pat's was the first shop to use Cheez Whiz on steaks. On weekend summer nights, lines can stretch for up to an hour at Pat's and Geno's, while the hungry, often tipsy masses angle for seats at the restaurants' picnic tables or on the Passyunk Avenue curb. Ordering at either shop requires a specific etiquette. Consult posted signs for the correct jargon ("Wiz, wit" as an example, means Cheez Whiz on the steak, with onions).

The verdict? Call it a tie, and instead consider visiting the city's other cheesesteak battleground in Roxborough, a northwestern Philadelphia neighborhood that borders Manayunk. Here you'll find **Dalessandro's Steaks** (215-482-5407; 600 Wendover St.) across the street from **Chubby's** (215-487-2575; 5826 Henry Ave.). These steak shops are less frenzied than their South Philadelphia cousins, serve big steaks with more available toppings, and offer alcohol (hard liquor and beer at Chubby's, beer only at Dalessandro's). Seating is limited at both, though Chubby's is bigger.

Of course, Philadelphia has dozens of steak shops. Other favorites include **Tony Luke's** (215-551-5725; 39 E. Oregon Ave.), where the steaks are always juicy—keeping the meat juicy is a bedrock challenge of the cheesesteak business—and **John's Roast Pork** (215-463-1951; 14 E. Snyder Ave.). Both are deep into South Philadelphia. If you wish to stay in Center City, **Jim's Steaks** (215-928-1911; 400 South St.) is usually excellent and **Campo's** (215-923-1000; 214 Market St.) is also pretty good.

There are those who comb the city regularly in search of new and undiscovered steak shops. Others are satisfied with the cheesesteaks served at their local diner. Cheesesteaks are greasy, delicious, and uniquely Philadelphian. Ultimately, though, either you like them or you don't.

What follows is a list of quality Center City restaurants that attempts to capture a diversity of cuisine, price, and location. It could not possibly be exhaustive, and recommendable restaurants have been necessarily left off.

Dining Price Code

Inexpensive	Up to $15
Moderate	$15 to $30
Expensive	$30 to $50
Very Expensive	$50 or more

Chinatown and Market East

Imperial Inn
215-627-2299
146 N. 10th St., Philadelphia, PA 19107
Open: Daily
Price: Inexpensive
Credit Cards: Yes
Cuisine: Chinese, dim sum
Serving: L, D
Handicapped Access: Yes

One can find good Cantonese or Szechuan food at any one of a dozen restaurants in Chinatown, but Imperial Inn has a rare and appealing old school vibe. The place has been around for decades, and its dark paneled walls, muted lighting, and fully stocked bar are straight out of *Glengarry Glen Ross*. The median patron age drops on the weekends, when the Imperial serves bargain-priced dim sum.

Morimoto
215-413-9070
www.morimotorestaurant.com
723 Chestnut St., Philadelphia, PA 19106
Open: Daily
Price: Expensive to very expensive
Credit Cards: Yes
Cuisine: Japanese
Serving: L, D
Handicapped Access: Yes

Chef Masaharu Morimoto from the Food Network's *Iron Chef* television show teamed up with renowned Philadelphia restaurateur Stephen Starr to open this magnificent Japanese fusion restaurant in 2001. There is so much to like, starting with the interesting, but unobtrusively chic dining room topped off by a bamboo ceiling. Even the simplest dishes get the star treatment on Morimoto's menu; the tempura, for example, is battered so lightly that it practically melts in one's mouth. Cha-soba green tea noodles are unusually light and invigorating. Sushi is similarly outstanding (the eel avocado roll gets consistent raves) and the dessert sorbets are heavenly. Morimoto is expensive for dinner but worth it. Save the tasting menu for special occasions. Lunch is a relative value, and offers its own set of terrific dishes like the rock shrimp teriyaki.

Ocean Harbor
215-574-1398
1023 Race St., Philadelphia, PA 19107
Open: Daily
Price: Inexpensive to moderate
Credit Cards: Yes
Cuisine: Chinese, dim sum
Serving: L, D
Handicapped Access: No

Dim sum served every day from 11 to 3 in a busy red dining room. Servers wheel around carts of food, so point at what you want and don't be afraid to try the curry squid. Seafood dishes are the most popular, and no meal is complete without sticky rice balls infused with flecks of roast pork. Dim sum is best enjoyed in a big group, and three or four dishes per person make for a very satisfying meal. Weekend dining at Ocean Harbor sometimes involves a wait, but the food will be at its freshest. Couples and single diners may be seated with strangers at a large table during prime times.

Sang Kee Peking Duck House
215-925-7532
www.sangkeephiladelphia.com
238 N. 9th St., Philadelphia, PA 19107
Open: Daily
Price: Inexpensive to moderate
Credit Cards: Cash only
Cuisine: Chinese
Serving: L, D
Handicapped Access: Yes

Gaze out the tall windows facing rush-hour traffic on the Vine Street Expressway and be glad you're digging into crisp, smoky Peking duck at Chinatown's premier duck house. The birds are served half or whole,

Sang Kee Peking Duck House

carved into small pieces to wrap in pan-cakes, and easy to share. If dining in a group, order your duck as part of a liberally portioned combination meal that includes soup and rice. Sang Kee has stood on this remote corner of Chinatown for 28 years and its duck routinely wins "Best of" honors among Philadelphia restaurants.

City Hall Vicinity
The Capital Grille
215-545-9588
www.thecapitalgrille.com
1338 Chestnut St., Philadelphia, PA 19107
Open: Daily
Price: Very expensive
Credit Cards: Yes
Cuisine: Steakhouse
Serving: L weekdays only, D
Handicapped Access: Yes

In the shadows of City Hall, the Capital Grille is a famous haunt for local politicos, lobbyists, and other garrulous folks in well-tailored suits. The dark, elegantly adorned room comes alive from Noon to 2 P.M. on weekdays, when regulars stop in for lobster bisque, club sandwiches, and enormous cheeseburgers. You can always get thick slabs of beef at the Capital Grille, though the midday menu lists some good entrée salads as well. The dinner crowd is often headed to or from the theater, and gets to enjoy dry aged, 24-ounce porterhouses that hold their own against any steak in the city. The Capital Grille's wine selection is superlative, as is the restaurant's acclaimed Stoli Doli cocktail: pineapples are bathed in vodka for a week, strained out, and then the pineapple-infused liquor is served cold in a martini glass.

Nineteen (XIX)
215-790-1919
www.nineteenrestaurant.com
200 S. Broad St., Philadelphia, PA 19102 (at Park Hyatt at the Bellevue)
Open: Mon.–Sat.
Price: Expensive to very expensive
Credit Cards: Yes
Cuisine: Continental
Serving: B, L, D
Handicapped Access: Yes
Special Features: Remarkable views

The nineteenth floor of the Park Hyatt at the Bellevue is devoted to this opulent gourmet room, which is actually a three-part arrangement: first there's the bar, with a lengthy list of specialty cocktails and the city's best weekday martini-loaded happy hour. Next there's a café menu for sand-wiches and breakfast all day. Finally, there's the restaurant, its tables assembled in a ring around the seafood bar and white pearl chandelier. If at all possible, sit near the terrace dining for phenomenal views, or at a private table outside the main room—either is plausible on weeknights. The menu is mostly seafood at dinner, complemented by a wine list befitting such a romantic venue.

Logan Square

Aya's Cafe

215-567-1555

www.ayascafe.net

2129 Arch St., Philadelphia, PA 19103

Open: Mon.–Sat.

Price: Moderate

Credit Cards: Yes

Cuisine: Mediterranean, Middle Eastern

Serving: L (weekdays only), D

Handicapped Access: Yes

Special Features: BYOB, eclectic

Hidden from Center City foot traffic on a demure residential block in Logan Square, Aya's is the restaurant that Philadelphia's foodies keep secret. Cuisine is as varied as it is recommendable, drawing influence from Italian, Egyptian, and Greek recipes. The Egyptian falafel is a perfect dinner appetizer, but leave room for kabobs, lamb stew, or pasta immersed in a wispy marinara sauce. The rotating lunch special is always a bargain, as are lamb pitas and shawarma for under $10. Service is excellent, and the tan and tawny dining room provides a gentle ambiance.

Fountain Restaurant

215-963-1500

www.fourseasons.com/philadelphia/dining/fountain_restaurant.html

1 Logan Square, Philadelphia, PA 19103 (at the Four Seasons)

Open: Daily

Price: Very expensive

Credit Cards: Yes

Cuisine: Continental

Serving: B, L, D, Sun. Brunch

Handicapped Access: Yes

Special Features: Jacket required for dinner; reservations recommended

Seasonal flavors with diverse international influences and a phenomenal tasting menu make this renowned restaurant one of Philadelphia's favorite places for a special night out. The décor builds off the hotel's placid sophistication, bringing together woods, flora, and fine art. The cuisine is classified as French, but the label fails to acknowledge the choreography of diverse European influences that informs the menu. Everyone gets the "yes sir" treatment from the expert waitstaff. The restaurant's only hint of hierarchy is the presence of select tables looking out on Logan Square's Swann Fountain. Sunday brunch is superb—a combination buffet and entrée setup with heavenly desserts—but can be a difficult reservation to get without some lead time.

Old City

Amada

215-625-2450

www.amadarestaurant.com

217–219 Chestnut St., Philadelphia, PA 19106

Open: Daily

Price: Expensive

Credit Cards: Yes

Cuisine: Spanish, tapas

Serving: L weekdays only, D

Handicapped Access: Yes

Old City restaurants are sometimes all sizzle and no steak, but Amada has the creative menu and ingredient quality to back up the voguish scene. Chef Jose Garces's menu is an original, affording sweet and smoky meats, silky Spanish cheeses, and Mediterranean-flavored beef, chicken, duck, lamb, and seafood dishes that comprise the perfect toolbox for crafting a tailor-made epicure. It's tapas, so order many plates; a good approach is to sample some fusion new American preparations and cheeses with a couple *Tradicional* choices like shrimp in a hot garlic broth or lamb meatballs in Manchego. Amada also goes out of its way to cater to vegetarians. Sangrias match the weather; sip Blanco in the summertime and spiced Tinto to warm up the winter. The contemporary dining room is full of surprises. A single elevated table is enclosed by a white curtain, while another is positioned street-side on a bed of rocks.

Buddakan

215-574-9440
www.buddakan.com
325 Chestnut St., Philadelphia, PA 19106
Open: Daily
Price: Expensive to very expensive
Credit Cards: Yes
Cuisine: Pan-Asian
Serving: L weekdays only, D
Handicapped Access: Yes

See and be seen at the high priest of Philadelphia's trendy restaurant movement. The hip crowd is as much a fixture as the 10-foot-tall Buddha who presides over the dining room or the gargantuan onion rings that sit atop the Asian barbeque pork—a popular sweet and spicy entrée. This is where the Starr restaurant empire got into its groove, and you won't find a better union of food and atmosphere in Philadelphia. With its reputation firmly entrenched, Buddakan could get away with second-rate cuisine, but the Asian fusion fare is exceptional from start to finish. Most dishes are served family style, so try a variety of appetizers, entrées, salads, and soups. Portions are generally quite large. Prices are surprisingly reasonable—check out Manhattan's Buddakan if you feel undercharged. A long sake list complements the quintessential Starr cocktail menu. And while there's no sense in making promises, Buddakan isn't a bad place to watch for celebrities.

Chlöe

215-629-2337
www.chloebyob.com
232 Arch St., Philadelphia, PA 19106
Open: Wed.–Sat.
Price: Expensive

Credit Cards: Cash only
Cuisine: New American
Serving: D
Handicapped Access: Yes
Special Features: BYOB

Inventive American dining across the street from the Betsy Ross House, Chlöe is romantic but casual, a perfect place to settle into some wine and a gourmet dinner. It does not take an expert gastronome to appreciate what Chlöe does with ingredients. The Moroccan lamb is characteristically inspired, with six large cubes alongside spicy tomatoes, couscous, and a smooth, invigorating cucumber raita. The chicken pot pie incorporates a traditional potato and vegetable medley with edamame, and is feather-light from the crust to the gravy. Trust the specials—there are usually many, listed on a chalkboard—and order the pillowy gnocchi when available. You do have to work for it a little. Chlöe is only open four days a week and won't take reservations or credit cards. The dining room seats about three-dozen people.

City Tavern

215-413-1443
www.citytaven.com
138 S. 2nd St., Philadelphia, PA 19106
Open: Daily
Price: Moderate
Credit Cards: Yes
Cuisine: American
Serving: L, D
Handicapped Access: Yes
Special Features: Good for families

The Tavern is an affectionate re-creation of the actual pub where delegates to the 1787 Constitutional Convention went to unwind, and forged the relationships that ultimately united opposing factions around the final document. City Tavern goes the extra mile to replicate the original. The waitstaff dresses in colonial-era garb and water is served in pewter goblets. What's remarkable is that actual Philadelphians eat here, which is a testament to the restaurant's quality. Dinner entrées are generously portioned, and preceded by a bread tray that includes Jefferson's favorite sweet potato biscuits. Jefferson was also the brains behind City Tavern's tasty honey wheat beer (beers incorporate recipes written by him and George Washington). The Tavern is a great place for families, and fun for large parties.

Cuba Libre

215-627-0666
www.cubalibrerestaurant.com
10 S. 2nd St., Philadelphia, PA 19106
Open: Daily
Price: Expensive
Credit Cards: Yes
Cuisine: Cuban
Serving: L, D, Sat. and Sun. Brunch
Handicapped Access: Yes
Special Features: Dance floor

With décor reminiscent of Old Havana, Cuba Libre makes for a fun and unique night of dining. The central dance floor is opened up at night for impromptu salsa, and the open-air veranda is heaven during the warmer months. A star of the menu is the renowned "Fire and Ice" ceviche appetizer, with just enough jalapeño to light up your mouth. Seafood entrées make the best main courses at Cuba Libre, and you won't go wrong with the house fish, which changes nightly. Share an order of fresh, crisp plantains for dessert. A wide variety of rums and superb mojitos make great accompaniments to most dishes, and servers are attentive even when the restaurant gets loud and busy.

Eulogy Belgian Tavern

215-413-1918
www.eulogybar.com
136 Chestnut St., Philadelphia, PA 19106
Open: Daily
Price: Moderate to expensive

Credit Cards: Yes
Cuisine: Belgian
Serving: L, D
Handicapped Access: No
Special Features: Beer list

Eulogy has six kinds of mussels delivered fresh from Maine every day and the half-pound burger is a perennial contender for tops in the city. Best of all is the international beer list, which is almost comically comprehensive; the dozens of Belgian beers only begin to scratch the surface. It's mostly a dark bar downstairs, with just a few tables, but there is more sit-down dining on the second level.

Haru Philadelphia

215-861-8990
www.harusushi.com
241 Chestnut St., Philadelphia, PA 19106
Open: Mon.–Sat.
Price: Expensive
Credit Cards: Yes
Cuisine: Japanese
Serving: L, D
Handicapped Access: Yes

The New York-based Japanese fusion brand arrived in Philadelphia in 2005, quickly becoming the best sushi in Old City. It's also a fun place to imbibe, with a fine sake selection and nectareous cocktail blends like the Momotini (peach puree and sake). Haru refitted an old bank building with soft woods and a stylish private lounge on the second level, but it refused to go too far. More than many Old City hotspots, it manages a sleek, modern feel without being obnoxious. Lunch boxes are terrific, particularly the trio yakitori, which features chicken, salmon, and beef teriyaki alongside tempura and a California roll. Sushi is generously portioned at both lunch and dinner. Those who would know rave about the sake. Non-aficionados can sample cocktails at happy hour from 5 P.M. to 7 P.M. on weekdays, and enjoy Sapporo draft beer.

The Plough and the Stars

215-733-0300
www.ploughstars.com
123 Chestnut St., Philadelphia, PA 19106
Open: Daily
Price: Moderate to expensive
Credit Cards: Yes
Cuisine: Irish
Serving: L, D, Sat. & Sun. Brunch
Handicapped Access: Yes

Don't be surprised to see the same people drinking and dancing into the wee hours of Saturday night return to the same table for brunch the next day. The Plough and the Stars is high-energy fun in the evenings and its Shepherd's Pie a perfect hangover treatment in the mornings. A youngish crowd takes over when the sun sets, but the big hamburgers and lunch salads are a good way for anyone to break up a long day touring Old City. If things get busy, request a table on the second level for quieter dining. Food and drinks are reasonably priced considering the neighborhood. One could hope for a few more Irish beers on tap, but the list is balanced with some solid local brew. Live Irish music is featured on Sundays.

Tangerine

215-627-5116
www.tangerinerestaurant.com
232 Market St., Philadelphia, PA 19106
Open: Daily
Price: Expensive
Credit Cards: Yes
Cuisine: Moroccan, Mediterranean
Serving: D
Handicapped Access: Yes

Do not come expecting traditional Moroccan cuisine, but do expect a fun evening in a cozy space. Tangerine pulls off modern and relaxed at the same time, with muted lighting emanating from above and a wall of candles sparkling to the side. The dining room is divided into two sections by a translucent black curtain and is bordered with stylish burgundy drapery. Tangerine also pays extra attention to the little things, most notably plate presentation. The artful menu likes to merge spicy and sweet, with lots of pronounced chili and garlic flavors submerged in olive oils or fruit-based sauces. After a breadstick basket, try the crudo sashimi appetizer, which changes often, or shrimp Pil-pil. A meaty seared tuna and a sliced pomegranate pork chop make excellent main courses. You can also snack and drink in style at Tangerine's lounge, which serves a special tapas menu and imaginative cocktails.

Rittenhouse Square

Alma de Cuba

215-988-1799
www.almadecubarestaurant.com
1623 Walnut St., Philadelphia, PA 19103
Open: Daily
Price: Expensive
Credit Cards: Yes
Cuisine: Cuban
Serving: L, D
Handicapped Access: Yes
Special Features: Outdoor seating

If at all possible, try and score a table on the second-level dining area of this chic Cuban restaurant—it's a good spot for people-watching, and ground floor diners endure a noisier, more hectic experience. Still, wherever you are in Alma de Cuba, you're in for a flavorful evening. Seafood, pork, and beef dishes comprise the bulk of the menu, so this is a haven for meat eaters who like a little zing. Portions are generous without being overbearing, which is a good excuse to start with a couple empanadas. Desserts are exceptional, particularly the famed Chocolate Cigar cake. And Alma's mojitos are pleasantly restrained, never cloyingly sweet.

Audrey Claire

215-731-1222

www.twentymanning.com
276 S. 20th St., Philadelphia, PA 19103
Open: Daily
Price: Moderate to expensive
Credit Cards: Cash only
Cuisine: Mediterranean
Serving: D
Handicapped Access: Yes
Special Features: BYOB; outdoor seating

Table for four at Audrey Claire

It seems like a new bistro opens and closes every week in Center City, but Audrey Claire—now entering its 12th year in Rittenhouse Square—has stood the test of time. The secret (alright, one of them) is the spices. Meat and seafood dishes are infused with an adaptable mix of garlic, tomato, onion, and olive flavors. The menu is broken into "smaller" and "bigger" dishes. Pick one of each to craft a filling meal. Begin with grilled flatbread or the highly regarded mussels starter served in a large glass bowl. Among the second coursers, the baby rack of lamb entrée is a good choice for its juiciness and couscous accompaniment. An unimposing dining room with open-air kitchen, simple wooden tables, and white walls keeps attention on the food. Reservations are taken on weeknights only.

Barclay Prime
215-732-7560
www.barclayprime.com

237 S. 18th St., Philadelphia, PA 19103
Open: Daily
Price: Very expensive
Credit Cards: Yes
Cuisine: Steakhouse
Serving: D
Handicapped Access: Yes

Twelve-foot mahogany walls, high ceilings, and white marble tabletops make this dark, distinctive steakhouse the perfect choice for a romantic dinner. Barclay Prime is also a popular after-work hangout for Philadelphia's business clique, with offices nearby and luxury condominiums above. The assiduous waitstaff can guide you through both the menu and the 16-page wine/champagne list in exacting detail. Steaks are served a la carte, with your choice of a half-dozen Japanese and German knives. While beef is king at Barclay Prime, including the famed $100 Kobe cheesesteak, don't ignore the right side of the menu for light, savory crab cakes, chicken, and seafood. You can even combine entrées to taste, so get creative and order scampi piled atop a porterhouse.

Caffe Casta Diva
215-496-9677
227 S. 20th St., Philadelphia, PA 19103
Open: Tues.–Sat.
Price: Expensive
Credit Cards: Cash only
Cuisine: Italian
Serving: D
Handicapped Access: No
Special Features: BYOB

This tiny Italian BYOB is quieter and more romantic than most restaurants in Rittenhouse Square, even on busy weekends. The mature, well-behaved crowd knows how to appreciate a properly prepared Italian meal served in an elegant room. Food is dependably fresh, from the mozzarella to the sorbet (dessert selections vary). Main courses are not especially large, though the three-quarter-inch-thick veal chop is a blissful exception. Make reservations if you can, and be sure to bring cash.

Lacroix at the Rittenhouse

215-790-2533
www.lacroixrestaurant.com
210 W. Rittenhouse Square, Philadelphia, PA 19103 (at the Rittenhouse Hotel)
Open: Daily
Price: Very expensive
Credit Cards: Yes
Cuisine: French, contemporary
Serving: B, L, D, Sun. Brunch
Handicapped Access: Yes
Special Features: Reservations recommended

Two momentous things occur on Sundays in Philadelphia: Eagles victories and brunch at Lacroix. And while football fans get 12 wins in a good year, brunch is served every Sunday at the city's most dependably creative, satisfying restaurant. Selections vary by season, but the ingredient diversity and culinary ingenuity is always there. The joy of Lacroix is in sampling from several dozen small plates and appreciating chef Matthew Levin's knack for surpassing even the highest expectations. The format allows Levin to experiment freely while keeping the menu accessible to all. On any given Sunday you might get caviar-topped oysters at the raw bar, octopus brochette, duck-stuffed croissant, lobster BLT, or strawberry Greek salad. But you're not even close to done. Venture into the kitchen for the hot dishes like king crab with couscous, quail egg with artichoke, pork belly fried rice, and carving stations featuring classics like beef tenderloin or innovations like scallop sausage; not to mention the chocolate fountains and accompanying fresh fruit. Dessert is a final act befitting the magnum opus that came before. Sky-high picture windows, a tastefully modern dining room, and live guitarist set the scene.

Truly an exceptional feast. Dinner here is similarly delightful and can be assembled a la carte or via the adaptable tasting menu.

Le Bec-Fin

215-576-1000
www.lebecfin.com
1523 Walnut St., Philadelphia, PA 19102
Open: Mon.–Sat.
Price: Very expensive
Credit Cards: Yes
Cuisine: French
Serving: L, D
Handicapped Access: Yes
Special Features: Reservations recommended

A perennial special occasion restaurant and Philadelphia institution since its 1970 opening at the original location on Spruce Street, this is famed chef Georges Perrier's masterwork—always a contender for tops in the city, and a AAA Five Diamond restaurant for 20 years. You'll often see the owner himself in the dining room greeting guests and making sure things are running smoothly. At press time, there was talk of redecorating the space and modernizing the shiny gold silk-paneled wall and antique mirror look that radiates elegance. The menu has seen some changes too; dinner is now a la carte, although a tasting menu remains available at lunch (offered in the main dining room Fridays and Saturdays only; the bar offers a lunch menu six days a week). It's fresh, accessible, rich French cuisine all the way, from the famed crab cakes starter to duck breast in wine sauce. And then the dessert cart comes out and vindicates the sum total of your life choices. No matter the work you've done, the people you've endured and the compromises you've made; at the very least it has culminated in dessert at Le Bec-Fin. This is what you're paying for. Servers present the choices with a tantalizing descriptiveness and put together a plate to your liking. The chocolate, rum-soaked Gâteau Le Bec-Fin is the classic, but it's all good.

Melograno

215-875-8116
2012 Sansom St., Philadelphia, PA 19103
Open: Tues.–Sun.
Price: Expensive
Credit Cards: Yes
Cuisine: Italian
Serving: D
Handicapped Access: Yes
Special Features: BYOB; reservations taken on weeknights; outdoor seating

The old location was a snug corner at Spruce and 22nd Streets. Close to press time, Melograno moved to a new location at Sansom and 20th. The menu remains the same: built around a dozen or so northern Italian dishes, prepared with fresh ingredients and served by friendly, capable staff. Bias yourself towards entrées that come alongside either buttery whipped potatoes or a zesty tomato salad. Dessert is suitably caloric and worth hanging around for. Friday and Saturday nights sometimes require a significant wait, but reservations are taken for other nights.

Monk's Café

215-545-7005
www.monkscafe.com
264 S. 16th St., Philadelphia, PA 19146
Open: Daily
Price: Moderate
Credit Cards: Yes
Cuisine: Belgian
Serving: L, D
Handicapped Access: No
Special Features: Beer list

Monk's is a great choice for sandwiches, burgers, pommes frites, and capably prepared mussels in high-rent Rittenhouse Square. The extensive beer list is a good place to start, with some Belgian brands that are difficult to find elsewhere in

Philadelphia. The dark dining room is crowded most nights during dinner, but the bar stays open until the wee hours, so feel free to keep draining those Chimays and Duvels until 2 A.M.

My Thai

215-985-1878
2200 South St., Philadelphia, PA 19146
Open: Daily
Price: Moderate
Credit Cards: Yes
Cuisine: Thai
Serving: L, D
Handicapped Access: Yes
Special Features: BYOB

My Thai

Do not be dissuaded by the slightly out-of-the-way location on the west end of South Street (not really "Rittenhouse Square" in the strictest sense). My Thai is a treat. The three-course dinner specials come with soup, appetizer, and a good-sized entrée. Old standbys like pad Thai are fine, but go for a fiery curry pot or a juicy assortment of barbequed chicken. The room's small size and floral décor make for a very pleasant dining environment. My Thai is also vegetarian friendly and most non-vegetarian dishes can be prepared without meat. The homemade ginger and coconut ice creams are perfect closers.

Parc Restaurant

215-545-2262
www.parc-restaurant.com
227 S. 18th St., Philadelphia, PA 19103
Open: Daily
Price: Expensive to very expensive
Credit Cards: Yes
Cuisine: French
Serving: B, L, D, Sat. & Sun. Brunch
Handicapped Access: Yes

It's normally a little risky to include recently opened restaurants in a travel guide since you never know if an establishment will last. That said, Parc ain't going anywhere. This hip Parisian brasserie on the ground level of a luxury condominium building is Stephen Starr's latest, and just a month after opening it has already secured a loyal contingent of brunch regulars. Outdoor seating lines the sidewalk across from Rittenhouse Square, making it great for people-watching. The tile-floor dining room is larger than it seems from the street; some refer to Parc ironically as a "mega bistro." The cheeseburger with pommes frites has enjoyed early raves, and the oatmeal crème brûlée makes for a surprisingly filling brunch.

The Prime Rib

215-772-1701
1701 Locust St., Philadelphia, PA 19103 (at the Radisson Warwick)
Open: Daily
Price: Expensive
Credit Cards: Yes
Cuisine: Steakhouse
Serving: D
Handicapped Access: Yes

There's a big menu, but impatient carnivores need look no further than the name. The restaurant specializes in mammoth cuts of prime rib, soaked in their natural juices and best served medium rare. The prime rib is straight out of another era. The floral-print booths, oversized black chairs, piano player, and animal-print carpet negotiate a thin line between classy and cheesy, but with beef this good, who cares? It's a little more casual than it once was—men no longer need to wear jackets in the dining room. Steaks and chops are a la carte, so share a side dish or two and a rich dessert. There are lots of appropriately muscular reds on the wine list. You can bring your own if you like, and the corkage fee is waived on Sunday nights.

Sansom Kabob House

215-751-9110
www.sansomkabob.com
1526 Sansom St., Philadelphia, PA 19102
Open: Mon.–Sat.
Price: Inexpensive
Credit Cards: Yes
Cuisine: Afghan
Serving: L, D
Handicapped Access: No

It can be easy to miss this little treasure, tucked below a sushi restaurant on an aesthetically unpleasing block. The Afghani couple who owns and operates Sansom Street Kabob (with an occasional assist from their daughter who doubles as maitre d') serve a delicious spread at bargain prices. Food is an appealing synthesis of Middle Eastern and South Asian cuisine, and the menu is heavy on chicken, ground beef, and vegetable choices, though dishes are generally less spicy than their Indian counterparts. As the moniker suggests, come for the kabobs—particularly the tender lamb. Dinner comes with salad, appetizer, and warm naan. Add on a wedge of dense baklava and a cup of coffee to round things out.

Square on Square

215-568-0088
www.squareonsquare.com
1905 Chestnut St., Philadelphia, PA 19103
Open: Daily

Price: Inexpensive to moderate
Credit Cards: Yes
Cuisine: Chinese
Serving: L, D
Handicapped Access: Yes

Regarded by savvy Philadelphians as some of the finest Chinese food outside Chinatown, the Square on Square menu emphasizes garlicky fusion dishes and lots of great seafood. The name is derived from the restaurant's location near Rittenhouse Square and from the orthogonal ceiling design, which actually predated the restaurant's opening in 2002. Fine choices include the satisfying Family Reunion, with beef, chicken, shrimp, scallops, and vegetables in a light brown sauce or the General Powell spicy chicken. Food is exceptionally fresh and service is both quick and polite.

Susanna Foo
215-545-8800
www.susannafoo.com
1512 Walnut St., Philadelphia, PA 19102
Open: Daily
Price: Expensive
Credit Cards: Yes
Cuisine: Chinese fusion
Serving: L weekdays only, D
Handicapped Access: Yes

Susanna Foo, at least a decade ahead of her time, brought Asian cooking with a French twist to downtown Philadelphia in 1986. The room's silk lanterns and unpretentious floral garnitures make for a congenial ambiance. At dinner the dumpling sampler is a practical starter, though chicken and mushroom dumplings are so savory that you might just want to order a whole plate. Folks swoon over the tea-smoked duck breast, but the punchy citrus shrimp, delicately fried and served with sweet rice, is even better. A dim sum prix fixe during lunch hours is a good way to capture a taste of the restaurant's fare. Large groups

should check on the availability of the Empress Den, a partially secluded dining room.

Warsaw Cafe
215-546-0204
www.warsawcafe.thekalon.com
305 S. 16th St., Philadelphia, PA 19102
Open: Daily
Price: Moderate
Credit Cards: Yes
Cuisine: Polish, other Eastern European
Serving: L except Sun., D
Handicapped Access: Entrance is one step up

Visit this intimate dining room with red tabletops and plentiful flora for outstanding pierogi, borscht, crepes, and other Eastern European delicacies from Poland, Hungary, Russia, the Czech Republic, and beyond. Warsaw is often packed on theater and concert nights, with its convenient location just two blocks off the Avenue of the Arts. Lunches are an excellent value, especially big plates of pierogi or potato pancakes alongside salad or fruit for under $10. Also consider the daily sandwich specials served on black bread. An ethereal beef stroganoff is a popular dinner entrée.

South Street
Tamarind
215-925-2764
www.tamarindsouthstreet.com
117 South St., Philadelphia, PA 19147
Open: Tues.–Sun.
Price: Moderate
Credit Cards: Yes
Cuisine: Thai
Serving: D
Handicapped Access: No
Special Features: BYOB

The best dining value on South Street, Tamarind works just as well for a romantic night out as for an impromptu dinner among friends. The menu has something for everyone, including traditional Thai noodle dishes, made to order curry entrées, and plenty of choices for vegetarians. Try to fit in a bowl of refreshing glass noodle soup, or a couple slightly spicy spring rolls. With consistently friendly service and a prime location a hundred yards from the waterfront, the place occasionally fills up. Make reservations for weekend dining.

Washington Square West

Jamaican Jerk Hut
215-545-8644
1436 South St., Philadelphia, PA 19146
Open: Daily
Price: Inexpensive to moderate
Credit Cards: Cash only
Cuisine: Caribbean
Serving: L except Sun., D
Handicapped Access: Yes
Special Features: Garden dining, BYOB

If the place looks faintly familiar, it's because this is where Toni Colette and Mark Feuerstein tied the knot in the 2005 film *In Her Shoes*. Even before this modest brush with celebrity, Jamaican Jerk Hut was known locally for outstanding jerk chicken, oxtail stew, and spicy Caribbean seafood. Go for dinner during clear spring or summer evenings, when you can be seated in the garden.

Mercato
215-985-2962
www.mercatobyob.com
1216 Spruce St., Philadelphia, PA 19107
Open: Daily
Price: Expensive
Credit Cards: Cash only
Cuisine: Italian
Serving: D
Handicapped Access: No
Special Features: BYOB

Dining alfresco at Mercato

Mercato separates itself from the herd of nouveau Italian BYOBs in Center City on the strength of its generous portions and dessert menu. Its fiercely loyal contingent of regulars swear by the "pyramid" pasta, a gorgeous plate of buttery conoids stuffed with shrimp and lobster. The large selection of salads and antipasti is a fine example of the menu's overall creativity. And there are rich treats everywhere, from tender short ribs in gnocchi to a chocolate tart that oozes caramel, which might be the best thing on the menu. Service is conscientious without being intrusive, and the room radiates a youthful energy not found in Center City's more stolid Italian restaurants. They can pack you in a little tight at busy times, but after the pre-theater crowd leaves—typically by eight—there's more personal space to be had. For a change of pace, bring your own bottle of vodka instead of wine. Mercato stocks Italian sodas, which make great mixers.

Ms. Tootsie's Soul Food Café

215-731-9045
1314 South St., Philadelphia, PA 19147
Open: Daily
Price: Moderate
Credit Cards: Yes
Cuisine: Southern, soul food
Serving: L (Fri.–Sun. only), D
Handicapped Access: Yes

Don't even try asking what's in the iced tea: everyone who knows has been sworn to secrecy. Whatever the recipe, it's a sweet fruity blend (hints of watermelon and citrus perchance?) and a welcome accompaniment to everything on the menu at Center City's hottest soul food restaurant. Most of the classic platters—smothered pork chops, moist and tender fried chicken—are generously portioned and come with one or two side dishes. For dessert, the sweet potato cheesecake and lemon butter pound cake both get consistent raves. Ms. Tootsie's

Restaurant Bar Lounge, a companion restaurant and lounge next door, has a swankier ambiance and similarly excellent food.

Vetri

215-732-3478
www.vetriristorante.com
1312 Spruce St., Philadelphia, PA 19107
Open: Mon.–Sat.
Price: Very expensive
Credit Cards: Yes
Cuisine: Italian
Serving: D
Handicapped Access: No
Special Features: Reservations recommended

Among the finest restaurants in Philadelphia since 1998, when chef and owner Marc Vetri brought his virtuoso Italian cooking to Center City. First-timers should put themselves in the kitchen's expert hands and order the tasting menu. Food varies depending on season and mood, but will generally include a couple antipasto dishes, handmade pastas, a meat dish, and dessert. The tasting menu typically incorporates some of the restaurant's classics. Spinach gnocchi with ricotta cheese, stuffed hen breast, and lavender olive oil sorbet are a few possibilities. Food and wine are unanimously first-rate, but the most appealing aspect of Vetri may be its lack of pretension. You can leave the suit and tie at home if you like, and engage in robust conversation without feeling rude. Vetri may not be cheap, but it is distinctly unsnobbish. It is about the pleasures to be had eating wonderful, imaginative food with friends and loved ones. The dining room, occupying the first floor of a Washington Square West townhouse, seats just 35 people, so getting a reservation is rarely easy. A few weeks advance notice can work for weeknights, but not for Saturday night dinners, when Vetri serves special tasting menus.

Food Purveyors

Center City has several top-notch coffeehouses, sandwich shops, bakeries, and pizzerias. But the king of food purveyors in Philadelphia shall always be **Reading Terminal Market** (215-922-2317; www.readingterminalmarket.org; 12th and Arch Sts.). If you eat just one lunch in Philadelphia, it should be at Reading Terminal. Located in the heart of downtown across the street from the Convention Center, the market brings together more than 80 vendors from all corners of the city and beyond. Some sell produce, raw meat, uncooked seafood, and non-food merchandise, but many are branches of area restaurants and food suppliers that serve breakfast and lunch fare at excellent prices. Wander around a bit and see what looks good. As a rule of thumb, you can't go wrong with turkey sandwiches from The Original Turkey carved fresh before your eyes, or colossal hoagies from Spataro's. Stop by the Pennsylvania Dutch vendors for baked goods, and Chocolate by Mueller for candies to go. The only problem is finding a place to sit. Tables fill up quickly during weekend lunchtime, so keep your eyes open. Parking is $3 at the garage on adjacent Filbert Street if you spend $10 and remember to validate.

Bakeries/Coffeehouses

Almaz Café (215-557-0108; 140 S. 20th St.). Gentle lime-green walls and two levels of seating make this a comfortable place to enjoy coffee and a sandwich. Some Ethiopian specialties are available as well.

Ants Pants Café (215-875-8002; 2212 South St.). Ostensibly a neighborhood coffee spot, you'll often find the front of Ants Pants occupied by area residents lingering over newspapers and laptops. But the small dining room in the back also serves a great breakfast and rich sandwiches.

The Bean Café (215-629-2250; 615 South St.). Epitomizes the South Street vibe, with local art, good coffee, and smoothies.

Double Shots Espresso Bar (215-351-5171; 211 Chestnut St.). Cozy neighborhood hangout in Old City. The Rocket Fuel latte comes with up to eight (yes, eight) shots of espresso. Any purchase also entitles you to some free Internet browsing.

ING Direct Café (215-731-1410; 1638 Walnut St.). A whimsical—and extremely orange—coffee spot brought to you by the multinational branchless bank. Patrons get complimentary Internet browsing and foam stress balls, plus free coffee on Fridays for anyone wearing orange.

Naked Chocolate Café (215-735-7310; 1317 Walnut St.). Chocolate, chocolate, chocolate, all day, every day. Drinking chocolates are served hot or frozen, blended, bittersweet, or spicy. Accompany with loose chocolates, chocolate-covered pretzels, or mocha fudge cake.

Tartes (215-625-2510; 212 Arch St.). Just a little sliver of a bakery peeking over the Arch Street sidewalk, with great cupcakes and other pastries to go.

Walnut Bridge Coffeehouse (215-496-9003; 2319 Walnut St.). Last chance for Illy brand coffee or hot chocolate before going over the Schuylkill River into West Philadelphia. Comfortable sofas and a friendly staff make Walnut Bridge a relaxing place to pass some time.

Refreshments at Franklin Fountain: the perfect way to break up a day touring Old City.

Candy, Ice Cream, and Water Ice

Capogiro Gelato Artisans (215-351-0900; 119 S. 13th St.). Fresh-made gelato every day on the premises, and a wonderful menu of more than two-dozen flavors. It's especially tough to refuse Madagascar Bourbon Vanilla. There is also a location near Rittenhouse Square at 117 S. 20th St.

The Franklin Fountain (215-627-1899; 116 Market St.). Retro ice-cream parlor makes a perfect milkshake and a near perfect egg cream. Gooey treats abound, like the habit-forming Southern Sympathizer, a rum raisin and pistachio concoction drenched in caramel.

Rita's Water Ice (215-629-3910; 235 South St.). The venerable northeastern chain serves up traditional syrupy, slushy Philadelphia water ice. While the ices are the main attraction, creamy frozen custard is also good. Additional locations are scattered throughout town.

Pizza, Sandwiches, Faster Food

Five Guys Burgers and Fries (215-972-1375; 1527 Chestnut St.). Juicy double burgers are cooked fresh with toppings to taste at this popular Virginia-based franchise. Snack on free unshelled peanuts while you wait.

Govidna's Gourmet to Go (215-985-9303; 1408 South St.). The Gourmet to Go counter at Govidna's is one of Philadelphia's best spots for a quick vegetarian lunch. The menu creatively works soy and rice into more than a dozen meals that even non-vegetarians enjoy.

Lorenzo & Son Pizza (215-627-4110; 305 South St.). Pizza that literally hangs off the plate. Slices are crisp and flavorful in addition to being big. Open until 4 A.M. on weekend nights in order to satiate the rumbling stomachs of South Street.

Primo Hoagies (215-496-0540; 2043 Chestnut St.). The red-and-white-striped awning signals big hoagies with lots of meat on fresh Italian bread. This Center City location is the best quick bite in the area; the original Primo is in South Philadelphia at 1528 Ritner Street.

Pumpkin Market (215-545-1173; 1609 South St.). Scrumptious gourmet sandwiches and top-flight chili that can be taken away or enjoyed in the creamsicle-colored room. Don't confuse it with the Pumpkin restaurant a block and a half away, which is a more formal eatery under the same ownership.

South Street Souvlaki (215-925-3026; 509 South St.). Yummy gyros at the sidewalk take-out window. Also good for a sit-down meal.

Recreation

Philly is a big sports town, no question, but recreational opportunities are limited within densely populated Center City. The city's professional sports teams all play in South Philadelphia (a controversial 2000 effort to bring a stadium to Chinatown failed) and municipal facilities are mostly located in peripheral neighborhoods where there's more room.

Bowling

Lucky Strike (215-545-2471; www.bowlluckystrike.com; 1336 Chestnut St.). Definitely not your grandfather's bowling alley, Lucky Strike is more like a chic downtown hotspot that also has bowling. The electronic scorekeeping even tracks ball speed. There's a strict dress code (no sweatpants, construction boots, or athletic jerseys) and after 9 P.M. it's 21 and over only. A strong happy hour on weekdays from 5–7 P.M. reduces your bar bill.

Family Fun

Dave & Buster's (215-413-1951; www.daveandbusters.com; 325 N. Columbus Blvd.). The popular chain has a branch on the Delaware River waterfront, chock full of arcade games, billiards, skeeball, etc.

Philly Mini Golf (Franklin Square, 6th and Race Sts.). Until just a couple years ago, Franklin Square was a shamefully rundown public space. Today it is a model of creative urban design, and includes an imaginative Philadelphia-themed miniature golf course. There is also a carousel, two playgrounds, and picnic areas.

On the Waterfront

Along the Delaware River is the area known as **Penn's Landing**, a partly public waterfront. On the northeast Center City border is the **Festival Pier** concert venue (www.livenation.com/venue/16764; Columbus Blvd. and Spring Garden St.). Penn's Landing is also a good place for a summertime stroll or to watch the sunrise.
Redevelopment of the area has been a divisive issue in Philadelphia for many years, as city officials, citizens, and businesses try to agree on a plan that merges growth with sufficient public space.

Fitness Facilities

The following downtown gyms offer daily rates for visitors. Most have a wide variety of machines and classes, and some include sauna, pool, and racquetball courts that can be reserved for an additional charge. Call ahead.

12th Street Gym (215-985-4092; www.12streetgym.com; 204 S. 12th St.)

Old City Ironworks (215-627-7002; 141 N. 3rd St.)

Philadelphia Sports Club (215-564-5353; www.mysportsclubs.com; 1735 Market St.)

Sweat (215-437-3222; www.sweatfitness.com; 1425 Arch St.)

Ice Skating

Blue Cross RiverRink at Penn's Landing (215-925-7465; www.riverrink.com; Columbus Blvd. and Market St.). Right next to the Delaware River, boasting a lovely view of the Ben Franklin Bridge. RiverRink is operational during the winter months, with skate rental on premises, and occasional special events. Open into the very late evening on Friday and Saturday nights.

Public Squares and Parks

Per William Penn's original design, Philadelphia has five public squares, most of which contain ample green space and are great places to relax. **Franklin Square**, referenced above, occupies the northeast quadrant, and has been recently reinvigorated. **Logan Square** in the northwest is where the Ben Franklin Parkway meets Race Street. It is the only public square that is actually a circle. Logan is mostly concrete, but has the attractive Swann Fountain at its center and numerous park benches around its perimeter. The middle of downtown gets **Centre Square**, which is consumed by City Hall (though this was not always the case). There is still activity in Centre Square, but it typically takes the form of press conferences and protests.

In the southeast, at Walnut and 7th Streets, you'll find **Washington Square**, a former burial ground for casualties of the Revolutionary War. It is now an attractive green space, good for lounging around with snacks and a book. The Tomb of the Unknown Revolutionary War Soldier memorializes the park's previous use. Finally, in the southwest is legendary **Rittenhouse Square**, its flowers, trees, fountains, and lovingly maintained lawns anchoring Philadelphia's ritziest neighborhood. It is equally beautiful in the wintertime. Rittenhouse hosts many festivals and special events throughout the year. **The Friends of Rittenhouse Square** (www.friendsofrittenhouse.org) maintains a good Web site to keep track of what's going on.

Center City parks are not limited to the original squares. Adjacent to City Hall is **JFK Plaza**, informally known as LOVE Park for the familiar Robert Indiana sculpture found in the center of the square. The Plaza is a popular lunch spot for municipal workers, as well as skateboarders who spiritedly oppose the city's controversial ban on the activity. Another park of note is **Welcome Park** at Walnut and 2nd Streets, where William Penn lived during his time in Philadelphia, and where you can find a map of the original city delineated in granite.

Shopping

The compact downtown grid has served Philadelphia's shoppers well since the first specie arrived on the Delaware River shore in the late 17th century. Today's broad range of stores caters to every imaginable customer. There is shopping scattered all over Center City, but handily divided shopping districts make browsing easy. The most specialized are **Antique Row** on Pine Street from 9th Street to 13th Street, and T-shaped **Jewelers' Row**, which runs down Sansom Street between 7th and 8th Streets and along 8th Street between Chestnut and Walnut. Antiquing on Pine Street is a fun diversion for even the most novice customer. The Jewelers' Row diamond district is where generations of Philadelphians have gone for wedding rings, necklaces, bracelets, earrings, and the like. The compact marketplace ensures easy comparison shopping and competitive pricing.

For a taste of how Philadelphians shopped many moons ago, drop by Macy's in the **Wanamaker Building** (215-241-9000; 1300 Market St.). Wanamaker's was among the first American department stores, and the grandiose interior harkens back to time when Wanamaker's decision to put price tags on all items was viewed as a radical concept. Macy's has occupied the Renaissance-style building since 2006.

High-end clothes shopping can be found along **Rittenhouse Row** (www.rittenhouserow.org), neatly mingled among art galleries, antique stores, and other curiosities. The Row, which is actually less a row than a rectangular shopping district, runs between Broad and 21st Street and along every crosstown street from Market down to Pine. The main artery is Walnut Street, where you'll find Ann Taylor, Armani Exchange, Brooks Brothers, Burberrys, Jacques Ferber Furs, and many more.

Also worth a look is **South Street** from 10th Street east to the river. Like its bars and restaurants, South Street boutique and specialty shopping draws a lot of college kids, hipsters, and erstwhile Bohemians.

The following list includes some noteworthy shops, strewn throughout Center City.

Antiques

Antiquarian's Delight (215-592-0256; 615 S. 6th St.). Two-dozen vendors at this one-stop-shop antique marketplace just south of South Street.

Freeman's (215-563-9275; 1808 Chestnut St.). This auction house's history dates back to the turn of the 19th century, and the business has never left the Freeman family. Fine art, European furniture, Oriental rugs, Americana, and a whole lot more. They still have live auctions at the Chestnut Street location as well as over the Internet.

M. Finkel & Daughter (215-627-7797; 936 Pine St.). Sixty-year-old Antique Row business, dealing principally in American needlework from the 18th and early 19th centuries.

Books

Barnes and Noble (215-665-0716; www.barnesandnoble.com; 1805 Walnut St.). Nice views of Rittenhouse Square from the second-floor café.

Book Corner (215-567-0527; www.libraryfriends.info; 311 N. 20th St.). The Friends of the Free Library of Philadelphia sell inexpensive used books right next door to the central library branch. Lots of interesting readings and special events.

Borders (215-568-7400; www.borders.com; 1 S. Broad St.) A sizeable branch in the heart of downtown.

Garland of Letters (215-923-5946; 527 South St.). New-age bookstore with material spanning world religions. Jewelry and music selections as well.

Clothing and Shoes

Benjamin Lovell (215-238-1969; 318 South St.). Funky shoe store with hard-to-find footwear from around the world, as well as a good selection of American brands like Michael Kors. There are three locations around the city, but the South Street branch has a popular sale rack.

Boyds (215-564-9000; 1818 Chestnut St.). Custom tailoring, complimentary valet parking, and an exceptionally high service standard. Boyds is the place to go for a carefully selected, perfectly fitted suit or designer dress. Open until 9 P.M. on Wednesdays.

Charlie's Jeans (215-923-9681; 233 Market St.). Mecca for designer women's jeans in every cut and size, with menswear on the other side of Market Street.

Daffy's (215-963-9996; 1700 Chestnut St.). Big, four-story discount clothing store for women and men, with huge price cuts on some chic attire. The Philadelphia branch of this northeast chain is one of the best. Takes some work to find the true bargains.

Grasshopper (215-925-3959; 727 Walnut St.). Independent labels and accessories at this posh boutique with mirrored ceilings. Some menswear, but the majority of customers are young women.

Leehe Fai (215-564-6111; 133 S. 18th St.). Swanky women's clothing store with fine party dresses and other apparel from haute designers.

Original I. Goldberg (215-925-9393; 1300 Chestnut St.). Well stocked Army-Navy and outdoors store with heavy-duty clothing and accessories. A good spot to hit before a hike or to just pick up some warm socks.

Smak Parlour (215-625-4551; 219 Market St.). Handmade clothes for women, designed and produced by the friendly co-owners who started the boutique.

Vagabond (267-671-0737; 37 N. 3rd St.). Old City women's boutique with a strong stock of vintage apparel, plus newer styles from local and independent designers. It doubles as a yarn shop, so you'll find many hand-knit garments as well.

Gifts

Blendo (215-351-9260; 1002 Pine St.). Eclectically stocked vintage store, stuffed to the limit with jewelry, dishware, clothing, and lots of other 50- and 60-year-old paraphernalia to rummage through.

Hello World (215-545-7060; 1201 Pine St.). Cute gift shop with presents for babies and adults alike.

South Street Florist (215-238-0504; 418 South St.). Fresh, creative arrangements and excellent customer service. Stays open for 48 hours straight prior to Valentine's Day and Mother's Day each year.

Gourmet Food

Di Bruno Bros. (215-665-9220; 1730 Chestnut St.). The famous Italian Market cheese sellers have a second gourmet food store in Rittenhouse Square. The staff is as sharp as the provolone, and happy to assist you in finding a perfect cheese. Also fresh bread, meats, olive oils, coffee, and other good stuff.

Old City Cheese Shop (215-238-1716; 160 N. 3rd St.). Lots of European cheeses to choose from, plus light sandwiches, salads, and soups for lunch and supper. The backyard garden is a wonderful hidden spot, folded inside the neighboring buildings, but removed from the 3rd Street commotion.

Malls and Complexes

The Bourse at Independence Mall (215-625-0300; 111 S. Independence Mall). Constructed near the turn of the 20th century as a commodities exchange, the Bourse now offers three levels of shopping and a food court to rejuvenate hungry, thirsty tourists in the historic district. The stores are mostly souvenir shops, making the Bourse a convenient place to pick up all your Liberty Bell pencil sharpeners and other Philadelphia paraphernalia. The handsome, late Victorian building uses a combination of red sandstone and brick for the exterior surface.

The Gallery at Market East (215-625-4962; Market St., between 8th and 12th Sts.). This cleverly designed multilevel urban mall is a planning triumph and a convenient Center City shopping hub. More than 170 stores, constructed in two phases and capped by a glass-covered atrium. Aspects of the mall are a little dated, and this is not the place to go for high-end shopping, but the Gallery retains a wide selection of clothing stores and food options. It is anchored in the west by a Burlington Coat Factory, and connects to the Market East subway and regional rail station.

Shops at the Bellevue (215-875-8350; Broad and Walnut Sts.). Attached to the famous hotel, this handful of mostly high-end shops is a quiet, pleasant spot to browse, especially

Mixed-use shopping and office space at the Bourse

in midafternoon. Nicole Miller, Polo Ralph Lauren, and Teuscher Chocolates are here, plus a big Williams-Sonoma. Food court downstairs.

Shops at Liberty Place (215-851-9055; 1625 Chestnut St.). Middle to high-end retail conveniently located between Philadelphia's oldest skyscrapers. Clothing stores for women like Ann Taylor Loft, and for men like JoS. A. Bank. The food court is a great place for lunch, with a wider variety of choices than typically offered, including Café Spice, a trendy Indian bistro, and gourmet slices at Peace a Pizza.

|INFORMATION

Ambulance, Fire & Police
The general emergency number for Philadelphia is 911. Call it for ambulance, fire, and police. Other emergency numbers:

Poison Control	215-386-2100
Rape Crisis Center	215-955-6840
Suicide & Crisis Intervention	215-686-4420
Women Against Abuse	215-386-7777

Area Codes & Town Government
The area code for Philadelphia is 215. Philadelphia is both a city and a county. It is governed by a 17-member city council and an elected mayor. Ten members represent districts, and seven members represent the city at large. For general information, call City Hall at 215-686-1776.

Banks
The **Wawa** convenience store chain has 24-hour stores strewn throughout Center City, all of which have ATM machines that do not charge withdrawal fees. See "Late Night Food and Fuel" for some locations. Many American banks also have Center City branches. Here are some main locations and telephone numbers:

Bank of America: 1-800-432-1000; 1428–1430 Walnut St.

Citizens Bank: 215-561-5800; 1234 Market St.

HSBC Bank: 215-592-0700; 1027 Arch St.

PNC Bank: 215-585-1166; 1600 Market St.

TD Bank: 215-282-7300; 121 S. Broad St.

Wachovia: 215-985-8237; 123 S. Broad St.

Recommended Reading
Philadelphia has served as the backdrop for many colorful lives and fascinating stories. Below is a sampling of recommended titles, arranged broadly by genre.

Autobiographies and Biographies

Ershkowitz, Herbert. *John Wanamaker: Philadelphia Merchant,* Conshohocken, PA: 1999. Profiles a remarkable personality who played a key role in Philadelphia retail during the Industrial Age.

Isaacson, Walter. *Benjamin Franklin: An American Life,* London: Simon & Schuster, 2003. Good biography on Philadelphia's most iconic Founding Father.

Paolantonio, S. A. *Frank Rizzo,* Philadelphia: Camino Books, 1993. A thorough, evenhanded book about Philadelphia's most controversial 20th-century mayor.

Fiction

Lippard, George. *The Quaker City,* Philadelphia: Leary, Stuart, 1876. Originally published in 1847, this is the seminal Philadelphia novel. Dark and arresting.

Roberts, Gillian. *Caught Dead in Philadelphia,* New York: Scribner, 1987. The first of Roberts's Amanda Pepper mysteries, set in Philadelphia.

Weiner, Jennifer. *In Her Shoes,* New York: Atria Books, 2002. Fun novel by local author, set in Philadelphia. Later a major motion picture.

Nonfiction

Batlzell, Digby E. *Puritan Boston and Quaker Philadelphia,* New York: Free Press, 1979. Delves into American social history, leadership, and class structure using Boston and Philadelphia as contrastive examples. A thoughtful, incisive book.

Bissinger, Buzz. *A Prayer for the City,* New York: Random House, 1997. Captivating reading about the inner workings of the Ed Rendell mayoral administration, which took the city's reigns in 1991.

Booker, Janice L. *Philly Firsts: The Famous, Infamous, and Quirky of the City of Brotherly Love,* Philadelphia: Camino Books, 1999.

Bowen, Catherine Drinker. *Miracle at Philadelphia,* Boston: Little, Brown: 1986. Tells the story of the Constitutional Convention in 1787. Bits and pieces about the city's early years give texture to the narrative.

Cotter, John L. and others. *The Buried Past: An Archaeological History of Philadelphia,* Philadelphia: University of Pennsylvania Press, 1993.

Keels, Thomas H. *Forgotten Philadelphia: Lost Architecture of the Quaker City,* Philadelphia: Temple University Press, 2007.

Nickels, Thom. *Philadelphia Architecture,* Charleston: Arcadia, 2005. Great overview of the city's architectural history and styles.

Warner, Sam Bass. *The Private City,* Philadelphia: University of Pennsylvania, 1968. An original scholarly argument about the Philadelphia's civic, social, and economic evolution.

Weigley, Russell F. ed. *Philadelphia: A 300 Year History,* New York: W.W. Norton, 1982. The definitive, 842-page history of the city, with a chapter on every era. Different writers were assigned each chapter, so tone and style vary a bit.

Federal Writers' Project. *WPA Guide to Philadelphia, 1988 edition,* Philadelphia: University of Pennsylvania Press, 1988.

Climate and Weather Reports

Philadelphia has a moderate mid-Atlantic climate, most pleasant in the spring and early fall when humidity is relatively low and daily temperatures top out at 70–80 degrees. It gets sticky in the summer, particularly late July and August, when humidity is high and noontime temperatures approach the triple digits. Winters are cold but not brutal, with average daily highs in the mid-40s.

Hospitals

Graduate Hospital: 215-893-2000; 1800 Lombard St.

Hahnemann University Hospital: 215-762-7000; Broad and Vine Sts.

Pennsylvania Hospital: 215-829-3000; 8th and Spruce Sts.

Thomas Jefferson University Hospital: 215-955-6000; 11th and Walnut Sts.

Late Night Food and Fuel

Look for **Wawa** (www.wawa.com) 24-hour food markets, which are several notches above your average round-the-clock newspaper and cigarette shop in both quality and variety. Sandwiches are made fresh to order, and the coffee is excellent. Wawa has closed a number of Center City locations in recent months, as it seems to be opening more gas station/food markets outside downtown in the Philadelphia metropolitan area. Locations that remain inside Center City include a store right off South Street in Society Hill (215-629-1050; 518-520 S. 2nd St.), a store in Chinatown (215-627-4121; 1038 Arch St.), a store near the Walnut Street Theatre in Washington Square West (215-923-1404; 912-916 Walnut St.) and a store near Penn Center on the north side (215-977-9558; 1707 Arch St.).

Boozy Philadelphia nights often require a hot meal. For late night sit-down dining try any of three **Midtown** restaurants or the popular **Little Pete's** in Rittenhouse Square. All serve satisfying comfort food and alcohol 24/7 to help you cut through the hangover before it even arrives.

Little Pete's (215-545-5508; 219 S. 17th St.)

Midtown II (215- 627-6452; 122 S. 11th St.)

Midtown III (215-567-5144; 28 S. 18th St.)

Midtown IV (215-567-3142; 2013 Chestnut St.)

There are few gas stations in Center City. One is the **Sunoco** at 2201 Walnut St.

Media

Magazines and Newspapers

Philadelphia City Paper (215-735-8444; www.citypaper.net; 123 Chestnut St.). Free alternative weekly newspaper with useful restaurant and entertainment listings. "I Love You, I Hate You" is a truly guilty pleasure—readers send in anonymous messages to loved ones and bitter enemies.

Philadelphia Daily News (215-854-2000; www.philly.com; 400 N. Broad St.). After the *Inquirer*, the most widely read newspaper in Philadelphia, published in tabloid format.

Philadelphia Gay News (215-625-8501; www.epgn.com; 505 S. 4th St.). A free weekly newspaper specializing in lesbian, gay, bisexual, and transgender issues. Over 30 years old, making it one of the first gay newspapers in the country.

Philadelphia Inquirer (215-854-2000; www.philly.com; 400 N. Broad St.). Philadelphia's eminent daily broadsheet newspaper. The weekend section is a useful resource to see what's going on around town.

Philadelphia Magazine (215-564-7700; www.phillymag.com; 1818 Market St.). Monthly magazine. Its "Best of Philly" awards are coveted by local businesses.

Philadelphia Metro (215-717-2600; philly.metro.us; 30 S. 15th St.). Short and to-the-point news stories in this ubiquitous daily.

Philadelphia Tribune (215-893-4050; www.phila-tribune.com; 520 S. 16th St.). The country's oldest African American newspaper, published five times a week.

Philadelphia Weekly (215-563-7400; www.philadelphiaweekly.com; 1500 Sansom St.). Free alternative weekly paper similar in style and breadth to *City Paper*. Available all around town.

Radio Stations
Many Philadelphia radio stations broadcast from the suburban side of City Avenue in Bala Cynwyd. This explains the 610 area codes for the stations below.

WBEN-FM 95.7 (610-771-0957), adult contemporary

WRDW-FM 96.5 (610-667-9000), hip hop

WOGL-FM 98.1 (610-668-5900), oldies

WBEB-FM 101.1 (610-667-8400), soft rock, mix of old and new

WIOQ-FM 102.1 (610-667-8100), top-40

WMGK-FM 102.9 (610-667-8500), classic rock

Television Stations
Channels and contact information for the major broadcast networks:

KYW TV Channel 3 (215-977-5300), CBS affiliate

WPVI TV Channel 6 (215-878-9700), ABC affiliate

WCAU Channel 10 (610-668-5501), NBC affiliate

WHYY TV Channel 12 (215-351-1200), PBS

WTXF TV Channel 29 (215-925-2929), FOX affiliate

WPSG Channel 57 (215-977-5700), CW affiliate

The news media convene at Independence Mall.

Visitor Information

Center City District (215-440-5500; www.centercityphila.org; 660 Chestnut St.). Partly a resource for local businesses and residents, but the organization's Web site is also a good way for visitors to check up on promotions and special events downtown. Look for Restaurant Week, when many terrific eateries offer discounted three-course meals.

Greater Philadelphia Tourism Marketing Corporation (215-599-0776; www.gophila.com). Does a superb job promoting the city and maintaining a Web site that features special events, assists in hotel booking, and recommends activities and entertainment to suit individual tastes. Also a useful resource for the surrounding counties.

Philadelphia Convention and Visitors Bureau (215-636-3300; www.philadelphiausa.travel; 1700 Market St.). General visitor information and convention scheduling.

3

GREATER PHILADELPHIA

Beyond Center City and into the Suburbs

Philadelphia's 135 square miles include almost 200 identifiable neighborhoods, depending on how narrowly one cares to subdivide. The vast majority of these lie outside Center City. Some occupy only a few blocks and a few dozen households, while others stretch for miles.

Many factors contribute to Philadelphia's identity as a "city of neighborhoods." Its old age and complex history are two big ones. Architecture also played a role. Philadelphia's rowhouse tradition distinguished its development from the growth in similarly high-density East Coast cities like Washington, D.C., and Boston. The prevalence of single-family homes as opposed to larger multifamily dwellings created the opportunity for more physical boundaries, which in turn created a larger number of small communities. There is no getting around the uglier side of this trend—an appalling history of segregation and redlining in certain parts of the city. But much of Philadelphia today boasts strong, diverse communities with a great deal of character. It is in these neighborhoods that you will find some of the city's finest restaurants, nicest parks, best shopping, and most interesting history.

Just south of South Street on the east side is **Bella Vista,** bordered by Washington Avenue in the south, 6th Street in the east, and 11th Street in the west. The heart of Bella Vista is the lively open-air Italian Market, where merchants sell fresh produce, seafood, meat, baked goods, and cheeses, as well as a wide variety of prepared foods. The neighborhood maintains an Italian flavor, though the Washington Avenue boundary is an eclectic thoroughfare with some terrific Vietnamese and Mexican food. The neighborhood is also home to most of the Passyunk Avenue shopping district, a distinctive strip of independently owned shops and an emerging restaurant row.

East of Bella Vista is **Queen Village,** the relaxed sister of Society Hill (its comparatively prim neighbor to the north). A stroll around Queen Village reveals some of the city's most picturesque residential blocks, a microcosm of Philadelphia's architectural diversity. Its quiet, walkable streets have made the area popular for young families with children and pets. The neighborhood was originally populated by some of the region's first Swedish colonists—the name refers to monarch Queen Christina.

Farther south is **Pennsport,** home to recently renovated Jefferson Square Park, where Union soldiers camped during the Civil War. Pennsport is another richly historic and tightly knit rowhouse neighborhood; some Irish American families have lived here for generations. On New Year's Day, hours after the Mummers have finished their march down

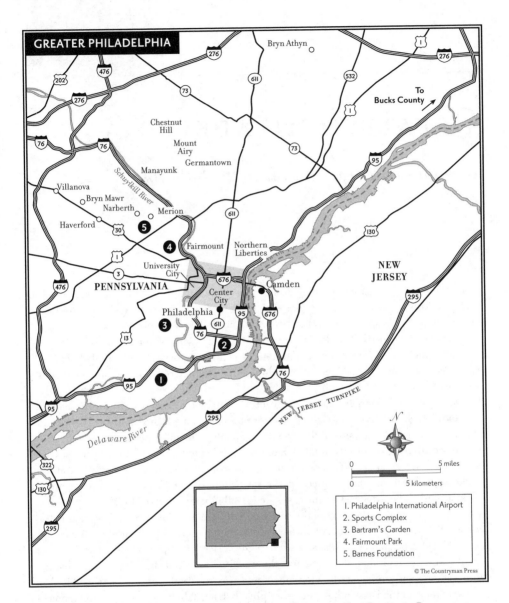

GREATER PHILADELPHIA

1. Philadelphia International Airport
2. Sports Complex
3. Bartram's Garden
4. Fairmount Park
5. Barnes Foundation

© The Countryman Press

Broad Street, the revelry continues along 2nd Street, known as Two Street, in Pennsport. (See the Mummers Museum write-up below for more on the tradition.)

Just north of Center City on the west side lies **Fairmount**, a diverse neighborhood that abuts Fairmount Park, the city's preeminent public space. The park itself stretches across the Schuylkill River, but the neighborhood is exclusive to the east side. Its Fairmount Avenue commercial strip thrives amid the unusual presence of Eastern State Penitentiary, a Gothic-style prison that looms over the avenue from centuries past. Eastern State is no longer a functioning penitentiary but is open for touring.

The northwest communities are perhaps the most interesting. Architectural enthusiasts fall head over heels for **Germantown**, originally a suburb of Philadelphia and the asylum of choice for wealthy city dwellers during the 1793 yellow fever epidemic. The advent of the railroad and the Industrial Revolution brought a second wave of major development in the mid to late 1800s. Because so much expansion came during this time, the area maintains a rare concentration of Victorian homes. While parts of Germantown struggle economically today, the neighborhood is improving. Farther northwest is **Mount Airy**, Philadelphia's proudest example of an integrated middle class community. Mount Airy gives way to the mansions and undulating byways of **Chestnut Hill**, a prestigious neighborhood with gourmet food stores and small shops that fills out to the suburban border. Germantown Avenue links the three neighborhoods and is a major commercial corridor. The avenue itself is something of a work in progress and a fickle blend of asphalt, granite blocks, and unused trolley tracks. A $17 million reconstruction project should be completed by press time, leaving the avenue in much better shape.

Northwest Philadelphia also includes **Manayunk,** formerly identified by its factories and today associated with boutique shopping. Manayunk is a study in contrasts, its hip Main Street shopping district adjoined by 19th-century churches and row-homes. The area has Philadelphia's steepest inclines, so visitors who intend to veer off Main Street should wear comfortable walking shoes. A 2-mile canal serves as a reminder of the neighborhood's previous incarnation as a manufacturing village. The canal towpath is a pleasant evening walk in the springtime. While you're in the area, adjacent **Roxborough** has two great steak shops and fine hiking at the Schuylkill Center for Environmental Education.

Nowhere has transformed faster or harder than **Northern Liberties,** a once sleepy community just north of Old City that has become a hub for Philadelphia's emerging art and music scene. Northern Liberties mingles artists' lofts with Federal rowhouses and a sparkling nightlife. New energy has also come to **University City,** the West Philadelphia locale anchored by an ever-expanding University of Pennsylvania and Drexel University, though this neighborhood is more complicated socially. The mix of students and families, temporary occupants and long-time residents is both an asset and a tension embodied in the area's restaurants, bars, schools, and newspapers. The largely Victorian housing stock makes for some picturesque blocks.

Chestnut Hill streetscape

Autumn is always beautiful at the University of Pennsylvania's Locust Walk.

And then there are the suburbs. Most famous are the neighborhoods of the **Main Line**—named for the railroad, today SEPTA's R5 line, extending west from Philadelphia into Montgomery County and eventually Chester County. Though it remains wealthy, the Main Line has evolved from the aristocratic enclave portrayed in the 1940 film *The Philadelphia Story* into a more voguish strip of bedroom communities with interesting stores and small colleges. It incorporates more than a dozen neighborhoods from **Overbrook** in the east (technically within the Philadelphia city limits) to **Paoli** in the west. A favorite to visit is **Narberth,** the most physically cohesive Main Line community. The Main Line suburb of **Wayne** was featured prominently in commentator David Brooks's *Bobos in Paradise*, presented as a model dwelling of "Bourgeois Bohemians"—a classification affectionately assigned to a new upper class that appreciates high-end food, avant-garde art, and designer clothing, but eschews traditional extravagances like luxury cars or yachts. The point can be taken too far (Wayne does not want for Mercedes Benzes), but there is an unstuffy air to the Main Line these days, and that was not always the case.

This is a difficult chapter to write, because with so much to do and see beyond Center City, worthwhile material will inevitably get left out. I have attempted to capture at least a taste of as many neighborhoods as possible.

Transportation

Penn's original grid extends outward from Center City. It can get frustrating, since many peripheral neighborhoods don't have the topography or development patterns that lend themselves to a grid. It is important to map routes to the outlying neighborhoods ahead of time. As a rule of thumb, traffic gets lighter and parking gets easier the farther one strays from downtown. Kelly Drive is a key artery that flanks Fairmount Park on the east side and delivers automobile traffic to Manayunk via the Schuylkill Expressway (I-76). In this northwest Philadelphia vicinity, I-76 also links up with US 1, home to the City Line hotels in the west. US 30 begins in University City and runs west through the Main Line, all the way to Lancaster, Pennsylvania.

You will find free street parking at most hours in south Philadelphia below Bainbridge Street. Ditto for University City so long as you are west of 40th Street. (There is metered parking and garage parking on and around the University of Pennsylvania and Drexel University campuses.) North of Center City can be a bit trickier. Manayunk, Mount Airy, Germantown, and Chestnut Hill have lots of metered parking. Northern Liberties has plenty of free street parking, but finding a spot can still be difficult on Friday and Saturday nights. Fairmount's northern section—past Fairmount Avenue—generally has available street parking, and there are inexpensive private lots near Eastern State Penitentiary.

SEPTA trains serve some of Philadelphia's peripheral neighborhoods and suburbs very well. The Market-Frankford El (blue line) stops at Spring Garden Street in Northern Liberties. Manayunk and sister neighborhood East Falls have stops on the R6 line. The R7 and R8 lines serve Chestnut Hill, and the R7 has multiple stops in Germantown and Mount Airy. The popular R5 train serves all the Main Line suburbs.

Lodging

Most Philadelphia visitors who stay outside Center City have a specific purpose: parents visiting children at college or business travelers attending a trade show. For this reason, lodging options outside downtown tend to exist in clusters. The main groupings are the airport district to the south and City Avenue at the Main Line border. This latter cluster exists in part to serve the corporate offices and broadcast headquarters that have cropped up in Bala Cynwyd on the suburban side. For leisure travelers these hotels don't make much sense, though Fairmount Park is close and the Main Line attractions are a short drive away.

University City's large Victorian mansions seem ideally suited for the bed & breakfast trade, and a few have taken hold. The area also has a couple larger hotels to serve travelers with business at the schools or hospitals. A small hotel and a midsized hotel in the Wayne area cater to tourists and parents with college-aged children. There are half a dozen schools within a 5-mile radius.

Rates

Inexpensive	Up to $60
Moderate	$60 to $120
Expensive	$120 to $200
Very Expensive	$200 and up

These rates do not include room taxes or special service charges that might apply during your stay.

Airport District

Eight miles from Center City in South Philadelphia are nearly a dozen hotels bunched around the airport. Lodging here is inconvenient to most major attractions, but you'll find lower rates than in Center City, free on-site parking, and better availability. There are some things to do in the area like visit the John Heinz Wildlife Refuge or Fort Mifflin, but not enough to fill more than a two-day trip. Airport hotels are frequented by business travelers, airline employees, and last-minute planners. The district became more stylish in August 2008 with the opening of **aloft Philadelphia Airport** (267-298-1700 or 1-877-462-5638; www.starwoodhotels.com; 4301 Island Ave.), Starwood's attempt at bringing some panache to the area. Hotel rooms have unusually high ceilings (hence the name), platform beds, and luxury amenities.

Here are some other reliable options in the airport district. Most are priced on the low end of the expensive bracket. The Marriott and Sheraton Suites are the costliest.

Embassy Suites Philadelphia Airport (215-365-4500; embassysuites1.hilton.com; 9000 Bartram Ave.)

Fairfield Inn Philadelphia Airport (215-365-2254 or 1-800-228-2800; www.fairfieldinn.com; 8800 Bartram Ave.)

Hilton Philadelphia Airport (215-365-4150 or 1-800-445-8667; www.hilton.com; 4509 Island Ave.)

Philadelphia Airport Marriott (215-492-9000 or 1-800-682-4087; www.marriott.com; 1 Arrivals Rd.)

Residence Inn Philadelphia Airport (215-492-1611; www.marriott.com; 4630 Island Ave.)

Sheraton Four Points (215-492-0400; www.fourpoints.com; 4101 A Island Ave.)

Sheraton Suites (215-365-6600; www.sheratonsuites.com; 4101 B Island Ave.)

Chestnut Hill

Chestnut Hill Hotel
215-242-5905 or 1-800-628-9744
www.chestnuthillhotel.com
8229 Germantown Ave., Philadelphia, PA 19118
Price: Moderate to expensive
Credit Cards: Yes
Handicapped Access: Yes

A lodging gem in the midst of Chestnut Hill, which was a vacation destination for affluent downtowners before it became the elite residential neighborhood it is today. An inn has occupied this spot since 1772 and the current building went up in 1864. The pastel yellow

The historic Chestnut Hill Hotel

hotel continues to thrive amid the shops and restaurants, offering its own excellent continental breakfast daily and three eateries on-site, including the venerable Chestnut Grill and The Melting Pot for fondue. There are 26 rooms in the main building plus another 10 in the adjacent annex properties, all with unique floor plans. One room above the Chestnut Hill Farmer's Market was built around the original cog and wheel that powered the elevator during the annex's previous incarnation as a grain barn. The bridal suite in the main building is an excellent choice for the added space.

City Avenue

Crowne Plaza Philadelphia Main Line

215-477-0200 or 1-800-642-8982
www.cpmainline.com
4100 Presidential Blvd., Philadelphia, PA 19131
Price: Expensive to very expensive
Credit Cards: Yes
Handicapped Access: Yes

Renovated two years ago and changed from a Holiday Inn to the higher end Crowne Plaza brand, this is the largest hotel on City Avenue (340 rooms). A highlight is the indoor pool area with a retractable roof that converts to an outdoor pool area when the weather is right. Parking is free on-site, and the hotel is right off I-76.

Hilton Philadelphia City Avenue

215-879-4000 or 1-800-445-8667
www.philadelphiacityavenue.hilton.com
4200 City Ave., Philadelphia, PA 19131
Price: Expensive to very expensive
Credit Cards: Yes
Handicapped Access: Yes

The most lavishly appointed of the City Avenue hotels, the Hilton's lobby is a galaxy of chandeliers. There are 209 modern guest rooms and a long list of amenities, like deluxe beds, a business center, newly renovated pool, and fitness facilities. Many rooms offer excellent views of Philadelphia's skyscrapers over the Belmont Reservoir, which is just west of Fairmount Park. Delmonico's—located just off the lobby—is a top steakhouse. The 35,000 square feet of meeting space make the Hilton popular with business folk.

Homewood Suites Philadelphia City Avenue

215-966-3000 or 1-800-225-5466
homewoodsuites1.hilton.com
4200 City Ave., Philadelphia, PA 19131
Price: Expensive to very expensive
Credit Cards: Yes
Handicapped Access: Yes

Homewood Suites is connected to the Hilton next door, making the two properties a hub for business travelers on City Avenue. This is also a good place for families thanks to the roomy accommodations, and it's a comfortable hotel for a lengthy trip. Suites are available in studio, one-bedroom, and two-bedroom configurations, all with kitchens featuring stoves, refrigerators, and dishwashers. The bright lodge area serves full hot breakfast, and evening refreshments Monday through Thursday (both included with your stay). Free parking near Homewood and the Hilton is sometimes available along Stout Road.

Main Line
The Radnor Hotel
610-688-5800 or 1-800-537-3000
www.radnorhotel.com
591 E. Lancaster Ave., St. Davids, PA 19087
Price: Expensive to very expensive
Credit Cards: Yes
Handicapped Access: Yes

Twelve miles west of Center City and a short drive from the Wayne shopping district, the 171-room, four-story Radnor is the Main Line's largest hotel. It is a good option for leisure travelers who might venture into Philadelphia once or twice during an extended trip, but wish to avoid the fuss of city lodging. The Radnor is also a popular choice for parents visiting their undergraduates at nearby Villanova University and the area's numerous liberal arts colleges. Guest rooms are all nonsmoking, with a floral motif and rose-colored bedspreads. Amenities include complimentary Internet access and a big fitness center with an outdoor swimming pool attached. Weddings are a regular occurrence in the Formal Gardens, a lively assortment of small trees, flowers, and a brick courtyard.

Wayne Hotel
610-687-5000 or 1-800-962-5850
www.waynehotel.com
139 E. Lancaster Ave., Wayne, PA 19087
Price: Very expensive
Credit Cards: Yes
Handicapped Access: Yes

Just over a hundred years old, this Tudor Revival hotel is an elegant building that fits seamlessly into the small town's attractive streetscape. With 40 rooms on four floors and gourmet dining at **Restaurant Taquet,** the Wayne is an intimate property that offers the amenities of a large hotel. Guest rooms are different sizes and layouts. Ornamentation varies as well, but you'll see a good deal of Victorian decoration accented by Asian art. Services and facilities are first rate—six months were spent on research to identify the most comfortable mattress available. The Wayne is owned by the same gentleman who owns the Radnor Hotel and guests are free to use its fitness room and pool. Look for packages featuring a bottle of wine and admission to nearby Chanticleer Garden (see "Recreation"), which is a must-see if you're in the area. An extensive continental breakfast is included with your stay.

University City
The Gables
Innkeepers: Don Caskey and Warren Cederholm
215-662-1918

www.gablesbb.com
gables@gablesbb.com
4520 Chester Ave., Philadelphia,
PA 19143
Price: Moderate to expensive
Credit Cards: Yes
Handicapped Access: No

A University City treasure, this
bountifully furnished Victorian
bed & breakfast was built in 1889
for prominent Philadelphia
physician Daniel Egan. Two generations later it was deeded to
the Catholic Church, advancing
the association between the
Egans and the diocese (during
Egan's time the local cardinal
would say mass on the home's
third floor). It was designed by
Philadelphia architect Willis
Hale, known for his showy take

Wraparound porch and garden at The Gables

on the Victorian Gothic look. The Gables has the style in spades, from the turret windows
down to the wraparound porch (now with mahogany deck). Common areas and guest
rooms are loaded with Victorian antiques mixed among a few of the innkeepers' select
family pieces. The Gables occupies six city lots, allowing for an unusually large backyard
where a Norwegian maple tree as old as the house itself shades the garden seating. There
are 10 guest rooms, eight of which have private bathrooms, and all of which offer modern
creature comforts set against the late 19th-century décor. Trolley cars stop just outside the
inn, making the trip to Center City in 10–15 minutes.

Inn at Penn

215-222-0200 or 1-800-445-8667
www.theinnatpenn.com
3600 Sansom St., Philadelphia, PA 19104
Price: Very expensive
Credit Cards: Yes
Handicapped Access: Yes

This luxury choice across from the University of Pennsylvania campus offers 268 rooms
and the University Club dining room on the lobby level (alumni should inquire about
membership). It is operated by the Hilton Corporation and resembles a high-end Hilton
property creatively integrated into a low-rise, mixed-use block. Arts and
Crafts–influenced décor gives it a warm and inviting feel. Decorative plaster friezes in the
common spaces depict sports scenes. The inn fills up quickly during major school-affili-
ated events like the Penn Relays and graduation, which together consume a big chunk of
the spring. An emphasis on workspace in the rooms also makes this a business-friendly
hotel.

Sheraton University City
215-387-8000 or 1-800-596-0369
www.philadelphiasheraton.com
3589 Chestnut St., Philadelphia, PA 19104
Price: Very expensive
Credit Cards: Yes
Handicapped Access: Yes

A second option within easy walking distance of Penn, the Sheraton is a 316-room high rise. Colorful murals by the front desk introduce guests to icons like City Hall and

But What About Camden?

Many outside the Delaware Valley who've heard of Camden, New Jersey, associate it with tragic poverty, political corruption, and a high crime rate. It is true that this 80,000-person city—a stone's throw from Philadelphia across the Delaware River—has seen better days. America's post-industrial urban decline was particularly unforgiving to places like Camden, which lacked the size and economic diversity to weather disinvestment without hemorrhaging its tax base.

A view of Campbell's Field from the Ben Franklin Bridge

But that's not the whole story. Behind Camden's difficulties lies an appealing little city with a nifty transit system, two major institutions in the large Rutgers campus and Cooper University Hospital, and a location teeming with potential. This potential has yet to permeate much of the inner city, but it is on display 365 days a year at Camden's waterfront, a clever, inviting public space that should be part of any extended trip to Philadelphia. There are four main things to do.

The big draw is the 200,000-square-foot **Adventure Aquarium** (856-365-3300; www.adventureaquarium.com; 1 Aquarium Drive), a high-octane family attraction that takes great pains to be experientially interesting for all ages. It opens with an African bird and hippo environment— a curious choice for an aquarium, but one that benefits from the animals' extroversion (and a stark contrast to the frustrating indifference you usually get from fish). The aquarium is divided into four "Adventure Zones," thoughtfully conceived to cover an exhaustive variety of exotic fish, arthropods, aquatic mammals, and starfish. Many exhibits are interactive, allowing visitors to touch sea creatures like jellyfish and stingrays. Zone D is devoted to sharks, viewable on all sides in a shark tunnel or from the sides of the 550,000-square-foot shark tank. You can even swim with the sharks if you schedule it

Boathouse Row. Amenities include a heated outdoor pool and business center. A lounge with continental breakfast is available for those who upgrade to Club guest status.

CULTURE

Architecture

Philadelphia's peripheral neighborhoods mostly developed after the early Georgian and Federal movements, so while there is an eclectic mix of architectural styles outside Center

ahead of time and pay the $165 fee. Penguins and seals fill out Zone B outdoors on the upper level, where you might catch a feeding. Spend two hours touring the premises and you probably won't get to everything. The aquarium is open 9:30–5 daily, year-round. It is most crowded on summer weekends, and is a popular attraction for local camp groups. Admission is $18.95 for adults, $13.95 for kids 2–12, not including extras like multidimensional theater shows. Look for combo tickets that include admission to the **Battleship New Jersey** (856-966-1652), which is docked nearby and can also be toured separately. The ship had involvement in World War II, the Korean War, the Vietnam War, and 15 years later during the conflict in Lebanon. Comprehensive tours are $17.50–$19.95 for adults.

Camden's aquarium inspired the naming of the Atlantic League baseball **Camden Riversharks,** who play their home games at Campbell's Field (1-866-742-7579; www.riversharks.com; 401 N. Delaware Ave.) by the waterfront April–September. Riversharks games are great fun and a perfect family night out. Endearingly kitschy contests between innings (dizzy bat, etc.) never fail to entertain, and if you're lucky you might get an appearance from Mr. Trash, who dances through the crowd with a plastic trash bag and collects refuse from fans. There's also rock climbing and a carousel for kids. Tickets are $7–$13 apiece.

Just down the river is the **Susquehanna Bank Center** (856-338-9000; www.livenation.com; 1 Harbor Blvd.), a 25,000-person amphitheater (until recently known as the Tweeter Center) and a great warm-weather venue for rock and country concerts. Lawn seating on the top tier is economical and fun. The roof comes up in the fall so the center stays operational during the colder months, albeit as a much smaller venue.

Camden still lacks much in the way of a dining scene, with concessions at the aquarium, stadium, and amphitheater pretty much the only games in town. A good play if you're spending the afternoon is to bring food to eat on the waterfront benches. There's a decent bar on the ground level of the Victor Luxury Lofts apartment complex called The Victor's Pub (856-635-0600; 1 Market St.) that serves food. The Victor was once an old manufacturing building—its transformation to loft apartments in 2004 was seen as something of a harbinger for Camden's revitalization. Time will tell, but there are reasons for optimism. One thing that seems certain is that Camden's fate is increasingly tied to Philadelphia's, as the valley completes its transformation to a regional economy.

PATCO (www.ridepatco.org) train service to Camden operates 24 hours a day, but most waterfront visitors come by car. There are lots at all the major attractions that charge for parking. If you have a bike, ride the pedestrian/bicyclist walkway on the Ben Franklin Bridge. It's open from 6 A.M. to 8 P.M. daily. From May through September you can take the two-tiered **RiverLink** ferry (215-925-LINK), which leaves from the Philadelphia waterfront by the Seaport museum.

City, you are less likely to find the balanced symmetry and brick exteriors that characterize Old City and Society Hill. That said, there are exceptions to the rule. Philadelphia's colonial-era elite often kept homes both inside and outside the city limits, and some exemplary Georgian summer houses survive. Most are located in Fairmount Park or Germantown. (For a complete rundown see "Fairmount Park Houses" and "Historic Homes and Sites" below.)

Philadelphia's neighborhoods developed differently from one another, but key periods in the city's growth explain today's streetscapes. Germantown was transformed from aristocratic retreat to upper middle class suburb with the coming of the railroads in the mid-19th century; a period identified with Italianate or Victorian construction. A similar trend guided West Philadelphia's 19th-century residential growth, which coincided with the University of Pennsylvania's move from Center City to west of the Schuylkill in 1870. This is no accident. As the Queen Anne–style houses sprang up around today's University City, they were joined by grand new university buildings like **Thomas Richards's College Hall** and Frank Furness's campus library.

Queen Anne architecture touched many middle class Philadelphia neighborhoods around the end of the 19th century, particularly in West Philadelphia. Its distinguishing bay windows, pitched gables, porches, and sundry nods to medieval architecture make it a personal favorite. Visit the **Powelton Village** historic district (32nd to 39th St. between Lancaster Ave. and Spring Garden St.) around Drexel University for some fine examples.

Residential building continued at a brisk pace from the early 20th century through the Great Depression. The different styles betrayed the city's wide economic disparity: low-rise row-homes packed together in North and South Philadelphia's immigrant neighborhoods and stone, country-style homes in Chestnut Hill. Post–World War II construction around Philadelphia brought remarkable buildings like Louis Kahn's **Richards Medical Research Laboratory** at the University of Pennsylvania. The laboratory, completed in 1961, is famous for integrating concrete and brick towers in a way that maximizes spatial utility.

Postmodern architecture in the peripheral neighborhoods includes the seminal **Vanna Venturi House** in Chestnut Hill, built by Philadelphia architect Robert Venturi for his mother. The not-quite-symmetrical design has a chimney ascending near the midpoint of the house, behind a yawning gap that partitions the roof. University City has some interesting, more recently constructed postmodern edifices like the colorful **Hub** building at 40th and Chestnut Streets—something like the video game Tetris reborn as a mixed-use housing/retail complex—and the **Fresh Grocer** supermarket at 40th and Walnut Streets, which conceals a cleverly designed parking garage. The **Cira Centre**, a new glass skyscraper resembling a quartz crystal sits next to 30th Street Station just west of the Schuylkill.

The most celebrated Main Line architecture are the suburbs' remaining estates, documented in William Morrison's *The Main Line: Country Houses of Philadelphia's Storied Suburb, 1870–1930*. While you're out there, take a peek at Kahn's **Erdman Residential Hall** at Bryn Mawr College, recognizable by its crisp geometry.

Art
Barnes Foundation
610-667-0290
www.barnesfoundation.org
300 N. Latch's Lane, Merion, PA 19066

Open: Sept.–Jun., Fri.–Sun. 9:30–5; Jul. and Aug., Wed.–Sun 9:30–5
Admission: $12

Merion's French Renaissance–style building houses a magnificent museum and art school, where wealthy art collector Albert Barnes placed his world-renowned collection of impressionist, post-impressionist, and early modern paintings, spread throughout two floors and 23 gallery rooms alongside African sculpture, Pennsylvania German chests, and other selected pieces. There are Renoirs, Cézannes, Matisses, and Picassos throughout, hung on Burmese burlap wall coverings—a clean, straightforward display surface that suits the artwork—and viewable by a closely regulated number of visitors each day. Visiting the Barnes is a special experience, but it takes some planning. Call at least a month in advance to make a reservation. Parking on-site is limited and carries a fee, though you can usually find street parking a few blocks away. Audio tours are available. Laminated cards in each gallery room provide titles, dates, and artist names. There is also an arboretum on the grounds.

The Barnes collection has been the subject of a five-year (and counting) fracas over a proposed move to the Ben Franklin Parkway within Philadelphia (Merion is just outside the city limits on the Main Line). The Foundation has run into financial problems owed in part to the limits on visitor volume. The move has been hotly contested by a local group—Friends of the Barnes—which has so far managed to stall the process. There is a case to be made for opening the Barnes to more people, which moving the collection to Philadelphia would do. On the other hand, it is hard to imagine a new facility retaining the intimacy and quiet appeal of the current space. Out in Merion, the Barnes is like no museum in the Delaware Valley; in the city its collection would likely blend into the Parkway's tourist scenery. At press time the Barnes remained operational in Merion.

Churches
Bryn Athyn Cathedral
215-947-0266
www.brynathyncathedral.org
ba.cathedral@verizon.net
PA 232, Huntington Pike at Cathedral Rd., Bryn Athyn, PA 19009
Open: Tues.–Sun. 1–4, tours every half hour
Admission: Free

The Church of the New Jerusalem emphasizes that no person is exactly like another, and so nothing in Bryn Athyn Cathedral is exactly like anything else. From the carvings in the key cabinet to the Monel door handles at the cathedral entrance, there are small stylistic differences everywhere—disruptions to symmetry, pillars of slightly different heights, and decorative spirals that wind in opposing directions. These many surprises were all conscious architectural choices, and they make a visit to Bryn Athyn an adventure. The cathedral itself is a Romanesque and Gothic masterwork completed in 1919 at the behest of Pittsburgh paint and glass magnate John Pitcairn.

Gloria Dei (Old Swedes' Church)
215-389-1513
www.old-swedes.org
info@old-swedes.org

916 Swanson St., Philadelphia, PA 19147
Neighborhood: Queen Village
Open: Daily, 9–5
Admission: Free

Philadelphia's original church, constructed at the turn of the 18th century for Swedish Lutherans and later absorbed by the Episcopal Church, Gloria Dei marked a departure from the log cabin style prevalent in New Sweden. The brick building was contracted to English colonists who had arrived in the Delaware Valley by the late 17th century and reflects an architecture common to their homeland. The cemetery grounds are a peaceful retreat integrated into residential Queen Village, just off busy Columbus Boulevard.

Merion Friends Meeting House
610-664-4210
www.merionfriends.org
615 Montgomery Ave., Merion, PA 19066
Open: Services 11 A.M., Sunday
Admission: Free

Completed nearly three hundred years ago, the Merion Friends Meeting House is a National Historic Landmark, and a reminder of the Welsh population that came to the Delaware Valley with William Penn. The meeting house is identifiably Quaker in scale and humility, but ironically Anglican in style, as Anglican persecution in Europe was a motivating factor for Quaker emigration to America. Weekly Meeting is still held every Sunday. A small cemetery on-site represents some of the region's oldest European bloodlines.

Fairmount Park

Fairmount Park (www.fairmountpark.org) is Philadelphia's playground. At over 4,000 acres, with every recreational amenity from bicycling to disc golf, it is a public space in the best sense of the term: a place used by all and cared for by everyone. No visit to Philadelphia, at least in the spring or summer, is complete without a visit to Fairmount.

The park's history effectively dates back to the Waterworks, Frederick Graff's hydraulic-powered water delivery mechanism that revolutionized the way Philadelphians lived. Set on the east bank of the Schuylkill River and completed in 1815, the Waterworks made the Schuylkill Philadelphia's principal source of drinking water (with the Delaware regarded as the commercial river). But Philadelphia's brisk 19th-century growth jeopardized the water's cleanliness, and when the city absorbed the suburban areas in 1854, it established Fairmount Park on both the east and west sides of the Schuylkill as a green buffer to keep industrial development at arm's length from the river.

It was a practical motive, but the park that emerged was as stunning as the most creative landscape architect could have dreamed. It gained worldwide attention and acclaim for hosting the 1876 Centennial, where attendees saw Hermann Schwarzmann's Memorial Hall and America's first zoo, which had opened two years earlier on the park's west side.

Today's Fairmount Park has a multifarious appeal: part recreational, part historical, and part architectural. It would take a hundred pages to detail every public sculpture or oblique pathway and spoil the park's marvelous ability to surprise. In that spirit, what follows is an imperfect overview of the areas east and west of the Schuylkill and the Fairmount Houses scattered throughout. Not included are the sports facilities at Fairmount Park. (See "Recreation" for a synopsis.)

East Park

Both the east and west parks stem from the Art Museum, located at the head of the Ben Franklin Parkway. The east side's main artery is Kelly Drive, which starts by the museum and runs along the east bank of the river. It is open to vehicular traffic, with a bike/jogging path that begins the **Schuylkill River Trail** hugging the river's edge.

The **Waterworks** stopped pumping water in 1911, but her riverside Neoclassical structures live on, reborn as the interactive **Fairmount Water Works Interpretive Center** (215-685-0722; www.fairmountwaterworks.com) and the **Water Works Restaurant and Lounge** (215-236-9000; www.thewaterworksrestaurant.com), a fashionable venue for brunch, dinner, and wedding receptions. The Interpretive Center is burrowed under the surface and features the actual turbine and pump that once powered the city's water-delivery system. There is a 15-minute theater presentation and fun kid-friendly exhibits. A full tour will leave you very well educated about the history and intricacies of big-city water management and environmental maintenance.

Just down the road is **Lloyd Hall** (215-685-3936), a recreation center with a snack bar where you can pick up park maps and rent a bicycle. It is the southernmost point of **Boathouse Row**, the Frank Furness–designed strip of Victorian and Italianate houses that are home base for Philadelphia's oldest boat clubs. The Schuylkill River is a nationally

Boathouse Row at Fairmount Park

A bike race in West Park. There's always something going on at Fairmount.

renowned venue for regattas, and you have a good chance at seeing some competitive row-ing any weekend morning in the warmer months.

The **Ellen Phillips Samuel Memorial Sculpture Garden** stretches along Kelly Drive north of Boathouse Row and incorporates numerous pieces by different sculptors into a creative expression of American history. Two nearby statues not in the garden but worth a peek are Carl Milles's mirthful **Playing Angels** on a pleasant riverside lawn great for pic-nicking and the **Ulysses S. Grant Statue** of the war general and president atop his horse at the mouth of Fountain Green Drive. Up the hill is the **Smith Memorial Playground** and Playhouse, a nifty spot for kids known for its enormous slide. The house dates back to the turn of the 20th century.

Barely past the East Park's northern end off Kelly Drive is **Laurel Hill Cemetery** (215-228-8200; www.theundergroundmuseum.org; 3822 Ridge Ave.), in use since 1836 and designed by prominent architect John Notman. It is a deeply serene place with picturesque river views, gazebos, and sculpture throughout. Thirty-nine Civil War generals are buried here, along with many noted Philadelphians. They celebrate General George Meade's birthday on December 31st every year as a prelude to New Year's Eve. Walk around for free, or pick up a companion guide to the grounds for $5.

If you continue biking or jogging along the Schuylkill River Trail, you will pass Wissahickon Valley Park. The bike route keeps going after the Drive ends, and if you follow it long enough it will take you all the way to Valley Forge (see "Recreation" below).

West Park

The West Park has a more pastoral and free-form milieu than the East Park. There is a lot to do, but plenty of room to spread out. This author confesses a slight preference for the West Park.

The West River Drive—also known as Martin Luther King Jr. Drive—runs along the river's west bank as Kelly Drive runs along the east. Other key roads in West Park are 34th Street and Lansdowne Avenue, which coalesce at W. Girard Avenue by the Philadelphia Zoo (see "Recreation").

The focal point of Philadelphia's 1876 Centennial Exposition and the heart of West Park today is **Memorial Hall.** A domed Beaux-Arts work crowned with sculpture and a bell tower, Memorial Hall is an imposing structure occupying more than an acre amid other-wise passive parkland. Figures on the skyline represent industry, commerce, agriculture, and mining, with a statue of Columbia on top. Memorial Hall was Philadelphia's original art museum and later became a police station. By the time you read this, it should be the new home for the expanded Please Touch Museum. While you're in the area, crane your neck to see the sky-high pillars of the **Smith Memorial Arch,** which pays tribute to Pennsylvania's Civil War heroes. Electroplate and typesetting industrialist Richard Smith is up there too; while not a war hero, he paid for the thing, so he can be there if he wants.

Past the hall are three gems. The first is **Shofuso** (215-878-5097), a Japanese house designed by Yoshimura Junzoo and gifted to Philadelphia in 1958 after a spell at the Museum of Modern Art. This one is truly a must-see. Constructed mostly from soft hinoki wood and fitted with paper walls, Shofuso portrays the idyllic setting of a traditional upper class Japanese home. A garden with koi pond completes the experience. Admission is $6, and fish food is half a buck. If you are in a large group call ahead; you may be able to take tea by the garden and learn the exacting rituals of a Japanese tea ceremony (the green tea is slightly bitter, but served with a sweet). You must remove shoes to tour. Those without socks can don paper slippers. Next door at the **Horticulture Center and Centennial Arboretum** (215-685-0096) see assorted plant life, a unique butterfly garden, reflecting pool, and sculpture on the spot where Horticulture Hall stood during the Centennial Exposition. A bit to the north is **Belmont Plateau,** the highest point in Fairmount Park. The view from the plateau is marvelous, capturing both the city skyline and the West Park's arboreal majesty. Locals picnic and play touch football games during the daytime and star gaze at night. It is, for what it's worth, my favorite spot in Philadelphia.

Break up the day with a snack or light meal at **Centennial Café at the Ohio House** (215-877-3055), northwest of the Horticulture Center. The gabled Victorian building was Ohio's contribution to the 1876 Exposition, made from the state's native materials. It was recently renovated and converted into this handsome café, serving breakfast until 11 and lunch through the late afternoon. Order coffee, cappuccino, soft drinks, salads, and sandwiches at the counter by the wall-sized mural depicting the exposition.

On the westernmost edge is the **Mann Center for the Performing Arts.** (See "Music and Dance" below for more on this venue.)

The Fairmount Houses

Like any good real estate broker, William Penn knew how to close a deal. During the early years of Philadelphia's birth, affluent colonists who agreed to purchase a tract in his new city were often given a large piece of land in the countryside to sweeten the bargain. These country plots became summer homes for the Philadelphia elite, who mostly maintained primary residences on the east side of Center City. After the 1854 consolidation act, the city government began purchasing these estates and incorporating them into the new Fairmount Park. Over time, many homes fell into disrepair and were destroyed, but those that remain are among the city's most dramatic examples of Federal, Georgian, and Neoclassical architecture.

As is often the case, previous centuries' charm makes today's tourism a logistical challenge. The houses are spread throughout the East and West Parks, often along winding, hilly roads. Signage is of variable quality, so it is best to pick up a park map at the Conservancy headquarters to help plot your trip. While it is possible to see the houses by foot or bicycle, a car makes things much easier.

Admission to each house is $5 per person, except at Belmont, where the $7 charge includes the Underground Railroad Museum exhibition.

Belmont Mansion
215-878-8844
www.belmontmansion.org
West Park, 2000 Belmont Mansion Drive
Open: Tue.–Sun. 11–5, (12–5 on winter weekends)

This is a 17th-century Palladian house and farm at the park's apex on Belmont Plateau, originally owned by abolitionist and loyalist judge William Peters. (The mansion was a station on the Underground Railroad.) The central hall's plaster ceiling is an architectural highlight—notice the carved scallop shells and musical instruments. The American Women's Heritage Society, which rescued the house in 1986, now manages the Underground Railroad Museum inside Belmont.

Cedar Grove
215-878-2123
West Park, Lansdowne Drive
Open: Tue.–Sun. 10–5, year-round

A stone country homestead in the Quaker farmhouse style, Cedar Grove was donated to the city and moved piece by piece from the city's northeast area into Fairmount Park in 1927. It had been occupied by prominent Philadelphia families since the mid-18th century, undergoing numerous expansions to accommodate increasing numbers of children. It was a rare summer home occasionally used during the winter, which explains the cast iron inset within the home's many fireplaces. Cedar Grove also contains numerous original Federal and Rococo furnishings actually owned by the families who lived here.

Laurel Hill
215-235-1776
East Park, E. Edgely Drive, off Reservoir Drive
Open: Apr.–Jun., Sat. and Sun. 10–4; Jul.–Dec. 14, Wed.–Sun. 10–4

Quaker widow Rebecca Rawle had this yellow Georgian summer house (stylistically comparable to Cedar Grove) built between 1764 and 1767, after her first husband's death and prior to her second marriage. A subsequent expansion produced the showcase octagonal room, noted for its Federal fireplace and furnished with a distinctive secretary bookcase.

This room also has wonderful acoustics and hosts the "Concerts by Candlelight" series every summer, which is a special experience—up to 80 guests are admitted to these intimate Sunday evening concerts put on by a rotating lineup of string quartets and other musicians. There are only a few concerts each summer and tickets are a bargain-priced $20, so call ahead to reserve. No matter when you visit Laurel Hill, be sure to take in the view from the backyard porch, which incorporates a picturesque stretch of the Schuylkill and the West Park's treetops. Other attractions include the heliographs in the front hallway depicting London street scenes. Laurel Hill is administered by the Women for Greater Philadelphia.

Lemon Hill
215-232-4337
East Park, Poplar Drive
Open: Apr.–Dec. 14, Wed.–Sun. 10–4

The large glass window panes make this Neoclassical house brighter than any other in the park, and the oval-shaped rooms make it unique. All the interior marble came from Valley Forge, with the exception of the Italian Carrara used to build the ground floor fireplace. The Lemon Hill site originally belonged to financier Robert Morris, a delegate to the Constitutional Convention who grew lemon trees in a greenhouse here, ultimately inspiring the name. When Morris's overinvestment in land decimated his finances, a part of this estate went to merchant Henry Pratt, who built the house in 1800. Lemon Hill was the first Fairmount house purchased by the city. Its 1844 sale actually predated the park's founding.

Mount Pleasant
215-763-2719
East Park, Mt. Pleasant Drive
Open: Tue.–Sun. 10–5, year-round

Its restoration completed in 2006, this Georgian house is marked by its handsome Palladian windows and the pediment mounted above its entrance. The rustic quoin on the exterior lends the estate a clean, attractive symmetry. Famously described by a visiting John Adams as "the most elegant seat in Pennsylvania," the house's interior goes to great lengths in achieving its genteel form, including mock doorway installations where necessary to preserve a room's balance. The mansion's first owner was John MacPherson, a privateer and shipper who built Mount Pleasant as part of a mostly unsuccessful effort to work his way into Philadelphia's social elite. Its second owner, traitorous Revolutionary War general Benedict Arnold, had to sell the place just a year after purchase and before he ever moved in.

Strawberry Mansion
215-228-8364
East Park, Near 33rd St. and Dauphin St.
Open: Jul.–Dec. 14, Wed.–Sun. 10–4

The largest of the Fairmount Houses, Strawberry Mansion is something between a historic home and a museum. The central part of the structure is a relatively humble Federal-style building constructed as a summer residence for English Quaker William Lewis around

Strawberry Mansion

1789. Wide Greek Revival wings were added in the early 19th century by lawyer, porcelain manufacturer, and Federalist politician Joseph Hemphill, who planted strawberry beds that would eventually earn the house its moniker (the subsequent owner sold the reputedly outstanding strawberries with fresh cream). The city eventually purchased Strawberry Mansion and its management was later entrusted to the Committee of 1926—an elite Philadelphia women's organization formed prior to the Sesquicentennial celebration. The committee's influence adds a measure of intrigue, supplying furnishings that vary greatly in era and style. One highlight is Civil War general George Cadwalader's refurbished French Empire chairs. Doll and toy collections occupy most of the attic. All this variety makes Strawberry Mansion one of the most interesting Fairmount house tours. Note that at press time the mansion was preparing to close temporarily for restoration work. The goal date for reopening to the public is August 2009, but call ahead to confirm.

Sweetbriar

215-222-1333
West Park, Lansdowne Drive
Open: Jul.–Dec. 14, Wed.–Sun. 10–4

Not a summer house like the majority of Fairmount mansions, Sweetbriar was a year-round estate for Federalist politico and merchant Samuel Breck. A three-story Neoclassical structure, Sweetbriar's high Italianate windows and chandeliers give the mansion immense gravitas. Furniture dates back to the authentic time period (the home was completed in 1797), though the carpets and drapes do not. The view over the Schuylkill River from the true front door (not the visitor entrance) is something special. Breck himself was an influential politician who wrote the Free School Law of 1834, bringing universal free public education to Pennsylvania.

Woodford

215-229-6115
East Park, Near 33rd St. and Dauphin St.
Open: Tue.–Sun. 10–4, year-round

Each Fairmount Park house has its own flavor that reflects its original purpose. Woodford's high ceilings and commanding architecture were designed to suit the influential merchants who owned it. Its second owner, David Franks, was an English businessman who provided for the British Army during the Revolutionary War. Franks took the Georgian house he purchased from merchant and judge William Coleman and added a second floor and rear expansion, turning the property into a grand gentleman's estate designed to impress visiting generals and area loyalists. (General Howe came by frequently during the British occupation of Philadelphia.) Woodford also demonstrates its owners' fondness for hierarchy. Compare the wide-plank wooden floors in the parlor to the thin flooring in the servants' quarters. The 11-room tour is a good mix of American history and a showcase for Woodford's antique objects collection, with items from Philadelphia collector Naomi Wood, whose trust administers the site. There is much to see, including Queen Anne furniture, delftware, and other rare pieces like the French barrel organ on display in the second-floor game room.

Film

The Main Line has managed to preserve three magnificent movie theaters that date back to the 1920s: The Anthony Wayne, the Bryn Mawr, and the Narberth. The Anthony Wayne Theatre opened in 1928 with five screens and a chromatic art deco look. The Bryn Mawr Theatre opened in 1926, and was rescued and restored by the nonprofit Bryn Mawr Film Institute in 2005. The twin-screen, Spanish Renaissance–style Narberth Theatre opened in 1927. In nearby Bala Cynwyd is another handsome old cinema that maintains its Egyptian Revival design and large center auditorium. All four have been recently renovated, and remain exceptional places to see a film.

Anthony Wayne Theatre (610-225-7247; 109 W. Lancaster Ave., Wayne)

Bryn Mawr Theatre (610-527-9898; 824 W. Lancaster Ave., Bryn Mawr)

Clearview Bala Theater (610-668-4695; 157 Bala Ave., Bala Cynwyd)

Narberth Theatre (610-667-0115; 129 N. Narberth Ave., Narberth)

Philadelphia also has three main theaters outside Center City.

The Bridge: Cinema de Lux (215-386-3300; 40th and Walnut Sts., University City).

Modern, full-service movie theater with a lounge on the premises that serves alcohol, plus stadium-style seating in the six auditoriums.

United Artists Main Street 6 (215-482-6230; 3720 Main St., Manayunk). Shows first-run features in a small shopping center next to the Manayunk Diner, a fun place for a post-film snack or cocktail.

United Artists Riverview Stadium (215-755-2219; 1400 S. Delaware Ave., South Philadelphia). Big multiplex south of Penn's Landing. Park for free under I-95.

Galleries

Institute of Contemporary Art (215-898-7108; 118 S. 36th St., University City). This big, lively museum space features changing exhibits that spotlight new talent in the modern art world and thoughtful exhibits that survey the work of better-known artists. It is an excellent reason to visit the Penn campus, and admission was recently made free to everyone. Season-opening receptions and lectures throughout the year are always enjoyable.

Main Line Art Center (610-525-0272; 746 Panmure Rd., Haverford). A 19th-century Federal building with a modern expansion. The center offers art classes, lectures, and multi-week workshops, and is mostly an institution for local residents—but if you're in the area see what's going on in the gallery space.

Samuel S. Fleisher Art Memorial (215-922-3456; 719 Catherine St., Bella Vista). A neighborhood treasure and resource for art education, this gift from textile manufacturer Samuel Fleisher displays competitively selected modern art. It has been a cultural hub from the turn of the 20th century. Since then, the original space has expanded to four buildings worth; you never know what you're going to see, but the faculty work is dependably interesting.

Gardens
Bartram's Garden
215-729-5281
www.bartramsgarden.org
info@bartramsgarden.org
54th St. and Lindbergh Blvd., Philadelphia, PA 19143
Neighborhood: Southwest Philadelphia
Open: Garden open Mon.–Fri. 10–5, Sat.–Sun. noon–4; house open Mar.–Dec. 14, Tues.–Sun. 12–4
Admission: Unguided garden visit free; house tour, adults $5, seniors $4

Deep into Southwest Philadelphia—a confounding part of the city marked by physical isolation and a heavy industrial presence—is this cherished public garden devoted to native plant life. It was founded by nature lover John Bartram in 1728, making it America's oldest botanic garden still standing. Enjoy a Center City view and tour the home, which is an adapted Swedish farmhouse.

Chanticleer Garden
610-687-4163
www.chanticleergarden.org
admin@chanticleergarden.org

786 Church Rd., Wayne, PA 19087
Open: Apr.–Oct., Wed.–Sun 10–5; Friday evenings, May-Aug., the garden stays open until 8
Admission: Adults $5, children under 16 free

If there exists a more enjoyable way to pass an afternoon in the Philadelphia suburbs than a stroll through Chanticleer, this author has yet to find it. The 35-acre layout is both a romantic space and a playful garden with an innovative design and subtle sense of humor. The stream garden appears organic and untouched until one ponders the planning required to achieve the effect. Everyone loves the Ruin and Gravel Garden, with the remnants of an old stone house tailored into a scrupulously clever centerpiece for the grounds. Find a drinking fountain at the base of the Ruin Garden walkup with a basin carved to resemble an oak leaf—turn the handle and water flows through its veins. Plant variety is superb, but one need not possess a botany degree to enjoy it. Speaking generally, it is the little things that justify the trip deep into the Main Line: the rabbits hiding under the brush, the garden furniture made by Chanticleer staff, or the hushed waterwheel. Pack a picnic lunch and settle in. You can even bring wine or champagne so long as you respect the garden and take out what you bring in.

Morris Arboretum
215-247-5777
www.upenn.edu/arboretum
100 E. Northwestern Ave., Philadelphia, PA 19118
Neighborhood: Chestnut Hill
Open: Apr.–Oct., Mon.–Fri. 10–4, Sat.–Sun. 10–5 (Jun.–Aug. open until 8:30); Nov.–Mar. 10–4
Admission: Adults $14, seniors $12, children $7

A lush retreat on the city edge, and Philadelphia's best place to clear your head. There are 21 striking attractions on the grounds, among them the winding Japanese Overlook and the inimitable Rose Garden. The seasonal Garden Railway is also nifty, its scale model trains snaking around the lush vegetation from late spring to early fall. The best way to tour is independently. Use the map as a starting point, but don't be afraid to venture off along Morris's hidden trails or loiter around a garden sculpture when the mood strikes. The University of Pennsylvania has operated the arboretum since 1932. Though it is a thoroughly relaxing place, walking the entire loop is good exercise and best on temperate spring days.

Historic Homes and Sites
Cliveden (Chew House)
215-848-1777
www.cliveden.org
info@cliveden.org
6401 Germantown Ave., Philadelphia, PA 19144
Neighborhood: Germantown
Open: Apr.–Dec., Thurs.–Sun. 12–4; last tour begins no later than 3:30
Admission: Adults $8, students $6; AAA members get 2 for 1 admission

A must for Revolutionary War buffs, this Georgian house was occupied by British troops

Ebenezer Maxwell Mansion, a stunning Victorian structure in Germantown

during the Battle of Germantown, three weeks after Washington's defeat at the Brandywine and the last fighting of the war before his famous winter spent in Valley Forge. The house belonged to Pennsylvania's provincial chief justice Benjamin Chew, whose ambivalence about the revolution led to his imprisonment by rebel forces during the war. Despite his neutrality, Chew was a member of the American elite, and the house still contains original furniture once owned by William Penn and a sheet of paper belonging to Ben Franklin.

Bullet holes and indentations remain in the walls as a tribute to the battle. Except for a brief period after the war, the Chew family occupied this house continuously through 1972. You can picnic on the grounds, amid weathered stone sculptures. Catch the annual battle reenactment during the first weekend of October.

Ebenezer Maxwell Mansion

215-438-1861
www.ebenezermaxwellmansion.org
emaxwellmansion@yahoo.com
200 W. Tulpehocken St., Philadelphia, PA 19144
Neighborhood: Germantown
Open: Apr. 17–Dec. 6, Thurs. and Sat. 12–4, but call ahead
Admission: $6

A sumptuously restored Victorian home, originally owned by cloth wholesaler Ebenezer Maxwell, who built the manse in 1859 after the railroad extended to Germantown. The house tour is an advanced class in Victorian-era American living, from the faux-marble fireplaces to the Paris china and Renaissance Revival–style sideboard in the dining room. The kitchen exhibits the creature comforts available to wealthy Philadelphia families during the Industrial Revolution, like a tool specifically designed to produce French cut string beans. Maxwell sold the house just a few years after building it, and subsequent owners redecorated the property with materials and styles showcased at the 1876 World's Fair. The mansion hosts a variety of special events and workshops, plus a Murder Mystery Weekend in October.

Edgar Allan Poe National Historic Site

215-597-8780
www.nps.gov/edal
532 N. 7th St., Philadelphia, PA 19123
Neighborhood: Northern Liberties
Open: Wed.–Sun. 9–5
Admission: Free

The Poe site is the last remaining of five Philadelphia residences that housed the distressed writer, as well as his aunt and ailing wife. Its dark cellar was a likely motivation for Poe's short story "The Black Cat," which was published during his brief stay here from 1843 to 1844. The house itself is a three-story brick build-

Raven statue at Edgar Allen Poe's old Philadelphia house

ing that changed ownership numerous times after Poe left, even serving as a flophouse during part of the 1920s and '30s. The writer's Philadelphia years were among his most prolific, though he battled his drinking and his childhood demons all the way through. A reading room has Poe's entire life's work in print, plus audio recordings from Christopher Walken and Vincent Price, among others. The raven statue outside the house has become a popular refuge for local birdlife.

Fort Mifflin

215-685-4167
www.fortmifflin.com
fortmifflin@earthlink.net
Island Rd. and Hog Island
Rd., Philadelphia, PA 19153
Neighborhood: Southwest
Philadelphia
Open: Mar.–Nov., Wed.–Sun.
10–4
Admission: Adults $6, seniors $5, children and veterans $3

Fort Mifflin's claim to fame
is its role in keeping over two
hundred British supply ships
out of Philadelphia during
the period of the Revolutionary War when General
Howe occupied the city. On

French General Comte de Rochambeau at Fort Mifflin in 1781.
Courtesy Fort Mifflin on the Delaware

an especially rough day of the six-week standoff, a thousand cannonballs rained down on Fort Mifflin in under an hour. The colonists eventually fled when they ran out of gunpowder, but held out long enough to allow General Washington valuable recuperation time at Valley Forge. The swampy island fort has been gradually restored, and played an active role in other American wars until it closed in 1954. Gaze around yourself and take in the sundry animal and plant life that live by the moat. Guided tours take you to the barracks, officer's quarters, open-air artillery shed, and the casemates, where enemy soldiers and traitors were held during wartime. The casemates are cold and spooky—some employees report paranormal experiences, and the fort runs fright-themed special events in October. Stay for a weapons demonstration if you can, or time your visit to coincide with the early November reenactment of the 1777 British siege.

Historic RittenhouseTown

215-438-5711
www.rittenhousetown.org
programs@rittenhousetown.org
206 Lincoln Drive, Philadelphia, PA 19144
Neighborhood: Germantown
Open: Jun.–Sept., 12–4, weekends only; all other times by appointment
Admission: Adults $5, seniors and children $3

The seemingly mundane papermaking industry was in fact a highly risky venture during the colonial era. The site of the first American paper mill is preserved today at Historic RittenhouseTown, where German immigrant Wilhelm Rittenhausen—later changed to William Rittenhouse—opened up shop in 1690. The operation produced roughly 1,000 sheets per day, and a small village of 40 buildings emerged around the original mill over the years as the business grew. The few that survive today include the Homestead and Bake

House, where the large hearth is still used for special events. Tours cover houses on the grounds and also show the papermaking process. Call ahead to see when you can make your own paper at a RittenhouseTown workshop, which is great fun for kids. The Rittenhouse name is legend in Philadelphia, mostly because of William's grandson David Rittenhouse, who was born on the site and later became an astronomer, inventor, and public intellectual. The RittenhouseTown Visitor's Center displays a clock David built in 1759 at just 16 years of age.

Johnson House

215-438-1768
www.johnsonhouse.org
6306 Germantown Ave., Philadelphia, PA 19144
Neighborhood: Germantown
Open: Thurs. and Fri. 10–4, tours by appointment; Sat. 1–4, tours on the half hour
Admission: $5

Incredible history at Johnson House

A main Germantown stop on the Underground Railroad, Johnson House was identifiable to escaped slaves walking along the Wissahickon Creek by the candlelight burning from a third-story window. The Johnsons were Quaker farmers, tanners, and steadfast abolitionists who hid escaped slaves on their property for decades prior to the Civil War. The house is a modest Colonial Georgian structure, its exterior built with Wissahickon schist from the immediate area. Due to the necessarily secretive nature of the Railroad, Johnson House remains ripe with mystery and discovery. Just a few years ago, a concealed attic door was found opening out onto the roof—likely an emergency hatch to help escaped slaves hide from bounty hunters. On a lighter note, a recent archeological dig uncovered numerous clam shells, revealing an apparent Johnson family affinity for seafood. Guided tours touch on the Underground Railroad's history, the family, and the development of Germantown.

Marian Anderson Historical Residence

215-732-9505
www.mariananderson.org
762 S. Martin St., Philadelphia, PA 19146
Neighborhood: South Philadelphia
Open: Tours by appointment
Admission: $10 suggested donation

Famously gifted contralto and goodwill ambassador Marian Anderson was born on a quiet block in South Philadelphia in 1897. Throughout her 96 years she earned plaudits for her rich, mellifluous voice and her immense gravitas. The historical residence, where Anderson lived for part of her career, is now a small museum with pictures, press clippings, a video presentation, and a scaled-down reproduction of the 8-foot bronze sculpture of Anderson on display at Georgia's Converse College. Founder Blanche Burton-Lyles (a remarkable musician in her own right) owns both the residence and Anderson's birthplace nearby, and is an expert on Anderson's life and talents. Either location can be seen with an appointment.

Stenton

215-329-7312
www.stenton.org
information@stenton.org
4601 18th St., Philadelphia, PA 19140
Neighborhood: Germantown
Open: Apr.–Dec., Tues.–Sat. 1–4
Admission: $5

Stenton is a brick Georgian mansion that once stood amid the 500-acre plantation of James Logan, a William Penn confidante, master of seven languages, and unofficial ambassador to the Native Americans. The house's interior has yellow, blue, and white lodging rooms (though the white is mostly pink), each with flying buttress canopy beds. Stenton was intended to resemble the estates of the English gentry, which put Logan's home at odds with the typically modest architecture of his fellow Quakers. The property is tucked away about a half mile off Germantown Avenue.

Wyck House

215-848-1690
www.wyck.org
wyck@wyck.org
6026 Germantown Ave., Philadelphia, PA 19144
Neighborhood: Germantown
Open: Apr.–Dec., Tues. and Thurs. 12–4, Sat. 1–4; call ahead to arrange a tour for another time
Admission: Adults $5, students and seniors $4

Home to nine generations of German Quakers dating back to 1690, Wyck house is a story told in many chapters, as structural changes altered the home's appearance and utility. The major renovation in 1824 by William Strickland (designer of the Second Bank downtown) made the house more open and adaptable. Much of the furniture and decoration is the original stuff, such as the parlor's Queen Anne chairs. Be sure to see the beautiful rose garden out back.

Libraries

Fisher Fine Arts Library

215-898-8325
www.library.upenn.edu/finearts
finearts@pobox.upenn.edu
220 S. 34th St., Philadelphia, PA 19104
Neighborhood: University City
Open: Hours vary
Admission: Free

Fisher Fine Arts Library at Penn, a Frank Furness masterpiece

One of the University of Pennsylvania's many remarkable constructions, the architecture here is a main part of the draw. Philadelphia's Frank Furness conceived the red sandstone building. Books and reference materials here are mainly on architecture, urban planning, and art history. The university's general collections are housed at Van Pelt Library nearby (the one with the button sculpture out front). Fisher is open to the public, but can get crowded during finals periods.

Friends Free Library

215-951-2355
www.germantownfriends.org
5418 Germantown Ave., Philadelphia, PA 19144
Neighborhood: Germantown
Open: Mon.–Thurs. 8–4, Fri. 8–3, shorter hours during the summer
Admission: Free

Among the first public libraries in America, the Friends Free Library dates back to 1845. It maintains ties to the Germantown Friends day school, a K–12 private academy with Quaker affiliation. It holds more than 55,000 books and magazines.

Germantown Historical Society

215-844-0514
www.germantownhistory.org
info@germantownhistory.org
5501 Germantown Ave., Philadelphia, PA 19144
Neighborhood: Germantown
Open: Tues. 9–1, Thurs. and Sun. 1–5
Admission: Adults $5, seniors and students $4, children $2; library admission extra

A three-room museum on the ground level displays the furnishings one would expect to find in Germantown homes from the colonial era through the Federal and Victorian periods. Germantown's unique role in American history comes alive with a little research in the upstairs library, where you'll find a wealth of newspapers and journals. If your family history touched Germantown, the library staff can help you trace it. A Civil War memorial in adjacent Market Square lists all the Germantown soldiers who died in the conflict or in the area afterwards.

Museums

American-Swedish Historical Museum

215-389-1776
www.americanswedish.org
info@americanswedish.org
1900 Pattison Ave., Philadelphia, PA 19145
Neighborhood: South Philadelphia
Open: Tues.–Fri. 10–4, Sat.–Sun. 12–4
Admission: Adults $6, seniors and children $5

As the Delaware Valley's original European immigrant group, the Swedish influence on Philadelphia is all too often forgotten. This superb presentation of Swedish social history in America is enhanced by an arts and crafts collection featuring Swedish rococo silver and glassware. Look up from the museum lobby to find Christian von Schneidau's bright ceiling painting depicting the early Swedes with the Lenape Indians, and tour the replicated log cabin to learn about everyday life in the Swedish colony. The star attraction is the ground floor's Golden Map Room, with its 360-degree map of 17th-century Swedish territories painted on bronze foil. There is also a tribute to John Ericsson, the Swedish American inventor who designed multiple Union warships during the Civil War. The museum is nestled snugly in South Philadelphia's Franklin Delano Roosevelt Park near the municipal golf course and can be a little difficult to find. Look for the signs along Pattison Avenue.

Eastern State Penitentiary

215-236-3300
www.easternstate.org
info@easternstate.org
22nd St. and Fairmount Ave., Philadelphia, PA 19130
Neighborhood: Fairmount
Open: Daily 10–5
Admission: Adults $12 seniors $10, students, children $8

A cell at Eastern State Penitentiary. Photograph by Michael Cevoli, courtesy Eastern State Penitentiary

A rare breed of tourist attraction that has something vital to say about the course of history and the human condition, Eastern State Penitentiary is the finest public site in Philadelphia. Creepy as all hell, it was once a fully operational prison that closed in 1971 and opened for visitors in the 1980s. Everything has been left pretty close to how it was the day the prison closed, with crumbling walls and abandoned fixtures strewn throughout. Opened in 1829, Eastern State was the most expensive building built in America at the time and became a model for prisons around the world. It was a Quaker-influenced design, with private cells intended to isolate prisoners for the purpose of introspection and spiritual healing. It was a progressive idea in theory, but tended to drive prisoners mad instead, and the concept was abandoned in the early 20th century. Eastern State's Terror Behind the Walls event takes place during the weeks leading up to Halloween. It trades on some alleged paranormal sightings within the penitentiary and the perception that the building is, if not haunted, then at least damned scary.

Glencairn Museum

267-502-2993
www.glencairnmuseum.org
info@glencairnmuseum.org
1001 Cathedral Rd., Bryn Athyn, PA 19009

Open: Sat. tours 11–1, call to reserve; museum open Mon.–Fri., 9–5 by appointment only
Admission: Tours are $7

This Romanesque palace exhibits Raymond Pitcairn's substantial collection of ancient and medieval objects, which reflect a lifetime spent collecting. The son of Pittsburgh glass and paint magnate John Pitcairn, Raymond also lived in Glencairn with his wife Mildred. Visit for the museum collection, but also for the building, which was constructed over 11 years (1928–1939) with granite, teak, stained glass, and topped with blue clay roof tiles. The diversity of materials and the inventive presentation will remind visitors of the Bryn Athyn Cathedral next door, Raymond's original project. Pitcairn believed in allowing construction to proceed organically, improvising and changing the building's design throughout the process. Saturday tours take about 75 minutes and begin with a ride up the original Otis elevator for a stunning terrace view that sometimes reaches the Philadelphia skyline. Visitors also get a sampling of the museum's galleries, including the Egypt room, cuneiform tablets in the ancient Near East room, and the popular Medieval European art collection. The Pitcairns' master bedroom is another highlight, featuring a teak bed with a pair of doves carved into each post, and a bird's-eye maple vanity in the corner. Tours conclude with a stop in Great Hall, a stunning mélange of glass mosaics, sculpture, and other Pitcairn treasures.

Insectarium
215-335-9500
www.myinsectarium.com
insectarium@aol.com
8046 Frankford Ave., Philadelphia, PA 19136
Neighborhood: Northeast Philadelphia
Open: Mon.–Sat. 10–4
Admission: $7

A creatively presented observatory for bug nuts, the Insectarium has multiple floors of arthropods, both living and dead. Founded in 1992 by a local exterminator, the museum makes exotic insects intimately knowable, humanizing such loathed creatures as the tarantula and Madagascar hissing cockroach. The context is jovial. The center of the second level features a model kitchen overrun by American roaches, making even the grubbiest bachelor pad seem habitable by comparison. Kids, or at least the unsqueamish ones, love this museum.

Mario Lanza Museum
215-238-9691
www.mario-lanza-institute.org
712 Montrose St., Philadelphia, PA 19147
Neighborhood: Bella Vista
Open: Mon.–Sat., 11–3
Admission: Free

An affectionate memorial to Mario Lanza, the Philadelphia-born singer and musical actor who starred in multiple MGM studio pictures during the 1940s and '50s before health problems and the tumult of fame took their toll, leading to his death at the age of 38. The single-room museum charts Lanza's life, from his roots in South Philadelphia through his World War II stint in the Special Services, his Hollywood films, his later work in Italian cinema, and his tragic death. The attached gift shop has the ultimate Lanza CD and audio-cassette collection, including the tenor's operatic recordings.

Mummers Museum
215-336-3050
www.mummersmuseum.com
mummersmus@aol.com
1100 S. 2nd St. at Washington Ave., Philadelphia, PA 19147
Neighborhood: Pennsport
Open: Tues.–Sat. 9:30–4:30; May–Sept., stays open until 9:30 on Thurs.
Admission: Adults $3.50 and seniors, students, and children $2.50

Mummers parades are great fun (see Chapter 2, "Seasonal Events"), but if you're not able to catch one, this museum is a good substitute. Gander at the extravagant costumes, chart the parade route's evolution, and dig into the history. String band concerts on Tuesday evenings from May–Sept. (call to confirm) are a treat. Even if you're not in town on Tuesday, you might catch the band practicing in the museum.

Please Touch Museum
215-581-3181
www.pleasetouchmuseum.org
info@pleasetouchmuseum.org
4231 Avenue of the Republic, Philadelphia, PA 19131 (Memorial Hall in Fairmount Park)
Neighborhood: West Fairmount Park
Open: Mon.–Sat., 9–5, Sun., 11–5
Admission: $15

Aimed solely at young children—ideally less than eight years old—the Please Touch Museum is an original set of interactive exhibits designed to entertain and engage. Some of the exhibits are purely for amusement, like Alice's Adventures in Wonderland, where kids can dine with the Mad Hatter and walk through a funhouse of doors and mirrors, while others have more real-world utility like the Supermarket, where kids practice grocery shopping and making change. This innovative museum just moved from its home on 21st Street in Center City to Memorial Hall in West Fairmount Park (the original art museum site), where it maintains its charm.

University of Pennsylvania Museum of Archeology and Anthropology
215-898-4000
www.museum.upenn.edu
websiters@museum.upenn.edu
3260 South St., Philadelphia, PA 19104
Neighborhood: University City
Open: Tues.–Sat. 10–4:30, Sun. 1–5; closed Sun. on Memorial Day and Labor Day weekends
Admission: Adults $8 and seniors, students, and children $5

The layout is a bit confusing, but the University of Pennsylvania's museum contains some very unusual stuff. You'll find pottery, jewels, stonework, weaponry, coinage, and thousands of other artifacts from all over the world. The Egyptian mummies and sphinx collection are famous, but the Greek, Etruscan, and Roman exhibits on the third floor are equally thorough and cogently presented. An interactive map allows you to track the course of the region's history from 3000 B.C. to A.D. 500. Other highlights are the African gallery and the magnific Chinese rotunda. A unique exhibition on the lives of native Alaskans was a specific interest of an early curator and is one of several collections that shed light on the nature of anthropological and archeological research. If time allows, relax in the courtyard.

Woodmere Art Museum
215-247-0476
www.woodmereartmuseum.org
9201 Germantown Ave., Philadelphia, PA 19118
Neighborhood: Chestnut Hill
Open: Tues.–Sat. 10–5, Sun. 1–5
Admission: Free

At the crest of Chestnut Hill's leafy roads is this quaint museum, which features work from Philadelphia's art community. The collection is surprisingly expansive for a small museum and includes some unique European sculpture. Look for work on display by Bucks County impressionists. The museum was once the home of oil executive Charles Knox Smith who posthumously endowed his mansion to become the Woodmere.

Music and Dance

Annenberg Center (215- 898-3900; www.pennpresents.org; 3680 Walnut St., University City). You can always count on an interesting season at Penn's Annenberg Center for the Performing Arts, which hosts theater, music, and dance performances featuring companies from all around the world. Dark during the summer.

Mann Center for the Performing Arts (215-893-1999; www.manncenter.org; 52nd St. and Parkside Ave., Fairmount Park). An open-air venue in West Fairmount Park for summertime concerts. Two-thirds of the 7,200 seats are beneath the big wooden roof. The seats farthest from the stage are unsheltered, but it's intimate enough that everyone feels like part of the show. Nearly all concerts fall in June, July, and August. The Philadelphia Orchestra and the Philly Pops do several performances each summer. Mann also hosts one-night shows from headliners and daytime concerts for kids. Check the Web site for the current season's schedule.

World Café Live (215-222-1400; www.worldcafelive.com; 3025 Walnut St., University City). A bi-level concert venue with drinks and dining on the cusp of University City. The big-ticket headliner shows play downstairs, while the upstairs lounge is more informal and hosts a good happy hour. WXPN-FM also broadcasts from here.

Nightlife

Bishop's Collar (215-765-1616; 2349 Fairmount Ave., Fairmount). A great neighborhood tavern with a loyal contingent of Fairmount regulars, a beautiful maple wood bar, and genuine church pews in the back.

Cavanaugh's Bar and Restaurant (215-386-4889; 119 S. 39th St., University City). Popular with both locals and college students, Cavanaugh's achieves a contentious harmony. Sit at the bar to watch sports or enjoy beer, food, and inexpensive mixed drinks (plus free wire-less Internet) at the booths.

Finnegan's Wake (215-574-9317; 3rd and Spring Garden Sts., Northern Liberties). An immense, boisterous three-story pub and a gateway to the revelry of Northern Liberties.

Johnny Brenda's (215-739-9684; 1201 N. Frankford Ave., Fishtown). Intriguing bar, restaurant, and music venue on the southern edge of Fishtown—commonly branded as Philadelphia's "next" neighborhood, home to an increasing number of artists and writers. Come for inexpensive local beers, excellent food, pool, and music acts. Call it "JB's" if you want to look like you've been here before.

McMenamin's Tavern (215-247-9920; 7170 Germantown Ave., Mt. Airy). A great beer selection, darts, and a chatty neighborhood crowd. Also some of the best pub grub in Philly; the beer-battered chicken tenders are mouthwateringly good.

Ortlieb's Jazzhaus (215-922-1035; 847 N. 3rd St., Northern Liberties). The menu has caught up with the jazz, and Ortlieb's is now an all-around fantastic night out; chow down on some of the city's best Cajun, served at candlelit tables, and soak in the music and atmosphere. Cover charge on Friday and Saturday nights.

Philadelphia Clef Club of Jazz & Performing Arts (215-893-9912; 738 South Broad St.). Just south of Center City, the club's 250-seat performance hall is a great spot for jazz concerts. Music classes are offered periodically and the space can be rented. Look for special event film screenings as well.

Royal Tavern (215-389-6694; 937 E. Passyunk Ave., Bella Vista). Dark woods, a flattened tin ceiling, and first-rate American cuisine at this Bella Vista pub and restaurant. Also one of Philadelphia's most reliable Sunday brunch spots, and not as crowded as Sabrina's Café nearby.

Seasonal Events
Devon Horse Show and Country Fair
610-688-2554
www.thedevonhorseshow.org
Lancaster Pike and Dorset Rd., Devon
Time: Late May to early June

This Main Line tradition goes all the way back to 1896. It's a week-and-a-half-long event, with horses and equestrian fans coming from around the globe to participate. Admission is charged.

Fairmount Park Holiday Trolley Tours
215-684-7863
www.fairmountparkhouses.org
West and East Fairmount Park
Time: Early to mid-December

Christmastime in Philadelphia means that Fairmount Park's mansions are festively decorated and open for special holiday tours. Visitors are ushered between houses via trolley. Check the Web site or call ahead to see which houses will be participating. Admission is charged.

Manayunk Arts Festival
215-482-9565
www.manayunk.com
Main St., Manayunk
Time: Last weekend in June

On the last weekend every June, Manayunk's main drag shuts down to car traffic while artists, vendors, and musicians take over the street. There's a juried art show and lots of fun to be had, particularly if the weather holds out. Free to attend.

Penn Relays
215-898-6145
www.thepennrelays.com
Franklin Field at the University of Pennsylvania, University City
Time: Late April

A leading amateur track and field competition with over 22,000 participants each spring, the relays draw athletes from high schools and colleges around the country. High attendance figures fill University City to the brink. Tickets should be purchased well in advance.

Terror Behind the Walls
215-236-5111
www.easternstate.org
22nd St. and Fairmount Ave., Fairmount
Time: Mid to late October

As if Eastern State Penitentiary wasn't scary enough on a normal day, try it during the lead up to Halloween, when the abandoned cellblocks are transformed into a haunted house. This is an exceptional venue for a creepy evening and Terror Behind the Walls is very popular. Admission is charged.

RESTAURANTS AND FOOD PURVEYORS

Some of the city's best dining is found outside downtown and the restaurants are as diverse as Philadelphia itself. Improved dining in the peripheral neighborhoods has followed a similar chronology to that of Center City, though lower rents in the neighborhoods allow distinguished restaurateurs to offer inexpensive menus and try new things. What follows are recommendations that—as elsewhere in the book—aim for variety in cuisine, location, and price. They are arranged by neighborhood.

Dining Price Code

Inexpensive	Up to $15
Moderate	$15 to $30
Expensive	$30 to $50
Very Expensive	$50 or more

Bella Vista

Anastasi's Seafood Ristorante

215-462-0550
1101 S. 9th St., Philadelphia, PA 19147
Open: Daily
Price: Moderate
Credit Cards: Yes
Cuisine: Seafood
Serving: L, D
Handicapped Access: Yes

The salty ocean smell of fresh seafood fills the air at this cozy fish market and café on the south side of the Italian Market. Many locals come just to buy raw fish to prepare at home, while others grab a table in the glass-enclosed dining room (weekend lunchtime is the most popular). You can order many dishes steamed, but Anastasi's fries its shrimp and scallops to such a perfect light golden brown that it just seems wrong. Sauces are famous, as is the raw bar, calamari, and jumbo crab cake. A "mini" combination plate at around $15 makes for a good-sized lunch. Quality espresso is a pleasing close.

International Smokeless BBQ

215-599-8844
600 Washington Ave., Philadelphia, PA 19147
Open: Mon.–Sat.
Price: Inexpensive to moderate
Credit Cards: Yes
Cuisine: Korean, Japanese, Vietnamese
Serving: L, D
Handicapped Access: No

Put yourself to work cooking chicken, beef, squid, and vegetables on the gas grills in the center of your table. Waiters bring the raw food, tongs, and butter, and light 'em up; after that, the onus is on the customer. A buffet of vegetables and assorted Asian side dishes allows you to eat your BBQ in the style of your choosing (sample the spicy kimchi or wrap your barbeque in big lettuce leaves). Tables seat four, six, or eight diners, and the place is great for groups. There are prepared foods too, including many excellent soups. International Smokeless BBQ is in the New World Plaza, one of two Bella Vista shopping centers packed with authentic Asian cuisine. The room is bright and boisterous, with a wall-length mural depicting agrarian China.

Ristorante Mezza Luna

215-627-4705
763 S. 8th St., Philadelphia, PA 19147
Open: Tues.–Sun.
Price: Moderate to expensive
Credit Cards: Yes
Cuisine: Italian
Serving: L (Tues.–Fri.), D
Handicapped Access: Yes
Special Features: BYOB

Now 10 years old, Mezza Luna is far from the oldest Italian restaurant in the city, but it's among the best. Eating here is an uncommonly warm and friendly experience, personified in gregarious co-owner Canio Pascale who jokes and philosophizes with diners on even the busiest nights. The food is top notch and classic Italian; big on homemade gnocchi, veal preparations, and branzino carved tableside (when available). A yellow and blue décor is crisp, simple, and modern, though you'll find a few crested moon accoutrements on the walls. Bring your own wine and order beer or mixed drinks from the fully stocked bar.

Sabrina's Cafe

215-574-1599
www.sabrinascafe.com
910 Christian St., Philadelphia, PA 19147
Open: Daily
Price: Moderate
Credit Cards: Yes
Cuisine: American
Serving: B, L, D
Handicapped Access: No
Special Features: BYOB

Sabrina's has earned an excellent reputation among Bella Vista residents for its fresh ingredients, reasonable prices, and creative fare. An extensive brunch menu (including a variety of salads and sandwiches) is available during dinnertime as well, and most choices are suitable for any meal. If given the option, try the sweet potato fries, which come dusted with powdered sugar. Look for sister restaurant **Sabrina's Café and Spencer's Too** in Fairmount (1802 Callowhill St.).

Salt & Pepper

215-238-1920
www.saltandpepperphilly.com
746 S. 6th St., Philadelphia, PA 19147
Open: Tues.–Sat.
Price: Expensive
Credit Cards: Yes
Cuisine: American
Serving: D
Handicapped Access: Outdoor seating
Special Features: BYOB

Almost everything changes with the seasons at Salt & Pepper, from the décor to the menu. The small, understated room with brown kraft paper table coverings serves a pleasing variety of fresh, elegantly presented appetizers and entrées. Menus offer just a handful of choices each night, but so much thought goes into the selections and so much attention is applied to the cooking that you really can't go wrong. Salt & Pepper is one of the few Philadelphia BYOB restaurants that serve reliably top-notch game—quail and venison preparations have both proven outstanding. Seafood is also a good bet, and the scallop appetizer is well regarded.

Taquería La Veracruzana

215-465-1440
908 Washington Ave., Philadelphia, PA 19147
Open: Daily
Price: Inexpensive
Credit Cards: Yes
Cuisine: Mexican
Serving: B, L, D
Handicapped Access: No
Special Features: BYOB

This casual spot on the Washington Avenue corridor serves some of the finest Mexican fare in Philadelphia. The mammoth burritos are just a little bit spicy and come packed with rice, onion, tomato, avocado, cheese, sour cream, and your choice of meat. Tacos are also excellent, served three to a plate for just $6. Menus are in Spanish, but anyone with a half semester's worth can get by. The dozen tables are highlighted with primary colors and a few select pieces of art complete the room. Wash it all down with glass-bottled Coca-Cola (made with real sugar rather than corn syrup) or a sweet fruit drink. Food can also be ordered to go.

Chestnut Hill
Cafette

215-242-4220
www.cafette.com
8134 Ardleigh St., Philadelphia, PA 19118
Open: Tues.–Sun.
Price: Moderate
Credit Cards: Yes
Cuisine: American
Serving: L (Tues.–Sat.), D, Sat. & Sun. Brunch
Handicapped Access: Partial
Special Features: BYOB

Cafette is a genuine find, nestled into a residential block in Chestnut Hill where few tourists ever venture. Their loss! Those willing to negotiate the meandrous back roads on the edge of the city will be rewarded with a bold menu that gives new life to comfort food, like turkey breast served with Cajun sauce or crab cakes coated with panko breadcrumbs (plus imaginative entrées for vegetarians and vegans). The kitchen is near the entrance at Cafette, but the multiple small dining rooms are secluded and comfortable. The best tables are in the floral sculpture garden outdoors, so request one if available. Cafette is BYOB, but also serves Boylan black cherry soda, which is an awfully hard beverage to improve on.

Cafette: a little tough to find, but easy to love.

McNally's Tavern

215-247-9736
mcnallystavern.com
8634 Germantown Ave., Philadelphia, PA 19118
Open: Daily
Price: Inexpensive
Credit Cards: Yes
Cuisine: American
Serving: L, D
Handicapped Access: Yes

Home to The Schmitter, the calorie-laden sandwich treat made with salami, cheese, onions, tomatoes, and special sauce on a layer of steak. It has become such an institution that versions of the sandwich are now served at Phillies and Eagles games (though the sandwich is *not* named for legendary Phillies slugger Mike Schmidt— don't get caught insinuating as much).

McNally's would be great even without the Schmitter, on the strength of its soups, beers, and daily dinner specials. It is also that rarefied species of family-friendly Philadelphia pub, so feel free to bring the kids.

Osaka

215-242-5900
www.osakachestnuthill.com
8605 Germantown Ave., Philadelphia, PA 19118
Open: Daily
Price: Moderate to expensive
Credit Cards: Yes
Cuisine: Japanese
Serving: L (Mon.–Sat.), D
Handicapped Access: No

No one will ever accuse patrician Chestnut Hill of being cool, but this is surely its hippest spot. The neighborhood's youngest couples (sometimes with children in tow) gather seven nights a week at Osaka, Chestnut Hill's answer to the bevy of Japanese fusion restaurants that began dotting Center City in 2001. The sushi is exceptional, and served from an innovative and thorough neo-Japanese menu with dozens of rolls. Other seafood entrées are also worth a look, like the drunken king crab, which comes in a thin buttery sauce alongside shrimp, oysters, and scallops. Start with a couple cold appetizers or a smoky somen noodle soup, and treat yourself to one of Osaka's syrupy cocktails. Reservations recommended on weekends.

Fairmount
Jack's Firehouse

215-232-9000
www.jacksfirehouse.com
2130 Fairmount Ave., Philadelphia, PA 19130
Open: Daily
Price: Moderate
Credit Cards: Yes
Cuisine: American

Serving: L (weekdays only), D, Sat. & Sun. Brunch
Handicapped Access: Yes

When Jack McDavid converted this 19th-century firehouse into a restaurant in 1989, it had for years been used to store scull boats—like the one that still hangs over the mahogany bar in the restaurant's center. Lots of nice touches here: locally grown ingredients, two-dozen wines by the glass, and alfresco dining on Fairmount Avenue's wide sidewalk or alongside the firehouse. The interior is bathed in dark woods and is a thoroughly genial space. Diners feel as comfortable wearing jeans and T-shirts as they do suits and ties. Meals start with corn muffins, buttermilk biscuits, and a home-made pineapple spread, and end with complimentary cookies. Steaks, seafood, chops, and ribs stand out on the dinner menu. If you plan on going for lunch, call ahead and reserve a three-course special that includes a ticket to Eastern Penitentiary.

L'oca

215-769-0316
www.locafairmount.com
2025 Fairmount Ave., Philadelphia, PA 19130
Open: Tues.–Sun.
Price: Expensive
Credit Cards: Yes
Cuisine: Italian
Serving: D
Handicapped Access: Yes
Special Features: BYOB

In the shadows of Eastern State Penitentiary, L'oca (Italian for "goose") serves northern Italian food that is rich without being heavy. It is the sort of BYOB bistro that represents the city's best culinary instincts: unpretentious, thoughtful preparations that maintain the cuisine's regional integrity. The first two antipasti dishes on the menu are standouts: smooth, buttery gnochetti, and the bagna cauda medley with grilled vegetables, cheeses, meats, and a delightfully creamy mushroom pâté. Skewered snails make a rare Philadelphia appearance as well. Split the antipasti and then try spaghetti served al dente with seafood or a simple but delicious penne. The stylish room, with hints of red on a clean white canvas, is small enough to afford intimacy, but large enough that you won't feel like you're dining on top of your neighbors. The apple tart dessert, when offered, is a treat.

Osteria

215-763-0920
www.osteriaphilly.com
640 N. Broad St., Philadelphia, PA 19130
Open: Daily
Price: Expensive
Credit Cards: Yes
Cuisine: Italian
Serving: L, D
Handicapped Access: Yes

Osteria rocketed to the top of Philadelphia foodies' lists after winning *Philadelphia* magazine's recognition as Best New Restaurant in 2007. The innovative northern Italian menu uses local ingredients and comes from chef and co-owner Marc Vetri, maestro of Vetri in Center City. Osteria is designed to be a bit more affordable than the comparatively expensive, much tinier Vetri, but a couple will have no trouble running up a $100 bill for dinner with wine. The wine list is a good place to start at Osteria; ask the sommelier to assist in selecting a quartina or two. Pastas are all recommendable, but portions are small. Consider sampling more than one, along with antipasti or thin-crust pizza (four medium slices to a pie) for the table. For an entrée course, the braised pork ribs fall off the bone and come in a light stew of polenta, vegetables, and sausage. Stay for gelato or a nutella pizza with coffee.

Zorba's

215-978-5990
www.zorbastavern.com
2230 Fairmount Ave., Philadelphia, PA
19130
Open: Tues.–Sun.
Price: Moderate
Credit Cards: Yes
Cuisine: Greek
Serving: L, D
Handicapped Access: Yes
Special Features: BYOB

A wall-length mural of the Mykonos Island coast stretches along one of three snug dining rooms at this bona fide Greek taverna in Fairmount's restaurant district. Plants and vines hang from the ceiling and walls, while small speakers lay down a peppy Greek soundtrack to suit the busy atmosphere. Pick up an excellent gyro or souvlaki to go during the daytime, or sit down for dinner and try tender lamb shank.

Northern Liberties

Bar Ferdinand

215-923-1313
www.barferdinand.com
1030 N. 2nd St., Northern Liberties
Open: Mon.–Sat.
Price: Moderate to expensive
Credit Cards: Yes
Cuisine: Spanish, tapas
Serving: D, Sun. Brunch
Handicapped Access: Yes

The tapas trend has barely touched Philadelphia, but Bar Ferdinand at the Liberties Walk development is a welcome exception. Cuisine is rich, garlicky Spanish cooking that employs lots of olive oil and cheeses. Beef, pork, and seafood dishes predominate. A good beginning is the *dátiles con tocino,* a semi-sweet empanada filled with dates and cream cheese. Three or four plates per person make a square meal, but share everything and split a pitcher of tart sangria or a nice Rioja

(wines are half price on Mondays). The busy dining room is decorated with fire-colored mosaics and dried roses dangling above the bar. On clear nights you might see the paella prepared fresh near the outdoor seating.

Honey's Sit 'n' Eat

215-925-1150
800 N. 4th St., Philadelphia, PA 19123
Open: Daily
Price: Inexpensive to moderate
Credit Cards: Cash only
Cuisine: Southern
Serving: B, L, D (weekdays only), Sat. & Sun. Brunch
Handicapped Access: Yes

You won't find a heartier brunch in Northern Liberties than at this comfy, country-style restaurant. The wait for a table can run long on weekends, as area 20-somethings pile in to Honey's for three-sided potato pancakes, fluffy omelets, and bottomless cups of strong coffee. Biscuits and gravy, speckled with bits of spicy sausage, are especially filling. The cuisine could be described as southern with Jewish influences, but it's nowhere near kosher; Lancaster County country bacon is the tastiest side on the menu. Sometimes you can get past the brunch wait by taking a seat at the counter. No separate dinner menu,

Honey's Sit 'n' Eat

though lunch is served until 10 P.M. on weekdays, and Honey's sandwiches are tremendous in both size and quality.

Il Cantuccio
215-627-6573
701 N. 3rd St., Philadelphia, PA 19123
Open: Mon.–Sat.
Price: Moderate
Credit Cards: Cash only
Cuisine: Italian
Serving: L, D
Handicapped Access: Yes
Special Features: BYOB

Not the place for the elaborate neo-Italian cuisine found at your typical Philadelphia BYOB, and not for everyone. But Il Cantuccio prepares unfussy pastas and seafood entrées quite well, and is a great value to boot. The dining room is tiny but colorful, with an open kitchen, tin ceiling, and tapestry of Florence hanging from the wall. A shelf in the rear displays the emptied wine bottles of diners-past. The handwritten menu doesn't break any barriers, but food is freshly prepared and properly spiced, the restaurant's loyal client base is friendly, and you will never leave hungry. Service can be brusque.

Koi
215-413-1606
604 N. 2nd St., Philadelphia, PA 19123
Open: Mon.–Sat.
Price: Moderate to expensive
Credit Cards: Yes
Cuisine: Korean, Japanese
Serving: L, D
Handicapped Access: Yes
Special Features: BYOB

There are those who quibble that the ultramodern décor tries too hard, but look past Koi's faux trendiness and focus on the versatile menu of sushi, mix-and-match tempuras, noodle dishes, and Korean dishes like bulgogi, which are hard to find in greater Philadelphia. Food at Koi is invariably fresh, well portioned, and different from anything else in Northern Liberties. The restaurant is small—only six or seven tables—so reservations are recommended, particularly if you have a large group.

Liberties Restaurant and Bar
215-238-0660
www.libertiesrestaurant.com
705 N. 2nd St., Philadelphia, PA 19123
Open: Daily
Price: Inexpensive to moderate
Credit Cards: Yes
Cuisine: American
Serving: L, D
Handicapped Access: No

More bar than restaurant, but a quality choice for lunch or dinner in Northern Liberties. The main room is nice and dim, boasting a classic Victorian bar and decorated in rich walnut. Like its counterpart in Manayunk, the place feels like it's out of a different era, but Liberties takes its food very seriously. Daily dinner specials are reliably excellent, and sandwiches are large and well priced. Choose from a dozen beers on tap.

Standard Tap
215-238-0630
www.standardtap.com
901 N. 2nd St., Philadelphia, PA 19123
Open: Daily
Price: Inexpensive to moderate
Credit Cards: Yes
Cuisine: American
Serving: D, Sat. & Sun. Brunch
Handicapped Access: No

The liveliest of Northern Liberties' bar and restaurant combos, Standard Tap draws a diverse crowd of artists, students, and young professionals from Center City. The bar area is dark and gets loud on weekend nights, but the second-story dining room (plus outdoor deck) is more relaxed. Food goes well beyond normal pub fare and includes entrées like octopus doused in balsamic vinegar and tender sliced lamb on a soft roll. Standard Tap also serves a terrific hamburger and a strong list of local beers.

Queen Village
Famous Fourth Street Delicatessen
215-922-3274
700 S. 4th St., Philadelphia, PA 19147
Open: Daily
Price: Moderate
Credit Cards: Yes
Cuisine: Delicatessen
Serving: B, L, D
Handicapped Access: Yes
Special Features: BYOB

Home to the biggest portions in Queen Village and probably in greater Philadelphia, the Famous Fourth piles its corned beef, pastrami, and turkey to comical heights. The "regular" sandwiches can feed an army. The Zegfeld sandwiches (a few dollars more) can feed an army, a navy, an air force, and most of the civilian population as well. A hot dog, potato knish, and Dr. Brown's soda make for a more manageable lunch. Dinner entrées are quite good, but the place thrives on the quality and size of its sandwiches. The minimalist dining area and friendly service lend an old school charm. Take home a couple desserts with your leftovers and enjoy for days.

Little Fish
215-413-3464
littlefishphilly.com
600 Catherine St., Philadelphia, PA 19147
Open: Daily
Price: Expensive
Credit Cards: Yes
Cuisine: Seafood
Serving: D
Handicapped Access: Yes
Special Features: BYOB, Sunday prix fixe

A very tiny room bounded by white painted brick and fish art on the wall, Little Fish is cozy, friendly, and tastefully cute. The menu is all seafood, all the time. Dishes change constantly, but come expecting light, healthful New American fillet preparations in an affable setting and you will not leave disappointed. The open-air kitchen takes up a third of the restaurant, but stays ancillary to the table space. There are two seatings on Sunday nights for a five-course prix fixe menu for under $30 that includes a choice of entrée and dessert.

University City
Abyssinia Ethiopian Restaurant
215-387-2424
229 S. 45th St., Philadelphia, PA 19104
Open: Daily
Price: Inexpensive
Credit Cards: Yes
Cuisine: Ethiopian
Serving: B, L, D
Handicapped Access: Yes

The restaurant is not exclusively vegetarian, but spicy, meat-free combination plates are the way to go at Abyssinia. There is no silverware. Meals are instead served with injera, the spongy Ethiopian flatbread used to scoop spicy lentil, yellow chickpea, and other wot (Ethiopian stew) off the plate. The kitfo beef dish is the non-vegetarian standout and comes out of the kitchen rare. Two can eat a satisfying lunch for around $20. Unfortunately, service is notoriously slow—a small staff attends to both the bar area in the front of the restaurant and the main dining room in the back—but the food is worth the wait.

Dock Street Brewery
215-726-2337
www.dockstreetbeer.com
701 S. 50th St., Philadelphia, PA 19143
Open: Daily
Price: Inexpensive to moderate

Making beer at Dock Street Brewery

Credit Cards: Yes
Cuisine: American
Serving: L, D
Handicapped Access: Yes

With fresh beer brewed on premises and scrumptious wood-fired pizza, Dock Street has injected new life into an old firehouse at the western end of University City. Garrulous owner Rosemarie Certo, who co-founded the Dock Street Brewing Company more than 20 years ago, loves to discuss the joys of zymurgy and her journey as one of America's few female brewers. Try a variety of beers if you have the time, sampling the more exotic brews in between pints of exceptional Rye IPA and Bohemian pilsner. The place sustains a youthful energy that marked the August 2007 opening, but its popularity has expanded and now draws patrons of all ages from around the city.

Fatou and Fama
215-386-0700
www.fatouandfama.com
4002 Chestnut St., Philadelphia, PA 19104
Open: Tues.–Sun.
Price: Inexpensive

Credit Cards: Yes
Cuisine: African, West Indian
Serving: L, D
Handicapped Access: Yes
Special Features: BYOB

You'll see both students and locals enjoying Senegalese and Caribbean delicacies at this casual lunch and dinner spot two blocks north of the University of Pennsylvania. Yassa dishes—fish, chicken, or shrimp in a mustard and lemon sauce—are especially zesty. Vegetarians swear by the surprisingly hearty peanut butter vegetable stew, while ginger juice and fried plantains make nice accompaniments to everything. A small buffet is under $10 and includes salad, chicken, rice, vegetables, and usually a seafood dish. Call ahead if you have a large party; the room is small, but the dozen or so tables can be rearranged.

Marigold Kitchen
215-222-3699
www.marigoldkitchenbyob.com
501 S. 45th St., Philadelphia, PA 19104
Open: Tues.–Sun.
Price: Expensive
Credit Cards: Yes
Cuisine: New Southern
Serving: D
Handicapped Access: No
Special Features: BYOB

Inspired, agile new southern cooking served in environs that feel like a favorite relative's sitting room. The restaurant occupies the first and second floors of a Victorian house on a cute residential block in University City. It was a tearoom in a previous life. The interior is contemporary and fresh; exterior bay windows and gabled roof are a bridge to the old days. Chef Erin O'Shea works wonders with the whole menu, but seafood and pork dishes in particular. Diver scallops are served as flavorful as any mollusk you've ever tried. Slow-cooked grits with shrimp are also terrific. Look for special seasonal three-course dinners offering appetizer, entrée, and dessert for $30. The strawberry shake makes a refreshing closer.

Nan

215-382-0818
www.nanrestaurant.com
4000 Chestnut St., Philadelphia, PA 19104
Open: Mon.–Sat.
Price: Expensive
Credit Cards: Yes
Cuisine: French, Thai
Serving: L (Mon.–Fri.), D
Handicapped Access: Yes
Special Features: BYOB

Vigorously flavored wine- and fruit-based sauces make the unusual pairing of French and Thai cuisine a success at this top University City restaurant. The pork tenderloin medallions are a fine example, bathed in a tart sauce, with cranberries, cherries, and a slight kick of thyme. You can also get old standbys like fresh pad Thai or a thick pepper-crusted filet mignon. Dinner entrées come with a side of vegetables and start with a hot roll. The mostly plain white dining room makes efficient use of the space, with four neat rows of tables, each marked by a lone fresh flower.

Pod

215-387-1803
www.podrestaurant.com
3636 Sansom St., Philadelphia, PA 19104
Open: Daily
Price: Moderate to expensive
Credit Cards: Yes
Cuisine: Asian fusion
Serving: L (Mon.–Fri.), D
Handicapped Access: Yes

Stephen Starr's only Philadelphia restaurant outside Center City, Pod delivers all the fun of Morimoto at half the price. The décor almost transcends description, but imagine the dining room of an art deco spaceship and you're halfway there. Fusion cuisine emphases Japanese and Thai flavors, with standouts like macadamia chicken stir-fry and lettuce wrap or crab spring roll appetizers. A good play is to share a few dishes, particularly if your party includes sushi lovers (who can anticipate the freshest and most flavorful spicy tuna rolls in town). Pod is a celebration of all things orbicular; a few tables ("pods") allow

The remarkable Pod dining room

diners to change the lighting to suit their mood. The restaurant fills up for dinner, but is also where University of Pennsylvania students and their hippest professors dine between classes.

Rx

215-222-9590
4443 Spruce St., Philadelphia, PA 19104
Open: Tues.–Sun.
Price: Inexpensive to moderate
Credit Cards: Yes
Cuisine: American
Serving: D, Sat. & Sun. Brunch
Handicapped Access: Yes
Special Features: BYOB

The name is owed to the building's former life as a drugstore and also to the restaurant's promise of "feel good food." Rx delivers on this pledge, serving up strong recipes of locally produced fare at brunch and dinner. The menu changes slightly from day to day. Expect old favorites artfully prepared during brunch, like French toast with strawberry compote or a superb huevos rancheros. Dinner gets more creative, with New American seafood preparations earning the most consistent praise. Similar meals cost $5–$10 more per plate in Center City bistros.

Northern Exposure

Philadelphia has hundreds of restaurants that could qualify as local favorites, and this chapter profiles a number of them. But the city is large and good food isn't always perfectly convenient. Some outstanding restaurants exist far off the tourist track in residential North and Northeast Philadelphia neighborhoods. Are they worth a special trip? It's a subjective question.

The Port Richmond neighborhood has gifted us **Tacconelli's** (215-425-4983; 2604 E. Somerset St.), tucked into an otherwise residential street and quite possibly the finest pizza in Philadelphia. The proper Tacconelli's experience takes a little planning: call a day in advance to make a reservation and tell them what you'd like (type of pie and toppings). Pies are served fresh (no pizza by the slice) with a thin crust, and heavy on the tomato sauce. Can't go wrong with a standard pie, but the white pizza is equally delicious. Tacconelli's is closed Monday and Tuesday.

Also in Port Richmond is Syrenka (215-634-3954; 3173 Richmond St.), a small luncheonette with delicious Polish fare. Food is served cafeteria style—the fresh soups, golabki, and kielbasa ladled and spooned onto your tray. A five-pierogi plate with a dollop of sour cream is just four bucks, and the whole menu is a similar bargain. Syrenka only works for lunch or an early dinner (hours are 11 A.M. to 7 P.M. weekdays, 10 A.M. to 6 P.M. Saturday), but it's excellent. Food is also sold to go.

The sleeper restaurant opening of 2008 was **Memphis Taproom** (215-425-4460; 2331 E. Cumberland St.), which serves a changing menu of delicious craft beers and cider alongside first-rate southern-influenced fare like chicken fried chicken and barbeque pork. For a neighborhood pub, the Taproom's menu is surprisingly diverse and unusually friendly to patrons with vegetarian and vegan restrictions. It is located close to the increasingly hip Fishtown neighborhood on the Port Richmond boundary.

Farther out in Northeast Philadelphia the city loses population density, but gains the **Country Club Restaurant and Pastry Shop** (215-722-0500; 1717 Cottman Ave.). Country Club is a wonderful diner and family owned for more than 50 years. Desserts are all baked on the premises, including the black and white cookies as moist as any you'll find on the Lower East Side of Manhattan. There is a Jewish emphasis to some dishes, like the handmade blintzes, matzo ball soup, knishes, and steamed cabbage (an oft-featured side dish), but you'll also find lots of standard coffee shop grub.

Food Purveyors

Any conversation about food purveying outside Center City needs to start with the **Italian Market**, which runs along 9th Street in Bella Vista between Fitzwater Street and Wharton Street. The outdoor stands capped by metal awnings perpetuate the Old World atmosphere, much as the strip looked a century ago. Many businesses you'll see today in the Italian Market have been family owned and operated since their inception. There isn't much you can't buy here—cheeses from the original **Di Bruno's**, seafood from **Micali Fish** or **Anastasi**, fresh cuts of meat and homemade sausage from **D'Angelo Bros.**, and a whole lot more. It's best to visit early in the morning—most businesses open at 9 A.M.

Bakeries/Coffeehouses

Anthony's Italian Coffeehouse (215-627-2586; 903 S. 9th St., Bella Vista). A storied institution on the Italian Market. Stop in for a fresh cup and buy the coffeehouse's own blends by the pound to take home.

Bean Exchange Coffeehouse (215-592-1960; 650 Bainbridge St., Bella Vista). A very attractive, peaceful coffeehouse just south of South Street in Bella Vista. Has a working fireplace, board games, and excellent java.

Bredenbeck's (215-247-7374; 8126 Germantown Ave., Chestnut Hill). Half bakery and half ice-cream parlor serving Bassett's brand flavors. The flawlessly shingled Victorian building on a stretch of redbrick sidewalk is off-the-charts adorable.

Cake (215-247-6887; 184 E. Evergreen Ave., just of Germantown Ave., Chestnut Hill). The bakery and restaurant is a converted greenhouse that retains park-like effects with its dense flora and fountain. The ownership even draped orange banners from the glass ceiling, which summon memories of Christo and Jeanne-Claude's "The Gates" exhibition in New York's Central Park. Cake is actually much more than a bakery; it's a popular full-service restaurant that specializes in brunch.

Chestnut Hill Coffee Company (215-242-8600; 8620 Germantown Ave., Chestnut Hill). Chestnut Hill Coffee Company roasts and grinds their own beans, as you might deduce from the big bags and whisper-quiet machinery on the second level. The food selection is limited to desserts and pastries, but this is a pleasant place for coffee.

Green Line Café (215-222-3431; 4239 Baltimore Ave., 4305 Locust St., and 3649 Lancaster Ave., University City). With three locations, all in University City, Green Line is the coffee shop of choice for Philadelphia's college and graduate students, many of whom live nearby and attend the University of Pennsylvania.

Isgro Pasticceria (215-923-3092; 1009 Christian St., Bella Vista). More than just the best cannoli, but you'd be foolish not to take some home. The vanilla and chocolate mousse cannoli in particular are divine.

Mugshots Coffeehouse and Café (267-514-7145; 2106 Fairmount Ave., Fairmount). A progressive coffeehouse even by progressive coffeehouse standards, Mugshots is run partially on wind power, brews fair trade coffee, and prepares its salads and sandwiches with locally grown food. There is a second location in Manayunk (215-482-3964; 110 Cotton St., off Main St.).

Pink Rose Pastry Shop (1-800-767-3383; 630 S. 4th St., Queen Village). Bubble-gum-colored tablecloths at this small, Victorian-tinged bakery with great cakes. Stays open late to serve the South Street spillover.

Roller's Espress-o (215-247-7715; 8341 Germantown Ave., Chestnut Hill). Piping-hot La Colombe coffee at this cozy luncheonette (once a neighborhood flower shop). Roller's serves good-sized breakfasts in the morning and nicely crafted sandwiches and salads through the afternoon.

Candy, Ice Cream, and Water Ice

Chloe's Corner (215-482-5600; 4162 Main St., Manayunk). Tiny frozen treat shop that faces the Manayunk canal from above.

John's Water Ice (215-925-6955; 701 Christian St., Bella Vista). The good stuff: home-made, sugar-sweet water ice in four classic flavors. The trick is to pace yourself so it melts just a little and you can drink the last bit without using the spoon. Try with some soft serve to make gelati.

Nonnie's at Bruno's (215-766-1470; 5 Northwestern Ave., Chestnut Hill). Imported gelato and Bassett's ice cream at this colorful Chestnut Hill parlor attached to Bruno's restaurant. A great place for refreshments after a bike ride or hike up Forbidden Drive (see "Recreation").

Pizza, Sandwiches, and Faster Food

The Couch Tomato Café (215-483-2233; 102 Rector St., Manayunk). A friendly neighborhood spot for gourmet pizza and salads, just off Manayunk's main drag. Choices can be a bit limited if you just want a slice, but they'll make you a pie with almost anything on it. Choose from eight sauces and over three-dozen toppings. Great for kids.

Drake's (215-247-5911; 8419 Germantown Ave., Chestnut Hill). The attraction here is the hidden garden in the back. Drake's prepares tea sandwiches and other foods to enjoy outside.

Koch's Deli (215-222-8662; 4309 Locust St., University City). Tremendously large sandwiches made with the highest quality meats, cheeses, and condiments, best eaten over the course of two days or after a prolonged fast. It can take some time to get to the head of the line, but they like to hand out free slices to help tame the hunger.

Main Line Deli-Café (610-664-9263; 109 N. Narberth Ave., Narberth). Casual luncheonette that pairs well with a matinee at the Narberth Theatre. Breakfast and lunch staples most of the time, but it stays open for dinner on Fridays with a special BYOB menu.

Rustica (215-627-1393; 903 N. 2nd St., Northern Liberties). Reliable gourmet pizza sold by the slice and excellent sandwiches.

Saad's Halal Place (215-222-7223; 45th and Walnut Sts., University City). Outstanding falafel, shawarma, and other Halal specialties served either to-go or sit-down. A filling dinner for around $7.

Sarcone's Deli (215-922-1717; 734 S. 9th St., Bella Vista). Always a contender for best sandwiches in the city. Big Italian-style hoagies on perfect bread, baked fresh next door at the Sarcone family bakery.

South Street Philly Bagels (215-627-6277; 613 S. 3rd St., Queen Village). For some reason Philadelphia isn't a great bagel city, but this place is a welcome exception. Come early in the morning and get 'em while they're hot.

Tommy Gunn's American BBQ (215-508-1030; 4901 Ridge Ave., Manayunk). On the east frontier of Manayunk find this little cube of a barbeque restaurant. Order a Carolina pulled pork sandwich or some Memphis-style ribs and settle down at one of the picnic tables outside.

RECREATION

Philadelphia has an oft-underappreciated parks network that utilizes the city's diverse geography. The system itself is operated by the Fairmount Park Commission, named for the flagship park (see "Fairmount Park"). Though Fairmount is wonderful, it is just one star in Philadelphia's recreational galaxy.

Hikers and bikers swear by 1,800-acre **Wissahickon Valley Park** in the northwest part of the city. The Wissahickon Creek runs through the park's 7 miles, from the northernmost boundary in Chestnut Hill to the southern endpoint where it empties into the Schuylkill River. The park is a densely wooded area popular with trawlers, bikers, equestrians, and anyone else looking to escape Center City's tempo with relative ease. The Wissahickon schist native to the region is the grayish, silver stone used to build many of the historic homes you'll find in the surrounding towns. **Friends of the Wissahickon** (www.fow.org) does valuable work preserving and advocating for the area.

Northeast Philadelphia boasts two great parks for bird-watching and hiking: 300-acre **Tacony Creek Park** and rambling **Pennypack Park** farther east, which is more than four times the size. Another personal favorite is **Penn Treaty Park** in Fishtown, heralded as the site where William Penn made peace with the Lenape. It is shadowed by nondescript commercial buildings and could be better maintained, but the park has a good view upstream from the Ben Franklin Bridge.

In University City, check out the year-round Saturday farmer's market at **Clark Park** (43rd St. and Baltimore Ave.), which is also open Thursdays from May to November. Clark Park also hosts music and theater events.

Baseball

The 2008 World Series Champion **Philadelphia Phillies** (215-463-1000; philadelphia.phillies.mlb.com; 1 Citizens Bank Way) play their 82 annual home games at Citizens Bank Park in South Philadelphia. The stadium is modern and fan friendly. Single game tickets cost $16–$50. Hot dogs go for a buck a piece during "Dollar Dog" days, roughly a half-dozen games each year.

Basketball

Philadelphia 76ers (215-339-7676; www.nba.com/sixers; 3601 S. Broad St.) bas-

Enjoying summer Shakespeare at Clark Park

ketball makes for a fun night at the Wachovia Center in South Philly. Tickets go for as little as $15. Drexel University takes its basketball seriously; the **Drexel Dragons** (1-866-437-3935; Market St., between 33rd and 34th Sts.) play at the 2,300-seat Daskalakis Athletic Center in University City. Nearby at the University of Pennsylvania, you can catch the **Penn Quakers** (215-898-6151; 215 S. 33rd St.) at the famed Palestra Gymnasium. Out on the Main Line, the **Villanova Wildcats** (610-519-4100; 800 Lancaster Ave., Villanova) play championship-quality ball.

Bicycling and Hiking

Philadelphia's most popular bike ride is the 23-mile **Schuylkill River Trail** (www.schuylkillriver.org), which begins in Center City, runs along the river's east bank, and concludes in Valley Forge. Only committed bikers do the entire round-trip with any regularity, but a segment from the Art Museum to Manayunk is a manageable and pleasant route. It is a paved trail, suitable for all bikes, and used by runners as well. Consult the aforementioned Web site or visit Lloyd Hall in Fairmount Park for a map. King Drive across the river is also good for bicyclists, and feeds into the hillier roads that pour through the West Park. On weekend mornings from April through October, King Drive is closed to vehicular traffic, making it even better for biking.

The Fairmount Park routes get packed on spring and summer weekends (King Drive to a lesser extent). On these occasions—any occasion for that matter—take a trip down **Forbidden Drive** in Wissahickon Valley Park. There is great urban history here: the 7-mile road, once a crucial thoroughfare servicing the mill-based economy on Wissahickon Creek, was deemed too serene for vehicular disturbance in 1899. Cars have since been forbidden, which explains the name. The drive is a wide gravel path that is fine for most bikes, though a little tread on the tires helps. There are a few small inclines here and

Valley Green Inn on Forbidden Drive

Amphitheater amid the Schuylkill Center for Environmental Education hiking trails

there; numerous hiking and mountain biking trails stem from Forbidden Drive if you're looking for more precipitous terrain. Refreshments are available at the **Valley Green Inn** (215-247-1730; www.valleygreeninn.com; Valley Green Rd. at Wissahickon), a historic property situated at the midpoint on the drive. Buy drinks, ice cream, sandwiches, and the like from the inn snack bar. The main dining room is a more formal affair. Another land-mark to look for on the drive is **Thomas Mill Bridge,** the lone remaining covered bridge in Philadelphia.

See Chapter 2 for places to rent a bike close to Center City. Here are two more, a little farther out:

Eastern Mountain Sports (215-386-1020; 130 S. 36th St., University City). A 10-minute ride from the southern end of the Schuylkill River Trail and King Drive.

The Human Zoom (215-487-7433; 4159 Main St., Manayunk). A big store, also a fine place to buy accessory equipment. Look for the main light fixture, which resembles a giant bicy-cle wheel.

The northwest portion of the city presents other opportunities for hikers. There are eight short trails (none more than a mile long) woven around the **Schuylkill Center for Environmental Education** (215-482-7300; www.schuylkillcenter.org; 8480 Hagy's Mill Rd., Roxborough). The trails vary in slope. The highest inclines are along the Ravine Loop—also the most interesting hike, touching marshland and bridges. Some trails are a little overgrown, but the area is small and the signage is good, so you can find your way around without much trouble. Multiple trails converge on an amphitheater and pavilion. The center itself is open Mon.–Sat., 8:30–4:30, and offers a children's exhibit and gallery space. The trails are open seven days a week.

Bird-Watching

Bird-watching is just one of many activities offered at **John Heinz National Wildlife Refuge at Tinicum** (215-365-3118; heinz.fws.gov; 86th St. and Lindbergh Blvd., Southwest Philadelphia). Named for the late Pennsylvania politician and environmental advocate, the refuge bounds a freshwater tidal marsh at Philadelphia's southwestern tip near the airport. Birds love to lurk in and around the marsh grasses, and over three hundred varieties have been spotted. A good walk around the main gravel pathway incorporates many promising bird-watching stations, including a bi-level pavilion. Also look for a narrow planked wooden bridge traversing the marsh on the east side with free binoculars. While you're at Heinz, visit the geothermal-powered **Cusano Environmental Center** near the parking lot. It has some nice exhibits on bird migration patterns and an indoor setup for bird-watching. The refuge is free and open from sunrise to sunset. The center is open daily, 8:30–4.

A bird-watching post at John Heinz National Wildlife Refuge

Bowling

North Bowl (215-238-2695; 909 N. 2nd St., Northern Liberties). A retro décor and two levels of bowling, 17 lanes total, in what was once a garage. A fun vibe and a popular hangout either pre- or post-barhopping in Northern Liberties. Valet parking available weekends, but good drink specials weeknights. The bike racks outside are among the most creative in the city.

Strikes Bowling Lounge (215-387-2695; 4040 Locust St., University City). A mostly younger crowd at this university-area alley with a well-stocked bar and an appetizer/sandwich menu. Bowling is supplemented by foosball, pool, and Ping-Pong.

Wynnewood Lanes (610-642-7512; 2228 Haverford Rd., Ardmore). Not too much flash, just good, old-fashioned bowling and friendly faces at this Main Line institution.

Fishing

You can purchase a temporary Pennsylvania fishing license over the Internet from the **Pennsylvania Fish and Boat Commission** (www.theoutdoorshop.state.pa.us) for $25–$33 depending on how long you want to fish. Pay by credit card and print the license from your computer.

Fishing on the banks of the Schuylkill River at Fairmount Park is a popular spring and summer pastime, as much for the environs as for the fish. You might see some bass or shad. Wissahickon Creek at Wissahickon Valley Park is nearby and more isolated. Trout, smallmouth bass, and carp are some possibilities. In the city's northeast at Pennypack Creek are these species and more.

Designated areas at the Heinz Wildlife Refuge allow fishing. Green sunfish, striped bass, American shad, and catfish are among the fish you might find in the lower Darby Creek. Do not eat them.

Football

The **Philadelphia Eagles** play at 67,594-seat Lincoln Financial Field (215-463-5500; www.philadelphiaeagles.com; 1 Lincoln Financial Way) near the new baseball stadium and basketball/hockey arena. Philly football fans root hard, and Eagles games are always fun. You can also tour the stadium at noon on selected dates in the spring and summer. Call 267-570-4510 for more information.

Golf

The Main Line has some spectacular private golf courses, including the East Course at the **Merion Golf Club** (610-642-5600; 450 Ardmore Ave., Ardmore), which will host the 2013 U.S. Open. Non-members can make due at Philadelphia's municipal courses.

Cobbs Creek and Karakung Golf Courses (215-877-8707; 7200 Lansdowne Ave., West Philadelphia). Adjacent 18-hole, par-71 courses; 6,202 yards at Cobbs Creek and 5,762 yards at Karakung. Putting green and chipping area. Fees for 18 holes: $35–$50.

Franklin D. Roosevelt Golf Course (215-462-8997; 1954 Pattison Ave., South Philadelphia). Par 69, 18 holes; 6,004 yards. A recreational course with wide fairways. Decently maintained, the greens give a relatively smooth roll.

Juniata Golf Course (215-743-4060; 1391 E. Cayuga St., Northeast Philadelphia). Par 66, 18 holes; 5,275 yards.

Walnut Lane Golf Course (215-482-3370; 800 Walnut Ln., Roxborough). Par 62, 18 holes; 4,509 yards. Fees: $16–$37.

Hockey

The **Philadelphia Flyers** (1-800-298-4200; flyers.nhl.com; 3601 S. Broad St.) take to the ice for 41 regular season games a year at the Wachovia Center. The minor league affiliate **Philadelphia Phantoms** (215-465-4522; Broad St. and Pattison Ave.) play nearby at the older Wachovia Spectrum, but not for long. The famed Spectrum will be demolished after the 2008–2009 season.

Horseback Riding

Riding on Forbidden Drive in Wissahickon Valley Park seems like fun, but you need your own horse. And while there are several boarders in peripheral Philadelphia, essentially the only place to ride what you don't own is at **Ashford Farm** (610-825-9838; River Rd., Lafayette Hill), where you can take lessons on the premises—no trail rides.

Ice Skating

University of Pennsylvania Ice Rink at the Class of 1923 Arena (215-898-1923; 3130 Walnut St., University City). Ice time is available to the public September through April, including open hockey during special hours. Skate rental and lessons available. Call ahead for public skate times.

Tennis

The courts at **Franklin D. Roosevelt Park** (215-685-1000; 2000 Pattison Ave., South Philadelphia) are lighted for night play. Fairmount Park's west side has several courts, like the **Chamounix Tennis Courts** (Chamounix Drive, off Belmont Drive). Consult the Fairmount Park Web site (www.fairmountpark.com) for more information.

Zoo

Philadelphia Zoo

215-243-1100
www.philadelphiazoo.org
34th St. and Girard Ave., Philadelphia, PA 19104
Fairmount Park
Open: Daily Mar.–Nov., 9:30–5, Dec.–Feb., 9:30–4
Admission: Mar.–Nov., adults $18, children $15; Dec.–Feb., adults $15, children $13

America's first zoo retains the beauty and charm of its 1874 opening, when admission was a quarter and much of consolidated Philadelphia was rural. There are more than two-dozen animal habitats and attractions arranged in a 42-acre half circle, including the newest exhibition of lions, tigers, jaguars, and other felines. The rare animal conservation center displays interesting creatures like the red-capped mangabey and a shifty looking group of mongoose lemurs. The primate preserve is a novel space, with spirited gorillas and information on zoological conservation efforts. Chickens wander freely around the Children's Zoo, and a peacock might sidle up next to you wherever you are. For a few extra bucks you can ride a camel, goof around on a swan paddleboat, or take a trip upward on the iconic hot-air balloon for a bird's-eye view of greater Philadelphia.

Paddling the day away on the Philadelphia Zoo's swan boats

Shopping

A few Philadelphia neighborhoods outside Center City have popular shopping districts. The two most trafficked are Main Street in **Manayunk** and Germantown Avenue in **Chestnut Hill.** They both tend towards higher-end merchandise, though not exclusively so by any means. You'll find apparel stores, gift ideas, and gourmet food shops at either one. Manayunk's Main Street has a newer, edgier feel and boasts some especially unique furniture stores, but Chestnut Hill has better restaurants and more to see. Either makes for a very pleasant Saturday morning stroll.

Below are just a few of the many notable stores in the city's peripheral neighborhoods, plus some Main Line shops to round things out.

Books

Bookhaven (215-235-3226; 2202 Fairmount Ave., Fairmount). A well-organized, deceptively large used bookstore. Just when you think you've seen the whole stock, a hidden doorway reveals a new room or staircase.

Readers' Forum (610-254-9040; 116 N. Wayne Ave., Wayne). Great independent bookstore with friendly, helpful owners.

University of Pennsylvania Bookstore (215-898-7595; 3601 Walnut St., University City). This cavernous shop carries both popular titles and textbooks for students, plus Penn logo gear. A special section on the second level stocks books written exclusively by Penn professors.

Clothing

Fresh Ayer (610-688-4933; 100 E. Lancaster Ave., Wayne). High-quality plus-sized women's clothing from designers like Trentacosta and Gayla Bentley at this corner boutique.

Sanctuary (215-242-3150; 8611 Germantown Ave., Chestnut Hill). Specializes in yoga clothing and accessories. The store itself is calming too.

Skirt (610-520-0222; 931 W. Lancaster Ave., Bryn Mawr). Popular women's clothing boutique on the Main Line.

Urban Outfitters (215-387-6990; 110 S. 36th St., University City). A large branch of the trendy-but-not-too-expensive clothing store right by the Penn campus.

While we're on the subject, Urban Outfitters was founded in Philadelphia and maintains its headquarters in South Philadelphia's old Navy Yard (S. 16th St. and Flagship Ave., South Philadelphia). The Navy stopped building ships here in 1995, at which point the city embarked on a quest to spur reinvestment in the area. Urban Outfitters moved to the Yard in 2006, transforming huge industrial buildings into a whimsical headquarters befitting the creative temperament for which the brand is known. It's a minor hassle to get to—a 15-minute drive to the Navy Yard from Center City (just head south on Broad Street)—but damned cool anyway. While most Urban Outfitters buildings are closed to visitors, you can drop by Building #543 and have a bite at the Shop 543 cafeteria or Jharoka coffee bar. Admire how the old materials were put to new use and how the designers maintained the building's soul.

Furniture

Dwelling (215-487-7400; 4050 Main St., Manayunk). A 24,000-square-foot showroom displays a fresh variety of home furniture. Lots of sharp, eye-catching pieces made with international materials that you can't find just anywhere.

The Furniture Workshop (215-483-6160; 4901 Umbria St., Manayunk). Good-looking, high-quality wood pieces, located a little off the beaten track northwest of the Main Street shopping district. The workshop also custom-builds wood furniture.

Malls and Complexes

Franklin Mills Mall (215-632-1500; www.franklinmills.com; 1455 Franklin Mills Circle, Northeast Philadelphia). Numerous factory outlet stores with bargain merchandise at this enormous shopping complex on the Philadelphia side of the Bucks County border, right off Exit 35 on I-95. The Nike and Saks Fifth Avenue outlets are among the most popular, but there are 200 stores in total, plus a 14-screen movie theater and food courts.

Suburban Square (610-896-7560; www.suburbansquare.com; Anderson and Coulter Aves., just off Lancaster Ave., Ardmore). A mix of retail and dining, this creatively planned shopping complex is a fun place to walk around. Lots of apparel options. You'll recognize

The courtyard at Ardmore's Suburban Square

most stores—Macy's, American Eagle, Talbots, etc.—and there's a farmer's market from Wednesday to Sunday. Suburban Square is conveniently located steps away from the Ardmore train station on the R5 line, a half-hour ride from downtown Philadelphia. It should be noted that Ardmore itself has a walkable retail district along Lancaster Avenue with some independently owned shops.

Sporting Goods and Clothing

The shops listed in "Biking" rent bikes and are also well stocked with clothing and accessories. One other excellent store is family-owned **Wayne Sporting Goods** (610-293-0400; 124 E. Lancaster Ave., Wayne), which sells apparel and equipment for a wide range of sports. Pick up everything from footballs to gym shorts at very competitive prices.

INFORMATION

Much of the information for Philadelphia's neighborhoods is the same as in Center City. Please consult the previous chapter for anything not listed here. What follows are services, books, newspapers, and other information unique to the peripheral neighborhoods and Main Line suburbs.

Area Codes

The area code for Main Line neighborhoods is 610. Philadelphia neighborhoods outside Center City use 215.

Recommended Reading

Autobiographies and Biographies

Buschel, Bruce. *Walking Broad: Looking for the Heart of Brotherly Love,* New York: Simon & Schuster, 2007. An absorbing journey through the author's life and the city's life as he walks down Philadelphia's Broad Street.

Longstreth, Thatcher W. with Rottenberg, Dan. *Main Line Wasp,* New York: W.W. Norton, 1990. Funny, charming autobiography of the late bow-tie-wearing mayoral candidate, city councilman, and Philadelphia institution.

Nonfiction

Clark, Dennis. *The Irish in Philadelphia: Ten Generations of Urban Experience,* Philadelphia: Temple University Press, 1973.

Conn, Steven. *Metropolitan Philadelphia: Living with the Presence of the Past,* Philadelphia: University of Pennsylvania Press, 2006. Puts its finger on the pleasures, problems, and eccentricities of this emerging regional web.

Juliani, Richard N. *Building Little Italy: Philadelphia's Italians Before Mass Migration,* University Park: Pennsylvania State University Press, 1998. A fascinating and important history of the Italian immigrants who preceded the late-19th century wave of migration to South Philadelphia.

Miller, Fredric and others. *Philadelphia Stories: A Photographic History, 1920–1960,* Philadelphia: Temple University Press, 1988.

Hospitals

Bryn Mawr Hospital: 610-526-3000; 130 S. Bryn Mawr Ave., Bryn Mawr

Chestnut Hill Hospital: 215-248-8200; 8835 Germantown Ave., Chestnut Hill

Children's Hospital of Philadelphia: 215-590-1000; 34th St. and Civic Center Blvd., University City

Hospital of the University of Pennsylvania: 1-800-789-7366; 3400 Spruce St., University City

Lankenau Hospital: 610-645-2000; 100 W. Lancaster Ave., Wynnewood

Late Night Food and Fuel

There are two 24-hour Wawa stores in University City, at 3604 Chestnut St. and 3744 Spruce St. Some late night sit-down dining options in the peripheral neighborhoods are:

Manayunk Diner (215-483-4200; 3722 Main St., Manayunk). Open 24 hours on Friday and Saturday nights and until 2 A.M. the rest of the week.

Minella's Diner (610-687-1575; 320 W. Lancaster Ave., Wayne). Food here is several notches better than at your average 24-hour diner.

Media
Magazines and Newspapers

Chestnut Hill Local (215-248-8800; www.chestnuthilllocal.com; 8434 Germantown Ave.). Neighborhood paper published weekly.

Main Line Life (610-896-9555; www.mainlinelife.com, 311 E. Lancaster Ave., Wynnewood). Weekly newspaper, covers Main Line issues with depth and attention to detail.

Mainline Magazine (610-667-8100; www.mainlinemag.com; 3 Bala Suite, Bala Cynwyd). Fashion, fine dining, art, and other topics of intrigue out in the well-heeled suburbs. A glossy bi-monthly publication.

Main Line Today (610-325-4630; www.mainlinetoday.com; 4699 West Chester Pike, Newtown Square). Monthly magazine with feature articles, dining, shopping, and more on the Main Line.

Main Line Times (610-642-4300; www.mainlinetimes.com; 311 E. Lancaster Ave., Ardmore). Another suburban paper.

South Philly Review (215-336-2500; www.southphillyreview.com; 12th and Porter Sts., South Philadelphia). A well-done community newspaper, printed weekly.

Visitor Information
If you find yourself wanting some guidance in Chestnut Hill, stop by the **Chestnut Hill Visitor's Center** (215-247-6696; 8426 Germantown Ave.) in the center of the neighborhood's main shopping district

4

BRANDYWINE VALLEY

Villages of the River

> The steam industry of the later nineteenth century smeared every natural beauty it touched with smoke, dirt, and waste. This was not true of water power. The capture of the swift currents of the Brandywine for work and profit was more like a seduction than a rape. The mills on its banks, the raceways on its margins, humanized nature in the eighteenth century way, changing the romance of the primitive into the sentiment of rural beauty.... It was not until the romantic novelists of the nineteenth century began to write of the Brandywine that crags, caves, solitude, and melodramatic beauty began to be observed by travelers to the river made famous by a battle.
>
> —Henry Seidel Canby, *The Brandywine*

To fully appreciate Canby's ode to the Brandywine, pack a picnic lunch and settle by the creek on a spring afternoon. None of the region's waterways can match its soothing effect—certainly not the lower Delaware, employed for industrial purposes since Penn's arrival, nor the Schuylkill, too closely identified with competitive sports to bring to mind anything other than life's interminable contests.

Speaking literally, the Brandywine is a slim, shallow river flowing southward from the rivulets of the Welsh Hills where exurban Chester County meets a more remote, mountainous terrain. The rivulets form two main streams that meet a few miles north of the Chester and Delaware County border near Chadds Ford, the archetypal Brandywine Valley town. The Brandywine flows past Chadds Ford, through northern Delaware state, and beyond downtown Wilmington, meeting the Christina and emptying into the Delaware River. Originally home to the region's Lenape tribes who lived off the river's fish, the Brandywine was quiet during its first hundred post-colonization years. Washington's abortive effort at the Battle of Brandywine interrupted things for a short while, but the valley emerged from the war as the same quiet string of rural villages it was before.

Things changed considerably at the turn of the 19th century when the Du Ponts landed on the American shore. The river's speed around the northern Delaware area made the Brandywine an ideal source of free energy. The Du Ponts acquired enormous swaths of northern Delaware, constructing mills and dams to manufacture gunpowder and farm the fertile soil. The DuPont Corporation evolved over time into a development company for

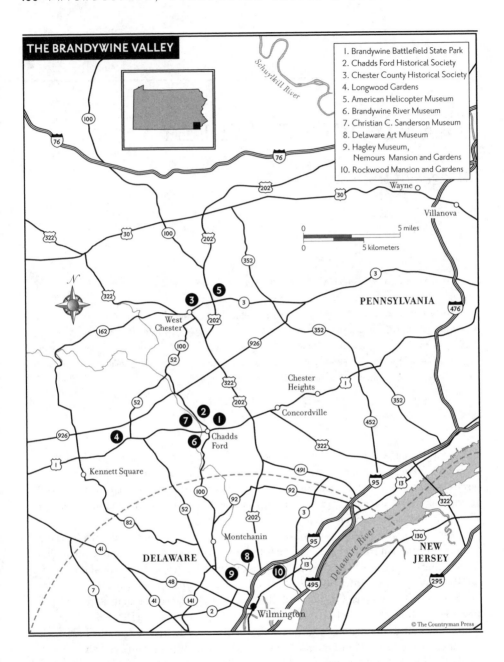

THE BRANDYWINE VALLEY

1. Brandywine Battlefield State Park
2. Chadds Ford Historical Society
3. Chester County Historical Society
4. Longwood Gardens
5. American Helicopter Museum
6. Brandywine River Museum
7. Christian C. Sanderson Museum
8. Delaware Art Museum
9. Hagley Museum, Nemours Mansion and Gardens
10. Rockwood Mansion and Gardens

© The Countryman Press

dynamite, chemical production, and materials science, but its presence in the Brandywine forever wedded industry to the creek and sewed a dominant family through the social fabric. It is impossible to imagine the Brandywine today without the Du Ponts. Their rolling estates at Winterthur and Nemours along with the original gunpowder mill at Hagley are one-of-a-kind attractions, and no hotel in the region can compare to Wilmington's Hotel du Pont.

It is similarly impossible to imagine the Brandywine without the Wyeths. As the artistic ingredient in the Brandywine stew, the Wyeth family's trademark landscapes serve as a peaceable foil to the Du Ponts' industrial juggernaut. This artistic tradition, known as the Brandywine School, began at the turn of the 20th century, when illustrator Howard Pyle held art classes in the Brandywine Valley. Among his students was New England transport N. C. Wyeth, who won prominence for his magazine illustrations. His son, Andrew Wyeth, inherited and expanded on this legacy, producing realist landscapes renowned for their tender interpretation of rural scenery. Andrew Wyeth remained prolific right up to his death in January 2009 at the age of 91. Locals remember him as a Brandywine fixture, dining at Hank's Place and painting the Pennsylvania countryside. Andrew's son, Jamie, is a noted painter as well, and a broad sampling of Wyeth art can be found at the Brandywine River Museum alongside other realist work.

For the purposes of touring, Brandywine Valley can be split into four localities. Each one maintains a unique identity while contributing to the totality of the Brandywine's mise-en-scène. The northern post is **West Chester,** large enough for a local newspaper but small enough that five or six main roads encompass nearly the entire downtown. Blessed with neat rows of Greek Revival buildings near the city center and grand Victorian residences in the periphery, West Chester comes close to Hollywood's conception of a small town. It is powered by the legal services industry and higher education, with Chester County courthouse in the heart of the business district, and 13,000-student West Chester University on the south side. The large student presence during the university's school year gives West Chester a dual identity not uncommon in the Delaware Valley's many college towns. The same bar filled with Budweiser-fueled undergraduates the evening before commencement becomes a dark, quiet tavern where locals go for red wine and prime rib au jus the evening after.

Just over the Delaware County line is **Chadds Ford,** with its landmarks and museums mixed into the scenery of a decentralized suburb. The township is an enthusiastic promoter of its history. Just one example of this is the annual Chadds Ford Days festival, an arts and crafts fair timed to mark the Battle of Brandywine every September. Chadds Ford is also the place to go for Wyeth art.

Eight miles west of Chadds Ford is **Kennett Square,** known most famously as the "Mushroom Capital of the World" since regional farms supply more than half of all cultivated mushrooms consumed in the United States. This amazing production is owed to the ingenuity of William Swayne, a Kennett Square farmer who traveled to England in the late 19th century and returned with mushroom spawn to grow in the greenhouse space beneath his carnations. From these fungal roots, Kennett Square has blossomed into a beautiful small town with streets of independently owned shops, bed & breakfasts, and restaurants that use produce grown on local farms to wonderful effect. Kennett Square is perhaps the most independent of the Brandywine communities; smaller than West Chester and more walkable than Chadds Ford. Kennett is the westernmost village, but still within easy driving distance of all Brandywine attractions. Longwood Gardens is about 2 miles from downtown.

The valley is anchored by greater **Wilmington** across the state line in Delaware. The river runs through Brandywine Park, a lovely urban green space with Delaware's only zoo, before it encounters the Christina. Brandywine Valley attractions identified as "Wilmington" are mostly north of the city limits in or around scenic communities like **Montchanin,** with its small luxury hotel equidistant from the Hagley Museum and

Canoeing on the Brandywine

Winterthur estate. Northern Delaware outside Wilmington is identifiably Brandywine—rolling countryside hills and lush greenery, dotted by an occasional stone house. The city is something else entirely, though misconceptions about Wilmington abound. It is known to many as just a way station along I-95 with tax-free shopping and the nerve center of the consumer credit industry. In truth, Wilmington has much to offer, including a first-rate concert venue, contemporary art center, and minor league baseball. If you are interested in neighborhoods, peruse Little Italy or the lively Trolley Square district, where you'll find shopping and sports bars. This chapter incorporates greater Wilmington, with parks, libraries, museums, and lodging both inside and outside the city limits.

Today's Brandywine Valley exists in that subtle place between bedroom suburb and country getaway. It has performed this difficult balancing act with great success for many years—a testament to Brandywine residents' reverence for their home and a commitment to maintaining the land's natural splendor. Managing the region's development is an everlasting campaign, but as re-enactors remind onlookers every September, when it comes to battles the Brandywine has survived much worse.

TRANSPORTATION

Interstate 95 is a straight shot from Philadelphia to Wilmington, but unless you're heading directly downtown, it is best to utilize the other highways. US 1, also known as Baltimore Pike, runs from Philadelphia straight through Chadds Ford and close to Kennett Square. West Chester Pike (PA 3) is crammed with stoplights but links Center City with West Chester directly. For a more circuitous—but potentially faster—route to West Chester, take the Schuylkill Expressway (I-76) west to US 322 South.

Traveling within the Brandywine Valley, US 202 is the key artery. It runs north-south between West Chester and Wilmington, intersecting US 1 at Chadds Ford. US 202 also hooks up with 322 briefly, just south of West Chester. Kennett Pike, known as DE 52 or PA 52 depending on the state, connects Kennett Square with Wilmington. It also connects Longwood Gardens to West Chester.

Automobile is the primary way to travel both to and around the Brandywine Valley. **SEPTA** shortsightedly closed down regional rail to West Chester in 1986. There is bus service to West Chester from the 69th Street Terminal in Upper Darby (the westernmost stop on the Market-Frankford line from Philadelphia), but the trip is long and inconvenient. SEPTA does offer rail service from Philadelphia to downtown Wilmington on the R2. AMTRAK also stops in Wilmington on its Northeast Corridor route. Wilmington is additionally served by **Greyhound** buses.

TOURING

A good place to start is the **Chester County Visitor's Center** (1-800-228-9933; www.brandywinevalley.com; 300 Greenwood Rd., Kennett Square), situated right next to Longwood Gardens off US 1. The building is an old Quaker meetinghouse that was active in the Underground Railroad, and maintains a permanent exhibition on that history. Pick up travel brochures, coupons, and maps.

Since the Brandywine Valley spans four towns and 72 square miles, it is usually best to stay within one or two areas each day. Downtown West Chester and Kennett Square are the best places to stroll. The self-guided **Kennett Square Walking Tour** (www.historickennettsquare.com/walkingtour.html), with 36 sites clustered around downtown, is a handy way to survey the borough's architecture. You can print the tour out online or pick it up at the visitor's center near Longwood Gardens. West Chester's guided **Historic Walking Tour** (610-696-2102) costs $10 and leaves Saturday mornings from spring through fall. Call for more details and to reserve a spot. For group tours of the valley, contact **American Heritage Landmark Tours** (610-647-4030; 14 Anthony Dr., Malvern).

If you're taking the whole family or just feel like gorging on potato chips somewhere you won't be judged, leave time for the **Herr's Snack Factory Tour** (1-800-637-6225; www.herrs.com; US 1 and PA 272). It's in Nottingham, about 20 miles from Kennett Square—drive south on US 1 from the valley.

LODGING

Bed & Breakfasts and Small Inns

Choosing accommodations in the Brandywine Valley means balancing priorities. There are many excellent bed & breakfasts and small inns around the countryside. One strategy is to select by location and choose lodging closest to the attractions you most want to see. This leads horticulturists to Kennett Square (proximate to Longwood Gardens), Wyeth fans to Chadds Ford, and shopaholics to West Chester for the QVC Studio Park. Location is certainly a worthy consideration, but remember that nothing in the Brandywine is more than a 30- to 45-minute drive from anything else. Keep an open mind, particularly if you are staying more than one night and plan on exploring more than one Brandywine town.

If you are booking a B&B, call or e-mail the innkeeper to ask about specials and packages. Some offer themed getaways, and others feature discounts to Brandywine attractions. Finally, keep in mind that hotels in downtown Wilmington rarely include free parking, so if you select a property in the city figure on $10–$25 per day on top of the room rate.

Rates

Inexpensive	Up to $60
Moderate	$60 to $120
Expensive	$120 to $200
Very Expensive	$200 and up

These rates do not include room taxes or special service charges that might apply during your stay.

Chadds Ford and Vicinity

Brandywine River Hotel

1-800-274-9644 or 610-388-1200
www.brandywineriverhotel.com
US 1 and PA 100, Chadds Ford, PA 19317
Price: Moderate to expensive
Credit Cards: Yes
Handicapped Access: Yes

A reliable little inn that delivers well-maintained guest rooms and a subdued Victorian style that prioritizes warmth over flamboyance. The staff is kind and helpful and the furnishings are agreeable. You won't get silk duvet covers on the beds, but staying here is less costly than at area B&Bs. Homemade cookies with tea are served in the late afternoon and daily continental breakfast is served in the morning. The location atop a small hill amid the Chadds Ford Barn Shops is at the valley's nexus. There are 40 guest rooms total, including suites with Jacuzzi tubs. The small lobby bar with fireplace is a great spot to unwind in the evening over a book and a mixed drink.

Fairville Inn

Innkeepers: Laura and Rick Carro
1-877-285-7772 or 610-388-5900
www.fairvilleinn.com
info@fairvilleinn.com
506 Kennett Pike (PA 52), Chadds Ford, PA 19317
Price: Expensive
Credit Cards: Yes
Handicapped Access: One room

The mostly Federal-style Fairville is three B&Bs in one, with 15 rooms and suites spread around the Main House, Carriage House, and Springhouse. Many rooms have private decks, the choicest of which are the two Carriage House suites equipped with sleeper sofas and upholstered seating. Decks face either the on-site garden or contiguous meadow. All rooms are gener-ously sized and all bathrooms have tubs. Breakfast is a cold buffet with pastries baked on the premises, accompanied by a choice of hot entrées prepared by Rick. A recent addition is the four-pin chip-ping/pitching course for golfers who can't wait to hit the area's fine courses. The Fairville's location just north of the Delaware border makes it convenient to most Brandywine Valley attractions.

Hamanassett Bed & Breakfast

Innkeeper: Ashley and Glenn Mon
1-877-836-8212 or 610-459-3000
www.hamanassett.com
stay@hamanassett.com
115 Indian Springs Dr., Chester Heights, PA 19017
Price: Expensive to very expensive
Credit Cards: Yes
Handicapped Access: No

Sets the standard for luxury accommoda-tions in the Brandywine area, with a stately opulence magnified by the innkeeper's gra-ciousness and enthusiasm. The mansion can be found at the apex of a Chester Heights development, slightly removed from the traditional Brandywine Valley, but close to the major attractions. The 1856 mansion, since expanded, has a Federal-style interior; especially impressive are the palatial dining room and billiard room on the ground floor. Guest rooms at Hamanassett are larger than you will typi-cally find at a B&B and come outfitted with extras like personal coffee makers, robes, and magnifying vanity mirrors. Innkeeper Ashley Mon's southern background lends a regional influence to her outstanding breakfasts. She has also dealt in antiques, and has an eye for furnishings that are as visually interesting as they are functional. Iced tea, lemonade, and cookies are served on an antique wash stand on the second floor. A rosewood half-tester bed in the Windsor Room is a magnificent piece as well. The 7-acre grounds include meadows, rose plantings, a beautifully decorated koi pond out front, and a Japanese magnolia tree. In addition to the seven guest rooms in the main house, larger groups can stay at the Hamanassett's well-appointed carriage house, which has two bedrooms and two and a half baths.

Palladian window from inside the Winterthur Room at Pennsbury Inn

Pennsbury Inn

Innkeepers: Cheryl and Chip Grono
610-388-1435
www.pennsburyinn.com
info@pennsburyinn.com
883 Baltimore Pike, Chadds Ford, PA 19317
Price: Expensive to very expensive
Credit Cards: Yes
Handicapped Access: Limited

This Colonial mansion, parts of which date back to 1714, survives as an exemplar of luxury in the early Delaware Valley. The place is nothing if not solid, held together by 18- to 24-inch walls and garnished with local bluestone granite. There is some debate as to whether the inn's wood floors are yellow pine or oak, but the music room features rare, orange-tinged pumpkin pine mantles. There are seven guest rooms with private bath to choose from, each boasting unique decorative flourishes. Note the thematic designer wallpaper in the Four Seasons Room and the spool bed in the John Marshall Room (often requested by vacationing lawyers). The Winterthur Suite is the most breathtaking, with deep soaking tub, vaulted ceiling, and oversized Palladian window overlooking the garden. There are featherbed mattresses in all rooms and electric fireplaces in most. Guests are free to enjoy the 8-acre grounds, which are replete with reflecting and fish ponds. The Pennsbury is a breathtaking place for a wedding, but book early. Such events are spaced out weeks apart so as not to over-tread the garden.

Kennett Square
Bancroft Manor

Innkeeper: Michael E. Snyder
610-470-4297
www.bancroftmanor.com
innkeeper@bancroftmanor.com
318 Marshall St., Kennett Square, PA 19348
Price: Expensive
Credit Cards: Yes
Handicapped Access: No

Innkeeper Michael Snyder purchased this hundred-year-old Victorian mansion in 2000, and spent the next three years refurbishing the property and stocking it with period antiques. The Bancroft is ideally located just a couple blocks from PA 82 and the Kennett Square shopping district, which gives the property a relaxed, country feel (and guarantees a good night's sleep). Architectural highlights like the Tuscan columns abutting the parlor room and the leaded glass windows are original to the house. Note also the 1930s wallpaper featuring a peacock and magnolia vine that appears on the Bancroft's logo. There are three bedrooms with private bathrooms. The Amish Room is smallest, but connects to a second-floor sun porch, the perfect place to share an evening glass of wine. Beds come in three sizes: king, queen, and full, with the smallest in the Amish Room and the king in the Longwood Suite, which also includes a sitting room with garden mural. Snyder prepares a changing hot breakfast; one popular specialty is his portobello mushroom served alongside seared tomato and eggs.

Garden mural in the Longwood Suite sitting room at Bancroft Manor

Stebbins-Swayne House

Innkeeper: Rosemary Malatesta
610-444-9097
www.sshbandb.com
history1842@yahoo.com
221 S. Union St., Kennett Square, PA 19348
Price: Expensive
Credit Cards: Yes
Handicapped Access: No

The deeply knowledgeable innkeeper is just one of many reasons to stay at Stebbins-Swayne, a mid-19th-century Georgian house that hints at a Victorian look—note the large front porch. It belonged first to Kennett Square doctor Sumner Stebbins, who ran a practice in the back of the house during the mid-19th century, and opened as a B&B in 2005. Malatesta grows vegetables in the garden—set amid native plant life and an old quince tree—using the fresh produce to garnish breakfast. The baked-from-scratch muffins, in all varieties from banana to rhubarb, complement fresh fruit and a hot entrée. There are three rooms, each with a distinct personality. The Garden Room has a second daybed in addition to a queen, and hand-painted Venetian blinds. The Empire Room is the most masculine, encircled by stout blue walls and equipped with dark wood furnishings and a sunken bathroom. It is also where actor John Turturro stayed during a recent visit to the Brandywine.

Sunrise Suites

Innkeeper: Lynn Sinclair
302-559-0923
www.sunrisecafe-tearoom.com
214 N. Union St., Kennett Square, PA 19348
Price: Expensive
Credit Cards: Yes
Handicapped Access: No

A sister property to the Sunrise Café and Tearoom nearby, this bed & breakfast rents one very large, first-floor, multi-room suite with exposed brick and a large sleigh bed in the bedroom (tenants occupy the second and third floors). The suite includes a full kitchen with refrigerator and stove, plus a DVD/VCR and cable television. The building, constructed in 1840, maintains its Federal character, though a decorative hip roof added in the 1870s changed the exterior look a bit. A night's lodging includes fresh coffee on-site, and breakfast or lunch the next day at the Sunrise Café. The café is open until 2 P.M., so sleep in if you like.

West Chester
1732 Folke Stone Bed & Breakfast
Innkeepers: Marcy and Walter Schmoll
1-800-884-4666 or 610-429-0310
www.bbonline.com/pa/folkestone
folkbanb@aol.com
777 Copeland School Rd., West Chester, PA
19380
Price: Moderate
Credit Cards: Yes
Handicapped Access: No

The beam ceilings and beehive oven in the entrance area lend this old stone house northwest of downtown West Chester an agrarian authenticity. There are three rooms, two with king beds and all three with private bathroom access. Décor varies by room, but all are carefully coordinated. Art and furniture are thematically integrated—the bursts of pink and lavender sprinkled around the Rose Room work especially well. The property shares a pond out back with the next-door neighbors, so feel free to introduce yourself to the family of swans that calls it home.

The Tory Inne
Innkeeper: Linda Waterhouse-Koski
610-431-2788
www.toryinne.com
toryinne@comcast.net
734 North Chester Rd., West Chester, PA
19380
Price: Expensive
Credit Cards: Yes
Handicapped Access: No

Three miles from downtown West Chester in a landmarked building that was slated for demolition until it was meticulously restored by Waterhouse-Koski, the Tory Inne is a wonderfully unique retreat. The building, formerly a general store and post office, stands along the road the British and their Hessian mercenaries used to take Philadelphia during the Revolutionary War. The innkeeper is a delight—enthusiastic,

attentive, and knowledgeable about the area's history (though she is partial to the British side of the conflict). In keeping with the theme, breakfast is English and includes an assortment of breads, puddings, teas, and egg and meat dishes that vary depending on Waterhouse-Koski's mood. This is the perfect bed & breakfast for history buffs, as well as anyone looking for a relaxing time in the northern portion of the Brandywine Valley.

Wilmington and Vicinity
The Inn at Montchanin Village
1-800-269-2473
www.montchanin.com
DE 100 and Kirk Rd., Montchanin, DE
19710
Price: Expensive to very expensive
Credit Cards: Yes
Handicapped Access: Yes

An ideal Brandywine Valley lodging experience, as notable for its luxurious accommodations as it is for its unique connection to northern Delaware. There are 11 buildings and 28 guest rooms spread across a lush 6-acre triangle in the heart of the area's best attractions. The village was once inhabited by mill workers employed by Dupont at the nearby mills supplying the gunpowder that helped the Union win the Civil War (today the Hagley Museum and grounds). There is no universal design style to the property, as housing was added over time to coincide with the extension of the railroads and the changing labor demands of the area economy. A mix of local stone, wood, and stucco fill out the cottage buildings, with all rooms modernized and outfitted with cable television, wet bars, and marble bathrooms. Suites are especially nice. Guest registration is in a mid-19th-century barn with a cavernous gathering room where you can enjoy a nightcap from the self-service bar or play a game of backgammon. The inn was named best hotel in the world under $250 by *Travel & Leisure* in 2006, earning it some well-deserved exposure for its quality and value. A new day spa should be open by press time.

Hotels and Larger Inns

Brandywine Valley hotels are clustered mostly in downtown Wilmington and along part of US 202 in northern Delaware. Smaller national chain hotels in the West Chester and Kennett Square areas are referenced under "Value Choices."

Brandywine Suites Hotel

1-800-756-0070
www.brandywinesuites.com
707 N. King St., Wilmington, DE 19801
Price: Moderate to expensive
Credit Cards: Yes

The hotel is a little worn down, but the suites are big and the value is tough to beat.

Not much more than $100 per night gets you two rooms, with a pair of televisions, spacious sitting area, and a marble shower near the Historical Society of Delaware in downtown Wilmington. A skylight makes the lobby a bright, convivial space, and Squires Pub downstairs lends this sleepy part of the city a little excitement.

Doubletree Hotel Downtown Wilmington

302-655-0400
www.doubletree.com
700 N. King St., Wilmington, DE 19801
Price: Moderate to expensive
Credit Cards: Yes

A fine, often affordable choice in downtown Wilmington. While the location is within walking distance of downtown's major attractions, there are few amenities within a two- or three-block radius. Fortunately, the hotel is well equipped with

The Doubletree Wilmington on US 202

a small fitness center, indoor pool, full-service restaurant, and room service. Doubletree's signature warm cookies at check-in are always a nice touch.

Doubletree Hotel Wilmington
302-478-6000
www.doubletree.com
4727 Concord Pike, Wilmington, DE 19803
Price: Moderate to expensive
Credit Cards: Yes
Handicapped Access: Yes

This recently renovated 244-room Doubletree is a bit more architecturally flashy than her cousin downtown. The brick exterior is capped with white cornice moldings. Rooms are modern, taupe colored, and fitted with flat-screen televisions. The hotel's location on Concord Pike (US 202) makes it a better choice for travelers interested in visiting north Delaware's traditional Brandywine attractions rather than center city Wilmington. Book a suite and receive a complimentary breakfast buffet at Palette's, the on-site restaurant.

Hotel du Pont
1-800-441-9019
www.hoteldupont.com
11th and Market Sts., Wilmington, DE 19801
Price: Very expensive
Credit Cards: Yes

Downtown Wilmington does not get any better than this beautiful Renaissance-style hotel, constructed in 1913 at the behest of Pierre S. du Pont, who also gave the Brandywine Valley its beloved Longwood Gardens. The refurbished guest rooms are outfitted with modern amenities but preserve the elegance that has enticed a long list of actors, politicians, and other celebrities into spending the night throughout 96 years in existence. Highlights include deep soaking tubs in the bathrooms and 24-hour room service. Afternoon tea is taken daily in the Lobby Lounge. The hotel's Green Room restaurant serves a renowned Sunday brunch under a gold leaf ceiling supported by gorgeous wood-panel walls. Lucky brides and grooms tie the knot in the opulent Gold Ballroom. The hotel is attached to the DuPont Theatre, and is located near Rodney Square and the Public Library.

Value Choices
Best Western Concordville (610-358-9400; www.bestwestern.com; US 322 and US 1, Concordville, PA 19331). Concordville stands at the intersection of two major Brandywine roads, 5 miles east of Chadds Ford. It is marked by a large, spiffy shopping center and this 115-room hotel and conference facility.

Comfort Inn & Suites Brandywine Valley (610-399-4600; www.comfortatbrandywine.com; 1310 Wilmington Pike, West Chester, PA 19382). Seventy-five guest rooms on three floors, including some good-sized junior suites.

Holiday Inn West Chester (610-692-1900; www.hiwestchester.com; 943 S. High St., West Chester, PA 19382). Located just outside the heart of downtown West Chester. The 141 rooms are small but functional, with free high-speed Internet service, coffee makers, and a fair amount of workspace. Rates tend to jump a little during the week of commencement at nearby West Chester University, but are otherwise consistent.

Hilton Garden Inn Kennett Square (610-444-9100; www.hiltongardeninn.com; 815 E. Baltimore Pike, Kennett Square, PA 19348). Ninety-two guest rooms with workspace and indoor pool, very close to Longwood Gardens.

Inn at Wilmington (302-479-7900; www.innatwilmington.com; 300 Rocky Run Pkwy., Wilmington, DE 19803). A recently renovated 71-room hotel on Concord Pike.

CULTURE

Architecture

Most of the Swedish log cabins decomposed a long time ago, but more durable Brandywine architecture dating back to the colonial period survives. Especially notable are the stone country houses built by English settlers in the early 18th century that dot the landscape near Chadds Ford and other rural areas beyond the valley's main towns. Local fieldstone was a useful (if unwieldy) building material, and it quickly became the foremost ingredient in the area's architecture. As quarrying techniques grew more sophisticated and the inhabitants better oriented to the land, the variety and complexity of stone construction grew. Surviving houses are made from materials like darkish Brandywine blue granite—a native rock so famous it inspired the name of the Wilmington Blue Rocks minor league baseball team (see "Recreation"). The John Chads House, profiled below, is partly made from Brandywine blue, as is the Pennsbury Inn above (see "Lodging"). For those interested in the particulars of the region's stone construction, the bible on the subject is *Stone Houses: Traditional Homes of Pennsylvania's Bucks County and Brandywine Valley,* by Margaret Bye Richie, John D. Milner, and Gregory D. Huber, with beautiful photographs by Geoffrey Gross.

Brandywine Battlefield State Park

610-459-3342
www.ushistory.org/brandywine
US 1, Chadds Ford, PA 19137
Open: Tues.–Sat. 9–5, Sun. 12–5; in winter, Thurs.–Sat. 9–5 and Sat. 12–5
Admission: Park is free, tours are $5

The September 11, 1777 Battle of Brandywine was a major setback for the Americans, forcing the Revolutionary Army into retreat and presaging a more lopsided defeat at Paoli 10 days later. General Washington's ineffectiveness at countering the British attack has led some to suspect traitorous activity; it is surely true that the prosperous and contented Brandywine farmers had more than a few Loyalists among their ranks.

The day began with General Washington positioned just east of Brandywine Creek near Chadds Ford. His army was met by General Howe's troops, which came from Kennett Square in the west. What Washington did not know was that Howe had split his army into two groups, and directed Lord Cornwallis to march 7,500 troops across the river north of Chadds Ford. Cornwallis caught Washington by surprise and the Americans suffered hundreds of casualties. The area's densely wooded terrain and the foggy weather that day made Howe's flanking movement easier to execute successfully.

The Brandywine Battlefield State Park was established in 1961 to mark this history. The battle itself was fought over a 10-square-mile area. Much combat took place at Sandy Hollow, which became a municipal park in 1949, but the state park on US 1 is the best place to start touring. The park's visitor's center screens a film on the battle and the history of the Revolution. American and British military equipment are on display, including some items excavated from Valley Forge and the Brandywine battlefield itself.

After you've seen the visitor's center, Washington's headquarters at the reconstructed Benjamin Ring House, and the nearby Gideon Gilpin House (talk to the park staff at the visitor's center to arrange tours), you can either wander the park grounds or purchase a driving tour map for $1.75. It will direct you to 28 sites around Chadds Ford that played a

Valley Forge

It was looking mighty bleak for General Washington and the Continental Army in the fall of 1777. The rebel army had been pummeled all over the Delaware Valley, losing successive battles at Chadds Ford, Paoli, and Germantown and surrendering Fort Mifflin after a six-week struggle. And so it was with an air of desperation that Washington led his 12,000 men to Valley Forge to camp for the winter. The site—15 miles northeast of West Chester and the Brandywine Valley—was a natural fortification. Its distance from British-occupied Philadelphia and its high altitude made it difficult to attack. The red-coats stayed away and the army emerged from the winter encampment a more professional, more prepared fighting force.

A reconstructed log hut at the Muhlenberg Brigade encampment

As part of the Bicentennial celebration, the rolling fields and forest became **Valley Forge National Historical Park** (610-783-1077; www.nps.gov/vafo; 1400 N. Outer Line Drive, King of Prussia), a 3,466-acre space that combines educational and recreational tourism. Few remnants of the legendary winter remain, but reconstructed log huts throughout the park signify the living quarters that Washington's men constructed for themselves. Look for a cluster along North Outer Line Drive at the Muhlenberg Brigade encampment, or near Washington's Headquarters on the west side. Other highlights include the Henry Knox Covered Bridge, the cannons at Artillery Park, and Washington Memorial Chapel: a Gothic Revival structure and an active church. The park is open year-round, but is most heavily visited during the summer when special events and themed tours shake things up.

Begin at the remodeled Visitor's Center. Displays track the area's Revolutionary-era history and exhumed artifacts bring it to life. There's an 18-minute video overview of the site's importance in the adjacent theater. You can also buy an audio driving tour for $15. The CD has an hour's worth of material and guides you through 10 major park sites, expounding on their historical import and helpfully recommending caution at busy intersections.

For all its educational merit, the park works even better as a recreational space. While the area is surrounded by Philadelphia's rapidly growing exurbs, the park itself is wooded and withdrawn. White-tailed deer are everywhere (to the point of problematic overpopulation). Paved and unpaved bike trails are carefully laid out, weaving riders through both the educational attractions and natural scenery. You can rent a bicycle from a vendor in the Visitor's Center parking lot for $10 an hour, with discounts for children and package pricing for families. There are also three designated picnicking areas.

role in the battle or its aftermath. The Birmingham Meeting House, still actively attended by area Quakers, was used as a hospital around the time of the war and maintains a large cemetery. The map will also guide you to the 1714 Barns-Brinton House (a colonial-era tavern), General Howe's headquarters, and many other sites. An entire driving tour takes at least an hour but can be trimmed.

Film

Theater N at Nemours (302-571-4699; 1007 Orange St., Wilmington, DE). Screens independent films in downtown Wilmington.

Galleries

Wander blindfolded around Chadds Ford or Kennett Square long enough and you'll walk into a Wyeth print. The region's artists tend to follow the Wyeth aesthetic, so local galleries are rich with landscape paintings and realist art.

Artworks Fine Arts & Crafts Gallery (610-444-6544; 126 S. Union St., Kennett Square). Mostly local artists' originals and prints, with diverse interpretations and variations on the Brandywine School.

Blue Ball Barn (302-577-1164; 1914 West Park Dr., Wilmington, DE). Open daily in Alapocas Run State Park, this converted dairy barn houses a compilation of Delaware folk art. The ground level also delves into the site's history and the finer points of dairy farming.

Chadds Ford Gallery (610-459-5510; www.awyethgallery.com; 1609 Baltimore Pike, Chadds Ford). A good place to go for Wyeth reproductions from all three generations, plus other realist work.

Longwood Gallery (610-444-0146; 200 E. State St., Kennett Square). Multifaceted gallery of regional paintings and a Kennett Square art institution.

Strodes Mill Gallery and Framing (610-429-9093; 1000 Lenape Rd., West Chester). Many local originals in this onetime mill and cider press. Strodes also does framing for the Brandywine River Museum and the Wyeths.

Gardens

Longwood Gardens
610-388-1000
www.longwoodgardens.org
US 1, Kennett Square, PA 19348
Open: Daily Apr.–Oct. 9–6, Nov.–Mar. 9–5
Admission: Adults $16, seniors $14, students $6, children 4 and under free

Folks come to the Brandywine Valley just to visit Longwood Gardens, and it does not take long to see why. Famed industrialist Pierre S. du Pont bought the land (at one time owned by William Penn) in 1906 and spent much of the remainder of his life transforming the grounds into the thousand-acre botanical wonderland it is today. There is much to see, so plan on spending the better part of a day. The Italian water garden is a perennial favorite, as is the magnificently designed Conservatory. Longwood is open year-round and there is almost always something going on, including concerts, tours, barbeques, fireworks, theatrical performances, and illuminated water shows at the Main Fountain Garden, so be sure to call or check the Web site for a calendar of events. The gardens are a surprisingly good family attraction, particularly with a new children's garden now open. Food and beverages are available, but canny visitors will bring along a bottle of water, along with comfortable walking shoes.

Marian Coffin Gardens at Gibraltar

302-651-9617
www.preservationde.org/gibraltar
garden@perservationde.org
1405 Greenhill Ave., Wilmington, DE
19806
Open: Daily 9–5
Admission: Free

Sculpture enlivens the Marian Coffin Gardens at Gibraltar.

Anyone who appreciates urban oases will fall in love with this Renaissance-style garden on the edge of Wilmington. The magnificently integrated flora and sculpture occupy 6 acres and adjoin the Gibraltar Mansion, which Hugh and Isabella Mathieu du Pont Sharp acquired in 1909. The couple asked landscape architect Marian Coffin to design the garden, which was restored and opened to the public 10 years ago. The pathways are made of Gibraltar rock, which is prevalent in the area and for which the house is named. Much of the limestone sculpture and assorted marble comes from Italy, where the Sharps vacationed often and acquired their taste for formal gardens. The grounds feature an especially unique collection of old trees, interspersed with roses, African lilies, a reflecting pool, and more.

Historic Homes and Sites

Barns-Brinton House

610-388-7376
www.chaddsfordhistory.org/houses/brinton.htm
info@chaddsfordhistory.org
US 1, a mile north of PA 52, Chadds Ford, PA 19317
Open: May–Sept. 12–5, weekends only
Admission: Adults $5 including John Chads House, children $2

An old Chadds Ford tavern that dates back to 1714, the Barns-Brinton House was a rest stop along what is today US 1. Blacksmith William Barns had the house constructed, but in 1753 it was acquired by James Brinton—grandson to a Brandywine Valley settler who purchased a great deal of property in the area. It is an exquisite brick edifice that features Flemish bonding, with a unique pent roof above the ground level that stretches around nearly the entire house.

John Chads House

610-388-7376
www.chaddsfordhistory.org/houses/chads.htm
info@chaddsfordhistory.org
PA 100, by the Chadds Ford Historical Society, Chadds Ford, PA 19317

Open: May–Sept., 12–5, weekends only
Admission: Adults $5 including Barns-Brinton House, children $2

A modest bank house built into a small hill with bluestone, this residence belonged to Quaker farmer and ferryman John Chads. His is the name behind the founding of Chadds Ford—the extra "d" added some years later. Note the large beehive oven and walk-in fireplace in the basement kitchen. There is no parking on the site, but visitors can use the lot across the street at the Chadds Ford Historical Society.

Nemours Mansion and Gardens

302-651-6912
www.nemoursmansion.org
1600 Rockland Rd., Wilmington, DE 19803
Open: May–Oct., tours Tues.–Sat. at 9, 11, 1, and 3; tours Sun. at 11, 1, and 3
Admission: $15

A bona fide gem and a Brandywine Valley must-see. Nemours is the 77-room, 47,000-square-foot, five-story French Neoclassical mansion and gardens that Alfred I. duPont built in an attempt to win the love of his second wife, Alecia Maddox duPont. It was completed in 1910 after just a year and half spent on construction—a feat nearly as remarkable as the grounds themselves. A $38 million restoration was finished in May 2008, and the home is again open for public tours. The mansion's style and furnishings are opulent beyond belief. It's an eclectic opulence, though. You'll find English furniture, French chandeliers, American art, Chinese porcelain, ivory birds, cast iron coat hooks, and much more. The vista from the mansion to the reflecting pool was inspired by Le Petit Trianon at the Palace of Versailles. Connections to the Du Ponts' native France are everywhere. (Nemours was the French town where Pierre S. du Pont had lived.) Marie Antoinette's incredible musical clock is just one highlight. Alfred was also an innovator—he registered two hundred patents during his lifetime—so the mansion is suffused with high-tech gadgets of the early 20th century. The heating and ice-making systems on the ground floor are especially impressive. Alfred also developed a water purification system for bottled drinking water that was decades ahead of its time. He thought of everything—soft cork flooring in the billiards room and kitchen to keep feet relaxed and overnight accommodations for visiting chauffeurs. Tours are expertly guided, two hours long, and include a video presentation on Alfred's alternately triumphant and tragic life. Visitors have the option to linger in the garden for 45 minutes after the house tour before the shuttle bus picks them up. If the weather is at all accommodating, be sure to stay. Call ahead at least two weeks in advance to make a tour reservation.

Rockwood Mansion Park

302-761-4340
www.rockwood.org
rockwoodpark@nccde.org
610 Shipley Rd., Wilmington, DE 19809
Open: Wed.–Sun. 10–3, with tours on the hour; gardens open daily
Admission: Adults $5, children $2

Perfect for a picnic or a morning stroll, Rockwood Park is also the former home of Joseph Shipley, a wealthy English Quaker who acquired gout and relocated to this specially designed late-19th-century mansion in north Wilmington. Shipley, a lifelong bachelor, shared the residence with the Bringhurst Family who eventually had the property deeded to New Castle County, Delaware. The 40-minute house tour re-creates the life lived by Shipley and the Bringhursts. While some rooms contain reproductions, many accoutrements are real, such as bookshelves stocked with Shipley's original volumes. The ground floor has three beautiful Victorian parlor rooms where guests can take afternoon tea (parties of 10–30 only, $18 per person—call in advance to reserve).

Libraries
Wilmington Public Library
302-571-7400
www.wilmlib.org
wilmweb@lib.de.us
10 E. 10th St., Wilmington, DE 19801
Open: Mon.–Thurs. 9–8, Fri. and Sat. 9–5

A proud Wilmington institution since its 1922 completion, the library stands regally on the south side of Rodney Square in the heart of downtown. Edward Lippincott Tilton's Beaux-Arts structure attracts attention for its poised ionic columns and ornamentation. The library's collections are extensive, and there's a used book sale on the ground level.

Museums
American Helicopter Museum and Education Center
610-436-9600
www.helicoptermuseum.org
info@helicoptermusuem.org
1220 American Blvd., West Chester, PA 19380
Open: Wed.–Sat. 10–5, Sun. 12–5
Admission: Adults $6, seniors $5, children and students $4

This nifty little museum is a good choice for kids, who love sitting in the cockpits of the various military and transport helicopters on display. A favorite exhibit is the vertiport model, which imagines a future of helicopter travel integrated into America's transportation network. Then there are the Ospreys, the Bells, and the Sikorskys, all the way back to the single-bladed Chinese propeller toy. There is also a small theater, where volunteers assist visitors in selecting film presentations. The museum is looking to expand, which would allow for more and larger displays, but it is still worth a visit at the current size.

Brandywine River Museum
610-388-2700
www.brandywinemuseum.org
inquires@brandywine.org
US 1 and PA 100, Chadds Ford, PA 19317
Open: Daily 9:30–4:30
Admission: Adults $10, seniors, students, and children $6; additional $5 charge for house and studio and farm tours

This riverside museum houses the art of the Wyeths—the three generations of Chadds Ford painters whose work gives the Brandywine its artistic identity. N. C. Wyeth, the elder, got his break illustrating the first edition of Robert Louis Stevenson's *Treasure Island,* and many of these colorful illustrations are on display here. His son Andrew's watercolor land-scapes and egg tempera paintings capture both the lushness and the intimacy of the valley. Don't miss the American Illustration exhibit on the second floor with rotating works from Howard Pyle, or Jamie Wyeth's beloved animal portraits. The museum itself is part of the attraction. It was adapted from a grist mill and outfitted with floor-to-ceiling windows overlooking the Brandywine River and bringing in a great deal of natural light. If there's time, take the N. C. Wyeth house and studio tour, to see where the Brandywine's artistic heritage began. You can also tour nearby Kuerner Farm, which motivated Andrew's style. Both tours leave via shuttle bus from the museum.

Chester County Historical Society

610-692-4800
www.cchs-pa.org
cchs@chestercohistorical.org
225 N. High St., West Chester, PA 19380
Open: Wed.–Sat. 10–5
Admission: Adults $5, seniors $4, students and children $2.50

Chester County is rightly proud of its history as a sanctuary for tolerance and innovation, and this museum in downtown West Chester illustrates the tradition well. There are five main gallery rooms, with the permanent exhibits on the second floor. These galleries highlight the contribution of immigrants to Chester's early communities and the founding of Lincoln University, America's first historically black institution of higher learning. There is also a tribute to Chester County's prolific clockmakers, and a children's history lab where kids can try on Victorian-era garb and inspect early American tools. First-floor exhibits are temporary and sometimes feature Brandywine Valley artists. The on-site library is a separate admission fee ($5) and is useful for tracking Chester County lineages.

Christian C. Sanderson Museum

610-388-6545
www.sandersonmuseum.org
1755 Creek Rd., Chadds Ford, PA 19137
Open: Mar.–Nov., Sat. and Sun. 1–4:30
Admission: Free

Until his death in 1966, Christian Sanderson was a Chadds Ford bon vivant: teacher, histo-rian, musician, radio commentator, friend to the Wyeth family, and most of all collector. Sanderson began collecting at 10 years old and never stopped. The Sanderson Museum is his life's compilation of Americana, housed in his old residence just off US 1. There are some exceptional items inside, like a piece of the bandage set on Abraham Lincoln just after he was shot, artifacts dug up from the Brandywine Battlefield, and the only pastel Andrew Wyeth ever produced. But the greatest pieces are in fact the "ordinary" items that Sanderson left behind: correspondence from friends, students' report cards, music posters, etc. It is these seemingly mundane objects that tell Sanderson's tale and give life to the American history written throughout his 84 years. To appreciate the collection requires more than a single afternoon's visit.

Delaware Art Museum

302-571-9590
www.delart.org
info@delart.org
2301 Kentmere Pkwy., Wilmington, DE 19806
Open: Wed.–Sat. 10–4, Sun. 12–4
Admission: Adults $12, seniors $10, students $6

Seventeen galleries of carefully chosen American art are housed in this recently renovated and beautifully designed museum. There is a bit of overlap with the Brandywine River Museum, as both incorporate a great deal of regionally significant American Illustration, but the Delaware takes more risks. John Sloan's realist cityscapes are alternately stimulating and haunting. The exhibition on American art mingles abstract expressionist painting with sculpture and photography. And spend some time exploring the Copeland Sculpture Garden, which wraps around the main parking lot. The Delaware Art Museum has also taken steps to make touring interactive. Visitors can stop at one of two computers on the main floor and create their own stories involving the museum's collections. This can be especially fun for kids, who also get their own interactive gallery on the lower level.

Delaware Center for the Contemporary Arts

302-658-6466
www.thedcca.org
info@thedcca.org
200 S. Madison St., Wilmington, DE 19801
Open: Tues., Thurs.–Sat. 10–5, Wed. and Sun. 12–5
Admission: Free

The Delaware Art Museum

This contemporary gallery with changing exhibits is large enough to be considered a museum and attractive enough to host weddings. The Center, founded in 1979, has been in this 35,000-square-foot building near the Christina River for more than eight years, predating much of Wilmington's riverfront redevelopment. The space was once a factory and later a warehouse, and the Center benefits from high ceilings that allow for dramatic installations. It certainly works well for large sculpture exhibitions, but the breadth of art on display at any given time—around 30 exhibits a year—usually includes paintings, sketches, and other mediums.

Delaware History Museum
302-656-7161
www.dehistory.org
deinfo@dehistory.org
504 Market St., Wilmington, DE 19801
Open: Tues.–Fri. 11–4, Sat. 10–4
Admission: Adults $4; seniors, students, and military $3; children $2

Converted from an old Woolworth Store, this museum is a sweeping trip across Delaware's role in history, beginning with the Lenape Indians and the state's contributions to the American Revolution. The thoroughness is impressive—there are even displays on the poultry industry and Delaware's niche as an inexpensive place to incorporate. It also makes a significant effort to appeal to kids. A rotating exhibit in the museum's front section changes a couple times a year. The museum is managed by the Delaware Historical Society, which is headquartered across the street at **Willingtown Square** (302-655-7161; 500 block of Market St.). The square's four Colonial and Federal period buildings are not open to visitors, but you can see them from the courtyard and drop by the society's excellent library.

Delaware Museum of Natural History
302-658-9111
www.delmnh.org
4840 Kennett Pike (DE 52, just south of Winterthur), Wilmington, DE 19807
Open: Mon.–Sat. 9:30–4:30, Sun. 12–4:30
Admission: Adults $6, children $5, seniors $4

A single-story interactive natural history museum featuring dinosaur bones, a giant squid, stuffed mammals, and one of the country's most extensive shell and mollusk collections. Don't miss the giant African snail exhibit, which charts how the pesky, crop-destroying species made its way from Madagascar to the United States. Leave time for the bird egg collection and the Discovery Room for children. An auditorium and central gallery offer temporary exhibits.

Delaware Sports Museum and Hall of Fame
302-425-3263
www.desports.org
info@desports.org
801 Shipyard Dr., Wilmington, DE 19801
Open: Apr.–Oct., Tues.–Sat. 12–5
Admission: Adults $4, seniors $3, children $2

Attached to Wilmington's minor league baseball stadium, this meticulously organized museum makes a good companion to an afternoon game or visit to the waterfront. There is a 12-minute presentation on Delaware sports history, followed by the main exhibition room, which presents the region's sports history starting with Lenape lacrosse. There is also a special exhibit on Judy Johnson, star third basemen in the Negro Leagues, and eventual Hall of Fame inductee. The museum's own hall of fame has 262 (and counting) members—all Delawareans who played, coached, wrote, or attained some other success in the sports world.

Hagley Museum and Library

302-658-2400
www.hagley.org
info@hagley.org
DE 141 between DE 100 and US 202, Wilmington, DE 19807
Open: Daily mid-Mar.–Dec. 9:30–4:30, Jan–mid-Mar. 9:30–4:30 Sat.–Sun., plus one tour at 1:30 weekdays
Admission: Adults $11, students $9, children $4

The Hagley Museum tracks the American story of Delaware's illustrious du Ponts, who began producing black gunpowder on these 235 acres in 1802. Small buses shuttle visitors to the main attractions, like E. I. du Pont's Eleutherian Mills, a Georgian residence that serves as a window into the lives of the du Ponts who lived and worked here. The house tour is comprehensive, but too long to interest young children, who are generally much happier watching gunpowder demonstrations in the Powder Yard. The Explosives Era display tells the story of E. I.'s canny business sense and early gunpowder production. Attractions are well executed, with great attention to detail, like the educational and interactive Science and Discovery exhibit that follows the corporation's evolution into materials science development. You will also find a tremendous research library focused on the history of American business, and a good restaurant. Bring sneakers if you intend to walk the grounds.

QVC Studio Park

1-800-600-9900
www.qvctours.com
studiopark@qvc.com
1200 Wilson Dr., West Chester, PA 19380
Open: Daily, tours at 10:30, 12, 1, 2:30 an 4
Admission: Adults $7.50, children $5

QVC has been broadcasting from West Chester since its founding over 20 years ago, and what started as a single host hawking shower radios for $11.25 has morphed into a billion-dollar, international business with a half-dozen distribution centers. The comprehensive tour starts with a video of QVC's pilot show, and ends with a bird's-eye view of the live broadcast. (QVC is on air live 24 hours a day, seven days a week except Christmas Day.) You'll also see how the company weeds out inferior products, learn how much dry ice the company uses to ship its perishables, and have a look at the bustling production room. True home shopping fans should call ahead to reserve a space as part of a studio audience; these shows are not shot every day, but audience members are often seen on air and are occasionally offered free samples. For a vaguely surreal experience, browse the studio store on the way out: It may be your only chance to buy a QVC product from outside the comfort of your own home.

Winterthur
302-888-4600 or 1-800-448-3883
www.winterthur.org
tourinfo@winterthur.org
DE 52, 5105 Kennett Pike, Wilmington, DE 19735
Open: Tues.–Sun. 10–5
Admission: Adults $20, seniors and students $18, children $10 for the grounds, exhibitions, and one-house tour

Perhaps the grandest of all the du Pont bequests to the Brandywine Valley, Winterthur was the sprawling estate of the late Henry Francis du Pont. The centerpiece is the 9-floor, 175-room manse, where you'll find the Montmorenci staircase transplanted from North Carolina, du Pont's Chinese Parlor with original 18th-century Chinese wallpaper, and countless pieces of 18th- and 19th-century Americana. Winterthur's enthusiastic staff changes the decoration of the house by season to give a taste of what it was like to live like a du Pont. Many house tours are themed based on season as well. The museum galleries display more furniture, dishware, and tools, which are mostly (but not entirely) American. At the soup tureen collection, look for a small exhibit detailing how Winterthur scientists and curators disproved the date of origin of what was thought to be an 18th-century German piece. And take time out to explore the estate's rolling gardens—you can opt for a narrated train tour, but the grounds are idyllic and best explored by foot. Young kids, who are barred from most house tours, love Enchanted Woods, a clever playground garden complete with fairy tale. There is so much to see here that admission tickets are good for two days. Take advantage and make your visit leisurely.

Music, Dance, and Theater
DuPont Theatre (1-800-338-0881; www.duponttheatre.com; 1007 N. Market St., Wilmington, DE). Top-notch performances of Broadway hits and assorted children's theater in this landmark showroom within the Hotel DuPont. Major shows tend to come for weeklong or extended weekend runs, so check the Web site to see what's in town. The first few rows of the center mezzanine are a good place to be.

Grand Opera House (302-652-5577; www.grandopera.org; 818 N. Market St., Wilmington, DE). Grand is the perfect word to describe this Second Empire–style building (once a Masons lodge) with adjacent proscenium. It is home to the Delaware Symphony, Opera Delaware, and First State Ballet Theatre, and is a regular venue for musical headliners.

Seasonal Events
Chadds Ford Days
610-388-7376
1736 N. Creek Rd., Chadds Ford
Time: Early September

The essential Chadds Ford event, commemorating the Battle of Brandywine and offering crafts and antique vendors the opportunity to sell their merchandise in the late summer sun. Crafts demonstrations, executed by folks in colonial dress, include trades like needlework and papermaking. The event is sponsored by the **Chadds Ford Historical Society** (www.chaddsfordhistory.org) and takes place at the grounds of the society's visitor center. Admission is free.

Kennett Square Mushroom Festival
610-925-3373
www.mushroomfestival.org
Kennett Square
Time: Early September

Everything a mushroom festival should be, from the mushroom soup cook-off to the mushroom judging contest. The annual event attracts over 100,000 attendees on the weekend after Labor Day to celebrate Kennett's history and its prized crop. There are also vendors, art demonstrations, and a car show. A modest admission fee is charged. The Mushroom Festival is held on the same weekend as Chadds Ford Days,

Delicious large cap mushrooms from Kennett Square

thus stoking the tacit rivalry between the Brandywine towns that simmers beneath the surface most of the year. Chadds Ford residents like to note that their event has been going on longer than the Mushroom Festival. They say it in a lighthearted way, but you can tell that deep down they're a little upset.

RESTAURANTS AND FOOD PURVEYORS

Dining in the Brandywine Valley has improved dramatically in recent years. Part of the pleasure is that many of the region's best restaurants allow patrons to bring their own alcohol; a good play is to visit some of the valley's wineries at the start of your trip and then bring along a bottle or two for dinner. These BYOB restaurants will open your wine and provide glasses either free of charge or for a small corkage fee.

Of the Brandywine Valley towns, West Chester has the superior restaurant scene. It boasts a healthy mix of gourmet continental fare and moderately priced taverns and bistros. Ethnic food has never been the Brandywine's strength, but West Chester's varied Japanese, Indian, and Italian restaurants—many of which opened recently—challenge that conventional wisdom. Kennett Square is also a good eating town, with restaurants incorporating area ingredients like the mushroom crop and locally raised game. Chadds Ford has fewer restaurants than the other towns of the Brandywine Valley, but a couple true standouts. The only disappointment is Wilmington, which lacks the diversity in fare that one hopes for—nay, expects—in a 72,000-person city. There are signs that this might be changing. The riverfront renewal aims to make Wilmington more of a destination city. If successful, it will undoubtedly draw new restaurateurs.

Dining Price Code

Inexpensive	Up to $15
Moderate	$15 to $30
Expensive	$30 to $50
Very Expensive	$50 or more

Chadds Ford and Vicinity

The Gables at Chadds Ford

610-388-7700
www.thegablesatchaddsford.com
423 Baltimore Pike, Chadds Ford, PA 19137
Open: Daily
Price: Expensive
Credit Cards: Yes
Cuisine: Continental, French
Serving: L (Mon.–Fri.), D
Handicapped Access: Yes

A converted dairy barn with a history that dates back to the earliest European presence in the Brandywine Valley, The Gables has become Exhibit A in the case for a newer, hipper Chadds Ford. A piano in the bar area hints at the lively evening ambiance, and you'll find contemporary dishes like tuna with udon noodles and a unique mushroom lasagna alongside classics like duck confit. A rustic look survives in the form of wood plank floorboards, exposed brick, and a hay pulley. Food is New American with French twists here and there; seafood dishes have proven reliable at both lunch and dinner. The wine list is extensive, including nine bottles under $25. Most dinner entrées come in "petite" portions, but regular-sized entrées aren't overwhelming. There are two levels of dining, plus an outdoor terrace where beads of water drip discreetly through the crevices of a rock wall.

Hank's Place

610-388-7061
US 1 and PA 100, Chadds Ford, PA 19317
Open: Daily
Price: Inexpensive
Credit Cards: Cash only
Cuisine: American
Serving: B, L, D (Tues.–Sat.; closes at 7 P.M.)
Handicapped Access: Yes

Good, hearty food, priced right and perfectly located. Hank's has been a Chadds Ford institution for a good long while, but the acclaim has not interfered with the restaurant's high quality and reasonable prices. The daily specials are usually the way to go, and the strawberry pie—served with a layer of cream cheese, a layer of sliced banana, and fresh strawberries—is as yummy as advertised. Sandwiches and burgers are consistently good, and there are few places in Brandywine to fill up for less. There may be a wait during prime breakfast and lunch hours.

Pace One, well worth the 10-minute drive from Chadds Ford

Pace One Restaurant and Country Inn

610-459-3702
www.paceone.net
341 Thornton Rd., Thornton, PA 19173, near Chadds Ford
Open: Daily
Price: Moderate to expensive
Credit Cards: Yes
Cuisine: New American
Serving: L (except Mon.), D, Sun. Brunch
Handicapped Access: Yes

This jewel of a restaurant is housed in a restored colonial barn with original stone walls, wooden floors, and hand-hewn ceiling beams. It's the best reason to visit Thornton, a small town about 5 miles northeast from Chadds Ford with the oldest continuously operational post office in the United States. While the country décor suggests unreconstructed comfort food, Pace One's menu is a great deal more ambitious. Call the cuisine New American for its willingness to give French, Italian, and Asian turns to old favorites, all prepared with dependable quality. Appetizers excel, so try a few starters at dinner—the mushroom bisque is a regional specialty, of course, and the powerfully flavored duck wontons are a rare treat. If at all possible, treat yourself to the Sunday brunch buffet and try not to fill up on waffles. The menu includes made-to-order omelets, smoked salmon, fresh fish, gourmet cheeses, New England pudding, and roasted turkey freshly carved from the breast with a thick honey, mustard, and rosemary glaze.

Kennett Square

Half Moon Restaurant and Saloon

610-444-7232
www.halfmoonrestaurant.com
108 W. State St., Kennett Square, PA 19348
Open: Mon.–Sat.
Price: Expensive
Credit Cards: Yes
Cuisine: American
Serving: L, D
Handicapped Access: Yes

With its unwavering faith in the gastronomical and nutritional virtues of wild game, Half Moon is that rare restaurant that lists the caloric content of emu, elk, and alligator on the menu. In addition to daily bison, look for specials like the rotating wild game hamburger—they say the boar is tops for juiciness, but an antelope burger is also quite tasty. The prevalence of game is both a refreshing culinary twist and a reminder of the Brandywine's proximity to rural Pennsylvania; Half Moon purchases its buffalo from a farm just 5 miles away in Unionville. Stick to local specialties and start with a peppery mushroom bisque or mushroom appetizer bathed in claret sauce. Half Moon is also great for drinks, offering Belgian, English, and German beers, plus a dozen "Moon-tinis" and a strong wine and tequila list. The main dining room, with mahogany trimmings and porcelain tile floors, is quite nice, but snag a table on the roof if you can. Rooftop diners are sheltered by a climate-controlled atrium during the colder months, with sliding windows that let in the spring and summer breeze. It is especially romantic at night.

Newton's on State Street

610-925-5055
www.newtonsonstatestreet.com
114 E. State St., Kennett Square, PA 19348
Open: Daily
Price: Inexpensive to moderate
Cuisine: American, pub fare
Serving: L, D, Sun. Brunch
Credit Cards: Yes
Handicapped Access: Yes

This large, bright Kennett Square pub and restaurant has quickly attained popularity with locals and families. The $6 lunch specials—including sandwich, soup, and salad combinations—are a bona fide bargain. An innovative dinner menu allows diners to combine an entrée with their choice of cooking style, sauce, and sides. With its bar sectioned off from the main dining room (the bar area can get smoky when busy), Newton's is also a great place for a quick drink. The wine list and beer selection are both extensive.

Sovana Bistro

610-444-5600
www.sovanabistro.com

696 Unionville Rd., Kennett Square, PA
19348
Open: Tues.–Sun.
Price: Moderate to expensive
Credit Cards: Yes
Cuisine: French, Italian
Serving: L (Tues.–Sat.), D
Handicapped Access: Yes

It is hard not to like this eclectic bistro a mile from downtown Kennett Square, owned and operated by gifted chef Nicholas Farrell, who launched the restaurant at just 23 years of age. The fusion of French and Italian cuisine is accompanied by a fusion in ambiance: a California mannered urban modernity (soft woods and temperate lighting) embellished by antique pieces sprinkled throughout. Cheeses are remarkable, whether spread on the pizzas and raviolis or served on their lonesome before dinner. The express lunch plate includes a half sandwich, soup du jour, and pile of salad alongside dessert: an inclusive taste of Sovana's menu. Organic ingredients are purchased locally whenever possible. After 10 years in business the restaurant has obtained its liquor license, and now serves seasonal cocktails and a hundred-bottle wine list. It remains BYOB with a $5 corkage fee.

Sinclair's Sunrise Café and Tearoom

610-444-8141
www.sunrisecafe-tearoom.com
127 E. State St., Kennett Square, PA 19348
Open: Daily
Price: Inexpensive
Credit Cards: Yes
Cuisine: American
Serving: B, L
Handicapped Access: Yes

The lavender walls display snapshots of the sun rising all over the globe—from Maine to Argentina—at this casual lunch and breakfast spot in downtown Kennett Square. Some breakfast customers are staying at Lynn Sinclair's nearby Sunrise Suites B&B, but you're just as likely to see local firefighters or attorneys scarfing down whole-grain buttermilk pancakes and fluffy omelets before the workday begins. The Sunrise specializes in deluxe teas, and you can reserve the private tearoom for afternoon parties with small sandwiches and desserts.

West Chester and Vicinity

Dilworthtown Inn

610-399-1390
www.dilworthtown.com
1390 Old Wilmington Pike, West Chester, PA 19382
Open: Daily
Price: Very expensive
Credit Cards: Yes
Cuisine: Continental
Serving: D
Handicapped Access: Yes

Without equal among Brandywine Valley restaurants, the Dilworthtown Inn is the kind of restaurant that will never go out of style. Its history dates back to 1754, when James Dilworth christened the village of Dilworthtown with a family home that soon became a tavern. The current incarnation has been open since 1972, and has been meticulously restored to resemble the original 18th-century property. There are 15 dining rooms with candlelit tables, all decorated in a warm Colonial style. The furnishings are consistent, but each room carries a unique intimacy—some accentuated by the placement of a fireplace and others by a particular piece of art. Menus change daily to keep the experience fresh, while classic preparations shine through. Caesar salads are prepared tableside by a skilled and attentive waitstaff (clad in black tie). The filet mignon, 2 inches thick at the very least, comes with a choice of rich sauces alongside vegetables and whipped potatoes. Opt for the "Chef's Duet" and have your filet joined by a South African lobster tail. Polite gasps monopolize the din at the sight of chateaubriand for two carved tableside. Dilworthtown is consistently recognized for its first-rate wine selection by *Wine Spectator*. Fans of the inn can take a gourmet cooking class nearby at the **Inn Keeper's Kitchen** (610-399-1390; 1390 Old Wilmington Pike).

Doc Magrogan's

610-429-4046
www.docmagrogans.com
117 E. Gay St., West Chester, PA 19380
Open: Daily
Price: Moderate to expensive
Credit Cards: Yes
Cuisine: Seafood
Serving: D
Handicapped Access: Yes

The place to go in West Chester for oysters, mussels, crab, lobster, and all ocean-dwelling delicacies, served late in a fun pub atmosphere. Doc Magrogan's earns plaudits for both dinner entrées and lower-priced sandwiches (the oyster po' boy is tops). The broiled stuffed shrimp comes loaded with crab and is a seafoodaholic's dream. They make a tasty filet mignon as well, served any of five ways. The waitstaff is among West Chester's friendliest, and the beer selection is great. Locals pack the place on Mondays for $1 oysters.

High Street Caffe

610-696-7435
www.highstreetcaffe.com
322 S. High St., West Chester, PA 19380
Open: Tues.–Sun.
Price: Moderate to expensive
Credit Cards: Yes
Cuisine: Cajun
Serving: L (Tues.–Fri.), D
Handicapped Access: Yes

There are now several excellent restaurants in West Chester, but the High Street Caffe

was among the first, and it remains the town's culinary pride. The litany of Cajun and Creole dishes are as flavorsome as they are filling. Start out with the peppery bisque du jour or gumbo, and don't be afraid to soak up the bowl with the house's homemade bread. Rotating dinner specials are unique, but classics like surf-and-turf scampi (with generous portions of shrimp and hanger steak) are expertly prepared as well. High Street now serves alcohol, but remains BYOB with a $5 corkage fee. Service is unfailingly friendly, and the small, pleasantly dark room works well for both couples and groups. Weekend jazz nights are a treat; make reservations if you want to dine before 9 P.M.

Iron Hill Brewery

610-738-9600
www.ironhillbrewery.com
3 W. Gay St., West Chester, PA 19380
Open: Daily
Price: Moderate
Credit Cards: Yes
Cuisine: American
Serving: L, D, Sun. Brunch
Handicapped Access: Yes

The delicious beers brewed on-site are not a surprise; what really impresses at Iron Hill is the quality of the food. Wood-oven pizza is great to share, as is the appetizer menu with fresh choices like buttermilk-fried calamari. You won't go wrong with salads or sandwiches either. Sunday brunch is popular and Sunday nights feature a prime-rib dinner. On nice days you'll want to sit outside by downtown West Chester's main intersection, but the cool wood-trimmed interior is cushy, especially if you're eating at one of the enormous booths. Nondrinkers should order foamy root beer, which is also brewed on the premises. The West Chester brewery is one of seven regional Iron Hills, including a location on the Wilmington waterfront.

Kooma

610-430-8980
www.koomarestaurant.com
151 W. Gay St., West Chester, PA 19380
Open: Daily
Price: Expensive
Credit Cards: Yes
Cuisine: Japanese fusion
Serving: L (Mon.–Fri.), D
Handicapped Access: Yes

The best sushi in the Brandywine, and also a hotspot on Friday and Saturday nights when sake sippers hang around until the late, great hours of the early morning. Its modernist dining room of burnished surfaces and nonfigurative polygons could not be more different than the dark pub look that characterizes many area restaurants. Sushi standards like yellowtail and spicy salmon are always well done, but the real fun is in the dozen specialty rolls. Kooma is also BYOB on Mondays. An expanded dining room should be completed by press time, which will help alleviate the occasional wait time for weekend seating.

Spence Café

610-738-8844
www.spencecaferestaurant.com
29-31 E. Gay St., West Chester, PA 19380
Open: Daily
Price: Expensive
Credit Cards: Yes
Cuisine: American, seafood
Serving: L (Mon.–Fri.), D
Handicapped Access: Yes
A classic West Chester restaurant that has skillfully adapted to the town's varied age demographics while maintaining its quiet

Inside Kooma

sophistication at lunch and dinner. Where else can you order a Macallan single malt Scotch followed by a bottle of Pabst Blue Ribbon? You will find pepper grinders on the tables and an L-shaped bar near the entrance, abutted by red walls with wood moldings. Spence promotes itself as a seafood haven—a large fish is suspended from the ceiling by the entrance—but steaks, pork, and fowl are all over the contemporary American menu as well. It is a business lunch hotspot on weekdays, serving entrée salads (the flat iron steak salad is a good choice) and sandwiches with waffle fries. Late at night Spence Café often transforms itself into a music venue; the reasonably priced, four-dozen-brand beer list is partly a nod to West Chester's college crowd, as are fun music events like Wednesday night reggae.

Trattoria Alberto

610-430-0203
116 E. Gay St., West Chester, PA 19380
Open: Mon.–Sat.
Price: Moderate to expensive
Credit Cards: Yes
Cuisine: Italian
Serving: L (weekdays only), D
Handicapped Access: Yes

Fresh Italian food served in a relaxed setting, with friendly West Chester service and a good wine list. There is much to choose from, so try sampling a few starters. Any pasta dish can be halved and served as an appetizer, typically prepared al dente. Also worth a look are the bruchetta and the delicately spiced beef carpaccio, either of which is perfect for splitting. There are always two or three excellent fish filet and shellfish specials. Main dining rooms are accented by murals of Tuscan farmland and porcelain dishware. Brick walls and blue shutters lend a different flavor to the secluded back room.

Charcoal Pit, famous for burgers

Wilmington and Vicinity
Charcoal Pit

302-478-2165
2600 Concord Pike, Wilmington, DE 19803
Open: Daily
Price: Inexpensive
Credit Cards: Yes
Cuisine: American
Serving: L, D
Handicapped Access: Yes

The thickest milkshakes in the Brandywine Valley and juicy, charcoal broiled hamburgers cooked to order that come in either quarter- or half-pound patties. The fries are good, but the onion rings are better, and the soup de jour is reliably excellent. A 1950s diner décor manages to be fun without going over the top; a few booths have jukeboxes. The Charcoal Pit is the Delaware Valley's only appearance in George Motz's seminal *Hamburger America: A State-by-State Guide to 100 Great Burger Joints.*

Krazy Kat's

302-888-4200
www.krazykatsrestaurant.com
DE 100 and Kirk Rd., Montchanin, DE 19710, at Montchanin Village
Open: Daily
Price: Expensive to very expensive
Credit Cards: Yes
Cuisine: Continental

Serving: B, L, D, Sun. Brunch
Handicapped Access: Yes

This well-regarded gourmet restaurant is a
romantic choice that serves a pleasingly
diverse New American menu with atten-
dant wines and Sunday brunch a la carte.
The dining room is formal but fun—tiger
print seating at the tables and portraits of
dogs and cats wearing military uniforms on
the walls. It is housed in an old brick and
stucco blacksmith's shop at the Inn at
Montchanin Village. Look for getaway
packages at the inn that include breakfast.

Krazy Kat's restaurant at Montchanin Village

Washington Street Ale House
302-658-2537
www.wsalehouse.com
1206 Washington St., Wilmington, DE
19801
Open: Daily
Price: Moderate to expensive
Credit Cards: Yes
Cuisine: American
Serving: L, D, Sun. Brunch
Handicapped Access: Yes

A dark pub with a wooden horseshoe bar, exposed brick walls, and votive cups of red and
white candles scattered throughout. The menu is high-quality pub fare with a few variations: unusually good salads for a bar/restaurant, and a satisfying chicken and waffles dinner entrée. There are over 20 beers on tap and numerous televisions broadcasting sports.
A separate section of the dining room is quieter and opens out onto the sidewalk, which is
nice at dinnertime after most of Wilmington has gone home. And don't say Washington
Street hasn't thought of everything; the men's room has a flat-screen television above the
sinks and complimentary mouthwash.

FOOD PURVEYORS

Bakeries
Country Bagel Bakery (610-696-8890; 145 E. Gay St., West Chester). Pretty good fresh
bagels. Also a location at 929 S. High Street.

Los Alondras (610-444-3966; 113 E. State St., Kennett Square). A Mexican bakery with
cases full of sweet treats, such as galletas (cookies), donuts, and other pastries.

Coffeehouses
eeffoc's (302-655-4959; www.eeffoccafe.com; Delaware Ave. and N. Clayton St.,

Wilmington). Baking is done on-site, and pastries go great with the excellent coffee and tea selection. Salads are huge. This is the Trolley Square location in downtown Wilmington, but there is another eeffoc's on the riverfront.

Harrington's Coffee Company (610-444-9992; 109 S. Broad St., Kennett Square). This handsome coffee shop and gift store resembles a colonial-era living room, with Windsor chairs and fireplace. You can purchase candles, mugs, and other decorative items. Good selection of Central and South American coffees.

Red Clay Cafe (610-388-2212; 880 Baltimore Pike, Chadds Ford). The hip coffee shop scene has finally come to Chadds Ford—Red Clay opened in spring 2008.

Presto! (302-777-3786; www.prestogourment.com; 1204 Washington St., Wilmington). The menu goes a lot farther than at most trendy coffeehouses, which is why Presto! bills itself as a coffee bar and bistro. Choose from half a dozen tasty omelet sandwiches at breakfast. Stays open through dinner.

Sprazzo (610-344-7435; www.sprazzocafe.com; 27 N. High St., West Chester). Best bet in West Chester for an espresso, but also for the phenomenal gelato, sorbetto, chocolate-covered pretzels, and many other treats.

Candy and Ice Cream

Éclat Chocolate (610-692-5206; 24 S. High St., West Chester). Arguably the best thing in

Sprazzo in downtown West Chester

West Chester. A superlative chocolate shop for mouth-watering caramels, truffles, and assortments.

La Michoacana Homemade Ice Cream (610-444-2996; 231 E. State St., Kennett Square). A small Mexican ice-cream shop with unique homemade flavors like rice pudding and avocado.

Gourmet Foods

Bistro to Go (610-388-8089; 1623 Baltimore Pike, Chadds Ford). Attached to the sleek **Bistro on the Brandywine** restaurant with a similar culinary sensibility. The French-influenced to-go menu includes sandwiches, salads, pizzas, and entrées. One of the few places to get food in Chadds Ford without committing to a sit-down meal.

Kennett Square Farmers Market (www.historickennettsquare.com/farmers). Area farmers come to downtown Kennett on Friday afternoons from mid-May through October. You'll find produce, meats, cheeses, jams, and much more. The market can be found in the downtown's center, near the State and Union Sts. intersection.

Talula's Table (610-444-8255; www.talulastable.com; 102 W. State St., Kennett Square). A gourmet food store to most, but a restaurant to a lucky few. Talula's is owned and operated by Aimee Olexy and Bryan Sikora, who sold their outstanding Philadelphia restaurant Django in 2005 to open Talula's in Kennett Square. There is a single pine table in the center of the store that seats 8–12 patrons for an evening tasting menu. The table is booked solid a year in advance; if you have your heart set on eating dinner here, call at 7 A.M. one year to the day before you intend to visit, and a spot could be yours. Otherwise, enjoy Talula's artisan cheeses, fresh breads, sandwiches, salads, and other takeaway food made from local ingredients during the store's 7 A.M. to 7 P.M. daily hours. There is some seating at the store and on the sidewalk out front, so an impromptu breakfast or lunch is possible. If you like the scenery at your B&B and it has a kitchen, take back a couple premade dinners, heat in the oven, and enjoy.

Pizza and Sandwiches

The Fresh Works (610-696-8474; 10 W. Market St., West Chester). Even the "half" size sandwich is huge at this downtown sandwich shop open until the early morning hours. The bacon-chicken cheesesteak is a favorite.

Jimmy John's Pipin' Hot Sandwiches (610-459-3083; 1507 Wilmington Pike, south of West Chester). See the electric train layouts around the shop and chow down on hot dogs, burgers, and other delightfully greasy comfort food.

RECREATION

Bicycling and Hiking

North of downtown Wilmington are two exquisitely designed and lovingly maintained state parks that together provide most every recreational opportunity imaginable in northern Delaware. They are **Bellevue State Park** (302-761-6963; 800 Carr Rd., Wilmington, DE) just off I-95 to the northeast of the city, and **Brandywine Creek State Park** (302-577-3534; 41 Adams Dam Rd., Greenville, DE), which is a larger, more densely wooded green

A quiet spot in the formal gardens at Bellevue State Park

space near Winterthur. Each carries an admission fee of $6 per car for out-of-state visitors and $3 per car for Delawareans. The fee is charged in season, which runs from March to the end of November.

Not only does Bellevue State Park offer good mountain biking, it provides the bikes for free. There are a dozen available for general use. Leave photo identification at the park office, and spend the day (8:30–4:30) exploring the 328-acre grounds. Trail markers show the way through the unpaved pathways of the nature preserve in the northern part of the park. The Northern Delaware Greenway Trail also has a paved stretch running through here that extends west to **Rockwood Park** (302-761-4340; 610 Shipley Rd., Wilmington, DE) where you can visit the Joseph Shipley estate (see "Historic Homes" above). This is a very good ride. A smart idea generally for designing a bike route in northern Delaware is to visit the **Delaware Greenways** Web site (www.delawaregreenways.org) and check the Northern Delaware Greenway map.

For hiking, it's hard to beat the trail variety at Brandywine Creek State Park. Three main trails are offered, each between 2 and 3 miles long. Be sure to pick up a detailed trail guide at the park office before you head out. Prepare to confront some taxingly vertical stretches and rapid drops as you wind around the park's 933 wooded acres. The Rocky Run Trail has an overall height of 300 feet, and is the trickiest to navigate (trailways can be rocky, as the name suggests). Less physically demanding are the walking paths at **Anson B. Nixon Park** (610-444-1416; N. Walnut St. near US 1, Kennett Square) in Pennsylvania. Nixon is an excellent multi-use park with a concert series in the summer.

Baseball

The **Wilmington Blue Rocks** are a Carolina League single-A affiliate of the Kansas City Royals. You can see them play at Judy Johnson Field in Daniel S. Frawley Stadium by the Wilmington waterfront (302-888-2015; www.bluerocks.com; 801 S. Madison St., Wilmington, DE).

Bird-Watching

Brandywine Creek State Park is the best place to bird-watch in the valley. **Hawkwatch Hill** on the park's southern end is a good place to start. Park staffers attest to numerous bald eagle and broad-winged hawk sightings from this area. Another option is to use the seating area in the Nature Center and Park Office building, outfitted with rocking chairs for optimal comfort. Carolina chickadees, red-bellied woodpeckers, and blue jays make frequent appearances, along with some hundred other species whose presence varies by season and is carefully tracked.

Canoeing and Tubing

There are a couple options for floating down the Brandywine if you don't have your own equipment. **Northbrook Canoe Company** (1-800-898-2279 or 610-793-2279; 1810 Beagle Rd., West Chester) is four hours upstream from Chadds Ford by boat, and rents canoes, kayaks, and inner tubes. If you're staying in Wilmington, try **Wilderness Canoe Trips** (302-654-2227; 2711 Concord Pike on US 202, Wilmington, DE); they will deposit you up the river so you can drift back down. If you own a canoe, either company can transport it for you for a fee. Pricing for canoe and tube trips varies by duration. A four-hour canoe trip is around $60–$70 per boat including transportation, with shorter and longer trips available. Tube rides cost in the neighborhood of $20 per tube for a two-hour trip. Make a reservation, especially for the weekend.

Also consider **Brandywine Outfitters** (610-486-6141; 2096 Strasburg Rd., Coatesville) which offers Brandywine River canoe and kayak trips that leave from farther upstream, a bit northwest of the valley.

Fishing

The pond at Bellevue State Park, encircled by a 1.25-mile fitness track (fun to walk or jog), is stocked with largemouth bass for catch-and-release. You do need a state-issued license to fish in Delaware, which costs $12.50 and can be purchased over the Internet (www.fw.delaware.gov). The Web site also lists places to pick up a license in person, of which there are a dozen in Wilmington. You may need a trout stamp (an extra $6.20) if you plan on trout fishing during designated periods. Trout can be found in the creek at Brandywine Creek State Park, along with smallmouth bass and bluegill.

Golf

Delcastle Golf Club (302-995-1990; 801 McKennan's Church Rd., Wilmington, DE). Par 72, 18 holes; 6,628 yards. Driving range and miniature golf. Fees: $21–$47.

Ed Oliver Golf Club (302-571-9041; 800 N. Dupont Rd., Wilmington, DE). Par 69, 18 holes; 6,125 yards. Driving range. Fees: $28–$48.

Loch Nairn Public Golf Course (610-268-2234; 514 Mccue Rd., Avondale). Par 70, 18 holes; 6,409 yards. Fees: $30–$54. This is a really good one, not impossible for high handicappers, but sporadically tricky for experienced golfers too.

Rock Manor Golf Course (302-295-1400; 1319 Carruthers Lane, Wilmington, DE). Par 71, 18 holes; 6,405 yards. Fees: $29–$65.

Horseback Riding

Brandywine scenery is ideally suited for touring on horseback. You can take a trail ride with **Gateway Stables** (610-444-1255; 949 Merrybell Lane, Kennett Square) even if you've never been riding before. Rates are $40 per hour up to four hours, and $35 per hour for rides longer than that.

Picnicking

Rockford Park (302-577-7020; www.destateparks.com/wilmsp/rockford .htm; Kentmere Pkwy. and Rockford Rd., Wilmington, DE). Adjacent to the Delaware Art Museum in one of the more scenic parts of Wilmington, this state park is a good spot to break for lunch before heading north to Hagley or Winterthur. It offers both wooded areas and carefully manicured lawns, along with tennis courts, baseball fields, and the stone Rockford Tower (one of the more attractive water towers you'll ever see, situated on Wilmington's highest point). You can go up the tower on weekends in May through October from 10 A.M. to 4 P.M.

Sandy Hollow Heritage Park (www.birminghamtownship.org/shhpark.html; S. New Street Rd. off Birmingham Rd., near Chadds Ford). Today it is a large, open green space encircled by woods and a walking path. On September 11, 1777, it was the scene of the bloodiest fighting during the Battle of Brandywine. More than the sum of its parts, this Birmingham Township park is a great place to stop, picnic, and soak in the region's history. Closes at sunset.

Zoo

Brandywine Zoo

302-571-7747
www.brandywinezoo.org
1001 N. Park Dr., Brandywine Park, Wilmington, DE 19802
Open: Daily, 10–4
Admission: Adults $5, seniors $4, children $3 in summer; slightly lower Oct.–May

A small, rarely crowded, well-landscaped zoo just off the namesake river that runs through Brandywine Park. Most animals come from the Americas or Asia, though there are also species native to Africa like the beautiful serval wildcat. Other highlights are the pygmy goats, seemingly mystified by the squawks from the nearby macaw cage. Visit a Siberian tiger, and don't miss the exotic animal house with assorted monkeys and a recently acquired toucan. The zoo is an easily navigable strip that concludes with a picnic area near the river otters' pool. It is open 365 days a year.

Rockford Tower

Shopping

West Chester and Kennett Square have the most interesting, walkable shopping districts. Chadds Ford is the place to go for Brandywine Valley antiquing.

Antiques

Brandywine View Antiques (610-388-6060; 1301 Brintons Bridge Rd., Chadds Ford). The location is new, but the building is old and so is the stock. Five dealers sell all sorts of odds and ends, including porcelain, jewelry, and furniture (look for Victorian furnishings). Closed Wednesday and Thursday.

Chadds Ford Antiques and Collectibles (610-388-3482; US 1 and PA 100 at the Village Barn Shoppes, Chadds Ford). A more diverse collection than your average antique shop. Browsers are as likely to come across an out-of-print illustrated novel as a porcelain dish set. If you can't find what you are looking for, it's definitely worth asking.

Pennsbury Chadds Ford Antique Mall (610-388-1620; 641 E. Baltimore Pike, Chadds Ford). More than a hundred dealers and a very wide variety of merchandise. Always fun to browse. Closed Tues.–Wed.

Books

Armadillo Books (610-696-8360; 109 N. High St., West Chester). Every book in the store is just $4—selection is mostly new copies of last year's titles.

Baldwin's Book Barn (610-696-0816; 865 Lenape Rd., West Chester). DUCK OR GROUSE read the signs that hang from the low wooden ceiling beams at this genuine dairy barn built in 1822 and converted to a bookstore in 1946. The front room, complete with Sunshine Oak wood stove, is rich with material on Wyeth illustrations and Chester County history. The rest of the five floors contain all kinds of used and rare books.

Kennett Square Resale Book Shoppe (610-444-6069; 113 S. Union St., Kennett Square). Large, well-organized used book store with titles arranged by subject and author.

Second Reading Book Store (610-692-6756; 32 N. Church St., West Chester). Small used book store with some terrific finds for those patient enough to look.

Thomas Macaluso Rare and Fine Books (610-444-1063; 130 S. Union St., Kennett Square). Very interesting stock, including rare antique maps and several titles of local interest.

Clothing

The Growing Tree (610-444-8484; 114 W. State St., Kennett Square). Located within the Mushroom Cap (see below) this small shop carries cute apparel for tykes.

Malena's (610-738-9952; 145 W. Gay St., West Chester). Extensive collection of vintage clothing, open seven days a week.

Moonflower (610-431-6607; 130 W. Gay St., West Chester). A new-age clothing and accessories store that does good business with university students.

Obvi (610-696-2477; 30 S. High St., West Chester). Stylish women's clothing in downtown West Chester.

Gifts

The 5 Senses (610-719-0170; 133 W. Market St., West Chester). Crafts intended to rouse all five senses. Look for the unique garden accessories.

The Mad Platter (610 431-1509; 111 W. Gay St., West Chester). New CDs, used CDs, and a good selection of rare records.

The Mushroom Cap (610-444-8484; 114 W. State St., Kennett Square). A fun store, and an edifying look at Kennett Square's proudest export. In addition to the mushroom para-phernalia—mushroom T-shirts, boxer shorts, etc.—there's an exhibition space with mate-rial on the growing process from Kennett's now-closed mushroom museum. Even better, you can buy freshly grown local mushrooms by the pound in over a half-dozen varieties. Not only are these mushrooms less expensive than the supermarket variety, but the differ-ence in taste is profound. Also pick up soups and sauces.

Simon Pearce (610-793-0949; www.simonpearce.com; 1333 Lenape Rd., West Chester). This Brandywine branch of the high-end glassware company has been operational since 2000. Each piece sold is hand blown and identifiable by its crisp, clean design. The ground floor has an exhibition and film on the glassblowing process and company history. The second level includes the store and a fine restaurant serving contemporary American cuisine where diners drink from Simon Pearce glasses and eat off Simon Pearce pottery. A slightly elevated upper tier affords all tables a view of the Brandywine River. Sunday brunch is a specialty, but lunch and dinner are served seven days a week.

"V" marks the spot at Va La Family Farmed Wines

Malls and Complexes

It's not in the valley exactly, but the gargantuan **King of Prussia Mall** (www.kingofprussiamall.com) is a 20-minute drive east of West Chester on I-76. "KOP" (as the kids call it) is so big that it's actually two malls: the Plaza and the Court, which together amount to more than four hundred stores. Shopping here is high end but within reach. Think Nordstrom's, Neiman Marcus, Lord & Taylor, DKNY, Cole Haan, and the like. Oversized chairs and benches throughout the mall give weary shoppers a chance to collect their thoughts and put down their bags. Dining is everywhere too, from gourmet snacks in the food court to Morton's Steakhouse. The popular Cheesecake Factory chain restaurant stays open past midnight on Fridays and Saturdays. Play around at the nearby Urban Outfitters while you wait for a table.

Sporting Goods and Clothing

Chester County Running Store (610-696-0115; 24 S. High St., West Chester). Running shoes for casual joggers and competitive sprinters alike.

Fairman's (610-344-9959; 43 W. Gay St., West Chester). A big, independently owned shop specializing in skateboarding, snowboarding, and surfing gear. Frequented by skateboarder and West Chester native Bam Margera (of MTV's *Jackass*).

Wineries

The Brandywine Valley Wine Trail (610-444-3842; www.bvwinetrail.com) is an association of Brandywine Valley wineries that offer tastings and vineyard tours and sponsor other special events throughout the year. The group also partners with area hotels to fashion getaway packages that include a wine-tasting component. There are currently six family-operated wineries on the trail. Oenophiles should consult the Web site to see what's going on and print the colorful trail map (warning: not to scale). The best known of the bunch is the **Chaddsford Winery** (610-388-6221; 632 Baltimore Pike, Chadds Ford), which has a presence throughout southeastern Pennsylvania. You can purchase their wines in places like Bucks County's Peddler's Village and Suburban Square on the Main Line. Tastings at Chaddsford Winery are fun, and the outdoor deck is a pleasant way to while away the afternoon. Another favorite is **Va La Family Farmed Wines** (610-268-2702; 8820-4 Gap Newport Pike, Avondale), located past Kennett Square on PA 41 south. The 7-acre vineyards produce a variety of interesting blended wines that are paired with locally made cheeses. You can take your glass upstairs and peruse the art gallery as you imbibe. Ten dollars for a three-wine tasting includes a logo glass to take home.

INFORMATION

Ambulance, Fire & Police

The general emergency number is 911. Call it for ambulance, fire, and police. Other emergency numbers:

Poison Control	1-800-222-1222
Rape Crisis Center	610-692-7273
Suicide & Crisis Intervention	302-633-5128

Police (non-emergency)

Chadds Ford	610-793-3333
Kennett Square	610-444-0501
West Chester	610-692-9600
Wilmington	302-654-5151

Area Codes & Town Government

The area code for Chadds Ford, Kennett Square, and West Chester is 610. Northern Delaware is 302.

Kennett Square and West Chester are boroughs within Chester County, each governed by a seven-member council and appointed borough manager. West Chester also has a mayor. Wilmington has its own city government, run by an elected mayor and elected city council. It is located within New Castle County (known as "the first county in the first state"). Chadds Ford is a township within Delaware County and has three elected supervisors. For general information call the county offices:

Chester County	610-344-6000
Delaware County	610-891-4000
New Castle County	302-395-5101

For questions specific to the borough, township, or city, try the following:
Chadds Ford—10 Ring Rd., 19317; 610-388-6368
Kennett Square—120 Marshall St., 19348; 610-444-6020
West Chester—401 E. Gay St., 19380; 610-692-7574
Wilmington—800 French St., 19801; 302-576-2100

Recommended Reading

Canby, Henry Seidel. *The Brandywine*, Altgen, Pennsylvania: Schiffer Publishing Ltd., 1997 (Second Edition). Illustrated by Andrew Wyeth, this is a comprehensive and deeply personal narrative of the river's history and meaning.

Gross, Geoffrey and others. *Stone Houses: Traditional Homes of Pennsylvania's Bucks County and Brandywine Valley*, New York: Rizzoli, 2005.

Westerman, Carla. *Chadds Ford: History, Heroes and Landmarks*, Gettysburg, PA: Thomas Publications, 2003. A fun read with great pictures by a Chadds Ford expert.

Books and exhibition catalogues on the Wyeths fill out the common rooms at local bed & breakfasts and are available for purchase at the Brandywine River Museum and Chadds Ford galleries. Some possibilities:

An American Vision: Three Generations of Wyeth Art, essays by James H. Duff, Andrew Wyeth, Thomas Hoving, Lincoln Kirstein. Boston: Little Brown & Co., 1987.

Hoving, Thomas, and Wyeth, Andrew. *Andrew Wyeth: Autobiography*, Boston: Bulfinch Press, Little Brown and Co., 1995.

Meryman, Richard. *First Impressions: Andrew Wyeth* (from the First Impressions series), New York: Harry N. Abrams, Inc., 1991.

Meryman, Richard. *Andrew Wyeth: A Secret Life*, New York: Harper Collins, 1996.

Hospitals

Alfred I. DuPont Hospital for Children: 1600 Rockland Rd., Wilmington, DE; 302-651-4000

Chester County Hospital: 701 E. Marshall St., West Chester; 610-431-5000

LifeCare Hospitals of Chester County: 400 E. Marshall St., West Chester; 484-826-0400

St. Francis Hospital: 701 N. Clayton St., Wilmington, DE; 302-421-4100

Late Night Food and Fuel

Three convenient **Wawa** locations (food and fuel) are 706 E. Gay St., West Chester; 901 E. Baltimore Pike near Kennett Square; and 3446 Naamans Rd., Wilmington, DE.

Media

Newspapers

Daily Local News (610-696-1775; 250 N. Bradford Ave., West Chester). West Chester's daily newspaper.

Kennett Paper (610-444-6590; 112 E. State St., Kennett Square). Local Kennett Square newspaper.

The News Journal (www.delawareonline.com). Gannett newspaper specializing in northern Delaware.

Radio Stations

WCUR-FM 91.7 (610-436-2478), West Chester University, college radio

WJBR-FM 99.5 (302-765-1160), Wilmington, adult contemporary

WSTW-FM 93.7 (302-478-2700), Wilmington, popular music

Visitor Information

The **Chester County Conference and Visitors Bureau** (610-719-1730; www.brandywinevalley.com; 17 Wilmont Mews, West Chester) and **Delaware County's Brandywine Conference and Visitors Bureau** (610-565-3679; www.brandywinecvb.org; 1 Beaver Valley Rd., Chadds Ford) are useful resources for Brandywine attractions in Pennsylvania. For the Delaware side, consult the **Greater Wilmington Convention and Visitors Bureau** (302-295-2210; wilmcvb.net; 100 W. 10th St., Wilmington, DE). Also consult the **Chadds Ford Historical Society** (610-388-7376; www.chaddsfordhistory.org; 1736 Creek Rd., Chadds Ford) for more information about Chadds Ford.

5

BUCKS COUNTY

Small Towns, Great Getaways

All of us who lived here in those dazzling days felt part of the parade. We cheered when our Pearl Buck won the Nobel Prize and our Oscar Hammerstein the Pulitzer. We relished Perelman's latest books, and roared at his scripts for the Marx Brothers' movies. I was stunned by the brilliance of how our neighbors, Samuel and Bella Spewack, produced the musical gem, Kiss Me Kate.... The bonds the tied me to that time and place never parted. Long after I moved away, my wife and I returned year after year to the Philips mill to reassure ourselves that Bucks County painters were still at their easels.

—James A. Michener,
Introduction to *The Genius Belt: The Story of the Arts in Bucks County*

Should you find yourself in a Philadelphia traffic jam (editorial policy compels disclosure that it's a distinct possibility) consider that somewhere—less than an hour's drive away—a deer is lapping water from a wooded creek. The magic of the Delaware Valley is its lightning quick shift from urban to rural, particularly at the northeast border, where crowded Philadelphia unfolds into Bucks County.

Bucks occupies more than 380,000 scenic acres north of the city and west of New Jersey along the Delaware River. One of the three counties originally settled by William Penn, it is rooted in the agrarian traditions of the valley. Its natural scenery can be found even in the more densely populated lower region, where Penn himself lived during the four years he spent guarding the colony's development. This is not to say that Bucks lacks traditional post–WWII suburbs; quite the contrary. Lower Bucks, as the inner ring is known, actually contains the second of William Levitt's original Levittowns. But unlike other suburban counties in the region, Bucks County's villages tend not to bleed into one another. They function more like independent hamlets, linked by state roads and parks rather than shopping centers. And once you travel just a little north to Central and Upper Bucks, you'll find a country retreat in its purest form.

An association of mill towns through the Industrial Age, Bucks took a new direction in the 1930s, when New York writers descended on the county to work and socialize amid the

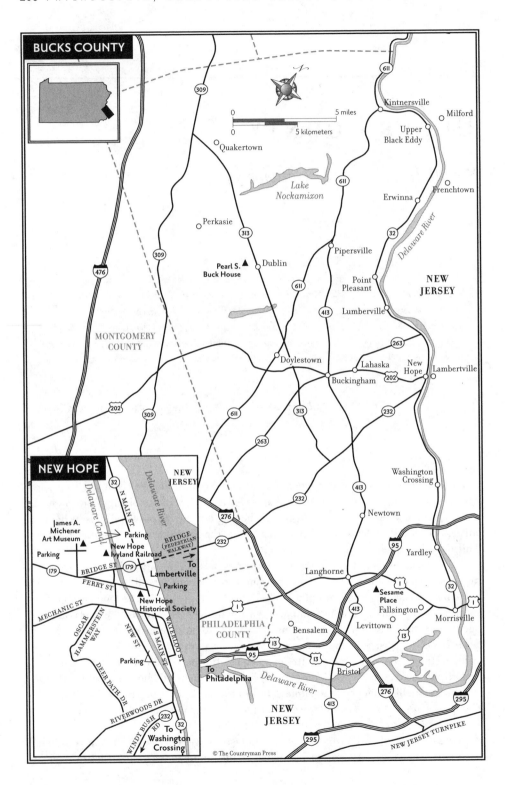

© The Countryman Press

bucolic surroundings. Colorful personalities like George S. Kaufman and Dorothy Parker, who once traded quips at the Algonquin Round Table in Manhattan, relocated to Bucks in the '30s and joined the budding artist's colony. There were the razor-tongued satirists like Parker, but also more decorous members like Pearl S. Buck, and eventually Bucks County native James Michener, who returned to the area in 1949 after his short-story collection, *Tales of the South Pacific,* won a Pulitzer Prize. Methodical writers and progressive public intellectuals, Buck and Michener spent many prolific decades in Bucks County. And the connections the area writers maintained with Broadway helped develop a local theater tradition, most visibly at the Bucks County Playhouse—still a thriving venue today.

But the writers were only part of what made Bucks such fertile ground for the creative class. A century before their arrival, Edward Hicks was painting his famous Peaceable Kingdom series in the area. Impressionists like Edward Redfield and Daniel Garber followed, inspired by the region's lush scenery. By 1929 local painters were holding juried exhibitions at Phillips' Mill in Central Bucks, and Henry Chapman Mercer marked 30 years spent producing Arts and Crafts tile work at his Moravian pottery center. Fifteen years later, the arrival of George Nakashima gave Bucks a visionary woodworker.

The influence of these painters, writers, lyricists, designers, and craftsmen is evident throughout Bucks County today. Their work is on display throughout the museums and galleries, and the tradition they began endures with new generations of artists who call Bucks County home. Though the region's fieldstone homes and country farms are idyllic, what sets Bucks apart is its cultural vitality and spirit; a visit here is as much a journey to the past as a toast to the future.

The epicenter of Bucks' tourist scene is **New Hope.** Located in Central Bucks County on the banks of the Delaware River, New Hope has drawn day-trippers and weekenders since summer theater debuted at its playhouse in 1939. Prior to the artists' arrival, it was a model Bucks County mill town, producing grain, cotton and lumber, among other goods, and using its geographically advantageous location to facilitate trade between New York and Philadelphia. The name dates back to 1790, when fire destroyed the town's mills—the rebuilt grist and saw mills were dubbed "New Hope Mills," and the name stuck. It is hard to guess what would have happened to New Hope had it not become an artist's colony after the industrial economy began to fade. The town's artistic bent made it a subsequent hotspot for counterculture tourism. It was among the first places in the United States to attract gay tourism and remains a popular vacation destination for gay travelers. Today's New Hope is deceptively complex, drawing a diverse group of visitors. From bikers to Goths, undergraduates on fall break to married couples on summer vacation, from across the Delaware and around the globe, New Hope maintains its vibrancy and distinctive appeal: a merge of country scenery with an art scene, modish shopping district, and bubbly nightlife.

Complementing New Hope's artistic energy is **Lambertville,** New Jersey, a short walk across a two-lane bridge linking the two downtowns. Lambertville's colonial and industrial history parallels that of New Hope, though it did not emerge as a getaway destination until decades later. Today, there are seasoned tourists loyal to the area who prefer Lambertville to New Hope, arguing that the former more authentically represents the spirit and artistic heritage famously found in the latter. The argument is silly; the towns are contiguous, each has a great deal to offer, and there's no reason to choose. Visit both.

Just south of New Hope and Lambertville on the Pennsylvania side is **Washington Crossing,** suitably named for the spot where General Washington traversed the Delaware

The New Hope countryside from 350 feet above sea level

River on Christmas night in 1776 to launch a surprise attack on Hessian mercenaries at Trenton. Washington Crossing is now a small community, home to Washington Crossing Historic Park, which commemorates the event and provides numerous recreational and educational opportunities.

Also in Central Bucks is **Lahaska,** a retail wonderland with major shopping complexes in Peddler's Village and discount merchandise at Penn's Purchase factory outlets. It is just down the road from **Buckingham,** a more rural variation on Central Bucks that lacks a walkable downtown, opting instead for roomier bed & breakfasts and a terrific winery.

In more than one sense, everything in Bucks revolves around **Doylestown,** the county seat near the area's geographic center and home to its best museums. It is largely a traditional small town, with a movie theater, shops, restaurants, and an inn. But Doylestown was decisively shaped by Henry Mercer, a collector and craftsman whose tile-making business and artifact museum branded the borough as a cultural hub in the early 20th century. Both the museum and tile works are must-see attractions, along with the Fonthill House, where Mercer lived. Michener endowed a superb art museum here as well.

Bucks' main cultural draws are concentrated in the central part of the county, but they are far from all the area has to offer. Lower Bucks has a medley of tourist attractions sprinkled throughout. Elegant Pennsylvania architecture can be found in **Bristol, Fallsington,** and **Newtown.** On the eastern fringe is **Morrisville,** near William Penn's original Pennsylvania estate, today reimagined, reconstructed, and open to the public. During the spring and summer, half of all elementary school-aged children in the Delaware Valley descend on Sesame Place in **Langhorne.** Parents may prefer horseracing and slot machines at Philadelphia Park in **Bensalem,** near scenic Neshaminy State Park.

The hidden gems in Bucks are the northernmost towns like **Erwinna, Upper Black Eddy,** and **Kintnersville** along the Delaware River. Wrapped on all sides by Pennsylvania greenery, these thinly populated villages maintain their rural character even during high tourism seasons in the summer and early fall. In parts of northern Bucks you are more likely to see a tack shop than a chain drugstore. This is also a prime region for recreation, with an especially picturesque segment of the Delaware Canal towpath and Nockamixon State Park: an ideal area to hike, bike, fish, sail, or swim. The tranquil pleasures of Upper Bucks are even more remarkable considering their location less than an hour and a half from New York City and Philadelphia.

Just as New Hope has Lambertville, the Upper Bucks towns have their New Jersey cousins across the river. **Frenchtown** is boundlessly charming, with its luncheonettes, galleries, and antique dealers. It is also a good place to rent a bike and start exploring the region. North of Frenchtown on the New Jersey side is **Milford,** which has some good restaurants.

Finally, in the western portion of Upper Bucks you'll find **Quakertown,** an affable 9,000-person borough best known for Fries's Rebellion of 1799, in which a local auctioneer organized the mostly German-born population to rebel against new taxes levied to fund a theoretical war against France. Quakertown is a good home base for a couple days spent recreating in nearby Nockamixon State Park. There are inexpensive chain hotels here and multiple campgrounds.

TRANSPORTATION

Bucks County incorporates 600 square miles, and a car is a necessity for visitors who want to see more than one town. **SEPTA** regional rail serves Lower Bucks very well, but service schedules are tailored more for commuters than tourists. The R5 terminates in Doylestown, about a 90-minute ride from downtown Philadelphia, and is a plausible day trip. The R3 stops in Yardley, which is 10 miles south of New Hope. With Trenton-Mercer Airport now closed to commercial air travel, the closest major airport is Philadelphia International. **Greyhound** (www.greyhound.com) offers limited service to Doylestown and Quakertown.

Bucks' river communities are an hour and a half from New York City, and an hour from Philadelphia. From New York and points north, use I-78 and I-278 to find US 202, which strings together Central Bucks County locales like New Hope, Lahaska, Buckingham, and Doylestown. Pennsylvania 32 connects Central Bucks to Upper Bucks, flanking the Delaware River. It becomes US 13 south of Morrisville near US 1 and eventually hits Philadelphia.

Pennsylvania 32 can be a little unreliable. The Bucks County river towns have endured three floods in recent years, with Hurricane Ivan in the fall of 2004, a second flood in the spring of 2005, and a third in the summer of 2006. In addition to damaging parts of

Delaware Canal State Park (including segments of the towpath—see "Recreation") and harming many riverside business, the floods also forced reconstruction projects for parts of PA 32. An alternative is NJ 29, which runs alongside the Delaware River on the New Jersey side. Several bridges connect NJ 29 to Pennsylvania.

Travel between Bucks County towns is accomplished mostly with US highways and two-lane state roads. Pennsylvania 611 is useful, extending north to the Poconos and south to Center City, Philadelphia, where it becomes Broad Street. Interstate 95 will take you speedily around Lower Bucks, but hooks into New Jersey south of Washington Crossing.

Parking is free and easy nearly everywhere in Bucks County, with the exception of New Hope where it is a deeply humbling experience. Save time, and don't bother looking for a complimentary spot on a side street. The borough government has all the angles figured out. Meters are ubiquitous and must be fed every day from 10 A.M. to 9 P.M. Quarters are the only denomination accepted and each one buys 20 minutes. The good news is that complimentary parking is included at most bed & breakfasts in the area, some of which are walking distance from Main Street. If you plan on driving into town, however, consider yourself warned and bring a roll of quarters. In a pinch, merchants will make change.

TOURING

Bucks County has three main Visitor Centers, any of which can provide useful information about attractions throughout the area. Coming from Philadelphia on I-95, take Exit 37 for a short drive to the Visitor Center near Bensalem, constructed to resemble a traditional country house. There is a second county center near Lahaska, and a northern one just outside Quakertown.

New Hope has its own **Visitors Center** (215-862-5030; 1 W. Mechanic St.) in a historic building near the heart of town. Get acquainted with the area here. New Hope also has some good specialty tours:

Bucks County Carriages (215-862-3582; 2586 N. River Rd., New Hope). Horse-drawn weekend carriage rides around New Hope or Lambertville. Tours of Lahaska are available as well.

Coryell's Ferry Historic Boat Rides (215-862-2050; 22 S. Main St., New Hope). Paddlewheel rides on the Delaware, offered May through September.

Ghost Tours of New Hope (215-343-5564; ghosttoursofnewhope.com). Ghost tours leave Saturday nights, June through the third week in November at 8 P.M. at the intersection of Main and Ferry Streets. Additional Friday night tours in October.

LODGING

The bed & breakfast industry was made for places like Bucks County. The lush natural scenery is reason enough, but fathom how much American history took place along its winding country roads—a people's history of early farm life and subsequent adjustments through the Industrial Age and the modern service economy. All facets of this narrative exist within its lodges. Spend three nights in Bucks, and you can stay on a 300-year-old farm, a stone house attached to a grist mill, and a modern luxury inn.

New Hope has the most options, which makes sense given its popular cultural attractions, shopping, and riverside location in Central Bucks. Many lovely B&Bs in Upper Bucks are just a 20- to 40-minute drive from New Hope and Doylestown. Lower Bucks has the county's chain hotels, generally patronized by business travelers, families (who are often, but not always, unwelcome at bed & breakfasts), and spillover from Philadelphia. Beyond the scope of this guidebook are a handful of New Jersey inns across the river from Bucks County. One dependable option is the 45-room **Inn at Lambertville Station** (609-397-4400; www.lambertvillestation.com; 11 Bridge St., Lambertville). Its restaurant is profiled later in the chapter.

Many of the B&Bs profiled below offer cable television, wireless Internet access, and rooms with private baths. It is best to check with the innkeeper.

Rates

Inexpensive	Up to $80
Moderate	$80 to $150
Expensive	$150 to $230
Very Expensive	$230 and up

These rates do not include room taxes or special service charges that might apply during your stay.

Central Bucks

The 1740 House

Innkeeper: Joyce Cooke
215-297-5661
www.1740house.com
innkeeper@1740house.com
3690 River Rd., Lumberville, PA 18933
Price: Expensive
Credit Cards: Yes
Handicapped Access: Call to inquire

Twenty-three rustic guest rooms with four-poster beds and balconies (terraces on the first floor) just 5 miles north of New Hope. The elongated layout, which resulted from house expansions and a barn conversion, means a riverside view from nearly every room. Rooms 16 and 14 share a balcony and work well for couples traveling together. The inn name is a touch deceiving: The original house was built around 1860, which is still old enough for wood-beam ceilings throughout and a stone fireplace in the living room. Well maintained, with a pool in the center of the property and continental breakfast seven days a week (plus eggs on weekends), the 1740 House is a solid choice for vacationers who want easy access to New Hope combined with a riverside setting. Grab a drink before or after dinner at the cash bar.

1790 Pineapple Hill Inn

Innkeepers: Kathy and Charles Triolo
215-862-1790 or 1-888-866-8404
www.pineapplehill.com
innkeeper@pineapplehill.com
1324 River Rd., New Hope, PA 18938

Price: Moderate to expensive
Credit Cards: Yes
Handicapped Access: No

Gracious country-style accommodations in this late-18th-century manor, perfectly located for recreationalists near Washington Crossing Historic Park, and a five-minute drive from downtown New Hope. A decanter of sherry beckons in the pumpkin pine—floored common room, along with soft drinks, snacks, books, and one of many gas fireplaces on-site. The original part of the house was built and settled by Irish farmers; its B&B days date back to the Bicentennial. Pineapple Hill has been managed by the current owners since 1994, when extensive renovations began. The Magnolia Apartment Suite is the inn's largest offering, and includes a full kitchen and 6-foot soaking tub. A 1998 expansion added three rooms, which feature floral prints and generally more modern furnishings. The backyard pool is cleverly integrated into the remains of a stone Dutch barn, and you'll find nearby the innkeepers' archeologically absorbing "Wall of Rust," which displays horseshoes, potbelly stove parts, and other items uncovered during the property's refurbishment. The nearby orchard produces pears, cherries, apples, and other deer food.

1814 House Inn

Innkeeper: Jeannine Rudolph
215-340-1814
www.1814houseinn.com
info@1814houseinn.com
50 S. Main St., Doylestown PA 18901
Price: Moderate to expensive
Credit Cards: Yes
Handicapped Access: Call to inquire
The central Doylestown location amid restaurants and shops also puts the 1814 House next door to the Doylestown Historical Society. It's a fitting backdrop for what is among the oldest standing build-

ings in the borough, and a good value for travelers interested in the nearby museums. The inn now has a stucco exterior, but original stone remains. Most rooms have poster beds and five out of the seven offer big Jacuzzis in the bedroom corners, brightened with Mercer pieces from the nearby tile works.

Aaron Burr House

Innkeepers: Nadine and Carl Glassman
215-862-2343
www.aaronburrhouse.com
stay@aaronburrhouse.com
80 W. Bridge St., New Hope, PA 18938
Price: Moderate to expensive
Credit Cards: Yes
Handicapped Access: Yes

Years after the legendary duel in which he killed Alexander Hamilton, Aaron Burr sought asylum in New Hope. Visitors of this attractive Victorian inn need not possess such weighty burdens to enjoy its tranquility. The house is fitted with black walnut wood floors, thematic touches (note the Burr biographies in the guest rooms), and common pantry rooms with coffee and fruit on hand throughout the day. If available, book a second-floor room or the lush third-floor suite. Enjoy continental breakfast every morning and tea on Saturdays.

Art's Fox and Hound

Innkeepers: Lisa Menz and Michael Cheung
215-862-5082
www.foxhoundinn.com
innkeeper@foxhoundinn.com
246 W. Bridge St., New Hope, PA 18938
Price: Moderate to expensive
Credit Cards: Yes
Handicapped Access: No

No, George Washington never slept here. But his troops camped on the site in the weeks prior to the historic surprise attack on Trenton. Sixty-four years later a Victorian-style home with a mansard roof occupied the site, since renovated and expanded to include eight guest rooms with private baths, and most with decks or patio access. Ask if you can take wine or coffee amid the quirkily attractive remains of the property's old stone barn. You can ask in many languages—together, the innkeepers are fluent in Spanish, French, and German, and speak some Chinese. A three-course daily breakfast includes a hot entrée preceded by fresh fruit and homemade pastry like zucchini bread or plum coffee cake. The Fox and Hound is also one of New Hope's notable B&B values. Rooms can be reserved for around $100 midweek, and guests can have the entire top floor, with two king-bed rooms and a private roof deck for $220 a night.

Art's Fox and Hound, a rooftop view

Doylestown Inn

215-345-6610
www.doylestowninn.com
info@doylestowninn.com
18 W. State St., Doylestown, PA 18901
Price: Expensive
Credit Cards: Yes
Handicapped Access: Call to inquire

More of a small hotel than a bed & breakfast (though pastry and coffee are included with your stay at the adjacent Starbucks), the 11-room Doylestown Inn was fused together from a shoe store and hat shop in 1871. A third building was integrated into the structure during a subsequent expansion. Crowned by a handsome turret, it is one of the town's two centrally located lodging options, renovated in 2001 and outfitted with Jacuzzi bathtubs. Standard rooms are a little on the small side but a fair value. Premium rooms come with fireplaces.

Golden Plough Inn

215-794-4004
www.goldenploughinn.com
PA 202 and Street Rd., Lahaska, PA 18938
Price: Expensive to very expensive
Credit Cards: Yes
Handicapped Access: Some rooms

Where tired shoppers rest their weary heads. The Golden Plough is integrated into Peddler's Village, Lahaska's massive specialty retail complex, and is within easy walking distance of the Penn's Purchase Factory Stores. Its 71 rooms and suites are large and thoughtfully appointed, most with fireplaces and some with whirlpools. The layout can be a little confusing, but at least each room has its own reserved parking space. A cheery floral motif dominates both public and private areas. Room rates include complimentary champagne in the fridge, snack mixes, and a breakfast or lunch credit for the next day.

HollyHedge Estate

Owner: Joe Luccaro
215-862-3136
www.hollyhedge.com
innkeeper@hollyhedge.com
6987 Upper York Rd., New Hope, PA 18938
Price: Expensive to very expensive
Credit Cards: Yes
Handicapped Access: Call to arrange

With 15 rooms and more than a wedding a week on average (75–80 per year), this lush retreat in the New Hope hills is busier than a traditional bed & breakfast. Originally a farm estate built around 1730, HollyHedge has expanded numerous times while maintaining original elements like its stone-walled summer kitchen. This is where you'll find the property's bridal suite, a magnificent room with hand-hewn wood ceiling and whirlpool tub; just one reason why so many couples choose to tie the knot here. The grounds are beautiful, adorned with native plantings like laurels, hickory, and black walnut trees, in addition to a landscaped fountain that was one of Bucks County's first swimming pools. Nuptials usually take place in an old bank barn made from Pennsylvania fieldstone that was a stained glass and wrought iron workshop in a prior life. Its pitched roof and large windows give the space a churchlike quality, which is apt. Other guest rooms are furnished in different styles, from Colonial to Victorian, and are generally quite large. Full hot breakfast on weekends and continental breakfast weekdays.

Honey Hollow Farm Bed & Breakfast

215-862-5336
www.honeyhollowfarm.com
2799 Creamery Rd., New Hope, PA 18938
Price: Moderate to expensive
Credit Cards: Yes to reserve room, but pay by cash or check
Handicapped Access: No
Special Features: Rooms available only on weekend nights and throughout extended holiday weekends.

A treat in so many ways, Honey Hollow is a working farm set on 103 acres about 4 miles from Main Street, New Hope. The property was part of a land grant from Penn to the Paxson family, which held 2,000 acres of southeastern Pennsylvania and constructed a Colonial fieldstone house here in 1700. Stay in any of four guest rooms, with stone fireplaces and clawfoot tubs. Anxious as you may be to shop and

eat in downtown New Hope, take some time to meet the lovable farm animals, many of whom came from Philadelphia to live here. George and Boris are the most charming pigs you'll ever know—Boris, as it happens, has a video posted on MySpace. You'll also find the first milking parlor in Bucks County. Guests need not love animals to appreciate the property; a pleasant evening can be spent relaxing outside the house and enjoying the view. High continental breakfasts use free-range eggs from the farm's chickens.

The Inn at Bowman's Hill

Innkeeper: Timothy Glandorf
215-862-8090
www.theinnatbowmanshill.com
info@theinnatbowmanshill.com
518 Lurgan Rd., New Hope, PA 18938
Price: Very expensive
Credit Cards: Yes
Handicapped Access: One room

A gorgeous, romantic property located at the base of Bowman's Hill across from Washington Crossing Historic Park, the inn is a luxury getaway of the highest caliber. The emphasis is on guests' privacy and amenities, from the Egyptian cotton towels

George the friendly pig at Honey Hollow Farm

and king-sized featherbeds in the guest rooms to the terrace that overlooks a heated in-ground swimming pool and hot tub. The recently added 450-square-foot Manor Suite is a fine example of the inn's lavish instincts; there are 11 showerheads in the suite's two-person shower. Since the inn was built in 1978, it did not have to equip an old building with modern amenities, so you can expect larger rooms and more conveniences than some of the older B&Bs in Bucks County can provide. Choose from three hot entrées for breakfast, with a full English breakfast always available. Breakfast can be taken in your room or a country-style dining area attached to a glass-enclosed sun porch. Birdfeeders are strategically placed around the wooded periphery to give sunbathing guests something to watch for.

Inn at Stoney Hill

Innkeeper: Judy Lawson
215-862-5769
www.innatstoneyhill.com
info@innatstoneyhill.com
105 Stoney Hill Rd., New Hope, PA 18938
Price: Moderate to expensive
Credit Cards: Yes
Handicapped Access: No

Another luxurious, modern alternative to the centuries-old stone house bed & breakfasts in Bucks County, the cedar wood Inn at Stoney Hill makes the most of its 5-acre grounds. You'll find eight spacious guest rooms here, many with private patios that overlook the backyard garden. A stream trickles through the yard, which includes a mowed path good for strolling. Guest rooms are themed—wooden giraffe figurines in the Safari Suite, soothing blue walls in the Ocean Room—and some feature large Jacuzzi tubs. The lavender-hued Amethyst Room has two queen beds, rare for the area. Unwind or socialize in the Great Room, a cozy shared space with stone

fireplace. The innkeeper's French toast soufflé is always a big hit whenever served at the full daily breakfast. The New Hope and Ivyland Railroad steam and diesel heritage locomotives whisk right past the inn, and guests can arrange for a personal pickup—making it the only stop on the railroad besides downtown New Hope and Lahaska.

The Lexington House

Innkeepers: Ed White and Michael McHale
215-794-0811
www.lexingtonhouse.com
info@lexingtonhouse.com
6171 Upper York Rd., New Hope, PA 18938
Price: Expensive
Credit Cards: Yes
Handicapped Access: No

A functioning well supplies fresh spring water for the sinks, showers, swimming pools, and coffee at this genial six-room B&B just outside downtown New Hope. The fieldstone main house dates to 1749, now warmly decorated and among the most comfortable lodging options in Bucks County. Notable features include genuine Mercer tiles around the home's fireplaces and an old smokehouse and corn-crib barn. Upon acquisition of the Lexington House in 2004, innkeepers Ed White and Michael McHale focused on adding life and color to the grounds, planting over four thousand perennials, so during all but the most frigid months there is something in bloom, and fresh flowers in the guest rooms. You'll occasionally see deer grazing around the half wooded 4-acre property. Guest rooms are named for the home's prior residents, and feature private baths and queen beds (sofa beds in some rooms as well). Visitors take breakfast at their leisure and the dining room contains a large center table and a pair of two-person tables. No television in the rooms, but cable and DVDs in the downstairs lounge.

New Hope's Lexington House

The Mansion Inn

215-862-1231
www.themansioninn.com
9 S. Main St., New Hope, PA 18938
Price: Expensive to very expensive
Credit Cards: Yes
Handicapped Access: One suite

Conveniently located on New Hope's Main Street surrounded by dining and shops, the Mansion is a seven-room Victorian lodge and a top-quality restaurant in its own right. The large front porch and mansard roof are immediately eye-catching, and the beauty extends to the interior's handsome spiral staircase. The Mansion is proud of its history, but the extraordinarily accommodating staff never slips into haughtiness. It was the first Bucks County property with running water, at one time owned by beloved New Hope physician and local art patron Kenneth Leiby. Modernized and outfitted for its new life as a bed & breakfast in 1996, it does retain original 19th-century windows and doors. The manor is three stories tall, with two luxury suites on the top floor and a handicap-accessible cottage house. Enjoy a complimentary cocktail upon arrival and breakfast on the garden patio or Victorian porch. The Mansion is also one of a few local B&Bs that has a swimming pool.

Mill Creek Farm Bed & Breakfast

Innkeeper: Kristi Jones
215-794-3121
www.millcreekfarmbb.com
innkeeper@millcreekfarmbb.com
2348 Quarry Rd., Buckingham, PA 18912
Price: Expensive
Credit Cards: Yes
Handicapped Access: No

This working horse farm, just off US 202 between New Hope and Doylestown, is refreshingly laid back. The innkeeper is lenient about checkout times, but don't exploit her good nature. Intriguingly, you can board a horse here if you're bringing it on the trip (the only Bucks County lodge where this is the case), and while you can't ride on-site you can still get to know some impressive thoroughbreds. Despite the countrified appeal, Mill Creek is modern where it counts—private bathrooms for all, and a lighted tennis court and pool are open for guests—but it's also a great place to stretch your legs and soak in Bucks' Arcadian pleasures, like fishing on premises in Lahaska Creek for bass, catfish, and huge carp. Rooms got a facelift a while back from the Bucks County Designer House—a fundraising organization that sends interior designers into area homes to redecorate. Designer House put a roof on the porch, which became the dining room. Bedrooms are named for presidents of variable quality from Lincoln to Coolidge. Mill Creek is one of few B&Bs that cater to families, preferably midweek; the Washington Suite has an adjoining room specially decorated for kids with a daybed and alcove bed.

Porches Bed & Breakfast

Innkeepers: John Byers and Billy Camburn
215-862-3277
www.porchesnewhope.com
info@porchesnewhope.com
20 Fishers Alley, New Hope, PA 18938
Price: Moderate to very expensive
Credit Cards: Yes
Handicapped Access: Two rooms

Literally a hidden treasure, Porches sits obscured amid dense foliage just a hundred feet from New Hope's Main Street on Fishers Alley. The peach-colored Federal-style Main House has a stunning second-story porch, where guests can have breakfast and enjoy a truly one-of-a-kind view overlooking the Delaware Canal and the house garden. The floral mélange of perennials, hundred-year-old hydrangeas, and other plant life is a wonder, particularly

if the innkeepers show you pictures of what it looked like before. Porches' 10 rooms (six in the Main House, four in the Gatekeeper's House) come in all different sizes, furnished with mostly French and English antiques. Rooms in the Gatekeeper's House tend to be larger, and two such rooms adjoin and can be reserved as a pair. Country breakfast is a highlight thanks to the innkeepers' ingenuity—many guests on extended stays never see the same item twice.

Upper Bucks
The Bucksville House

Innkeepers: Barb and Joe Szollosi
610-847-8948
www.bucksvillehouse.com
4501 Durham Rd., Kintnersville, PA 18930
Price: Expensive
Credit Cards: Yes
Handicapped Access: Yes

Cozy fireside dining at The Bucksville House

The Bucksville House is a special place. All bed & breakfasts in northern Bucks County offer seclusion, but only Bucksville contains Barb and Joe Szollosi's antique collection, which makes the property a veritable museum as well. The treasure trove of dolls, tablet drawings, and, if you book the Nicholas Buck Room, an authentic pie safe—among many other pieces—are the product of more than 20 years spent scouring auctions and stores. The house itself owns a great deal of history too: It opened in 1795 as a wheelwright shop, was converted to a hotel and tavern in 1830, and spent the next hundred years as a way station between Easton and Philadelphia. The inn became a speakeasy during Prohibition, and when the Szollosis began rehabilitating the house in 1984, discarded liquor bottles were found buried below. On warm spring and summer mornings, Barb serves her "chef's choice" American breakfast outdoors. Choose from five rooms, each with queen beds and working fireplaces. The Attic Room on the house's top floor includes a living room, and is perfect for honeymooners seeking extra privacy.

Bucksville House: Haunted?

There are marked "cold spots" throughout the inn, and several items have been lost—and then found in the most unexpected places. Maids have reported conversations coming from empty rooms, soft touches on their shoulders, and shadowy forms drifting through the rooms. Disembodied footsteps—sometimes very pronounced footsteps on the tile floors—have been and still are common. The Szollosis even have several photographs which were taken during their renovation and contain anomalies which are difficult to explain and, Barbara believes, may be actual pictures of their otherwise invisible inhabitants.

—Charles J. Adams III, *Bucks County Ghost Stories*

Bridgeton House on the Delaware
Innkeepers: Bea and Charles Briggs
610-982-5856 or 1-888-982-2007
www.bridgetonhouse.com
info@bridgetonhouse.com
1525 River Rd., Upper Black Eddy, PA 18972
Price: Expensive to very expensive
Credit Cards: Yes
Handicapped Access: No

The innkeepers have been here since 1981 and make the most out of Bridgeton House's idyllic location upriver on the banks of the Delaware with a postcard vista. The views incorporate the Upper Black Eddy–Milford Bridge and are truly extraordinary; rooms overlooking the river cost a little bit more than those that don't, but are well worth it. For truly special occasions, the Boathouse Cottage and Penthouse Suite are the finest lodging to be had in Bucks County. Attention to detail in both spaces is characteristic of the property as a whole, but creates an especially romantic aura here—part country retreat, part luxury inn. Choose the Penthouse for its wraparound terrace and wood-burning fireplace or the cottage for its cavernous living room Jacuzzi. The innkeepers have a keen appreciation for art, and the dining room doubles as a gallery that hosts changing exhibits. Frankly, all 12 guest rooms are artistic installations in their own right, diversely decorated and smartly furnished. The River View Suite is just one example, its ceiling painted with sinuous clouds layered on blue sky. All rooms have featherbeds, modern amenities, and include access to Bridgeton's dock, where you're welcome to jump into the Delaware's temperate water. A multi-course breakfast can be taken in the rooms or on the private decks.

Golden Pheasant Inn on the Delaware
Innkeepers: Barbara and Michel Faure
610-294-9595
www.goldenpheasant.com
barbara@goldenpheasant.com
763 River Rd., Erwinna, PA 18920
Price: Moderate to expensive
Credit Cards: Yes
Handicapped Access: Call to inquire

A 150-year-old stone house situated between the canal and river on an enviable Erwinna plot located down the hill from the Sand Castle Winery. The Faures have owned and operated the Golden Pheasant since 1986, with Michel's considerable skills at work in the restaurant: a popular gourmet room serving a seasonal menu that supplements classic French with contemporary fare. Barbara's decorative tastes create a beautiful first floor stocked with rare French Quimper pottery with its brightly colored glazes and detailed imagery (available for purchase) and second-floor guest rooms with European antiques. Cottage house lodging includes a sofa bed and porch, and is family friendly.

Indian Rock Bed & Breakfast Inn
Innkeepers: Tom and Beverly Schweder
610-982-9600
www.indianrockinn.com
owners@indianrockinn.com
2206 River Rd., Upper Black Eddy, PA 18972
Price: Moderate to expensive
Credit Cards: Yes
Handicapped Access: No

A bit rough around the edges, but a fine value and the quintessence of Bucks County seclusion. Indian Rock is one of the few remaining Bucks County lodges that still serves its original purpose of feeding and sheltering travelers along River Road. Both the six-room inn and the road have undergone name changes since the early 1800s, but Indian Rock is so well insulated from development, even by Upper Bucks County standards, that you can really envision the stagecoaches and their weary voyagers stopping here for the night. Rooms are adorned with country furniture and all have private bathrooms. The on-site restaurant is a nice rustic space, serving gourmet American cuisine with Mediterranean influences. A canoe shell hangs over the attached bar.

Tattersall Inn
Innkeepers: Lori and John Gleason
215-297-8233
www.tattersallinn.com
info@tattersallinn.com

37 River Rd., Point Pleasant, PA 18950
Price: Expensive
Credit Cards: Yes
Handicapped Access: No

The small town of Point Pleasant has just one inn, but it's a beauty. Constructed in 1753, the Tattersall is a regal manor house that for two centuries belonged to the Stover family: wealthy Bucks County millers who owned vast tracts of land between Point Pleasant and Erwinna and who turned the house into a stop on the Underground Railroad for a time. Looking out from the Tattersall's second-story porch you can still see the top of the Stover's old mill, now a private residence. The inn's decoration has an English bearing, like the thematic tattersall material on the walls outside the ground-floor common room. Fieldstone emerges from one dining room wall as a reminder of the home's look prior to Victorian-era renovations. Choose the Royal Lavender Room for its lace canopy bed or the Winter Green Suite for its remarkable U-shaped design that isolates the seating area and affords extra intimacy. It should also be noted that the Tattersall is immaculately maintained (equal to or better than any B&B in this book) and spotlessly clean, reflecting the owners' devotion to the property.

Value Choices
Quakertown and its environs have a handful of moderately priced lodging options for those who wish to explore Upper Bucks without staying at a bed & breakfast. Here are a few:

Best Western Motor Inn (215-536-2500; book.bestwestern.com; 1446 W. Broad St., Quakertown, PA 18951). Two-story property with 40 rooms in the middle of Quakertown.

Comfort Inn & Suites (215-538-3000; www.comfortinn.com; 1905 John Fries Hwy., Quakertown, PA 18951). Part of a hotel cluster by I-476 west of the town center; 60 rooms.

Hampton Inn (215-536-7779; www.hamptoninn.com; 1915 John Fries Hwy., Quakertown, PA 18951). Seventy-nine rooms, indoor pool, and hot tub.

Holiday Inn Express (215-529-7979; www.ichotelsgroup.com; 1918 John Fries Hwy., Quakertown, PA 18951). Seventy-eight guest rooms on three floors, indoor pool.

Lower Bucks
Chain hotels dominate Lower Bucks, where many overnight visitors are traveling with children, often using their rooms solely as a place to rest after a tiring day at Sesame Place. They get business travelers here too, as well as impromptu visitors driving up or down the East Coast who want to see Philadelphia but avoid Center City rack rates. Some reliable options:

Bensalem Courtyard (215-639-9100; www.bensalempacourtyard.com; 3327 Street Rd., Bensalem, PA 19020). Marriott's economy brand, 167 rooms, recently renovated.

Comfort Inn (215-638-4554; www.comfortinn.com; 2779 US 1 North, Trevose, PA 19053). Eighty-eight rooms on three stories.

Courtyard Philadelphia Langhorne (215-945-7980; www.marriott.com; 5 No. Cabot Blvd., Langhorne, PA 19047). Ask about complimentary service to Sesame Place; 118 rooms.

Residence Inn Philadelphia Langhorne (215-946-6500; www.marriott.com; 15 Cabot Blvd. East, Langhorne, PA 19047). One hundred suites with kitchens and workspace.

Sheraton Bucks County Hotel (215-547-4100; www.sheraton.com/buckscounty; 400 Oxford Valley Rd., Langhorne, PA 19047). Indoor pool and sauna and 186 rooms.

Sleep Inn & Suites (215-244-2300; www.sleepinn.com; 3427 Street Rd., Bensalem, PA 19020). Sixty-four rooms adjacent to Philadelphia Park casino and racetrack.

CULTURE

Architecture

Like the Brandywine Valley, Bucks County has preserved many of the colonial-era stone houses built when William Penn made his original land grants to his fellow settlers. Some live on as bed & breakfasts. Others, like the **Parry Mansion** in New Hope, are open for touring.

Lower Bucks has the county's oldest towns, and local efforts to preserve historic architecture have resulted in comprehensive walking tours. A good one is **Historic Fallsington** (215-295-6567; www.historicfallsington.org; 4 Yardley Ave., Fallsington), the town where William Penn attended Quaker meeting, and where much colonial-era architecture endures alongside some notable Victorian homes. You can stop in at the Visitor's Center on Yardley Ave. and take a complimentary itinerary. Call ahead if you'd like a guided tour of the area ($5), which includes a visit inside two colonial-era stone homes and an original log house. **Bristol** (www.bristolhistory.org) and **Newtown** (www.newtownhistoric.org) also offer self-guided historic walking tours of their downtowns.

An architectural pleasure somewhat unique to Bucks County is the area's supply of covered bridges. Famously known as "kissing" bridges (their deceptive privacy and romantic country environs made them nice places to smooch), the dozen surviving examples date back to the 19th century and enjoy a dedicated following. The **Bucks County Covered Bridge Society** (www.buckscountycbs.org) has the details. Nearly all covered bridges are in Bucks' northern section where the relative lack of vehicular traffic has made their preservation more practical. The exceptions are the Van Sant Covered Bridge near New Hope and the reconstructed Schofield Ford Covered Bridge in Newtown's Tyler State Park.

While it gets limited attention, **Lambertville** architecture is a visual feast. The Victorian homes spill out from the main shopping district and have a spry egalitarianism. The homes are private, but their exteriors present diverse, colorful elements of 19th-century architecture and are fun to see. After antiquing and gallery-hopping for a while, stroll west from the bridge along Union Street. A striking site is the Second Empire–style A. H. Holcombe House, known as **Lambertville City Hall.**

Lambertville City Hall

Art

Art played a vital role in Bucks' past, and continues to help define the region's cultural identity. Pennsylvania landscapes are understandably popular in the county's many galleries, but you'll also find a fair share of funky, contemporary work in New Hope and Lambertville. The commitment to public art is also strong, with sculpture installations courtesy of **New Hope Arts** (215-862-9606; 2 Stockton Ave., New Hope). The organization's building just off Main Street is a hub for the town's art scene, hosting special events and exhibitions.

Miles of Mules has installed fiberglass mules all over the county.

You may also notice colorful fiberglass mule sculptures along the county's river towns. They are part of **Miles of Mules**, a network of pieces done by local artists and installed in 2003 all around the eastern Pennsylvania canals, as far north as Luzerne County and all the way down to Bristol.

Churches

National Shrine of Our Lady of Czestochowa

215-345-0600
www.czestochowa.us
info@czestochowa.us
654 Ferry Rd., Doylestown, PA 18901
Open: Daily
Admission: Free

Look for the distinctive 240-foot tower topped with a cross, which beckons from the hills just outside central Doylestown. This shrine is a sacred place that functions as both a Catholic church and a celebration of Polish traditions and faith. It was finished in 1966 to mark one thousand years of Polish Christianity. There is much to see, like the colorful main church interior, visitor's center, cemetery, and the Ave Maria Retreat House for overnight lodging. An exhibition gallery featuring Polish art, crafts, exhibits on Polish military history, and tributes to Pope John Paul II is open on Sundays from 11–3. The cafeteria and deli serve excellent food on Sundays as well. An annual Polish American Festival takes place in the late summer on the shrine grounds.

Film

County Theater (215-345-6789; 20 E. State St., Doylestown). A handsome twin-screen art deco theater in the middle of Doylestown, screening first-run, mostly independent titles. Catch some classic films on selected Monday and Wednesday nights during the summer.

Newtown Theatre (215-968-3859; 120 N. State St., Newtown). One of the oldest theaters in the U.S. still showing films, this historic landmark is a great place to take in a flick. Choose a balcony seat to take full advantage.

Galleries

George Nakashima Woodworkers

(215-862-2272; 1847 Aquetong Rd.,
New Hope). Only open to the public
1–4:30 P.M. on Saturdays, but a defi-
nite must-see if you're in town.
Nakashima furniture is as beautiful as
it is unique, most often made with
black walnut or cherry, and organically
designed such that the finished product honors the natural contours of the
wood. Though George passed away in
1990, his daughter, Mira, continues to
produce and display exceptional work.

The George Nakashima Woodworkers Gallery, open on Saturdays

Gratz Gallery (215-862-4300; 30 W.
Bridge St., New Hope). The place to go
in New Hope for American oil paintings and Pennsylvania landscapes in particular.

Jim's of Lambertville (609-397-7700; 6 Bridge St., Lambertville). A fine space for
Pennsylvania impressionism, this 7,000-square-foot gallery specializes in local work by
big-name Bucks County artists.

Sidetracks Art Gallery (215-862-4586; 2A Stockton Ave., New Hope). Edgier than your
average Bucks County gallery; takes some risks but not at the expense of quality. Definitely
worth a look when you're in the area.

Historic Homes and Sites

Margaret R. Grundy Memorial Museum

215-788-9432
www.grundymuseum.org
info@grundyfoundation.com
610 Radcliffe St., Bristol, PA 19007
Open: Tue.–Sat., 1–4
Admission: Free

A bit off the beaten path, but an impressive Victorian mansion on the Bristol waterfront
endowed by local businessman and pol Joseph Grundy. Grundy was a textile manufacturer
and pro-tariff Republican, the latter of which accounts for the elephant figurines found
around the house. There are many other nifty Victorian trinkets to appreciate as well. The
maple, golden oak, and cherry wood interior is luscious, and the Jeffersonian window
opens to a pretty Delaware River view. Tours take about half an hour. The free library next
door is also worth a visit.

Parry Mansion

215-862-5652
www.parrymansion.org
newhopehs@verizon.net
45 S. Main St., New Hope, PA 18938

Open: May–Oct., Sat. and Sun., 1–3
Admission: Adults $5, seniors and students $4

New Hope industrialist Benjamin Parry's home, built in 1784 after his early business success, and inhabited by Parrys for five generations. An expansion is noticeable from the street, as some of the exterior is done in blue fieldstone, and some in red. The New Hope Historical Society acquired the Georgian building in 1966 and spruced up the rooms using mostly Parry family furniture to portray different periods in the home's history—Colonial, Federal, Empire, and Victorian. It's a clever conceit that gives visitors four American decorative styles for the price of one. The Victorian Music Room is the most complete, adorned with Waterford Crystal, Chelsea China, and a coffin piano that commands attention. The Colonial rooms also do an especially admirable job, from the straw mattress on the pencil-post bed to the red clay dishware in the kitchen. Guided tours are the only way to see the house.

Pearl S. Buck House

215-249-0100 or 1-800-220-2825
www.pearl-s-buck.org
webmaster@pearlsbuck.org
520 Dublin Rd., Perkasie, PA 18944
Open: Tues.–Sat., tours at 11, 1, and 2; Sun. tour at 2
Admission: Adults $7, seniors $6

After spending most of her first 40 years in China as a daughter to a Presbyterian missionary, Pearl S. Buck moved to Green Hills Farm in Central Bucks County in 1935, where she became a vital piece of the emerging literary scene. This National Historic Landmark house and adjoining grounds tap into the soul of a remarkable woman, whose immense literary contributions were matched by her work for civil rights and the mainstreaming of bi-racial adoption. Buck adopted and cared for several children herself, and the Pearl S. Buck International humanitarian organization has offices on-site, continuing to do tremendous work placing adopted children and assisting underprivileged youth in Asia. Her novels brought Chinese culture into the American consciousness, making her a uniquely influential Bucks County writer. Visiting here is refreshing, because unlike so many historic homes in the Delaware Valley, this house looks lived in. Buck died in 1973 and aside from some minor rearrangement and nods to historic preservation, you can envision the place functioning as it did some 40 years ago. Delightful volunteers give tours peppered with stories about Buck's life and famous practicality, like how she and husband Richard Walsh had the corners rounded off his antique American table because they kept blocking access through the kitchen. The writer's distaste for decadence leaves the property free of overzealous decoration, but there are still many interesting pieces. Recently uncovered was the typewriter on which she wrote her Pulitzer Prize–winning *The Good Earth*. There is also a beautiful collection of silk robes from Asia.

Pennsbury Manor

215-946-0400
www.pennsburymanor.org
info@pennsburymanor.org
400 Pennsbury Memorial Rd., Morrisville, PA 19067

Open: Apr.–Nov., Tues.–Sun. 9–5; tour times vary
Admission: Adults $7, seniors $6, children $4 for tour; grounds passes are $3

The site where William Penn lived during his brief time in Pennsylvania, rebuilt as a New Deal public works project to resemble what historical and archeological evidence indicates the estate was like. Penn's original home was lost to neglect years after he died in England. Highlights of the 43-acre grounds are the reconstructed manor house including servants quarters, a barn with farm animals, a formal English garden, utilitarian kitchen garden, and model bake and brew house where Penn's servants brewed beer for themselves. (Penn likely availed himself of superior beer shipped from Philadelphia.) Admission covers the house tour and a video presentation on Penn's life (60 to 90 minutes total). Before or afterwards, take a stroll around and admire the pristine view of the Delaware River from the estate's edge. Pennsbury Manor is an excellent attraction, but the tragedy of Penn's life has a sobering effect—he lost his first wife and multiple children to terminal illness, died broke after a term in debtor's prison, and faced recurring harassment for his Quakerism.

Washington Crossing Historic Park
215-493-4076
www.ushistory.org/washingtoncrossing
1112 River Rd., Washington Crossing, PA 18977
Open: Tues.–Sat. 9–5, Sun. 12–5
Admission: Adults $7, seniors $6, children $4

George Washington crossing the Delaware River on December 25, 1776 is surely among the most iconic scenes in American history. While the famous painting by Emanuel Leutze shows a bright sky and triumphant Washington, the crossing was a brutal 11-hour affair amid a vicious evening storm. The weather was in some sense a blessing in disguise, maintaining the element of surprise that allowed the Revolutionary Army to defeat the Hessian mercenaries stationed in Trenton. It has been credited as an early turning point in the war, a maneuver which forced the British to take Washington seriously and drew the world's attention to the conflict.

The complete history is on display at Washington Crossing Historic Park, often confused with Washington Crossing State Park in New Jersey. The Pennsylvania park is in Bucks County, 7 miles south of New Hope, where the crossing began. Every Christmas Day historical interpreters reenact the event (conditions permitting).

The park is divided into two parts, with historical attractions sprinkled throughout. The southern part, known as the McConkey's Ferry Section, has a Visitor Center with a looping 15-minute video on the crossing (free) and four buildings to tour. McConkey's Ferry Inn is the star attraction here, as the only south park building that dates back to the 1776 crossing. It's a fine example of a colonial-era tavern. Guides take you along the creaky floors and discuss the period furniture, pewter drinking mugs, and a hearth with 6-foot-deep beehive oven. Captured Hessian officers were detained here on the third floor—and reportedly complained about the accommodations. The southern section also features the Durham Boat House, where the flat-bottomed boats used in the reenactments are stored; the handsome Federal-style Mahlon K. Taylor House; and the more modest Hibbs House.

The north part of the park, named the Thompson's Mill Section, is anchored by the Thompson-Neely House, where ailing Revolutionary Army soldiers were treated for battlefield injuries and illness. Nearby, take an exceedingly steep drive up to Bowman's Hill

Tower. After a short elevator ride and winding staircase, you'll find yourself 380 feet above sea level, with a tremendous view of the valley's treetops, houses, golf courses, baseball diamonds, and the sinuous curve of the Delaware River..On a clear day it is breathtaking.

A $5 combination ticket gets you entry to all attractions, and can be purchased at the Visitor Center, Thompson-Neely House, or tower. Tours take place every hour. Call ahead to make sure the tower is open, and look for special events like cooking demonstrations and crafts workshops.

Libraries

David Library of the American Revolution
215-493-6776
www.dlar.org
1201 River Rd., Washington Crossing, PA 19877
Open: Tue.–Sat. 10–5
Admission: Free

Quiet fun for history buffs. The David Library contains every book imaginable on the American Revolution and Revolutionary era, from land records and legal papers to popular biographies on the Founding Fathers.

Museums

Fonthill Museum
215-348-9461
www.fonthillmuseum.org
fhmail@fonthillmuseum.org
E. Court St., and Swamp Rd., Doylestown, PA 18901
Open: Mon.–Sat. 10–5, Sun. 12–5
Admission: Adults $9.50, seniors $8.50, children $4

Henry C. Mercer was Doylestown's Renaissance man: archeologist, collector, tile maker, and founder of the Bucks County Historical Society. He spent his last 18 years at Fonthill, a 44-room concrete Gothic residence specially designed to exhibit his collection of ceramic art. Mercer, who owned and operated a tile works, produced much of

Henry Mercer's illustrious Fonthill. Photograph by Barry Halkin, courtesy Mercer Museum

the home's art himself. The mansion is a spectacular labyrinth of narrow staircases and Arts and Crafts decoration. Many of the wall and ceiling arrangements tell stories, from the exploration of the New World to a dozen-panel illustration of an October harvest. Other highlights include Babylonian clay tablets on the ground floor and Mercer's novel guest rooms. Guided tours take an hour and are the only way to see Fonthill. Call (ideally a day in advance) to make reservations.

James A. Michener Art Museum
215-340-9800

www.michenermuseum.org.
jamam1@michenerartmuseum.org
138 S. Pine St., Doylestown, PA 18901
Open: Tues.–Fri. 10–4:30, Sat. 10–5, Sun. 12–5
Admission: Adults $6.50, seniors $6, students and children $4

This site was once used for the Bucks County Jail, but since 1988 its main captives have been landscape paintings, sculpture, and decorative art produced by local talent. Michener believed in giving back to the communities from whence he came, and as a Doylestown native who found success in the arts, the museum remains a fitting gift. Work from the most distinguished county painters is on display in the Visual Heritage of Bucks County and Pennsylvania impressionism galleries, featuring artists like Edward Hicks and Daniel Garber. The latter gallery also displays Bucks County art pioneer Edward Redfield's "The Burning of Center Bridge," an intense effort done in short, rapid brushstrokes that will have special resonance for anyone who has crossed the current bridge from New Jersey to the northern New Hope hills (the fire flickered up when lightning hit the old bridge in 1923). Also a must-see is the Nakashima Room, furnished with the designer's inspired style of wood furniture—check out the massive slab of a coffee table in the room's center— and enclosed on two sides by shoji window screens. A re-created Michener workspace, complete with editor's notes, and an outdoor sculpture garden round out the collection. The garden features the exoskeleton of what a Bucks County prison cell looked like.

James A. Michener Art Museum

215-862-7633
www.michenermuseum.org.
jamam1@michenerartmuseum.org
500 Union Square, New Hope, PA 18938
Open: Jan.–Mar., Wed.–Sun. 11–5; Apr.–Dec., Tues.–Sun. 11–5
Admission: Adults $5, seniors $4, children $2

Not a misprint. A sister to the Michener Museum in Doylestown, the single-story New Hope Michener annex is smaller, but nonetheless worth a visit. As in Doylestown, the well-executed permanent collection is a celebration of Bucks County's artistic history. A 10-seat screening room plays film clips that were written, produced, or scored by Bucks County residents (including Oscar Hammerstein II and Stephen Sondheim). The museum's two front gallery rooms host changing exhibits. This is New Hope, though, so parking at the museum is metered and strictly policed.

Mercer Museum

215-345-0210
www.mercermuseum.org
info@mercermuseum.org
84 S. Pine St., Doylestown, PA 18901
Open: Mon. and Wed.–Sat. 10–5, Tues. 10–9, Sun. 12–5
Admission: Adults $9, seniors $8, children $4

This remarkably comprehensive museum of early American paraphernalia reveals Henry Mercer's noble curatorial instincts. The six-story building is a tribute to 18th- and 19thary American trades, and includes over 60 exhibits on vocations like blacksmithing, oemaking, lumbering, and spinning. The surgical tool display will make you glad to be alive in the age of modern medicine. Mercer was a believer in the relevance and beauty of "everyday" items, which he procured from auction houses and antique dealers throughout his life. Chairs, wagons, and a whale boat hang from the atrium ceiling—Bucks County's answer to the suspended squid and whale at New York's Museum of Natural History. The Mercer Museum goes to extra effort to draw kids; visit the Imagination Gallery on the top floor for children's books and puppets. For extra enrichment, check out the Spruance Library on the third floor. A $12 combination ticket includes admission to Mercer and Fonthill.

Moravian Pottery and Tile Works

215-345-6722
www.buckscounty.org/government/departments/tileworks
moravianpotteryandtileworks@co.bucks.pa.us
130 Swamp Rd., Doylestown, PA 18901
Open: Daily, 10–4:45 (last tour at 4)
Admission: Adults $3.50, seniors $3, children $2

A companion to Fonthill, this is where Henry Mercer's Arts and Crafts tile business began in 1898, producing colorful clay tiles as a rebellion against the cold rigidity of Machine Age decorative trends. It still makes beautiful tiles from red clay native to Bucks County; an apprentice program trains up-and-coming tile makers. The tour is partly self-guided, taking you through Mercer's Byzantine, medieval, and Pennsylvania Dutch inspirations. It then gets into the nitty-gritty of tile production, including a visit to the downstairs Clay Room—an especially refreshing respite during muggy summer days. The tile works building resembles a Spanish mission and incorporates its self-produced mosaics into both the interior and exterior. An introductory video explains the business history and processes in detail. Pick up your own tiles in the shop on the way out.

Nightlife

Popular New Hope night spots include **Havana Bar** (215-862-9897; 105 S. Main St., New Hope), a music venue and nightclub with good food. Space heaters around the outdoor bar keep this spot busy year-round. Weekly karaoke contests are a lively event. Another popular locale is the patio at the **Logan Inn** (see "Dining"), which buzzes most nights until late. Located in the heart of Main Street, it's a good place for people-watching. A younger scene can be found at locals favorite **John & Peter's Place** (215-862-5981; 96 S. Main St., New Hope), which features live music every evening. Most of the musicians are area talent, but John & Peter's has also featured acts as varied as Norah Jones, George Thorogood, and Iron Butterfly. Dark wood-paneled walls and booths provide atmosphere. For those seeking a more cosmopolitan experience, **90 Main** (215-862-3030; 90 S. Main St., New Hope) is a good option. This bar/restaurant offers an extensive martini menu and bottle service. It's a relatively recent addition to New Hope nightlife, and brings to mind South Beach with its clean, contemporary look.

Nightlife outside New Hope is limited, though Doylestown can be a fun place to barhop. Smokers should visit the **Classic Cigar Parlor** (215-348-2880; 12 N. Main St., Doylestown), which is open until 11 on Friday and Saturday nights.

Wanna Bet?

Southeastern Pennsylvania has never been an easy place to make a wager. The Quaker ethos, so deeply ingrained in the region's history, originally banned drunkenness, swearing, and competitive sports; it should come as no surprise that gambling was also frowned upon. But times change, and the region has not been impervious to the spread of legalized gambling across America.

Parimutuel betting came to Bucks County in 1974, with the opening of the Keystone Racetrack in Bensalem. The Keystone has since been renamed **Philadelphia Park** (1-888-442-6366; www.philadelphiaparkcasino.com; 3001 Street Rd.) and expanded from a horseracing venue to a racino, with two floors devoted to slot machines, video poker, and electronic table games. There remains live horseracing year-round. If you can't make it to Philadelphia Park but feel like playing the ponies anyway, you can wager on horseracing off-site, at Turf Club locations throughout the area. There's a centrally located **Turf Club** in downtown Philadelphia (215-246-1556; 1635 Market St.). Watch and wager in either the upstairs clubhouse or the downstairs pit.

South of Philadelphia in the hardscrabble city of Chester, Pennsylvania—a 20-minute drive from Philly on I-95—is seasonal harness racing four days a week at **Harrah's Chester** (484-490-1800; www.harrahs.com;). The attached casino (slots, video poker, and electronic table games only) never closes, and houses a pretty good lunch and dinner buffet. Just beyond the Pennsylvania-Delaware border in Wilmington is **Delaware Park** (1-800-41-SLOTS; www.delawarepark.com; 777 Delaware Park Blvd.), the region's oldest racino.

And Philadelphia is a 75-minute drive from Atlantic City, with its boardwalk casinos and beach. There are a dozen hotel/casinos to choose from here, like the incessantly hip **Borgata** (1-866-MY-BORGATA; www.theborgata.com) in the marina district.

The minimum age for horse betting in Pennsylvania and Delaware is 18, and the minimum age for casino gambling is 21.

Seasonal Events
New Hope Automobile Show
215-862-5665
www.newhopeautoshow.com
New Hope–Solebury High School, New Hope
Time: Mid-August

A weekend for notable cars, as area collectors bring their antique and classic automobiles to show. Attendees cast ballots for their favorites. Admission fee is charged; the money raised goes to scholarships for local high school students and other charitable organizations.

Washington Crossing the Delaware
215-493-4076
www.ushistory.org/washingtoncrossing
1112 River Rd. at Washington Crossing Historic Park, Washington Crossing
Time: December 25th
A fun annual event where historical interpreters reenact the famed crossing from Pennsylvania to New Jersey. If you're not in town on Christmas Day, there's also a public dress rehearsal in mid-December.

Bucks County Playhouse, a converted grist mill

Theater

Bucks County Playhouse (215-862-2041; www.buckscountyplayhouse.com; 70 S. Main St., New Hope). A converted grist mill deftly adapted for live theater in 1939, the Bucks County Playhouse is a magnificent auditorium and a national treasure. The likes of Kitty Carlisle, Bert Lahr, and Walter Matthau, among many others, graced its stage at one time or another. At points in its history, the playhouse debuted new shows before they opened on Broadway. It currently plays host to roughly 16 musical productions a year, as well as an assortment of children's shows and special events. Tickets for most shows cost $23–$25 each, with discounts for students, children, active military, and subscribers. The playhouse is also associated with the **Washington Crossing Open Air Theatre** across the river in Titusville, New Jersey, which showcases summer productions of Shakespeare, among other performances (609-737-4323; 355 W. Pennington Rd.–Washington Crossing, NJ Rte. 546).

Musicals in Lower Bucks can be found at the **Bristol Riverside Theatre** (215-785-0100; www.brtstage.org; 120 Radcliffe St., Bristol). And there is much campy fun to be had at **Murder Mystery Dinner Theater** (215-794-4000; www.peddlersvillage.com; Peddler's Pub at the Cock 'n' Bull Restaurant) on Friday and Saturday nights in Lahaska.

RESTAURANTS AND FOOD PURVEYORS

Bucks County has excellent restaurants. Many are located in and around New Hope, though Doylestown's restaurant scene continues to improve in both overall quality and diversity of fare. In Upper Bucks you'll encounter old taverns with modernized menus, typically riffing on American fare. Keep in mind the New Jersey side of the river, particularly in the north.

Dining Price Code

Inexpensive	Up to $15
Moderate	$15 to $30
Expensive	$30 to $50
Very Expensive	$50 or more

Doylestown
Café Alessio

215-340-1101
www.cafealessiodoylestown.com
24 N. Main St., Doylestown, PA 18901
Open: Daily
Price: Moderate
Credit Cards: Yes
Cuisine: Italian, American, sushi
Serving: L, D
Handicapped Access: Yes

The strikingly remodeled dining room, outfitted with marble tables, stone columns, and exposed brick, has attracted new crowds to this already popular fusion restaurant. The double-sided menu—not counting the sushi selection—promises Italian food, but delivers classic American salads and sandwiches as well. Reasonably priced Sicilian entrées and generously portioned pastas work best for dinner. Cheeseburgers are suitably big and juicy for lunch, or try a grilled rib-eye steak sandwich. The location, within easy walking distance from the County Theater, makes Café Alessio a good date spot. Score a plush booth if you can, or dine alfresco and watch Doylestown motorists negotiate the pesky intersection at State and Court.

Chambers 19

215-340-1940
www.chambers19.net
19 N. Main St., Doylestown, PA 18901
Open: Daily
Price: Moderate to expensive
Credit Cards: Yes
Cuisine: American
Serving: L, D, Sun. Brunch
Handicapped Access: Partial access

A popular Doylestown restaurant that puts numerous twists on American bistro fare—some effectively Italian, others non-regional but inspired nonetheless. The best dishes are those unique to Chambers, like a tangy strawberry salad fortified by red onion and poppy seed dressing, or a zinfandel chicken pasta flush with mushrooms and spinach. (All pastas can be prepared with angel hair, penne, or linguine.) At lunch, try the duck-breast sandwich. This is also a great place to go for steaks, chops, and burgers. The room is dark in the evenings and very attractive, featuring exposed brick near the entrance bar, and a vivid mosaic with oval mirror as a backdrop to the main dining room. Live music on Thursday, Friday, and Saturday nights. Chambers is attached to The Other Side, which serves the same excellent menu but is more of a bar scene.

Siam Cuisine at the Black Walnut

215-348-0708
www.siamcuisinepa.com
80 W. State St., Doylestown, PA 18901
Open: Tues.–Sun.
Price: Moderate to expensive
Credit Cards: Yes
Cuisine: Thai, French
Serving: L, D
Handicapped Access: Yes

Sterling fusion cuisine that tends more in the Thai direction at lunch and more French at dinner. The petite dining rooms are painted breezy lavender or pink, balanced by darker wood floors and a nice collection of wall art. Alfresco tables are strung along a modestly busy block of State Street in central Doylestown. Dual-course lunch specials include either soup or salad and a well-portioned entrée. As is befitting of a true fusion restaurant, Siam Cuisine is big on ingredient variety—even applied to Thai mainstays like drunken noodles in a slightly hot chili sauce. The ample desserts are available throughout the day. Try generously portioned homemade ice cream served in a sundae glass or a rich French tart.

Lahaska

Waterlillies

215-794-8588
www.waterlilliesrestaurant.com
5738 US 202, Lahaska, PA 18931
Open: Daily, no dinner Mon.
Price: Moderate to expensive
Credit Cards: Yes
Cuisine: Italian
Serving: B, L, D
Handicapped Access: Yes
Special Features: BYOB

This soulful little spot near Peddler's Village is intimate without being cramped, decorated with red walls and tablecloths, white trim, and floral accents in the art. The convivial waitstaff adds pep to an already lively dining room. Sesame-seed bread opens the show at dinner, served with a tart red sauce rather than butter. You won't go wrong with seafood here. House scampi is excellent, and penne arrabiata comes out just right, with meaty scallops and shrimp in a light, tangy gravy. The Chicken Kimberly gets raves too. Entrées are thoughtfully presented, accompanied by fresh seasonal vegetables and preceded by soup or salad. Close with a homemade dessert and coffee in a glass mug. They serve three meals a day at Waterlillies— somewhat unusual for a restaurant of this quality, but a welcome surprise. The breakfast menu lists a dizzying array of omelets.

Lambertville

Bell's Tavern

609-397-2226
www.bellstavern.com
183 N. Union St., Lambertville, NJ 08630
Open: Daily
Price: Inexpensive to moderate
Credit Cards: No
Cuisine: Italian, American
Serving: D
Handicapped Access: Yes

Somewhat removed from the densely packed antique and gallery district in Lambertville is this bright tavern where locals assemble around the oval bar and cheerful tourists are welcomed with open arms. The inexpensive beers, wines, and mixed drinks go nicely with pasta in home-made sauces, an excellent half-pound burger, and daily specials. Bell's is not haute cuisine, but after a long day spent shopping or hiking it can be just what the doctor ordered.

Lambertville Station Restaurant

609-397-8300
www.lambertvillestation.com
11 Bridge St., Lambertville, NJ 08530
Open: Daily
Price: Expensive
Credit Cards: Yes
Cuisine: New American
Serving: L, D, Sun. Brunch
Handicapped Access: Yes

Anyone attempting to convert a historic building into a restaurant should see this cavernous multi-level restaurant and take diligent notes. It's located on the New Jersey side of the New Hope–Lambertville Bridge adjacent to a 45-room hotel. The original stone railroad station, once part of the Belvidere Delaware and later Pennsylvania Railroad, somehow maintains a casual ambiance amid the polished brass and dark woods. Large railroad photographs in the basement pub and other train antiques keep things thematic. The dinner menu is more ambitious than the lunch; in the evening match a wild game appetizer with a classic entrée like prime rib or rack of lamb. The wine list accentuates Italian, French, and American bottles.

Milford

The Ship Inn

908-995-0188
www.shipinn.com

61 Bridge St., Milford, NJ 08848
Open: Daily
Price: Moderate to expensive
Credit Cards: Yes
Cuisine: English
Serving: L, D
Handicapped Access: Yes

Given the relative paucity of dining variety in Upper Bucks County, be grateful for Milford—a quiet New Jersey town across the river from Upper Black Eddy—and for the Ship Inn. Unabashedly English, the choices go way beyond fish and chips and Yorkshire pudding, though both are available. Entrées enmeshed in peppery brown gravy are good, like the Crosby steak and mushroom pie. Housed in a Victorian edifice, its interior festooned with mugs, nautical gear, and all things British, the fun pub feel is overt. They brew five terrific beers here, including golden wheat and a silky smooth porter. If you call ahead you can arrange a group tour of the brewing process and take a box of beer home after the meal.

New Hope
The Blue Tortilla
215-862-5859
18 N. Main St., New Hope, PA 18938
Open: Daily
Price: Moderate to expensive
Credit Cards: Yes
Cuisine: Mexican
Serving: L, D
Handicapped Access: Partial access

Good Mexican food, including homemade corn tortillas, highly recommended enchiladas, and pork tacos. Dishes are mostly spiced lightly, though the pickled onions have some zip, and you can add jalapeño peppers pickled or raw. The alfresco dining streetside behind a white picket fence is a nice place to eat. Portions are a little too small and prices are a little too high, but life goes on.

Café Lulu's
215-862-3222
110 S. Main St., New Hope, PA 18938
Open: Daily
Price: Moderate
Credit Cards: Yes
Cuisine: American
Serving: B, L, D
Handicapped Access: Yes

Part juice bar, part café, Lulu's serves pita sandwiches and other unpretentious fare that goes well with most of the choices on the restaurant's long juice and smoothie menu. The dining room is jaunty and colorful, adorned by local art. Outdoor seating is nice, and the patio is big enough that you can usually get a table. Café Lulu's also offers excellent vegetarian and vegan options for those with dietary restrictions. An inexpensive takeout menu at lunchtime is a good option for an impromptu picnic on the banks of the Delaware.

Café Lulu's on a summer weekend

The Landing
215-862-5711
www.landingrestaurant.com
22 N. Main St., New Hope, PA 18938
Open: Daily
Price: Moderate
Credit Cards: Yes

Cuisine: American
Serving: L, D
Handicapped Access: Yes

Outdoor seating on a pictorial terrace
makes this reliable New Hope restaurant
among the town's most popular eateries in
the spring, summer, and fall. The cheery
alfresco atmosphere is contagious, as locals
and visitors alike come to trade stories
under the large patio umbrellas. Tables
look out on the rocky shore of the Delaware
River, where geese and ducks like to con-
gregate, occasionally working their way up
the deck to saunter around diners' toes.
Cuisine is creative American, with some
international hints and a few surprises. A
meatloaf sandwich on French bread is
toothsome, and the multifarious salads go
well with most appetizers (starters here are
a bit more adventurous than entrées).
When available, open with a refreshing gaz-
pacho. Lunch and dinner offerings come
off the same menu, so have a pulled pork
sandwich for supper if your heart so
desires. Extensive wine and beer lists are
well priced for the area. Find complimentary parking in a small adjacent lot.

Logan Inn

215-862-2300
www.loganinn.com
10 W. Ferry St., New Hope, PA 18938
Open: Daily
Price: Expensive to very expensive
Credit Cards: Yes
Cuisine: American
Serving: L, D, Sat. & Sun. Brunch
Handicapped Access: Yes

Dine on the sheltered patio if you can,
which faces New Hope's Main Street activity
and remains pleasing even during a light
drizzle. The patio bar is also a fun place to
linger after the sun goes down. The Logan
Inn's American fare is mostly steaks and
seafood at dinner, with seafood appetizers,
sandwiches, and salads at lunch. Parking is

free on premises for diners and guests at
the Logan's 16-room hotel. The site is rich
in history: in the early 18th century, when
the area was sparsely populated and mostly
inhabited by Native Americans, the Logan
Inn (then called the Ferry Tavern) provided
respite to travelers on horseback.

Marsha Brown

215-862-7044
www.marshabrownrestaurant.com
15 S. Main St., New Hope, PA 18938
Open: Daily
Price: Expensive to very expensive
Credit Cards: Yes
Cuisine: Cajun steak and fish house
Serving: L (weekends only, after 2), D
Handicapped Access: Yes

What looks like a Methodist church from
across the street (which it once was) is
actually one of New Hope's premier upscale
restaurants. The conversion from church to
restaurant is remarkable. Take special note
of "Redemption," a large mural depicting
the fight between man and lion that overlooks the second-floor dining room. Come
here for big, juicy steaks served on sizzling
hot plates, and for the best seafood in New
Hope; the raw oyster bar gets consistent
raves. Renowned appetizer specialties
include crab cheese cakes and lollipop lamb
chops. Most entrées are a la carte, but portions are large and side dishes can be
shared—both the sautéed and creamed
spinach are terrific. Service is outstanding,
and the low music and candlelit tables
make Marsha Brown a fine choice for a
romantic dinner. Make reservations for
weekend dining or during peak tourism
seasons.

Mother's Wine Bar & Restaurant

215-862-5857
www.mothersnewhope.com
34 N. Main St., New Hope, PA 18938
Open: Daily

Price: Expensive
Credit Cards: Yes
Cuisine: American
Serving: L, D, Sat. & Sun. Brunch
Handicapped Access: Yes

As perfect for an afternoon glass of chardonnay as it is for an anniversary dinner, Mother's serves New American cuisine alongside a compelling wine list. Start with a flight sampler—three 3-ounce pours of different wines—and stay with your favorite. The oenological emphasis extends to the walls, where you'll find sketches, paintings, and photographs of wine bottles and grapes on the vine. Food is fancier at dinner, but recommendable all the time. The menu changes occasionally. You can rely on pizzas and duck salad at lunch and steaks and chops for dinner. Especially appealing is the bar area, which has a luminous feel owed to the big front windows and open space under a pitched roof. Dining areas are comfortable but avoid pretension. The wood-beam ceilings in the main dining room are a rustic contrast to the carpeted floors and white tablecloths.

Mother's Wine Bar and Restaurant

Tastebuds
215-862-9722
www.tastebuds-newhope.com
49 W. Ferry St., New Hope, PA 18938
Open: Wed.–Sun.
Price: Expensive
Credit Cards: Cash or check only
Cuisine: American
Serving: D
Handicapped Access: Call to inquire
Special Features: BYOB

A rare Bucks County BYOB, Tastebuds has stood for 15 years on Ferry Street, held at arm's length from the boisterous New Hope nightlife. The 19th-century building with wood floors and beam ceilings is identifiably Bucks, while the silken lighting evokes an upscale urbanity that would not look out of place beside Rittenhouse Square. The seasonal menu changes five times a year, with a short (but always inspired) bill of contemporary American fare. A Mediterranean accent is felt mostly in the appetizers—spring preparations like lamb meatballs with gnocchi, for example. On the entrée side, seafood dishes get the most creative treatment, but the place knows its way around a steak as well. Stay for dessert.

Wildflowers Garden Restaurant
215-862-2241
8. W. Mechanic St., New Hope, PA 18938
Open: Daily
Price: Inexpensive to moderate
Credit Cards: Yes
Cuisine: American, Italian, Mexican, Thai
Serving: L, D
Handicapped Access: Call to inquire
What began as a cookie shop more than 20 years ago is now New Hope's most eclectic casual restaurant. Co-owners Robert Madrick and Grant Waldman serve up four cuisines and place special emphasis on desserts. Sandwiches and Thai specials make the best lunch choices; the many American comfort foods are reliable and

filling for dinner. Spring and summer meals are best enjoyed on the cozy garden patio that overlooks the canal. During the cold months, a heated canopy keeps diners warm with an assist from the homemade apple cider.

Quakertown
McCoole's at the Historic Red Lion Inn
215-538-1776
www.mccoolesredlioninn.com
4 S. Main St., Quakertown, PA 18951
Open: Daily
Price: Moderate to expensive
Credit Cards: Yes
Cuisine: American
Serving: L, D
Handicapped Access: Yes

The lifeblood of Quakertown dining, patronized by young and old alike. The Red Lion Inn played a significant role in the Fries Rebellion (you can purchase Paul Douglas Newman's excellent book on the subject at the restaurant), but the McCoole name predates the 1799 event. Wood panel and fieldstone walls evoke the Revolutionary-era Quakertown, with a few Victorian-style furnishings intermingled for effect. The menu is reliable and comprehensive American cuisine (good wings and sandwiches at lunch). Dinner entrées include sides like potato du jour or vegetable medley, with a long draft beer list to wash it all down. Chicken bruchetta is a solid choice—two large filets slathered in diced tomato with a layer of mozzarella melted on top. There is typically live entertainment two to three nights a week.

Pipersville
Piper Tavern
215-766-7100
www.pipertavern.com
PA 413 and Dark Hollow Rd., Pipersville,

Grand old Piper Tavern

PA 18947
Open: Tues.–Sun.
Price: Moderate to expensive
Credit Cards: Yes
Cuisine: Continental, American
Serving: L, D
Handicapped Access: No

Prodigious portions and great service at this beautiful Victorian structure built in the late 19th century on the site of a Revolutionary-era tavern. Situated midway between Doylestown and the river towns in Upper Bucks, lunch at Piper is a perfect way to break up a day of museum-hopping with a quiet evening at your B&B. Ambiance is refined but unstuffy, with three dining rooms, white tablecloths, an open kitchen, and large windows all around. Steaks, chops, and seafood are the way to go at dinner—Piper serves first-rate prime rib and a big pork chop. Lunchtime salads and sandwiches are similarly huge, with some creative choices like open-face crab melt and veal panini. Have a drink before dinner in the cozy bar area.

FOOD PURVEYORS

Bakeries

C'est la Vie (215-862-1956; 20 S. Main St., New Hope). Actually tucked a bit behind Main Street, so it can be easy to miss. Pick up a French magazine and enjoy viennoiseries with excellent coffee. Good sandwiches on freshly baked French bread as well.

Rolling Pin Pastries (610-847-8383; 4331 Durham Rd., Bucksville Shopping Center, Kintnerville). Pies worth taking home from Upper Bucks and exceptional sticky rolls.

Candy and Ice Cream

Cherry Top Drive In Snack Bar (215-766-8400; 6784 Easton Rd., Pipersville).

Raspberry root beer ice-cream sodas are a creamy cup of ice cold heaven. Burgers and sandwiches go for around two bucks each.

The Chocolate Box (609-397-1920; 39 N. Union St., Lambertville). Great variety of international chocolates and assorted confections.

Gerenser's Exotic Ice Cream (215-862-2050; 22 S. Main St., New Hope). Old shop in the heart of New Hope, dishing out many unusual flavors made on-site. The rose petal ice cream, when available, is especially refreshing.

Penn View Dairy Farm (215-249-3395; 1433 Broad St., Perkasie). Without a doubt, the freshest milk money can buy. A deposit is required on the glass milk bottles, so not a practical choice if you're just passing through. Look for cows crossing the street.

Coffeehouses

Saxbys Coffee (215-345-0795; www.saxbyscoffee.com; 22 N. Main St., Doylestown). A well-appointed branch of the popular regional coffeehouse chain. Excellent coffee, plush couch, free wireless Internet, and a large conference room in the basement.

Coffee and Cream (215-348-1111; 6 E. State St., Doylestown). They roast their own beans here and store them in glass jars by the entrance, which is why the place smells so good.

Homestead General Store (610-982-5121; 1670 Bridgeton Hill Rd., Upper Black Eddy). Country store with seating area and a light food menu.

Lambertville Trading Company (609-397-2232; 43 Bridge St., Lambertville). More than just a coffeehouse, Lambertville Trading serves exclusive brews like Ethiopian Longberry Harrhar. Mugs, dishes, gourmet foods, and other gifts available.

Gourmet Foods

A Gourmet's Pantry (610-294-9763; 905 River Rd., Erwinna). Homemade jams, plus lots of hard-to-find oils, vinegars, spices, and gourmet ingredients.

Cupteavity (215-862-9031; 88 Main St., New Hope). A modern looking tea lounge with lime green walls and jet black furnishings that serves more than five-dozen teas in and a selection of desserts. Hand-painted teapots for sale.

Pizza, Sandwiches, Faster Food

Dilly's Corner (215-862-5333; PA 263 and PA 32, New Hope). Comfort food at a cross-roads. Snack on immense ice-cream creations and 1/3-pound "Dilly Burgers."

Dragon's Chinese Restaurant (215-579-0155; 2841 S. Eagle Rd., Newtown). Looks rather ordinary tucked into a Newtown shopping center, but this is excellent Chinese food if you're in the area—either takeout or sit down.

Nifty Fifty's (215-638-1950; 2555 Street Rd., Bensalem). Frosty milkshakes, fresh-cut fries, superior cheeseburgers, and the Travolta/Thurman *Pulp Fiction* vibe. Great for families, with a mini-golf course on the premises.

Hoagie Works (215-348-7066; 44 E. State St., Doylestown). Just what a hoagie should be. Nice soft bread, overflowing with quality meats, cheeses, and veggies. Underpriced too, at around $5 for a huge lunch.

Spatola's Pizza (215-862-6041; 82 S. Main St., New Hope). Respectable pizza, and one of New Hope's few inexpensive dining options.

Wine Stores

Wonderful World of Wines (609-397-0273; 8 S. Union St., Lambertville, NJ). Bless you sweet New Jersey, where the living is easy and the liquor stores aren't state owned. Choose from a wide variety of international bottles. Beer and hard liquor too.

RECREATION

Biking and Hiking

When the Pennsylvania coal industry took off in the early 19th century, the state constructed a 60-mile canal along the Delaware River from the industrial hub of Easton (north of Bucks County in the Lehigh Valley) down to Bristol, where it helped power the Industrial Revolution in Philadelphia. The canal has not been used in over 75 years, but it lives on as **Delaware Canal State Park** (610-982-5560; headquartered at 11 Lodi Hill Rd., Upper Black Eddy). The canal's towpath is a great place to bike. Since the trail runs parallel to the river for most of the park, it is easy to stop for a swim or picnic on the banks. There are also many historical attractions in and around the towns scattered along the Delaware. Unfortunately, large segments of the park have been closed due to the recent flooding. One nice section that has not closed is the 6-mile stretch from Upper Black Eddy south to Smithtown. To compensate for the closed areas, try looping around one of the Delaware River bridges and bike along the river's edge in New Jersey, where the trail is smoother. Call the park office to confirm where you can and cannot go.

A single-lane bridge at Delaware Canal State Park

Places to rent a bicycle along the Delaware River:

Cycle Corner of Frenchtown (908-996-7712; www.thecyclecorner.com; 52 Bridge St., Frenchtown, NJ)

New Hope Cyclery (215-862-6888; newhopcyclery.com; 404 York Rd., New Hope)

Since the floods, many cyclists choose to ride inland. Committed bikers often design routes to incorporate some of the county's covered bridges. Such routes can be hilly, but promise extensive exposure to Upper Bucks' natural scenery. The Bucks County Conference and Visitor's Bureau has a covered bridge ride posted on its Web site (www.experiencebuckscounty.com) along with other routes throughout the county.

A paved bike trail and several hiking opportunities await at **Nockamixon State Park** (215-529-7300; 1542 Mountain View Drive, Quakertown), which is Bucks County's best park for pretty much everything. Nockamixon is a massive, rolling green space with a 1,450-acre lake in its center, and scores of activities around the circumference. Hiking trails can also be found at most other parks in Upper Bucks.

While you're in Upper Bucks make a stop at **Ringing Rocks Park** (Ringing Rocks Rd., Upper Black Eddy) and bring a hammer. Many rocks in the park's boulder field make a high-pitched ringing noise when struck. The boulder field is a very short hike from the main parking area, where there are picnic tables.

Bird-Watching

The **Bucks County Audubon Society** (www.bcas.org) manages a Visitor's Center at the Honey Hollow Watershed (215-297-5880; 2877 Creamery Rd.), just five minutes from central New Hope. Open 9–5 Monday through Saturday. Lots of good special events for bird lovers and families, including occasional early morning guided bird walks around the 700-acre grounds.

Boating and Tubing

Hop on a yellow school bus and have **Bucks County River Country** (215-297-5000; www.canoeonline.com; 2 Walters Lane, Point Pleasant) shuttle you upriver so you can float back down on an inflated tube. While you'll hit an occasional rapid, the water is generally quite calm. River Country is most famous for tubing, but they'll also rent you a canoe, kayak, or raft. Call or visit the Web site to make reservations.

In the center of Nockamixon State Park is **Lake Nockamixon**, where you can rent motorboats, canoes, sailboats, rowboats, and paddleboats in the summer. Bring your own (properly registered) watercraft and launch from any of the four public areas. In Lower Bucks, **Tyler State Park** (215-968-2021; 101 Swamp Rd., Newtown) rents canoes seasonally for use on Neshaminy Creek. Electric or non-powered boats are welcome here as well. Or try a Delaware River launch from **Neshaminy State Park** (215-639-4538; 3401 State Rd., Bensalem). If your boat is registered outside of Pennsylvania, you will need a launching permit from the Pennsylvania Fish and Boat Commission (www.fish.state.pa.us), which can be purchased online.

It only happens once in November and once in March, but if you happen to be near Upper Bucks on the right weekend, be sure to catch the whitewater release from Lake Nockamixon (call Delaware Canal State Park offices at 610-982-5560 for exact dates). The release turns the mostly tame **Tohickon Creek** into a speedy waterway, and skilled kayakers and boating enthusiasts negotiate the Class 3 and 4 rapids.

Camping

There are only a few lodging options in Upper Bucks around the Delaware River, particularly for families with children, which makes camping an appealing alternative during the spring and summer. Inexpensive camping can be found at **Tinicum Park** (215-757-0571; River Rd., Erwinna), a fun park right off the Delaware, great for picnicking and a woodsy round of disc golf. Another small campground at **Tohickon Valley Park** (215-297-0754; Cafferty Rd., Point Pleasant) has 22 sites close to Bucks County River Country tubing, and a public swimming pool near the camping area. There are also four cabins for rent. Call ahead for either of these to obtain a permit. Nockamixon State Park has a "Cabin Colony" with 10 rentable units, one of which is handicap accessible.

Privately owned campsites can be found throughout Upper Bucks:

Colonial Woods Family Camping Resort (610-847-5808; www.colonialwoods.com; 545 Lonely Cottage Dr., Upper Black Eddy, PA 18972). Large facility with 208 campsites, electric, water and cable hookups for an additional fee. Cabins and trailers available for rental as well.

Dogwood Haven Family Campground (610-982-5402; 16 Lodi Hill Rd., Upper Black Eddy, PA 18972). Fifty-five sites with water and electric hookups, close to Delaware River attractions.

Quakerwoods Campground (215-536-1984; www.quakerwoods.com; 2225 Rosedale Rd., Quakertown, PA 18951). Over 150 sites, electric, water and cable hookups available, discounts for extended stays, and special events and activities.

Tohickon Family Campground (1-866-536-2267; www.tohickoncampground.com; 8308 Covered Bridge Rd., Quakertown, PA 18951). More than 100 sites, water and electric hookups with sewage available as well.

Fishing

Fishing in Upper Bucks is excellent. You'll need a temporary Pennsylvania fishing license, which can be purchased online (see Chapter 3). Try your luck in the Delaware River where permitted, but as with many recreational pursuits in Bucks County, Nockamixon State Park is the coin of the realm. There's a small fishing pond and also a pier on the enormous lake. Largemouth bass fishing is good here, and you'll also find carp, muskellunge, panfish, and others. For a change in scenery, head 20 miles south to **Ralph Stover State Park** (610-982-5560; 6011 State Park Rd., Pipersville) for smallmouth bass and catfish in Tohickon Creek.

Family Fun

Despite relatively few lodging options for families, Bucks County does excellent family tourist business on the strength of singular draws like Sesame Place, which can occupy the better part of a whole day trip. Although Central Bucks lacks traditional family attractions like arcades and putt-putt golf, there are two outstanding courses near Lambertville at **Pine Creek Miniature Golf** (394 NJ 31, www.pinecreekgolf.com; West Amwell) in New Jersey. Drive south to Lower Bucks and visit **Snipes Farm and Nursery** (215-295-1138; 890 W. Bridge St., Morrisville), which boasts two miniature golf courses (farm and jungle themed) as well as seasonal family-friendly activities such as apple picking and hayrides.

If you find yourself in Doylestown with children, it is worth stopping by **Kids' Castle** (215-348-9915; 425 Wells Rd., Doylestown) in Central Park, which is a very nifty eight-story castle/playground complex. The castle is seasonal.

And for those heading north, consider a stop at downtown Easton's **Crayola Factory** (610-515-8000; www.crayola.com/factory; 30 Centre Square, Easton, PA 18042), which is not really a factory and not in Bucks County, but has interactive attractions for young kids and an exhibit showing how crayons are made. The Crayola Factory is 30 miles from Doylestown on PA 611. It is open daily during the summer, and Tues.–Sun. in the fall, winter, and spring. Call for hours.

Major family attractions in Bucks are:

New Hope and Ivyland Railroad

215-862-2332
www.newhoperailroad.com
info@newhoperailroad.com
32 W. Bridge St., New Hope, PA 18938
Open: Year-round, but days of operation and departure times vary
Admission: $14.50–$22.50

A breezy hour-long ride on an early 20th century passenger train powered by an authentic steam or diesel locomotive. The round-trip starts in New Hope at the depot on Bridge Street, where you can souvenir shop before the ride, and chugs west to Lahaska. Seasonal and themed trains are targeted at adults (dinner rides and murder mystery dinner theater) or kids (a Christmas train with free hot cocoa and Santa Claus). But it's a comfortable way to see Bucks County for anyone.

Sesame Place

1-866-GO-4-ELMO

www.sesameplace.com
100 Sesame Rd., Langhorne, PA 19047
Open: May–Oct., Hours vary
Admission: $51; discounted twilight tickets available

This novel theme park, based on the Sesame Street television program, is a must-do for kids 10 and under. Rides range from the vigorous (the Vapor Trail kid-friendly roller coaster) to the sedate (floating down the park's Lazy River on an inner tube). Many are water rides, so bring a suit. Sesame Place also features a daily parade down the park's Main Street and performances throughout the day incorporating the show's characters. Cookie Monster, Big Bird, and the rest of the gang are available for meet-and-greet picture opportunities: check the daily listed schedule and ask employees for confirmation. Parking is available on-site for $15.

Golf

Bucks County Country Club (215-343-0350; 2600 York Rd., Jamison). Par 71, 18 holes; 6,275 yards. Semi-private course south of Doylestown. Fees: $26–$53.

Fairways Golf and Country Club (215-343-9979; 750 Country Club Ln., Warrington). Par 65, 18 holes; 4,503 yards. Seven miles south of Doylestown. Fun course, no par fives. Fees: $19–$42.

Makefield Highlands Golf Club (215-321-7000; 1418 Woodside Rd., Yardley). Par 72, 18 holes; 6,619 yards. Fees: $32–$75.

Horseback Riding

Haycock Stables (215-257-6271; www.haycockstables.com; 1035 Old Bethlehem Rd., Perkasie). Pick a horse and spend an hour or two riding around the equestrian trails at Nockamixon State Park. Closed on Mondays, but open year-round.

Hunting

"What are the hunting regulations around here?" I asked a Bucks County innkeeper once. "Like all the laws in Pennsylvania," he replied. "Weird."

The Pennsylvania Game Commission (610-926-3136; www.pgc.state.pa.us) issues something like two-dozen types of hunting licenses. A seven-day license for nonresidents to hunt small game is $31. It is best to call ahead at least four weeks in advance to determine what license you need and to give the Game Commission time to process your application and mail it out. With the requisite license, visitors can hunt deer, rabbit, and other game in selected parts of Nockamixon State Park or **State Game Land 157** (1-877-877-9470) nearby.

Nature Preserves

Bowman's Hill Wildflower Preserve

215-862-2924
www.bhwp.org
bhwp@bhwp.org
PA 32, New Hope, PA 18938
Open: Daily, 8:30 to sunset, Visitor Center 9–5
Admission: Adults $5, seniors $4, children $2

Great for either a quick hike along any number of trails or a full day spent tracking down the countless plants in bloom. Bowman's has close to a thousand different types of flora native to Central Bucks County. The Penn's Woods arboretum is a haven for unusual trees and is especially striking in the autumn. Mid to late summer is perfect for visiting the trails on the preserve's west side. After you're done exploring, take a load off in the Visitor Center where you can bird-watch through a wall of large picture windows.

Plane Rides
Rent a glider or small plane from **Sport Aviation, Inc. at Van Sant Airport** (610-847-8320; 516 Cafferty Rd., Erwinna). A good way to see Bucks scenery from above.

Polo
Tinicum Park (908-996-3321; 963 River Rd., Erwinna) features horse polo on Saturdays in the spring, summer, and early fall. The only admission charge is $5 per car for parking.

Swimming
There are public pools at Neshaminy State Park, Tohickon Valley Park, and Nockamixon State Park. Be very cautious about swimming in the Delaware River, which is legal, but potentially dangerous. Swimming is not allowed in Lake Nockamixon.

SHOPPING

The New Hope shopping district pops with activity year-round. It's an eclectic scene with an emphasis on funky boutiques and novel gift stores that dot Main Street and the perpendicular side roads amid the galleries and restaurants. There's something for everyone with an open mind. Doylestown is more conservative, but also a nice place for an afternoon of browsing. And of course Lahaska, with its factory outlets and retail village, is a shopping destination.

Antiques
Bucks is good for antiquing, but the undisputed regional champion is Lambertville. You can park the car in the morning, spend the rest of the day shop-hopping, and still not hit them all. There are three-dozen antique shops in downtown Lambertville, plus a massive operation on Wednesdays, Saturdays, and Sundays at the **Golden Nugget Antique Flea Market** (609-397-0811; 1850 River Rd., Lambertville), 2 miles south. Many antique shops can also be found along US 202 in Bucks between New Hope and Lahaska, as well as in downtown New Hope itself. Weekends are best, since nearly all shops are open then. The following list is a sampling.

America Antiques and Design (609-397-6966; 5 S. Main St., Lambertville). All sorts of decorative art. Specializes in enormous clock tower dials, which dominate the room.

A Stage In Time Antiques (215-862-6120; 12 W. Bridge St., New Hope). Great selection of Arts and Crafts furniture.

Cockamamie's (215-862-5454; 6 W. Bridge St., New Hope). Art deco furnishings, specifically lamps from the 1920s, '30s, and '40s.

Gardner's Antiques (215-794-8616; 6148 Lower York Rd. on US 202, New Hope). Marvelous French antique furnishings from multiple eras.

Kline's Court Antiques (609-397-9886; 11 Kline's Court, Lambertville). Six antique dealers, and an inclusive presentation of everything from chess sets to rare books.

The People's Store (609-397-9808; 28 N. Union St., Lambertville). More than 40 dealers, with some notable collectibles and foreign pieces. A highly eclectic mix of merchandise.

Peter Wallace, Ltd. (609-397-4914; 3 Lambert Ln., Lambertville). Watch for chandeliers grazing the top of your head when you walk in. This packed multi-level shop has an international variety of lamps, furniture, paintings, and much more. A garden in the rear displays fountains and statues.

Riverview Antiques (610-982-5122; 1738 River Rd., Upper Black Eddy). A real find in Upper Bucks, especially for silver and porcelain dishware.

Books

Doylestown Bookshop (215-230-7610; 16 S. Main St., Doylestown). The largest independent bookstore in Bucks County, this shop has regular book signings from locally and nationally recognized authors.

Farley's Bookshop (215-862-2452; 44 S. Main St., New Hope). Popular local bookshop with especially extensive magazine selection. The children's section is also thorough, stocked with titles like the Berenstain Bears series penned by long-time Bucks County residents.

Lion Around Books (215-529-1645; 302 W. Broad St., Quakertown). Cute name, mostly used book store with a large children's section.

Phoenix Books (609-397-4960; 49 N. Union St., Lambertville). Just what a used book store should be; very well organized, including out of print material, and a jam-packed biography section. Michener novels have local relevance.

Crafts

A Mano Galleries (215-862-5122; 128 S. Main St., New Hope, and 42 N. Union St., Lambertville). With locations in both New Hope and Lambertville, A Mano sells beautiful American crafts, including an interesting selection of jewelry and decorative pieces for the home.

Gothic Creations (215-862-2799; 15 N. Main St., New Hope). Unique, comprehensive gargoyle collection featuring both reproductions and original interpretive work.

Made in Italy (215-862-9454; 45 N. Main St., New Hope). A variety of Italian imports, including pottery and jewelry made from Venetian glass.

Clothing

Lilies of the Field (215-353-0350; 1 S. Main St., Doylestown). A small, friendly women's clothing store that's upscale without being overpriced. Lots of accessories too, like beaded jewelry and hats.

Planet Wear (215-862-1174; 32 S. Main St., Suite 1, New Hope). Sportswear promoting dozens of countries all around the globe. Located in the 4 Seasons Mall.

Sterling Leather (215-862-9669; 97 S. Main St., New Hope). All sorts of leather products—coats, boots, belts, hats, etc.—for men and women and in every style. Patrons are as likely to be bankers as bikers (and sometimes both). They also have a store at Peddler's Village in Lahaska.

Vestiti (215-348-5261; 37 E. State St., Doylestown). High-end men's clothing.

Gifts

Celt-Iberia Traders (215-862-4922; 15 S. Ferry St., New Hope). An intriguing merge of Irish and Spanish merchandise. The genuine Irish sweaters and caps are top quality.

Fiddleheads (609-397-3716; 19 Bridge St., Lambertville). Excellent local florist, creative bouquets and gift baskets.

F. P. Kolbe (1-866-377-5852; 6 River Rd., Point Pleasant). Home and garden heaven, with fountains, ornaments, furniture, ceramic pots, and other merchandise literally spilling out of the store. A selection of model ships inside as well.

Hot Plates (1-888-869-3220; 40 S. Main St., New Hope). Kitchen wares are the main attraction at this store, which stocks one of the largest Fiesta dish selections around. Also original china and collectibles.

Lazer Illusions (215-862-9710; 11 Bridge St., New Hope). Novelty store specializing in holograms to hang on the wall. Lots of other stuff, from figurines and posters to gag gifts.

Strawberry Jam (215-862-9251; 44 S. Main St., New Hope). Not an inch of space is wasted at this fun shop, which sells jewelry, paper products, CDs, and perfumes among other things. A retail institution in New Hope, Strawberry Jam has been open 25 years.

Malls and Complexes

Peddler's Village (215-794-4000; www.peddlersvillage.com; US 202 and PA 263, Lahaska). Seventy-five shops are spread throughout this buyer's paradise, which takes at least a half day to explore. Lots of unique clothing and gift stores, gourmet food shops, and diversions for kids at the Giggleberry Fair entertainment center. Peddler's Village stays open extra late during the holiday season. Check into the Golden Plough Inn on-site and enjoy a shopping-themed vacation.

Penn's Purchase (215-794-0300; www.pennspurchase.com; US 202, Lahaska). The second fist in the one-two punch that is Lahaska shopping. Penn's Purchase has more than four dozen mostly upscale factory outlet stores like Coach, Brooks Brothers, and Nine West. While jaw-dropping bargains are rare, the discounts are considerable.

Rice's Sale & Country Market (215-297-5993; www.ricesmarket.com; 6326 Greenhill Rd., New Hope). A large outdoor flea market where vendors hawk clothes, jewelry, crafts, food, and a great deal more. Open Tuesdays all year and Saturdays from March to December. Hours are 7 A.M. to 1:30 P.M. Arrive during the last hour and enjoy maximum negotiating leverage, as sellers grow antsy and prepare to go home.

Unique

It's Christmas every day at **Byers' Choice Factory** (215-822-0150; www.byerschoice
.com; 4355 County Line Rd., Chalfont), where Joyce Byers turned her caroler figurine
hobby into a thriving business with husband Bob and their two children. Byers carolers are
fun, affectionate pieces, crafted in traditional and Victorian styles. The plaster figures are
still made by hand—Byers currently employs more than 150 artisans—and each piece is a
bit unique. A visit to the factory takes you down a cobblestone London street, through several exquisitely detailed caroler dioramas, and up an observation deck where you can see
the workshop in action. Byers' Choice is open Mon.–Sat. 10–5 and Sun. 12–5. The factory
is 7 miles west of Doylestown, just off US 202. Exhibitions are free, and you can purchase
carolers in the large factory gift shop. If you just can't get enough, follow up with a visit to
New Hope's **Christmas Past** (215-862-0501; 142 S. Main St., New Hope) for enough ornaments to last a lifetime.

Byers' Choice Carolers

Shopping in New Hope is a weekend pastime for many in the Delaware Valley. It is
packed with interesting shops that can't be found in your average small town. Some notables include:

Against the Grain (215-862-4900; 82 S. Main St., New Hope). Definitely worth a look,
even if you aren't a connoisseur of swords, fine handmade knives, and the other medieval
merchandise you'll find. Be careful handling the merchandise; as the signs say, you bleed
on it, you buy it.

Love Saves the Day (215-862-1399; 1 S. Main St., New Hope). An eclectic novelty and
clothing shop, perfect for assembling a Halloween costume or finding gag gifts and an
unusual figurine. Have Professor Renerb print your fortune for a quarter.

Grownups (215-862-9304; 2 E. Mechanic Ave., New Hope). Lingerie aplenty and other
risqué merchandise for adults eyes only.

Mystikal Times (215-862-5629; 127 Main St., New Hope). Tarot card readings and an
opportunity to stock up on pagan paraphernalia like candles, cauldrons, and whatnot.

Suzie Hot Sauce (215-862-1334; 19A W. Bridge St., New Hope). See how much heat you can take. The store's wide (international and domestic) variety of hot sauces is dished out in free-sample-sized servings.

Wineries

Bucks County has a climate and economy well suited for wine production, and there are excellent wineries in all county regions. A personal favorite is **Crossing Vineyards and Winery** (215-493-6500; www.crossingvineyards.com; 1853 Wrightstown Rd., Washington Crossing) where seven reds, six whites, and an assortment of specialty wines are produced and sold. The Cabernet Franc and Chardonnay are popular choices, but taste and decide for yourself. Crossing is famous for its many special events, like an inexpensive summer concert series where area musicians perform under a tent while attendees sip to their hearts' content. Open every day from noon to 6.

No trip to Upper Bucks is complete without a stop at **Sand Castle Winery** (1-800-722-9463; www.sandcastlewinery.com; 755 River Rd., Erwinna). The building is a work of contemporary art, with a tan exterior that resembles a large sand castle. It sits at the crest of a hill, from which you can see the vineyards themselves and the undulating Bucks valley landscape. Sand Castle offers three weekend tours of varying depth, all of which include some wine tasting. Call ahead or visit the Web site to reserve a spot for the more extensive tours.

For a more casual experience, try **Buckingham Valley Vineyards** (215-794-7188; www.pawine.com; 1521 PA 413, Buckingham), where you can graze the vineyards at your own pace and pick up more than a dozen bargain-priced wines. Not far east is **New Hope Winery** (1-800-592-9463; www.newhopewinery.com; 6123 Lower York Rd., New Hope). No vineyards here, but some tasty bottles sold in an old barn building.

INFORMATION

Ambulance, Fire & Police

The general emergency number is 911. Call it for ambulance, fire, and police. Other emergency numbers:

Abused Women's Hotline	1-800-220-8116
Crisis Services	1-800-499-7455
Poison Control	215-386-2100
Suicide Hotlines	
Lower Bucks:	215-355-6000
Central Bucks:	215-340-1998
Upper Bucks:	215-536-0911
Police (non-emergency)	
Bristol	215-785-4040
Buckingham	215-794-8813
Doylestown	215-348-4201
New Hope	215-348-7400
Newtown	215-860-7835
Quakertown	215-795-2931

Area Codes & Town Government

The area code for Bucks County is 215.

Bucks County is governed by a three-member board of commissioners who serve four-year terms. Individual towns and boroughs within the county have their own governmental structures. Doylestown, for example, has a mayor who works with a nine-member city council. New Hope has a seven-member council, with a president and vice president elected from and by council members.

The county chair is in Doylestown at 55 E. Court St., where the general services phone number is 215-348-6000. For questions specific to a borough or township, try the following administrative offices:

Bristol: 215-785-0500; 2501 Bath Rd., 19007
Buckingham: 215-794-8834; 4613 Hughesian Dr., 18912
Doylestown: 215-345-4140; 57 W. Court St., 18901
New Hope: 215-862-3347; 41 N. Main St., 18938
Newtown: 215-968-2109; 23 N. State St., 18940
Quakertown: 215-536-5001; 35 N. 3rd St., 18951

Banks

Bank of America: 215-489-7510; 100 Progress Dr., Doylestown

First National Bank & Trust: 215-862-2600; 408 Old York Rd., New Hope

Hudson United Bank: 908-996-2918; 21 Bridge St., Frenchtown, NJ

PNC Bank: 215-862-1521; 2 N. Main St., New Hope

TD Bank: 215-348-4063; 425 S. Main St., Doylestown

Wachovia Bank: 215-862-9455; 336 W. Bridge St., New Hope

Recommended Reading

Adams III, Charles J. *Bucks County Ghost Stories,* Reading, PA: Exeter House Books, 1999. A fun read; includes stories about several places mentioned above.

Battle, J. H. ed. *The History of Bucks County,* Spartansburg, SC: Reprint Co., 1985. Painstakingly detailed history.

Bush, George S. ed. *The Genius Belt: The Story of the Arts in Bucks County,* Doylestown PA: James A. Michener Art Museum in association with the Pennsylvania State University Press, 1996. Looks at the writers, painters, and craftsmen who shaped Bucks' art scene.

Hospitals

Doylestown Hospital: 595 W. State St., Doylestown; 215-345-2200.

Frankford Hospital—Bucks County: 380 N. Oxford Valley Rd., Langhorne; 215-949-5000

Lower Bucks Hospital: 501 Bath Rd., Bristol; 215-785-9200

Warminster Hospital: 225 Newtown Rd., Warminster; 215-441-6600

Late Night Food and Fuel

Doylestown Gulf (fuel), 216 S. Main St., Doylestown

Eagle Diner (food), 6522 Lower York Rd., New Hope

Lukoil (fuel), 350 W. Bridge St., New Hope

Wawa (food), 341 W. Bridge St., New Hope

Media
Magazines and Newspapers

Bucks County Town & Country Living (215-968-0321; www.buckscountymagazine.com; 510 B. Durham Rd., Newtown). Dining, entertainment, culture, and travel tips, published quarterly.

Bucks County Courier-Times (215-949-4250; 8400 Bristol Pike, Levittown). Daily newspaper.

Bucks County Herald (215-794-1096). Free weekly paper, focuses on the central and upper part of the county.

Half a dozen local newspapers serve Bucks' larger towns. A couple you may come across:

Doylestown Patriot (215-340-9811; 329 S. Main St., Doylestown)

New Hope Gazette (215-862-9435)

Radio and Television Stations

Bucks County receives radio signals from Philadelphia stations. Its broadcast television channels are the same as in Philadelphia.

Visitor Information

The **Bucks County Conference and Visitors Bureau** (215-639-0300; www.experience buckscounty.com; 3207 Street Rd., Bensalem) regularly updates its easily navigable Web site. Thorough lodging, dining, shopping, and cultural listings are posted. Their hard-copy promotional materials have detailed maps, including demarcations for the county's covered bridges.

6

Lancaster County's Amish Country

Finding Peace with the Pennsylvania Dutch

> Romantic images of the Amish abound in the American imagination. Popular myths portray them cling-
> ing to their frontier ways—washing clothes by hand and cooking over open hearths. The Lancaster
> Amish do diverge from modern ways, but they also sip sodas, bounce on trampolines, and use in-line
> skates. Amish life offers a peaceful pace and pleasant satisfaction, but it's not idyllic. The sweat of
> toil and earnest struggles to harness social change lace their daily world.
>
> —Donald B. Kraybill, *The Amish of Lancaster County*

The tour buses arrive virtually every day in the spring and summer from all along the eastern seaboard. Many carry teenagers unprepared to countenance the idea that children
their age could live happily without television or the Internet. But the Amish who live in
eastern Lancaster County are a mystery to nearly everyone.

Visiting Amish Country is a many-sided experience. The delicious food, the gorgeous
countryside, the shopping opportunities, and the bed & breakfasts afford vacationers the
rest and relaxation they seek. Family diversions are fun, and often unique. But Amish
Country is also instructive. The Amish rejection of modern creature comforts is grounded
in the worry that a full embrace of technology would undercut community values they hold
dear. And while the Amish lifestyle seems unusual, within its traditions lie some credible
indictments of mainstream American society—the dissolving of family dinnertime, the
compulsion to keep up with the Joneses, etc. Visiting the Amish not only illuminates the
workings of a starkly different culture, it compels us to point the spotlight back at ourselves.

First, a little history. In 1517 Martin Luther nailed his famed grievances to Wittenberg
Castle Church in Saxony, triggering the Protestant Reformation and catalyzing reform
movements across Europe. One such group took hold in Switzerland organized around the
practice of adult baptism. Anabaptists, as they were called, argued that the decision to

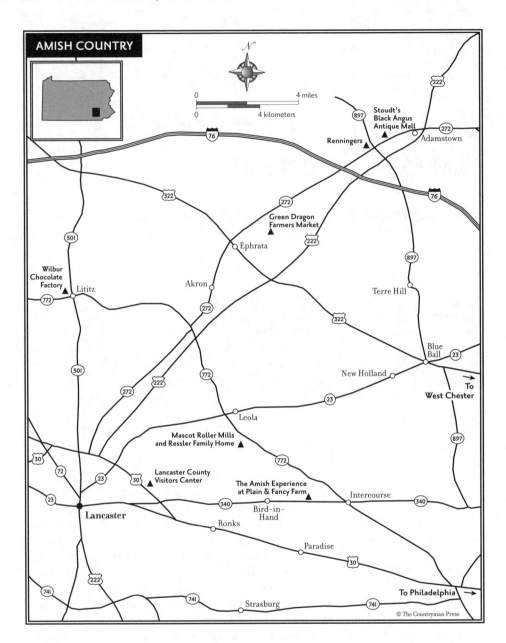

accept Christianity should be made during adulthood, and only then after careful consideration. Religiopolitical leaders of the day considered the Anabaptists extremely radical. They faced persecution from the movement's infancy, forcing geographical mobility on the adherents. This became one motivating factor behind subsequent splits from within the original sect.

After the founding, Anabaptist history becomes tricky to follow. Different Anabaptist groups cropped up around Europe in places like present-day Germany, France, Austria, and the Netherlands. Central tenets of the movement remained universal: adult baptism, opposition to intentional killing for any reason, and a general, overarching adherence to Christian doctrine.

The Amish settlements in today's Lancaster County are rooted in a late-17th-century Anabaptist branch that sprang up around Switzerland and Germany. It was founded by conservative reformer Jakob Ammann, whose last name inspired the "Amish" label. By 1693, the Mennonite sect had been around for over a hundred years, and Ammann refused to accept what he saw as deviations from the faith. Ammann engineered a split from the Mennonites, creating a church more averse to change and cultural assimilation. Today's Pennsylvania Amish and Mennonite populations live in the same area, identify with a similar cultural heritage, and are friendly with one another, but Mennonites are less resistant to American modernity. Visit a Pennsylvania farmer's market and you can see the differences before your eyes: Amish farmers arrive towing their goods via horse and carriage, while Mennonite farmers bring their produce in Ford vans.

Amish arrived in Pennsylvania shortly after its creation, drawn by William Penn's promise of religious freedom. High birthrates, durable ties to the community, and hard work have sustained and expanded the group's presence in Pennsylvania since that time. While Ohio and Indiana have sizable Amish populations as well, Pennsylvania's is the largest, and nowhere else is as widely associated with Amish tourism as Lancaster County. The evolution of Amish Country as a tourist destination arose from several related factors: the county's location near dense population centers like Philadelphia, convenient access to ancillary attractions like factory outlet shopping, the invigorating Lancaster countryside, and of course interest in the Amish themselves.

Donald Kraybill, a leading scholar on the Amish, often highlights the "ironic twists" woven through the area's tourist culture. "Paradoxically," he writes in *The Riddle of Amish Culture*, "the Amish defiance of modern life has brought them not persecution but admiration and respect—enough to underwrite a massive tourist industry. The course of history has converted these descendents of despised heretics into esteemed objects of curiosity.... And surprisingly, the tourism that appears to threaten their solitude may actually strengthen their cultural identity." It is hard to say whether Amish Country's thriving tourist market is quite this non-zero sum, but Kraybill touches on something poignant. It is best to view Amish Country tourism as a symbiotic relationship, and to respect the rules and customs of the local community while enjoying the cultural opportunities it has to offer. For more information on the Amish and Mennonite communities in Lancaster County, see "Recommended Reading" later in the chapter, or stop by the **Amish Mennonite Information Center** (717-768-0807; PA 340, Intercourse).

Pennsylvania's Amish Country, loosely defined, comprises the eastern half of Lancaster County, which is where the most densely concentrated Amish settlements lie. There exists an Amish presence elsewhere in Lancaster and elsewhere in the state, but this chapter focuses on the east for its distinctly Amish character. This does not include the city of Lancaster itself or western Lancaster County, which are fine areas to visit but beyond this book's reach. It does cover three unique communities—Lititz, Ephrata, and Adamstown—in the north part of the county that are near Amish settlements but are not always identified as part of Amish Country.

Since we're already knee-deep in boundaries and terms, here's one more: Pennsylvania Dutch Country. Dutch Country commonly refers to an area far larger than the land inhabited by Amish and Mennonite families in the eastern half of Lancaster. It incorporates several southeastern Pennsylvania counties west of the Philadelphia metropolitan area settled by German immigrants during the colonial era ("Dutch" in this context is derived from "Deutsche" and refers not to Netherlanders but to Pennsylvanians of German ancestry). I use the terms "Amish Country" and "Pennsylvania Dutch Country" interchangeably in this chapter, but to be wholly accurate, Amish Country is a part of Dutch Country.

Horse and cart at a produce auction

Whatever you want to call it, the heart of the area is found in **Bird-in-Hand** and **Intercourse**, separated by 4 miles along PA 340. These villages are twin meccas for Amish tourism, packed with furniture shops, buggy rides, food stores, and markets stocked with regional comfort foods (pretzels, jams, pies, etc.). Multi-attraction complexes like *The Amish Experience* in Bird-in-Hand and *Kitchen Kettle Village* in Intercourse have lodging on-site. Bird-in-Hand is a good starting point. Intercourse has a greater diversity in stores and attractions, and feels more like a town. There is, of course, the matter of the funny name, without which there would be fewer visitors and lewd T-shirt sales. Situated within a short drive from nearby Blue Ball and Berks County's Virginville, the area has saved countless stand-up comedians long nights spent writing new material. South of Bird-in-Hand and Intercourse are **Ronks** and **Paradise:** twin towns along US 30 dotted with motels, restaurants, and souvenir stores.

The Amish and Mennonites are the most readily identified Pennsylvania Dutch, but there is a similarly fascinating history to be learned about other Christian sects with German roots in the area. One such sect has vanished entirely: the disciples of Conrad Beissel, who formed the northern Lancaster settlement of **Ephrata** in 1732 to pursue a secluded existence of celibacy, sleeping on wooden pillows, and eating a single meal each day, with an unshakable belief that the Second Coming of Christ would occur between midnight and 2 A.M. during Beissel's lifetime. The story of Beissel and his followers is a good one, today told in depth at the Ephrata Cloister where the colony existed (see "Historic Sites" below). The town of Ephrata, built up around the Cloister over time, is a nice place to stay. Look for bed & breakfasts, a couple good restaurants, and some distinctive shopping.

West of Ephrata is the small village of **Lititz,** founded as a refuge for members of the Moravian Church in 1757. The Lititz Moravians were (and remain) a practical people, with a legendary work ethic that powered the community from its beginnings, allowing it to exist in relative isolation for its first hundred years. Property ownership was disallowed for non-Moravians through the mid-19th century, when Lutheran and Brethren congregations sprouted quickly. In the original Lititz, only one citizen was permitted to practice any given trade at any time, emphasizing the community's belief in a collective purpose. It acquired a new identity with the coming of Wilbur Chocolate in 1900, which along with the Sturgis Pretzel Bakery made Lititz a snack food hotspot, though it remains hard to top nearby Hershey, Pennsylvania, in this realm. Personally, I'm a sucker for Lititz. Walk the downtown strip, sample some chocolate, and stay at one of the superb bed & breakfasts buried deep within the periphery.

In the county's northeast corner is **Adamstown**, which has no unusual religious history other than a sacred devotion to antique dealing. Once known principally for its hat-making industry, Adamstown has evolved into an antiquing Shangri-La. The shops and markets are clustered mainly along PA 272 like casinos on the Las Vegas Strip. "If it's old and American, chances are it's in Adamstown," wrote Robert Schroeder in a 2002 article for the *Washington Post*. Of course there are loads of foreign antiques as well, plus fine dining and great beer at Stoudt's (see "Dining" below).

Finally, what antiquing is to Adamstown, railroads are to **Strasburg**. South of Ronks and a touch isolated from Amish Country activity, Strasburg has carved out its own personality around the Strasburg Railroad, which closed in the 1950s but has been preserved and adapted as a hub for teaching the state's railroading heritage. The town has three train-themed museums and historic train rides on the old coal-burning passenger trains themselves.

TRANSPORTATION

Getting There

Amish Country is 55 to 70 miles west of Philadelphia, depending on where you're headed. The fastest thoroughfare is I-76, a toll road most of the way; it becomes the Pennsylvania Turnpike near Valley Forge. It drifts northward before it can hit Lancaster, which makes it very convenient to Ephrata, Adamstown, and Lititz, but inconvenient to Bird-in-Hand, Intercourse, and Strasburg. State roads like PA 897 can be helpful in linking the turnpike with the southern Amish Country towns.

US 30 links Philadelphia with greater Lancaster, but is slow much of the way due to high volume and traffic signals. It runs west through the Main Line and past Paoli, where a bypass begins, splitting the route into a business road and a stoplight-free parkway. They link back up in West Sadsbury, 8 miles east of Paradise. If you are traveling to Bird-in-Hand or Intercourse, find PA 340 (also known as Old Philadelphia Pike), which branches off US 30 in between Downington and Coatesville.

Alternatives to car travel are limited if you're traveling without a privately arranged coach bus tour. **Greyhound** also has service to downtown Lancaster, and limited service to Ephrata. **AMTRAK** has a station in Lancaster. Very limited commercial air traffic goes through **Lancaster Airport** (717-569-1221; www.lancasterairport.com; 500 Airport Rd., Lititz). **Harrisburg International Airport** (1-888-235-9442; www.flyhia.com) is 40 miles from Amish Country and is served by eight commercial airlines.

Getting Around

Once you are within Amish Country, look to the state roads to connect the towns. Pennsylvania 340 links Bird-in-Hand with Intercourse, where it intersects PA 772—a straight shot to Lititz. Find PA 272 for travel to Ephrata and Adamstown. These roads are all quite scenic and you'll see grazing livestock and farm stands along the way. When driving around Amish Country, be conscious of horse and buggies traveling at slow speeds. They keep to the side of the road, but most Amish Country thoroughfares lack a shoulder. Passing the horse and buggies is often permissible, so pay attention to road signs. Look out for oncoming traffic and try not to use the car horn, which can scare the horses.

TOURING

Touring Amish Country by horse and buggy is a popular family and group activity. Amish, Brethren, and Mennonite tour guides trek around the winding rural byways while educating passengers on the community's customs and lifestyle. Tours may stop at farm stands, quilt shops, and other Amish-run businesses. Note that while Amish and Mennonites in the area speak German and the Pennsylvania Dutch (or Pennsylvania German) language, many—including horse and buggy tour guides—also speak fluent English.

AAA Buggy Rides (717-989-2829; Kitchen Kettle Village on PA 340, Intercourse). Three different-length tours are offered from AAA, which is easy to find in the Kitchen Kettle Village retail complex.

Aaron and Jessica's Buggy Rides (717-768-8828; 3121 Old Philadelphia Pike, Bird-in-Hand). Tours leave from the Plain & Fancy Farm complex in between Bird-in-Hand and Intercourse every 10 minutes.

Abe's Buggy Rides (717-392-1794; 2596 Old Philadelphia Pike, Bird-in-Hand). Amish drivers offer 2- and 4-mile rides.

LODGING

The tyranny of choice rears its head all over Pennsylvania Dutch Country when it comes to lodging. There are so many places to stay that it can become overwhelming. Some travelers just settle for the first motel they see on US 30, while others make it their mission to uncover an Amish farm B&B way off the tourist track. For an all-encompassing look at your options, contact the **Pennsylvania Dutch Convention and Visitors Bureau** (1-800-723-8824; www.padutchcountry.com), which has an extensive list that includes several working farms where you can stay. The majority are in the western part of the county, but not all.

Rates

Inexpensive	Up to $80
Moderate	$80 to $150
Expensive	$150 to $230
Very Expensive	$230 and up

These rates do not include room taxes or special service charges that might apply during your stay. All hotels are handicap accessible unless otherwise noted.

Bed & Breakfasts and Small Inns

Lancaster County has by some counts two hundred bed & breakfasts, making it among the most bed & breakfast–loaded areas in America. Not all these are in Amish Country, but many are. This section profiles a sampling of some good ones, deliberately chosen to represent different locations and price brackets. For more information and guidance, contact the **Lancaster County Bed-and-Breakfast Inns Association** (717-464-5588 or 1-800-848-2994; www.padutchinns.com). An upside to the ready supply of B&Bs is that room rates are quite reasonable. Expect to pay $20–$40 less per night in Dutch Country than you would for a B&B of similar quality in the Brandywine Valley or Bucks County.

Wherever you stay, ask your innkeeper about meeting Amish residents. Many proprietors have longstanding relationships with area Amish, from whom they often purchase food and manpower. Some can arrange for you to share a meal with an Amish family. Talk with the innkeeper about this before booking a room if it is something you want to do. As a rule of thumb, inns near Intercourse, Paradise, and Bird-in-Hand are the most likely to have connections to the Amish.

Bird-in-Hand, Intercourse & Vicinity

Carriage Corner Bed & Breakfast

Innkeepers: Gordon and Gwen Schuit
1-800-209-3059 or 717-768-3059
www.carriagecornerbndb.com
innkeeper@carriagecornerbandb.com
3705 E. Newport Rd., Intercourse, PA 17534
Price: Moderate
Credit Cards: Yes
Handicapped Access: No

Well-priced and impeccably located within a three-minute drive from central Intercourse, the Carriage Corner is a 40-year-old country house that exudes warmth. Gordon and Gwen have managed the property for 15 years and know their way around the area. All five rooms—each named for a fruit—include cable television and desk space, a rare feature in the area. The Lemon Room is the largest and most expensive, but still a bargain at barely $100 with tax. If you stay here, consider booking the Meandering package, which fits in all the major Amish attractions and saves you the effort.

The Creekside Inn

Innkeepers: Cathy and Dennis Zimmermann
1-866-604-2574 or 717-687-0333
www.thecreeksideinn.com
cathy@thecreeksideinn.com
44 Leacock Rd., Paradise, PA 17562
Price: Moderate to expensive
Credit Cards: Yes
Handicapped Access: No

Come for the inviting country-style rooms (with modern conveniences, of course) and stay for the innkeepers. Cathy and Dennis are not just friendly hosts, but a tremendous resource for discovering the parts of Amish Country off the usual tourist beat. They maintain longstanding relationships with many local Amish, from whom they've purchased several finely crafted chests, beds, and bookcases found at the inn. Cathy's Torquay pottery collection and a coal-burning stove in the kitchen lend extra character. Creekside is very well-priced considering the location and quality of the experience. History is also a special part of the attraction here. The stone house was built in 1781 by David Witmer, hemp miller and friend of George Washington, who (as the story goes) was dissuaded from constructing a hemp mill on his own estate when Witmer botched a private demonstration for the General. An original over mantle from the house is now on display at Winterthur in the Brandywine Valley.

Frogtown Acres

Innkeepers: Joe and Gloria Crawshaw
1-888-649-2333 or 717-768-7684
www.frogtownacres.com
joe@frogtownacres.com or gloria@frogtownacres.com
44 Frogtown Rd., Paradise, PA 17562
Price: Moderate
Credit Cards: Yes
Handicapped Access: One room

This rustic four-room inn is a surrounded on all sides by Amish farms, which supply the hearty breakfast menu. Innkeepers Joe and Gloria bring a friendly, lighthearted approach to the business that is simultaneously jokey and exceptionally accommodating. They once flew the Danish flag outside the inn to mark the arrival of a guest from Denmark, and Joe regularly organizes special events for guests like marshmallow roasts and recreational activities on the 3-acre grounds. Former educators, the innkeepers allow well-behaved children five years old and up. Bedrooms are spread throughout two floors of an 1810 fieldstone and barn lumber building, which housed a chicken coop throughout much of its life. You'll find hand-sewn Amish quilts on all beds, and a unique wooden balcony off the appositely named Balcony Room. Internet and television are restricted to the common area—an old horse stable that also stocks dozens of board games and an air hockey table. A frog theme stems from the creatures' presence on and around the grounds. Look for the frog figurines scattered throughout the buildings and parking lot humor (cars not belonging to guests will be "toad").

Mill Creek Homestead Bed & Breakfast

Innkeepers: Bob and Lori Kepiro
717-291-6419
www.millcreekhomestead.com
lkepiro@comcast.net
2578 Old Philadelphia Pike, Bird-in-Hand,

The pleasant dining room at Mill Creek Homestead

PA 17505
Price: Moderate
Credit Cards: Yes
Handicapped Access: No

A classic fieldstone house rooted in 18th-century Lancaster when the grounds were occupied by log cabins. Four themed guest rooms riff on time-honored B&B themes. Reds, whites, and blues mark the Patriot Room, but décor is restrained rather than brash. Italian lace and floral patterns differentiate the Magnolia Room, which also overlooks a magnolia tree. The innkeepers, who also operate a second B&B, **Homestead Lodging** in nearby Smoketown, have revamped the front lawn to offer better views from the front porch, and it's a pleasant place to watch horse and buggy traffic over morning coffee. The large in-ground pool and outdoor Jacuzzi are seasonal attractions.

Ephrata

Inns at Doneckers

1-800-377-2206

www.doneckers.com
318-324 S. State St., Ephrata, PA 17522
Price: Inexpensive to expensive
Credit Cards: Yes
Handicapped Access: Yes

Doneckers began as a mail-order dry goods business and evolved into an Ephrata empire with high-end fashion and furniture stores, dining, and this venerated lodging complex. Though the clothing store and restaurant were closing at press time, the furniture galleries (see "Shopping") and inns remain open. If you wish to stay at Doneckers you have some choices to make—the 31 rooms exist within four buildings and come in different shapes and sizes. One option is to stay in the Victorian-style Guesthouse, which strings together three townhomes (19 guest rooms total) on a residential section of State Street and feels a bit like living in Ephrata. Rooms in the Guesthouse all include Internet access and are a very good deal, sometimes as low as $75 a night for the smaller ones. Nearby is the 1777 House, once inhabited by an Ephrata clockmaker, which rents generally larger rooms, including the lavish Conrad Beissel Suite (an ironic title considering Beissel's austere lifestyle). Even larger suites can be had in the 1777 House's Carriage House. Daily continental breakfast comes with a hot item or two and is included with your stay.

Kimmell House Bed & Breakfast
Innkeepers: Dave and Bonnie Harvey
1-800-861-3385 or 717-738-3555
www.kimmellhouse.com
info@kimmellhouse.com
851 S. State St., Ephrata, PA 17522
Price: Moderate to expensive
Credit Cards: Yes
Handicapped Access: No

A meticulously restored Georgian Colonial house made of sandstone, with an unusually extensive array of the era's interior architectural features. Note the cross and bible doors on the dining room cupboard, which encloses butterfly shelves. Kimmell House was originally a corn and wheat mill, converted to a tavern in 1811. A small creek runs through the backyard, obscured from the house by the perky azalea garden and other foliage. Bonnie is a crafts aficionado who once owned an area store and still maintains a small gift shop in the house. A good lodging choice is the Shaker Room—known informally as the "treehouse room" since trees brush against all three windows.

Smithton Inn
Innkeeper: Dorothy Graybill
1-877-755-4590 or 717-733-6094
www.historicsmithtoninn.com
smithtoninn@dejazzd.com
900 W. Main St., Ephrata, PA 17522
Price: Moderate to expensive
Credit Cards: Yes
Handicapped Access: No

Smithton was built in 1763 during the age of activity at the Ephrata Cloister—its original occupants were Householders who worshipped with the cloister's brothers and sisters nearby. (Householders did not practice celibacy or live at the hermitage, but shared other traditions with Beissel and his

Smithton Inn from the backyard

followers.) It has served as an inn since horse-drawn carriages were the only transportation to come through Ephrata. Most rooms follow color themes, like the Purple Diamond, which features cherry wood flooring and windowsills to balance the violet undertones. A deviation from the color theme is the bi-level South Wing Suite, with a Dutch door that opens onto a private porch. The suite has the highest square footage of any room at the inn, and was an expansion onto the original sandstone house in the mid-19th century, serving as a tailor shop for a time. Some rooms will accommodate a single child or third adult who can sleep in a pull-out trundle bed. An unusual (and cushy looking) cupboard bed awaits in the suite. The innkeeper's late husband designed, built, and in some cases painted much of the Smithton's exquisite furniture.

Lititz

The Cooper's Inn

Innkeepers: Audrey and Dane St. Clair
717-626-2658

Lititz: come for the history, stay for the pretzels.

www.thecoopersinnbb.com
537 Hackman Rd., Lititz, PA 17543
Price: Moderate
Credit Cards: Yes
Handicapped Access: No

When the St. Clairs decided to expand the Cooper's Inn 12 years ago, prior to its life as a bed & breakfast, they did it the old-fashioned way. Animals hauled the raw materials, and all the poplar and oak lumber was milled on the premises. The resulting Pennsylvania German farmhouse is a monument to fine craftsmanship and attention to historical detail. Antique door latches and German locks re-create the house much as it would have looked more than two centuries ago. Pictures in the Gathering Room trace Audrey's family lineage, present in the area for six generations. The Keeping Room, where family-style breakfast is served, boasts a functional open hearth fireplace, reconstructed by Dane and outfitted with era-appropriate spoons, pots, peel, and crane. The bounty of interesting (and often personal) antiques is draw enough, but the inn's location just beyond downtown Lititz is tranquil even by Lancaster County standards. So long as the corn doesn't grow too high you can see four counties from outside the fields—a 270-degree view used by Union troops as a lookout post during the Civil War.

The General Sutter Inn

717-626-2115
www.generalsutterinn.com
generalsutter@dejazzd.com
14 E. Main St., Lititz, PA 17534
Price: Inexpensive to expensive
Credit Cards: Yes
Handicapped Access: Limited, call to inquire

A 250-year-old inn named for Swiss-born adventurer and entrepreneur John Sutter, who established an agricultural empire by the American River in California in 1840. It

Well-stocked bar at the General Sutter Inn's 1764 Restaurant

was overrun by thieves and vagrants in 1848 when word got out that there was gold on his land. The event set off the Gold Rush, and catalyzed a series of catastrophic events for Sutter, who eventually lost all his land and property. Sutter's tumultuous life ended in Lititz in 1880, seven years after his arrival and 24 years after the town's Moravian populace opened the community to outsiders. He lived across the street from this hotel, named for him after his death. There are 16 rooms for all budgets and needs, from singles priced at under $80 a night to the enormous third-floor apartment with full kitchen and deck. The floorboards creak with history, but renovations and steady attention to the property ensures a comfortable, authentic experience. A ballroom on the ground level hosts events for up to 125 people and there is fine dining at the 1764 Restaurant. The inn also allows children and pets.

Swiss Woods Bed & Breakfast and Inn

Innkeepers: Werner and Deborah Mossimann
1-800-594-8018 or 717-627-3358
www.swisswoods.com
innkeeper@swisswoods.com
500 Blantz Rd., Lititz, PA 17543

Price: Expensive
Credit Cards: Yes
Handicapped Access: No

You can tell from the winding gravel road that slopes through lush woodland to the inn's entrance that this is not your typical bed & breakfast. It is Werner and Debbie's Swiss Woods, a luxurious 30-acre hideaway in the Lititz hills, richly informed by the couple's many years spent in Switzerland. The inn was constructed 22 years ago and is so nimbly integrated into the grounds that it is hard to imagine the land without it. A soft pine décor gives the place a cheery feel. Perennials are everywhere, accented by annuals and a diverse stock of trees. Eight beehives are maintained on the premises, so plant life is chosen partly with the bees' tastes in mind. Swiss influences predominate—bedside chocolates are the most obvious examples, but conversation pieces from Switzerland can be found in guest bedrooms like the generously sized Matterhorn Suite and Appenzell Room. These rooms and the Lake of Geneva Room are on the top floor, and have the best views. Visitors can also enjoy the extensive tea selection and use of a first-floor kitchen. Full breakfast every morning.

Sandstone fireplace and furnishings at Swiss Woods

Terre Hill
Artist's Inn and Gallery
Innkeepers: Jan and Bruce Garrabrandt
1-888-999-4479
www.artistinn.com
relax@artistinn.com
117 E. Main St., Terre Hill, PA 17581
Price: Expensive to very expensive
Credit Cards: Yes
Handicapped Access: No
A one-of-a-kind property, situated in the tightly knit town of Terre Hill in northern Amish Country, where cigar wrapper production once powered the local economy (tobacco plants still grow on many farms). Innkeepers Jan and Bruce are as kind as they are talented. The first-floor gallery displays Bruce's colored pencil artwork, and Jan has an encyclopedic knowledge of the area's hidden gems. Cute touches abound at the Artist's Inn—guests of the green-and-red-accented Kris Kringle room get Santa Claus pajamas. Another fine choice is the Garden Suite, with hand-painted walls, a Jacuzzi bath, and private porch access allowing for a fine country-side view (the "Hill" in Terre Hill is there for a reason). Four-course breakfasts are unusually gourmet for Dutch Country. You're less likely to find traditional pancake and egg breakfasts than deluxe pastry and sausage partnered with vegetable-filled roulade and Mornay sauce. These outstanding meals also close with a dessert course. Check with the innkeepers about themed tour packages.

Small Hotels and Motels
Bird-in-Hand Family Inn (1-800-665-8780; www.bird-in-hand.com; 2727 Old Philadelphia Pike, Bird-in-Hand). This large motel is a reliable choice for families, and one of a few inns owned and operated in the area by the Smucker family, which also manages the on-site restaurant. Diversions for kids are conveniently on-site, including a big indoor/outdoor pool area, miniature golf course, and game room. A stay at the Family Inn, or any Smucker property for that matter, includes a two-hour country farm bus tour.

Hampton Inn & Suites Ephrata (717-733-0661; www.hamptoninn.com; 380 E. Main St., Ephrata). Highly recommended 72-room hotel at a high point in Ephrata with nice valley views. Well maintained and includes continental breakfast, fitness center, and indoor pool.

Orchard Inn (717-768-3644; www.orchardinnpa.com; 44 S. Harvest Rd., Bird-in-Hand). Single-story motel tucked away a half mile from the Bird-in-Hand attractions. The inn is very well taken care of and a good value.

Sleep Inn & Suites (717-687-0226; www.sleepinn.com; 2869 Lincoln Hwy., Ronks). A great location and recently built. They advertise Jacuzzi rooms.

Dairy farms abound in the Lancaster countryside.

CULTURE

Churches

Lititz Moravian Church
717-626-9027
www.lititzmoravian.org
8 Church Square, Lititz, PA 17543
Open: Fri. and Sat. 10–4

The spiritual and architectural nexus of
Lititz, this church was the fifth structure
where the community's Moravians came to
worship. It is a crisply designed building,
completed in 1787 and restored after a 1957
fire. Note the belfry, and find the adjacent
limestone Corpse House where bodies were
traditionally kept between death and burial.
There is also a gift shop on the grounds.

Film

Ephrata Main Theaters (717-733-9098;
124 E. Main St., Ephrata). Two-screen theater in downtown Ephrata showing first-
run movies.

Historic Homes and Sites

**The Amish Experience at
Plain & Fancy Farm**
717-768-3600
www.amishexperience.com
padutch@amishexperience.com
3121 Old Philadelphia Pike, Bird-in-Hand,
PA 17505
Open: Apr.–Oct., Mon.–Sat. 8:30–5, Sun.
10:30–5; Nov.–Dec., Mon.–Sat. 9:30–5,
Sun. 10:30–5. Farmlands tours leave at
10:30 and 1:45 Mon.–Sat., and at 11:30 on
Sun. Apr.–Oct. Tours leave daily at 11:30 in
Nov., and on Sat. and Sun. in Mar. and Dec.
Call or visit Web site for more information
about tour varieties and availability.
Admission: Varies by activity. Theater is
$10 adults, $6 children. Homestead tour is
$9 adults, $5 children. Farmlands tour is
$29 adults, $12 children. Look for packages
combining activities. A pass to all three is
$39 for adults and $19 for children.

An effective educational attraction with a
dash of Amish Disneyland, the Experience
is difficult to classify. A sort of one-stop-
shop for Amish tourism, it brings together
theater, lodging, dining, shopping, a mock
Amish homestead, and a coach bus tour
around the countryside. The center of the
Amish Experience is Plain & Fancy Farm,
which offers the educational attractions. Its
theater shows "Jacob's Choice," a fictional
account of a young man reared in an Amish
household but unsure of whether he wants
to join the church. A film component combined with experiential special effects
keeps kids' attention and provides a good
overview of Amish life. The house tour
offers further enrichment, taking visitors
through an imagined Amish home built in
1959, replete with the furniture and clothing that an Amish family would own (the air
conditioning is inauthentic, but there for
your comfort). Guides here are very helpful, and this is a good place to ask any questions one might have about Amish culture.
The farmlands bus tour leaves from the
Experience and takes two and a quarter
hours including stops, which vary from day
to day and tour to tour, but typically include
an Amish-owned business. A large souvenir store connects to family-style dining
at Plain & Fancy Farm (see "Restaurants
and Food Purveyors" for the write-up), and
this is also where Aaron and Jessica's Buggy
Rides commence. On-site is also the
Amish View Inn & Suites (1-866-735-
1600; www.amishviewinn.com), which is a
modern, well-appointed hotel with breakfast, pool, and in-room kitchenettes. Rates
vary by season and room size.

Ephrata Cloister

717-733-6600
www.ephratacloister.org
info@ephratacloister.org
632 W. Main St., Ephrata, PA 17522
Open: Mon.–Sat. 9–5, Sun. 12–5 (tours on
the hour)

Admission: Adults $9, seniors $8, children $6

Conrad Beissel realized his dream of a life spent connecting with God at Ephrata Cloister in 1732. It came after years of persecution in Germany where the orphaned baker refused to follow the dictates of the church. Soon after his arrival in Pennsylvania he and a band of disciples built Ephrata, where they lived a sober, celibate existence. Members slept on 18-inch-wide wooden planks using blocks as pillows, and ate a single meal each day. They rested for precisely six hours a night, with a two-hour interruption between midnight and two: the time Beissel believed the Second Coming of Christ would occur. The Second Coming did not happen during Beissel's lifetime (as he had promised his followers), and upon his death in 1768 the cloister began to dissolve. It was later sold to the state of Pennsylvania, which preserves the site as a historic attraction including eight original buildings. The guided tour incorporates the three largest structures and takes just under an hour. White-robed guides show visitors sites like the Sisters' House residence, and the Meetinghouse where members convened for Saturday prayer. Note the German side-lapped shingles and the low ceilings, which kept the buildings easy to heat. Take a map and walk the rest of the grounds.

Johannes Mueller House
717-627-4636
www.lititzhistoricalfoundation.com
137–145 E. Main St., Lititz, PA 17543
Open: Memorial Day through the last Saturday in Oct., Mon.–Sat., 10–4
Admission: Adults $5, seniors and AAA members $4, students $3

When the Moravians established the Lititz settlement in 1757, a rule mandated that only a single local craftsman be allowed to practice each vocation. It was by this law that Johannes Mueller became Lititz's sole dyer of cloth. He practiced his trade in this 1792 house, across the street from the Moravian Church and attached to the town museum, where you can purchase tickets for the 45-minute house tour. The tour is highly informative, opening with a primer on Moravian traditions that date back to Jan Hus and his criticisms of the Catholic Church at the turn of the 15th century. Fast forward 260 years to rural Pennsylvania, where tradesmen like Mueller lived and worked the industrious life demanded by the times. The house as presented today puts a fine point on that frugal, utilitarian culture. Mueller's seemingly ordinary life is a perfect window into the egalitarian society of the time. More than one hundred tools and household items are on display throughout, and costumed guides know the significance of every one. You'll also be taken upstairs where Mueller's periodic apprentices stayed.

Mascot Roller Mills and Ressler Family Home
717-656-7616
www.resslermill.com
443 W. Newport Rd., Ronks, PA 17572
Open: Mid-May through mid-Oct.,

Mascot Roller Mills

Tues.–Sat., 10–4
Admission: Free

An informative attraction on light industry that eludes far too many Dutch Country visitors, despite its convenient location on PA 772 near Intercourse. The Ressler family owned and operated this grain mill from 1864 to 1977, serving the local Amish community while also shipping white and whole wheat flour out of town. For a period the site housed a small post office and subsequently acquired the "Mascot" name (a fun story, told on the tour). The machinery still works, and you'll see hard corn being cut into cornmeal. At the Ressler house next door to the mill find original family items like a beautiful Mason and Hamlin organ. Touring both takes about 90 minutes.
Museums

American Military Edged Weaponry Museum
717-768-7185
www.usmilitaryknives.com/amewm.htm
3562 Old Philadelphia Pike, Intercourse, PA 17534
Open: May–Nov., Mon.–Sat. 10–5
Admission: $3

This jam-packed single-room museum begins with a socket bayonet used in the American Revolution and exhibits hundreds of knives, pistols, muskets, rifles, and other weaponry used throughout the country's military history through every major war. It's an engrossing collection, even for visitors unfamiliar with the subject matter. The concluding exhibit on experimental fighting knives is notable. A couple dollars buys you a bullet found at the Battle of Gettysburg from the sale item display case.

Candy Americana Museum
1-888-294-5287
www.wilburbuds.com
48 N. Broad St., Lititz, PA 17543

Open: Mon.–Sat. 10–5
Admission: Free

Attached to the Wilbur Chocolate Company's terrific chocolate and candy store is this small museum, well stocked with chocolate-related paraphernalia like molds, boxes, and pots. A video presentation informs about the history and logistics of chocolate production as well as the benefits of chocolate consumption. Visitors can also see selected confections produced live and in person.

Intercourse Pretzel Factory
717-768-3432
www.intercoursepretzelfactory.com
info@intercoursepretzelfactory.com
3614 Old Philadelphia Pike, Intercourse, PA 17534
Open: Mon.–Sat., Year-round except Jan. and first half of Feb., 9–5; tour times vary, call for information
Admission: Free

This small pretzel factory produces two thousand pretzels a day—around a hundred pounds worth—and gives short informational presentations on how it's done in the factory room. It's not as detailed a pretzel education as visitors get at Julius Sturgis (see below) but it's free. Pretzels, hard and soft, and lemonade can be purchased in the shop, and there are used books for sale on the upper level.

Julius Sturgis Pretzel Bakery
717-627-4354
www.juliussturgis.com
info@juliussturgis.com
219 E. Main St., Lititz, PA 17543
Open: Mar. 15–Dec., Mon.–Sat. 9–5; Jan.–Mar. 15, 10–4; tours on the half hour
Admission: $3 adults, $2 children

You can't bake the pretzels yourself, but at least they let you twist them. You'll also see the original Sturgis ovens—which began

producing pretzels in 1861 as the first commercial pretzel maker in the United Sates—
and learn how the key heat comes from the
bricks. Sturgis's sourdough pretzels available on-site are a nice, chewy snack.

Lititz Museum

717-627-4636
www.lititzhistoricalfoundation.com
137–145 E. Main St., Lititz, PA 17543
Open: Memorial Day through the last
Saturday in Oct., Mon.–Sat. 10–4
Admission: Free

An extension of the Johannes Mueller
house tour, this museum explores Lititiz's
fascinating Moravian roots, showcases
articles belonging to former Lititz resident General John Sutter, and closes with a
circumspect look at 20th-century
Americana, much of which is somehow tied
to the community. As with the Mueller
House, the Lititz Museum is big on tools
and objects: a reflection of the utilitarian
culture that took root here in the late 18th
century. The exhibits on toys and everyday
items are an interesting group, located
adjacent to a beautiful fan collection.

National Toy Train Museum

717-687-8976
www.traincollectors.org
info@nttmuseum.org
300 Paradise Lane, north of PA 741,
Strasburg, PA 17579
Open: May–Oct., 10–5; hours vary the rest
of the year
Admission: Adults $5, seniors $4, children
$2.50

A meticulous collection of model trains that
puts your old basement set to shame. There
are hundreds of pieces here. Some sit still
behind display glass, while others wind
their way around the five creative layouts.
Visitors can push buttons to flash beacon
lights and sound diesel horns. The museum
is operated by the 30,000-member Train

*Expressionless dolls, a token of Amish humility, for
sale at People's Place Quilt Museum*

Collectors Association, so exhibits are as
historically detailed as they are colorful and
fun. See generations of Lionel models,
including a sample from the Mickey Mouse
set that helped the company weather the
Great Depression. The live steam models
are also fascinating; the American,
German, and English trains on display were
powered with actual boiling water just like
their full-sized equivalents.

People's Place Quilt Museum

1-800-828-8218
www.ppquiltmuseum.com
PA 340, Intercourse, PA 17543
Open: Mon.–Sat. 9–5
Admission: Free

Colorful yet modest, stitched together with
diamond, triangle, block, and star patterns,
Amish quilts embody the resourcefulness
and assiduousness for which the community is known. This free museum occupies
the second floor of the Old Country Store
complex in Intercourse. See century-old
Amish quilts, learn about the history of the
art and test yourself on the interactive
question posts. Changing exhibits often
highlight prominent quilters from outside
the Amish community. When you're done

touring, browse the shopping floor and take home a handmade quilt for yourself (expensive, yes, but also incredibly labor-intensive) or some samplers.

Railroad Museum of Pennsylvania
717-687-8628
www.rrmuseumpa.org
info@rrmuseumpa.org
PA 741, Strasburg, PA 17579
Open: Mon.–Sat. 9–5, Sun. 12–5, closed Mon. Nov.–Mar.
Admission: Adults $10, seniors $9, children $8

After you've visited Strasburg's toy trains, drive less than half a mile and see the real deal. There are more than a hundred classic locomotives and railroad cars at this comprehensive museum. Some you can get in and explore yourself, like Instruction Car No. 492445, where Pennsylvania Railroad employees learned how to use the Westinghouse brake system without having to leave the job. Each engine and car has an information panel detailing vital stats and trivia. Learn about the 118.5-ton No. 5741 steam engine, a 10-wheel locomotive and predecessor to the electric trains that shuttle today's commuters around the Delaware Valley on SEPTA. Kids can operate a signal board and hang out at the Stewart Junction Railway Education Center, which has nine model train layouts, including a couple Lego villages. Inquire about guided tours of the rail yard.

Seasonal Events
Mud Sales
www.padutch.com/mudsales.shtml
Throughout the County
Time: Mid-February through mid-April

A fun Lancaster County tradition, these auctions and sales are held by local volunteer fire companies just before the spring growing season as a way to raise money. The farm equipment is rarely of use to visitors, but the Amish-made goods (often sold at bargain prices) certainly are. From February through April there's usually at least one mud sale per weekend—see the Web site above for locations and dates.

Theater
Rainbow Dinner Theatre (717-687-4300; www.rainbowdinnertheater.com; 3065 Lincoln Hwy., Paradise). It's heartening to see dinner theater alive and well in Lancaster County. The shows are all comedies—one month you'll get a Neil Simon classic, the next month something from a new playwright. Performances run for six to twelve weeks each. The menu changes as well, but is generally beef, chicken, and/or fish with standard American sides. Prices are from a bygone era: between $40 and $50 buys dinner and the show. Wine is extra, but reasonably priced. Call for performance dates and times.

RESTAURANTS AND FOOD PURVEYORS

They say that the four Amish food groups are fat, cholesterol, starch, and sugar. The produce is also excellent (Lancaster County soil is exceptionally rich), but more often than not you'll find it wedged into a pie crust. Surrender to temptation and stock up on the classics: soft and hard pretzels, sweet jams, wet-bottom shoofly pie, chow chow (a sweet relish), and whoopie pies (two chocolate cake–like discs sandwiched around vanilla icing). Many visitors develop a taste for Amish root beer, which is a less bubbly, more intense drink than the soda pop sold in most American grocery stores. Amish foods are widely available at the markets and shops around Intercourse and Bird-in-Hand. You can also drive along PA 340 or PA 722 and buy from roadside farm stands. Bring home raw fruits or vegetables, and get your hands on some cobbler.

"Hearty" is the word most commonly applied to Dutch Country cuisine, and the label fits. Chicken, beef, ham, eggs, oatmeal, and potatoes are some staples. In truth, the Amish diet is a bit more diverse than many assume, and is continually evolving, but Amish Country restaurants typically stick to the basics. Fried chicken, beef in gravy, baked ham, and buttered noodles are some common dishes. Most restaurants serve either family-style meals or all-you-can-eat buffets. The offerings are close to homogenous around Amish Country tourist hotspots. If you are only staying here for a day or two, you should probably eat at a popular eatery like Miller's or Good 'n Plenty to get the experience. After that, consider heading a little off the tourist track.

Adamstown

Stoudt's Black Angus Restaurant & Pub
717-484-4386
www.stoudtsbeer.com
2800 N. Reading Rd., Adamstown, PA 19501
Open: Daily
Price: Expensive
Credit Cards: Yes
Cuisine: Steakhouse
Serving: L (Fri.–Sun.), D
Handicapped Access: Yes

A romantic steakhouse with big portions to meet the appetite earned from a day spent antiquing in Adamstown. The exterior commands attention, its enormous steer set against the colorful Victorian ornamentation and adjacent to a more contemporarily designed microbrewery (which was among the state's first, now more than 20 years old). The interior dining rooms are softly lit, and loaded with antiques, mingled among pictures of the owner's relatives and pieces of political memorabilia. You could spend a half hour just surveying the walls. Big steaks come slathered in mush-

The iconic steer sign at Stoudt's

rooms and onions, with potato, vegetable, salad, and good bread baked on-site. German-style lagers, ales, and seasonal brew from the microbrewery are a highlight.

Bird-in-Hand & Intercourse

Dienner's Country Restaurant
717-687-9571
www.dienners.com
2855 Lincoln Hwy. East, Ronks, PA 17572
Open: Mon.–Sat.
Price: Inexpensive
Credit Cards: Yes
Cuisine: Pennsylvania Dutch, American
Handicapped Access: Yes
Serving: B, L, D (open to 6 P.M. most days, 8 P.M. Fri.)

Dienner's Amish and Mennonite cooks whip up superb, uncomplicated fare at inflation-defying prices. Huge cheeseburgers go for under $4 and half a chicken with all the trimmings is $8. The all-you-can-eat buffet lays out at least two-dozen items from three serving islands. The breakfast buffet is just $5 and includes freshly prepared bacon, home fries, scrambled eggs, French toast, pancakes, scrapple, sausage, fruit, and more. Lunch and dinner are more identifiably Pennsylvania Dutch. Best of all, everything tastes great. The restaurant's popularity ensures that buffet trays are refilled regularly so food stays fresh. The hours can be restrictive for dinner, which is served from 3 to 6 except on Fridays. Arrive early to avoid lines.

Family Cupboard Restaurant and Buffet
717-768-4510
www.familycupboard.com
3029 Old Philadelphia Pike, Bird-in-Hand, PA 17505
Open: Daily
Price: Inexpensive
Credit Cards: Yes
Cuisine: Pennsylvania Dutch, American
Serving: B, L, D
Handicapped Access: Yes

Most patrons go for the all-you-can-eat buffet at this homey restaurant enclosed in an adapted barn. The fare is traditional comfort food like meatloaf, rotisserie and fried chicken, stuffing, beef in gravy, vegetables, with a few Pennsylvania Dutch twists. Quantity is the draw, but quality isn't bad. Many tables enjoy nice farm views from the big windows. It is owned by the Dienner family, which operates Dienner's Country Restaurant as well (see above). Dienner's is a slightly better value, but Family Cupboard has more convenient hours.

Good 'n Plenty Restaurant
717-394-7111
www.goodnplenty.com
150 Eastbrook Rd., Smoketown, PA 17576
Open: Daily
Price: Inexpensive to moderate
Credit Cards: Yes
Cuisine: Pennsylvania Dutch, American
Serving: L, D
Handicapped Access: Yes

The company can be hit or miss at this con-verted farmhouse—you're seated with strangers—but the food is reliable. Everyone shares the bounty, which includes all the classically filling Dutch Country goodies: ham, roast beef, fried chicken, and chow chow to name a few. Good 'n Plenty also operates a bake shop on the premises and sells baked goods at the Bird-in-Hand Farmer's Market. The breads and desserts are especially good here.

Kling House Restaurant
717-768-2746
www.kitchenkettle.com
3529 Old Philadelphia Pike, Intercourse, PA 17534
Open: Mon.–Sat.
Price: Moderate
Credit Cards: Yes
Cuisine: American
Serving: B, L
Handicapped Access: Yes

A quality breakfast and lunch spot in the Kitchen Kettle retail complex, with alfresco dining and friendly service. Kling House pulls a neat trick, taking the area's plentiful fresh ingredients and whipping them into more diverse and healthful dining options than you'll typically see on Dutch Country menus. Lunch offers a half-dozen entrée salads, and breakfasts come with samplings of excellent locally produced jams and fruit spreads.

Miller's Smorgasbord
717-687-8436
www.millerssmorgasbord.com
2811 Lincoln Hwy. East, Ronks, PA 17572
Open: Daily
Price: Inexpensive to moderate
Credit Cards: Yes
Cuisine: Pennsylvania Dutch, American
Serving: B, L, D
Handicapped Access: Yes

A top all-you-can-eat smorgasbord in the Bird-in-Hand/Intercourse vicinity, Miller's stands out for ingredient freshness and overall quality. Lunch and dinner include freshly carved sirloin au jus, turkey and ham, plus peel-and-eat shrimp, salad bar, and a dozen other American staples, though you'll see occasional international influence in the hot dishes. Serving islands form a circle around the carving station in the restaurant's center. The dining room is very large, but high ceilings, warm country décor, and ample natural light keep it from feeling institutional. For half the price of a full lunch or dinner buffet you can get unlimited soup, salad, and rolls. Miller's is also one of the few area restaurants to serve alcoholic beverages.

Plain & Fancy Farm

717-768-4400
www.plainandfancyfarm.com
3121 Old Philadelphia Pike, Bird-in-Hand, PA 17505
Open: Daily
Price: Inexpensive to moderate
Credit Cards: Yes
Cuisine: Pennsylvania Dutch, American
Serving: L, D
Handicapped Access: Yes

Located alongside The Amish Experience compound, Plain & Fancy gets good business from school groups, the coach bus trade, and day-trippers in town for a quick shot of Amish-flavored tourism. While you can order a la carte off the menu, the family-style Feast is the main draw. Conceptually similar to Good 'n Plenty, you eat at a long table with strangers and pass the usual suspects (egg noodles, chow chow, fried chicken, pot pie) down the line until everyone's had their share.

East Earl

Shady Maple Smorgasbord

717-354-8222
www.shady-maple.com
129 Toddy Dr., East Earl, PA 17519
Open: Mon.–Sat.
Price: Inexpensive to moderate
Credit Cards: Yes
Cuisine: American
Serving: B, L, D
Handicapped Access: Yes

It's a 15-minute drive northeast from Intercourse, but this is the 800-pound gorilla of the all-you-can-eat smorgasbords in Lancaster County. The hearty country fare is fresher, tastier, and more creatively prepared than anywhere else in the region. Credit goes to the multiple live-action cooking stations where the choices vary depending on the day (steaks on Monday nights, seafood on Tuesdays, etc.), but standards like meatballs in a sweet sauce, tender roast beef, barbeque pork, stuffed chicken breast, and a big salad bar are also recommended. It's hard to say how big the dining room is, but it appears to be at least the length of a football field. Booths are upholstered with burgundy vinyl to match the tabletops and brass chandeliers hang from above. The smorgasbord is located on the second floor of one building within the even more gargantuan Shady Maple shopping complex. A 40,000-square-foot gift shop occupies the first floor, and adjoining buildings include a supermarket and furniture store.

Ephrata

Lilly's on Main

717-738-2711
www.lilysonmain.com
124 E. Main St., Ephrata PA 17522
Open: Daily
Price: Expensive
Credit Cards: Yes
Cuisine: New American
Serving: L, D, Sun. Brunch
Handicapped Access: Yes

Interesting, reasonably priced fusion cuisine in a bright and airy room, this is a trustworthy pick for a romantic dinner in

Ephrata. The menu is ambitious—innovative sauces and glazes on traditional foods and a smattering of unusual choices like calves liver au poivre. It can be difficult not to fill up on honey whole wheat cranberry bread, baked on the premises. The grilled pork and beef meatloaf entrée, sandwiched between scoops of whipped potato, is stellar and available in both lunch and dinner portions. Extensive wine list too, including some half bottles. Lilly's can be a little tough to find, tucked into a business center next to the town's twin-screen movie theater. Nod to the security guard at the front desk and follow the red staircase past the wall of water into the contemporary art deco room with big windows overlooking downtown Ephrata (not exactly Manhattan, but cheery during the daytime and serene in the twilight).

The Udder Choice

717-733-4300
1812 W. Main St., Ephrata PA 17522
Open: Daily
Price: Inexpensive
Credit Cards: Yes
Cuisine: Sandwiches, ice cream
Serving: B (Mon.–Sat.), L, D
Handicapped Access: Yes

This endearingly coy spot serves good sandwiches and homemade ice cream. Food is underpriced (sandwiches at or below $5) and can be ordered to go, but there is table service for dine-in guests. Seven specialty sundaes are named for cows; try the simple but delicious Guernsey, drizzled in warm caramel and crushed nuts. Vintage ice-cream signs hang on the walls, a glass display showcases ice-cream dippers up to a century old, and the legs of some wooden booths are shaped and painted to resemble cow hoofs. Eat under the sky-high ceiling supported by massive wooden beams. Turkey sandwiches, carved fresh off the breast, are a

strong choice. Open for breakfast every day except Sunday, when the restaurant opens at 2 P.M.

Lititz

Café Chocolate of Lititz

717-626-0123
www.chocolatelititz.com
40 E. Main St., Lititz, PA 17534
Open: Daily
Price: Inexpensive to moderate
Credit Cards: Yes
Cuisine: Eclectic, chocolate
Serving: B, L, D (Fri.–Sat.)
Handicapped Access: No

When in Rome do as the Romans do, and when in Lititz order chocolate. Wilbur Chocolate is the town's famous chocolatier, but Café Chocolate of Lititz also works wonders with the stuff, serving a full menu from morning to night (most days) that uses *real* dark chocolate, not the ordinary

Inside Café Chocolate

overly sweetened junk. Breakfast is available all day, and is highly recommended. Whatever you order, accompany it with a cup of hot chocolate, made fresh from steamed milk and 60-percent cocoa solids so it isn't too sweet. In the morning add a shot of espresso for under a buck. On the food front, it's very hard to argue with the sunshine crepes, stuffed with fresh fruit and drizzled in chocolate with a dollop of organic whipped cream. Lunch and dinner choices include gourmet sandwiches, soups, and pizza, and a few dishes that maintain the café theme (chili con chocolate). A good move is to order something salty and something sweet. Overall, an exceptionally friendly and fun place for either a full meal or dessert.

FOOD PURVEYORS

Bakeries/Coffeehouses

Achenbach's Pastries (717-656-6671; 375 E. Main St., Leola). A marvelous bakery in business for over 50 years. Really good sticky buns and bread.

Bird-in-Hand Bake Shop (717-656-7947; 542 Gibbons Rd., Bird-in-Hand). A fine place to pick up wet-bottom shoofly pie or some cookies.

The Brew House & Bistro (717-721-1980; 52 E. Main St., Ephrata). Homey little coffee shop with wireless Internet and tasty iced coffee drinks.

Candy and Ice Cream

Lapp Valley Farms (717-354-7988; 244 Mentzer Rd., New Holland). Fantastic ice cream made with milk from Jersey cows. Lapp Valley also has a stand at the Green Dragon Farmer's Market in Ephrata.

Gourmet Foods

Bird-in-Hand Farmers Market (717-393-9674; 2710 Old Philadelphia Pike, Bird-in-Hand). A convenient way to purchase the classic Dutch Country foods, since they're all here: relish from Jake and Amos, jams from Kitchen Kettle, shoofly pie from Good 'n Plenty. There's a lunch counter, a couple produce stands, and crafts as well.

Centerville Bulk Foods (3501B Scenic Rd., Gordonville, north of Intercourse). In part an ordinary grocery store, but also a fine place to pick up locally made flours, locally grown produce, and deluxe seasonings. Many area Amish and Mennonites shop here.

Intercourse Canning Company (717-768-0156; 3612 E. Newport Rd., Intercourse). Jammed goods of all sorts. Free samples abound—try the jams on oyster crackers and salsas on corn chips.

Stoltzfus Meats & Deli (717-768-7287; Cross Keys Village Center, Intercourse). The high-quality raw meat probably won't do you any good unless you're heading home that day, but try a Stoltzfus sausage sandwich prepared fresh on the grill. It goes great with a Dutch Country soda.

Weaverland Auction, Inc. (717-355-0834; 1030 Long Lane Rd., New Holland). If you've never seen a produce auction and you're an early riser, it's worth stopping in at

Weaverland. The lots are too big for leisure travelers to consider purchasing, but you're free to watch as the area's Amish and Mennonite farmers trot out their fruits, vegetables, and flowers for bid. Auctioneers mumble prices at a furious pace; it's amazing to see how this could ever work, but it does. Auction times change depending on season. During prime growing season they tend to occur five times a week (never Sunday) and start around 8 or 9 A.M. Call ahead to be sure.

Wine Stores
Mount Hope Wine Gallery (717-665-7021; PA 340 between Intercourse and Bird-In-Hand). The wine is made an hour away in northwest Lancaster County's Mount Hope Estate and Winery on PA 72, which also hosts the annual Pennsylvania Renaissance Faire from mid-August to mid-October. The selection is vast, and the shop sells all the accessories a wine drinker could want.

RECREATION

Baseball
There's no baseball in the countryside, but catch the Atlantic League **Lancaster Barnstormers** (717-509-4487; 650 N. Prince St., Lancaster) downtown. The stadium is a 20-minute drive from Bird-in-Hand.

Biking and Hiking
Amish Country is a fine place to bike ride, so long as you keep alert and watch for speeding vehicles and road-hogging trucks on the slim backcountry roads. The **Lancaster Bike Club** (www.lancasterbikeclub.org) has a great list of rides on its Web site that include some Amish Country routes. There are two recommended rides from Lancaster to Lititz that can be easily adapted to go the other way around and incorporate some picture-perfect stretches of northern Lancaster County. You'll hit a few covered bridges on each. The Strasburg Stoker ride is a brisk 23 miles, and a great way to take in both the train-related attractions and see the countryside.

A favorite hiking spot is **Money Rocks Park** (1000 Narvon Rd., Narvon) in the Welsh Mountains, a 20-minute drive northeast from Intercourse on the edge of Lancaster County. As legend has it, local farmers used to hide money in crannies between the area's boulders for safekeeping. No legend is required to explain the "Rocks" half of the name: the three park trails are very stony and a little steep. The Money Rocks Overlook trail is a fun, quick hike uphill to a scenic vantage point over and through the black birch trees. It is especially striking in the fall. There are two other trails here, including the Cockscomb Trail, which is a longer loop. Wear bright clothing at Money Rocks; the park contains approved hunting areas (shotgun, muzzleloader, and archery).

Camping
Area campgrounds do lots of business with RV travelers and are among the most modern facilities in southeast Pennsylvania. It's always good to call ahead to confirm availability since they occasionally fill to capacity during high travel seasons like Fourth of July weekend.

Beacon Hill Camping (717-768-8775; 128 Beacon Hill Dr., Intercourse, PA 17534). Forty-seven sites and three cabins with water, sewer, electric hookups, and wireless Internet access. No children under 16.

Country Haven Campground (717-354-7926; 354 Springville Rd., New Holland, PA 17557). Fifty-two sites with water, sewer, electric, and wireless Internet access.

Mill Bridge Village Camp Resort (717-687-8181; 101 S. Ronks Rd., just off PA 30, Paradise, PA 17572). Lots of amenities on-site, including a pool and arcade. Good for families.

Family Fun

Choo-Choo Barn—Traintown, USA

717-687-7911
www.choochoobarn.com
PA 741, near Fairview Rd., Strasburg
Open: Mid-Mar.–Dec., 10–5
Admission: $6 adults, $4 children

A very cool 1,700-square-foot Lancaster County themed model train layout (look for the model Dutch Wonderland theme park and Amish barn raising). There's so much to see at this family-operated and longstanding Strasburg attraction; the best details take a little hunting.

Dutch Wonderland

1-866-386-2839
www.dutchwonderland.com
2249 Lincoln Hwy. East, Lancaster
Open: May–Dec., hours vary
Admission: $31

Tykes enjoy this medieval-themed, 48-acre park, located just a couple miles west of Bird-in-Hand. Dancers and storytellers perform throughout, and kids can choose from three-dozen rides that include roller coasters, slides, and water flumes. Break up the day with lunch at the Castle Café or a visit to Duke's Lagoon, which requires a bathing suit. Dutch Wonderland is a nice size—there's enough to see and do to occupy a whole day with some time left over to revisit favorite attractions. It is best for children 10 and under.

Strasburg Railroad

717-687-7522
www.strasburgrailroad.com
PA 741 East, Strasburg
Open: Call ahead
Admission: Varies

The coal-burning trains leave up to 11 times a day from this old East Strasburg station across the street from the Railroad Museum and the heart of Strasburg's deeply ensconced train culture. Rides take 45 minutes around the Lancaster countryside and are a bargain. Adults can take the posh President Car or book a weekend wine and cheese ride when offered. There's also a lot to do around the station, especially for kids, who love riding on the pump cars and miniature steam trains. Famed storybook and television personality Thomas the Tank Engine appears a few times a year for special-event rides, presumably at the behest of Sir Topham Hatt.

Waters Edge Mini Golf
1-800-665-8780
PA 340, Bird-in-Hand
Two attractively landscaped 18-hole courses on the premises of the Bird-in-Hand Family Inn.

Golf
Foxchase Golf Club (717-336-3673; 300 Stevens Rd., Stevens). Par 72, 18 holes; 6,055 yards. Fees: $22–$55. Northeast of Ephrata. Driving range.

Overlook Golf Course (717-569-9551; 2040 Lititz Pike, Lititz). Par 70, 18 holes; 6,153 yards. Fees: $21–$43.

Tanglewood Manor Golf Club (717-786-2500; 653 Scotland Rd., Quarryville). Par 72, 18 holes; 6,452 yards. Fees: $29–$49. South of Strasburg.

SHOPPING

Pennsylvania Dutch Country is a shopper's paradise. In addition to the numerous shops and farm stands selling delicious Amish baked goods and produce, there are Amish and Mennonite furniture manufacturers, antique dealers in Adamstown, and gimmicky gift stores (the "Intercourse" name lends itself to racy puns you'll often find splashed across mugs and T-shirts). Lancaster County also boasts two major factory outlet malls just west of Bird-in-Hand. And the area is mere minutes from Reading, Pennsylvania, where outlet shopping was born.

Antiques
Pennsylvania 272 in Adamstown has a density of antique shops and markets like nothing else in southeastern Pennsylvania. The area bills itself as "Antiques Capital U.S.A." and folks come from around the country just to shop here. Antiquing in Adamstown is a pleasure for casual browsers. There are several antique markets with hundreds of vendors each, so it's a low-pressure environment where you can peruse and ask questions at your own pace. If at all possible try to visit Adamstown on a Sunday. Not only are most antique stores and markets open, but almost everything else in Amish Country is closed. A handful of the many antique markets in Adamstown:

Adams Antiques (717-335 3116; 2400 N. Reading Rd., Adamstown). With over 200 vendors, this showcase gallery is open seven days a week. Very strong on antique furniture and decorative items, but has a little bit of everything.

Mad Hatter Antique Mall (717-484-4159; PA 272 and Willow St., Adamstown). Housed in an old hat factory—hence the name—this one is a brighter, roomier space than your typical antique market. Open daily except Tuesday and Wednesday, 10–5.

Renninger's Antiques Market (717-336-2177; 2500 N. Reading Rd., Adamstown). A personal favorite for the exceptional diversity in available merchandise. With close to 400 vendors indoors every Sunday, you're as likely to stumble on a walnut bookcase as a neon beer sign. Open Sunday, 7:30–4. An outdoor market opens at 5 A.M.

Shupp's Grove (717-484-4115; off PA 897, Adamstown). A fun outdoor market in business since 1962 with sociable vendors and a loyal base of visitors. Open seasonally on weekends, April through October.

Stoudt's Black Angus Antiques Mall (717-484-2757; 2800 N. Reading Rd., Adamstown). A huge Sundays-only affair, with both indoor and outdoor dealer areas. It connects to Stoudt's restaurant and brewery for after-shopping eats.

Books

Aaron's Books (717-627-1990; 43 S. Broad St., Lititz). Inexpensive used books, very extensive shelves on mystery and romance novels.

The Book Shoppe (1-800-828-8218; 3510 Old Philadelphia Pike, Intercourse). Located within the Old Country Store shopping annex, the Shoppe is stocked mostly with titles about the Amish. Look for excellent cookbooks featuring Lancaster County recipes.

Clay Book Store (717-733-7253; 2450 W. Main St., Ephrata). A big Mennonite bookstore supplying a wide selection of religious titles and scholarly volumes on Amish and Mennonite religious traditions. Also a good selection of assorted used books sold for a dollar or two.

Crafts and Gifts

Dutch Haven (717-687-0111; 2857A Lincoln Hwy. East, Ronks). Large gift shop with sunglasses, shirts, mugs, and many other trinkets. Dutch Haven also sells sharp Amish root beer, soft pretzels, and whoopie pies.

Glick's Food & Crafts (717-656-1343; 248 Monterey Rd., Bird-in-Hand). Superior handmade quilts and shoofly pie. Hang around to see furniture being made and feed the animals.

The Old Candle Barn (717-768-8926; 3551 Old Philadelphia Pike, Intercourse). A copious variety of homemade candles, with scents that range from roasting chestnuts to fresh linen. Call ahead to check the schedule for candle-making demonstrations.

Dutch Haven souvenir store

The Outhouse (717-687-9580; 2853 Lincoln Hwy. East, Ronks). Whimsical souvenir shop full of gag gifts and snarky merchandise that also sells its own fudge. Bring some quarters for the carnival-style joke machines like the man-eating chicken.

Ten Thousand Villages (717-721-8400; 240 N. Reading Rd., Ephrata). A progressive, non-profit retailer that pays artisans from Third World countries a fair wage for their merchandise. The store is arranged in color groupings. You'll find home furnishings, jewelry, and a huge selection of Oriental rugs. There are Ten Thousand Villages stores all over the country, but Ephrata's is the largest.

Furnishings and Furniture

Cherry Acres (717-626-7557; 23 E. Main St., Lititz). Lumber from deconstructed barns is converted into attractive furniture, including some oak pieces. Great stuff, plus other decorative articles for the home.

Lapp's Coach Shop (717-768-8712; 3572 W. Newport Rd., Intercourse). Specializes in high-quality hickory furniture, mostly built by Amish craftsmen.

Riehl's Quilts & Crafts (717-656-0697; 247 East Eby Rd., Leola). Conveniently located, with a good selection of Amish-made wares, set on an Amish dairy farm.

Stoltzfus Carpet Shop (39 Pequea Valley Rd., Kinzers). Friendly shopkeeper Moses Stoltzfus sells beautiful cotton filler rugs (with or without shag) and brooms of exceptional quality.

Malls and Complexes

When it comes to massive retail complexes in Pennsylvania Dutch Country, it's not just about the antiques. Ephrata's farmer's market is where locals go on Fridays. And the dual factory outlet complexes east of downtown Lancaster on PA 30 are where bargain hunters go year-round.

The Green Dragon (717-738-1117; 955 N. State St., Ephrata). Open every Friday from 9 in the morning to 9 at night, this positively enormous farmer's market sells everything from freshly grown produce to collectible crafts, knickknacks, and clothing. A handful of the 400 vendors are Amish or Mennonite farmers and cooks. Try a pit beef sandwich in the prepared foods area. Arrive early to avoid traffic backup and to find convenient parking. The Green Dragon closes an hour early in January and February.

Kitchen Kettle Village (1-800-732-3538 or 717-768-8261; www.kitchenkettle.com; 3529 Old Philadelphia Pike, Intercourse). You can't miss this little faux village with shopping, lodging, and dining on PA 340, anchored by a large canning kitchen that is Intercourse's best place to sample jams and relishes (spoon 'em delicately onto the complimentary oyster crackers and buy a jar or two of your favorites). Kitchen Kettle offers much more than snack food—there are over three-dozen stores total—but the sweet popcorn, pretzel, chocolate, and candy sellers are definitely a highlight. Fifteen inn rooms are available on the premises for those who wish to stay the night.

Finding the best nectarines at Green Dragon

Rockvale Outlets (717-293-9595; 35 S. Willowdale Dr., Lancaster). More than a hundred factory outlet stores promising huge bargains. Most are apparel outlets like Bass and Dress Barn, but you'll also find books, luggage, toys, and outdoor recreation stores.

Stoudtburg Village (www.stoudtburgvillage.com; just off PA 272 in Adamstown). The commercial component is not yet complete, but what does exist is a marvel of mixed-use development: a European-inspired residential and shopping community laced with eye-grabbing bright colors and movie set streets. Some residents own the shops that occupy their homes' first floor. There are gift stores, galleries, some light food options, and the Vito Vino Wine Shop, which is a highlight.

Tanger Outlets (717-392-7260; 311 Stanley K. Tanger Blvd., Lancaster). As with other Tanger outlets around the country, the Lancaster stores are upscale brands like Brooks Brothers, Coach, Eddie Bauer, and Nine West. Apparel and shoes predominate.

INFORMATION

Ambulance, Fire & Police
The general emergency number is 911. Call it for ambulance, fire, and police. Other emergency numbers:

Crisis Intervention	717-394-2631
Poison Control	1-800-521-6110
Rape Crisis Hotline	1-888-727-2877
Suicide Hotline	717-299-4855
Police (non-emergency)	717-299-4321

Area Codes & Town Government
The area code for Lancaster County is 717.

The county is governed by three commissioners who serve four-year terms. The commissioners' mailing address is 50 N. Duke St., P.O. Box 83480, Lancaster, PA 17608. The general information phone number is 717-299-8381.

Banks
Ephrata National Bank: 717-733-4181; 31 E. Main St., Ephrata

Graystone Bank: 717-661-7676; 361 W. Main St., Leola

Recommended Reading
Kraybill, Donald B. *Amish and the State,* Baltimore: Johns Hopkins University Press, 2003.
Kraybill, Donald B. *The Riddle of Amish Culture,* Baltimore: Johns Hopkins University Press, 2001. Revised edition. Explains and confronts Amish experience in contemporary society. An excellent volume, comprehensive and even-handed.
Kraybill, Donald B. *The Amish of Lancaster County,* Mechanicsburg, PA: Stackpole Books, 2008. A brisk overview of the mores and values that characterize Amish life in southeastern Pennsylvania.

Hospitals

Ephrata Community Hospital: 717-733-0311; 169 Martin Ave., Ephrata

Lancaster General Hospital: 717-544-5511; 555 N. Duke St., Lancaster

Late Night Food and Fuel

Sheetz (food and fuel): 4179 Oregon Pike, Ephrata, and 701 Furnace Hills Pike, Lititz

Wawa (food and fuel): 2501 Lincoln Hwy. East, Ronks

Media

Newspapers

Intelligencer Journal (717-291-8811; www.lancasteronline.com; 8 W. King St., Lancaster). Daily newspaper, serving greater Lancaster.

Lancaster New Era (717-291-8811; www.lancasteronline.com; 8 W. King St., Lancaster). An afternoon daily paper, published by Lancaster Newspapers, Inc., which also prints the Intelligencer Journal.

Radio Stations

WDAC-FM 94.5; Lancaster, Christian radio
WLAN-FM 96.9; Lancaster, top-40
WIOV-FM 105.1; Ephrata, country music

Television Stations

Channels and contact information for the major broadcast networks:

WGAL TV Channel 8 (717-393-5851), NBC affiliate
WLYH TV Channel 15 (717-238-2100), CW affiliate
WHP TV Channel 21 (717-238-2100), CBS affiliate
WHTM Channel 27 (717-238-0964), ABC affiliate
WITF TV Channel 33 (717-704-3000), PBS
WPMT TV Channel 43 (717-843-0043), FOX affiliate

Visitor Information

Consult the **Pennsylvania Dutch Convention and Visitors Bureau** (1-800-PA-DUTCH; www.padutchcountry.com; 501 Greenfield Rd., Lancaster)

Amish Country is horse country.

General Index

Lodging by Price

Inexpensive: Up to $100
Moderate: $100 to $150
Expensive: $150 to $250
Very Expensive: $250 and up

Downtown Philadelphia

Inexpensive to moderate
Apple Hostels of Philadelphia, 47
Comfort Inn at Penn's Landing, 47
Hampton Inn, 48
Holiday Inn Express Midtown, 48
Holiday Inn Historic District, 48
Philadelphia Travelodge, 48

Moderate to expensive
Alexander Inn, 46–47
Radisson Plaza Warwick Hotel, 45
Thomas Bond House, 44

Expensive
Courtyard Philadelphia Downtown, 39
Hilton Garden Inn, 41
Penn's View Inn, 43–44

Expensive to very expensive
Best Western Independence Park, 43
Crowne Plaza Philadelphia City Center, 40
Embassy Suites, 42
Hyatt Regency at Penn's Landing, 43
Latham Hotel, 45
Loews Philadelphia Hotel, 41
Marriott Residence Inn, 40
Morris House Hotel, 47
Philadelphia Marriott, 41–42
Sheraton Center City, 42
Sheraton Society Hill, 46
Westin Philadelphia, 46
Windsor Suites Philadelphia, 42–43

Very expensive
Doubletree Philadelphia, 40
Four Seasons, 42
Hotel Sofitel Philadelphia, 44–45
Omni Hotel at Independence Park, 43
Park Hyatt Philadelphia at the Bellevue, 40
The Rittenhouse, 45
Rittenhouse 1715, 45–46
Ritz-Carlton Philadelphia, 40–41

Greater Philadelphia

Moderate to expensive
Chestnut Hill Hotel, 110–11
The Gables, 112–13

Expensive
aloft Philadelphia Airport, 110
Embassy Suites Philadelphia Airport, 110
Fairfield Inn Philadelphia Airport, 110
Hilton Philadelphia Airport, 110
Philadelphia Airport Marriott, 110
Residence Inn Philadelphia Airport, 110
Sheraton Four Points, 110

Expensive to very expensive
Crowne Plaza Philadelphia Main Line, 111
Hilton Philadelphia City Avenue, 111
Homewood Suites Philadelphia City Avenue, 111–12
Radnor Hotel, 112

Very expensive
Inn at Penn, 113
Sheraton University City, 114–15
Wayne Hotel, 112

Brandywine Valley

Inexpensive
Best Western Concordville, 175
Comfort Inn & Suites Brandywine Valley, 175
Hilton Garden Inn Kennett Square, 175
Holiday Inn West Chester, 175
Inn at Wilmington, 175

Moderate
1732 Folke Stone Bed & Breakfast, 173

Moderate to expensive
Brandywine River Hotel, 170
Brandywine Suites Hotel, 174
Doubletree Hotel Downtown Wilmington, 174–75
Doubletree Hotel Wilmington (Concord Pike), 175

Expensive
Bancroft Manor, 171–72
Fairville Inn, 170
Stebbins-Swayne House, 172
Sunrise Suites, 172
The Tory Inne, 173

Expensive to very expensive
Hamanassett Bed & Breakfast, 170–71
Inn at Montchanin Village, 173–74
Pennsbury Inn, 171

Dining by Price

Inexpensive: Up to $100
Moderate: $100 to $150
Expensive: $150 to $250
Very Expensive: $250 and up

Downtown Philadelphia

Inexpensive
Imperial Inn, 79
Sansom Kabob House, 88

Inexpensive to moderate
Jamaican Jerk Hut, 90
Ocean Harbor, 79
Sang Kee Peking Duck House, 79–80
Square on Square, 88–89

Moderate
Aya's Cafe, 81
City Tavern, 82–83
Monk's Café, 87
Ms. Tootsie's Soul Food Café, 91
My Thai, 87
Tamarind, 89–90
Warsaw Cafe, 89

Moderate to expensive
Audrey Claire, 84–85
Eulogy Belgian Tavern, 83
The Plough and the Stars, 84

Expensive
Alma de Cuba, 84
Amada, 81–82
Caffe Casta Diva, 85–86
Chlöe, 82
Cuba Libre, 83
Haru Philadelphia, 83
Melograno, 87
Mercato, 90–91
The Prime Rib, 88
Susanna Foo, 89
Tangerine, 84

Expensive to very expensive
Buddakan, 82
Morimoto, 79
Nineteen (XIX), 80
Parc Restaurant, 88

Very expensive
Barclay Prime, 85
The Capital Grille, 80
Fountain Restaurant, 81
Lacroix at the Rittenhouse, 86

Le Bec-Fin, 86–87
Vetri, 91

Greater Philadelphia

Inexpensive
Abyssinia Ethiopian Restaurant, 147
Fatou and Fama, 148
McNally's Tavern, 143
Taquería La Veracruzana, 142

Inexpensive to moderate
Dock Street Brewery, 147–48
Honey's Sit 'n' Eat, 145–46
International Smokeless BBQ, 141
Liberties Restaurant and Bar, 146
Rx, 150
Standard Tap, 146–47

Moderate
Anastasi's Seafood Ristorante, 141
Cafette, 142–43
Famous Fourth Street Delicatessen, 147
Il Cantuccio, 146
Jack's Firehouse, 143–44
Sabrina's Cafe, 141–42
Sabrina's Café and Spencer's Too, 142
Zorba's, 145

Moderate to expensive
Bar Ferdinand, 145
Koi, 146
Osaka, 143
Pod, 149–50
Ristorante Mezza Luna, 141

Expensive
Little Fish, 147
L'oca, 144
Marigold Kitchen, 148–49
Nan, 149
Osteria, 144
Salt & Pepper, 142

Brandywine Valley

Inexpensive
Charcoal Pit, 193
Hank's Place, 188
Sinclair's Sunrise Café and Tearoom, 190

Inexpensive to moderate
Newton's on State Street, 189

Moderate
Iron Hill Brewery, 191

Dining by Cuisine